Environmental Management

in the Soviet Union and Yugoslavia

Environmental Management
in the Soviet Union and Yugoslavia

Structure and Regulation
in Federal Communist States

Barbara Jancar

Duke Press Policy Studies

Duke University Press   Durham 1987

Library of Congress Cataloging-in-Publication Data
Jancar, Barbara Wolfe, 1935–
Environmental management in the Soviet Union and Yugoslavia.
(Duke Press policy studies)
Bibliography: p.
Includes index.
1. Environmental policy—Soviet Union.   2. Environ-
mental policy—Yugoslavia.   3. Environmental law—Soviet
Union.   4. Environmental law—Yugoslavia.   I. Title.
II. Series.
HC340.E5J35   1987   363.7′06′0947   87-5412
ISBN 0-8223-0719-7

To Lia, Saša, Vanja, Stanislav and Andrei

Contents

Contents

Tables and Figures

Tables

Figures

Acknowledgments

Primary research for this study was made possible by a S.U.N.Y.-Moscow University Research exchange and an IREX-Fulbright Grant in 1980–81 to the USSR, Czechoslovakia, and Yugoslavia. Subsequent return visits to the Soviet Union and the SFRY were made in 1983, 1984, and 1985. The author wishes to express her appreciation to the many government officials and scholars interviewed in the three countries for contributing their time and expertise to shed light on the successes and problems of environmental management in their countries. The author took notes at these interviews and has tried to present the views as she understood them at the time of the interview. Any misunderstandings or misconceptions are hers alone and she takes responsibility for all opinions and findings contained in the study.

For her hard work and perseverance in typing the manuscript, I would like to thank my niece, Julia Loomis. I would also like to express my appreciation to my students who helped me in the research and final editing of the book: Troy Lopez, Julia Lubeck, Stacey Rosenblum, Julie Wallace, and Julia Weidman. My special thanks to Ike Nwosu for the hours he spent in the library, and to Saundra Hampton and Jeffrey Loeb for their help with the index and proofreading. Last but not least, my deep thanks to John C. Webster, without whose help and enduring support this book would not have been possible.

1

The Environmental Problem:
Regulation or Structure

This book is about the failure of environmental protection. It does not aim to attack the environmental policies of any one country. Rather, it hopes to shed some light on why our best-laid environmental plans go astray. Environmental pollution now affects all the communist countries. The following newspaper quotations provide an idea of the dimensions of the problem in the Soviet Union and Yugoslavia.

"The problem of protecting air quality in cities has become so serious, that someone described it humorously in this way: either people do something to reduce the amount of smoke in the air, or the smoke will do something to reduce the amount of people."[1] "If I were not an optimist, I would have dropped this problem long ago."[2] "Unfortunately not always and not everywhere did local [government] use [its] full authority in its relations with businessmen who do not observe environmental protection legislation."[3] "The mass death of fish occurred in the river 16 years ago, . . . [when] the pharmaceutical plant and certain other industrial enterprises discharged a large dose of production wastes into the Sura [a tributary of the Volga]. The river still cannot set itself right from what happened. Pollution of the river continues. See for yourself."[4]

"Considerable sums have been allocated for antipollution measures and the construction of purification installations. It is quite inadmissible when, because of violations of operating rules, unsatisfactory technical conditions or insufficient staffing, they do not operate at full capacity. . . . The use of mineral fertilizers and chemical pest and weed killers in the fields is on the increase."[5] "Motor transport has now become one of the chief atmospheric

1

pollutants in cities."[6] "Only 8–9 percent of the republic is forested. Urban acreage in trees and shrubs is half the specified standard. Thirty percent of mammal and reptile species and 20 percent of bird and amphibian species are presently listed as rare and endangered. The main reasons for all this are that laws on the books are not being implemented completely or in a prompt and timely manner, and conservation measures targets regularly fail to be met."[7] "Despite the growing water shortage, there are still numerous cases of waste of irrigation water, pollution of drinking water, and waste of mineral water. Too many industrial enterprises dump polluted water into the river system."[8] "Research has shown . . . that on the average or at times of maximum concentration, smoke pollution [in the city] was 11.6 times greater than the maximum permissible levels, soot 27 times, coal dust 31 times, . . . and nitrate dust 10 times above permissible levels in 1976."[9]

"Analyses show that there is not a single river in the province whose water quality could be classified as first class." The Sava (a tributary of the Danube) is a "river without life."[10] "The republic committee for environmental protection warns that Macedonia is on the verge of becoming a very polluted area. Skopje is already polluted. Daily measurements have been showing that in some parts of the city, the pollution is so high that it impedes normal breathing."[11] "Thus we have the phenomenon of the growth of large polluted cities and the abandonment of smaller villages and agricultural land resulting in harmful consequences for the country's economy, for life, and for defense. In our cities, there are at most 10 square meters of open, green space for every inhabitant, but experience around the world shows these areas should be at least 40 square meters per inhabitant."[12] "Rijeka is probably the most threatened area in the Northern Adriatic. . . . This is a direct result of discharging all the industrial and municipal waste water directly into the sea."[13] "On the territory of Serbia there are as many as 2,500 industrial installations and engine plants that pollute the air. Neither rivers nor lakes are spared from ever increasing pollution, while there is a type of catch word that says that investments in protecting the human environment are a 'luxury.'"[14]

These reports were not made by Western observers; they were written by local journalists for local newspapers. As such, they highlight the fact that environmental degradation (ED) has become a matter of open public concern in the communist states. The Solidarity interlude in Poland saw the publication for the first time of data indicating the actual scale of the disaster there. Environmental degradation is now publicly admitted to be at crisis levels in Czechoslovakia. It is growing more serious in Yugoslavia every year. In the USSR, the increase in press reports of pollution and the waste of natural resources is testimony to rising official awareness of the Soviet environmental problem.

Until the end of the sixties, the Soviet Union and the rest of the socialist bloc dismissed environmental problems as the evil result of capitalism. Citizens were assured that the socialist system, particularly the public ownership of production, prevented such abuses from occurring in the socialist countries. The eruption of national and then international scientific concern over Lake Baikal brought recognition that the USSR, like capitalist nations, did have pollution problems, but that these problems were being taken well in hand by the party and government. In the early seventies, Soviet and East European scientists and journalists began to give systematic consideration to the scope and the depth of the ecological problems in their countries.[15]

In the West, rising popular interest in ecological issues aroused public curiosity about environmental conditions in the East. Were "they" doing better than "we"? The American environmental movement of the sixties was the product of widespread public disillusion with private enterprise, particularly as regarded its ability to engage in sound resource management and environmental protection. The negative effects of the profit motive and the market mechanism were ready targets for groups concerned with the increasing visibility of environmental abuse. Collective management by nonprofit government agencies was seen as the answer to the perceived insensitivity of private enterprise to environmental problems.[16] In the early seventies, Goldman and Pryde published studies indicating that the Soviet experience in collective management might not be the panacea for environmental degradation. The studies provoked more questions than they answered, and research on environmental degradation in the communist countries took off. Analyses and descriptions of the problem now not only include the Soviet Union but Eastern Europe and China as well.[17] Environmental degradation in the USSR has been the subject of a number of thought-provoking dissertations.[18] The growing literature on the subject is

3

proof of the fascination the environmental problem in the communist bloc continues to exert on Western students of the communist world.

How could environmental degradation reach such proportions in a system with a centrally planned economy and the total absence of private enterprise? Kelley, in a 1976 study, concluded that the Soviet Union might have a long-term advantage in dealing with environmental problems because of its political and administrative centralization and "a pattern of social and cultural norms which emphasizes deference to authority and a collectivist ethic."[19] McIntyre and Thompson also argued in favor of the greater long-term ability of the Soviet state-owned and centrally planned system to deal with environmental deterioration because of its comprehensive information-management capabilities.[20]

Many of the answers to communist environmental "misuse," to use Fred Singleton's word, have been sought in the economic realm. Goldman has summed up the most common arguments: no attempt to assess externalities; shortcomings in cost-benefit analysis; and emphasis on gross national product or economic growth as opposed to the concept of net national well-being.[21] Others with Goldman have offered a bureaucratic-administrative explanation. Goldman describes "a Department of Public Works mentality." Powell argues the lack of a central agency to develop and oversee environmental policy, the absence of autonomous interest groups, and "departmentalism," a variant of Goldman's public works mentality.[22] Kelley faults the Communist party elite for failing to accept the political costs of reordering national priorities to initiate adequate abatement programs, while Ziegler compellingly argues that administrative reorganization is the key.[23] Ideology has also been used, notably by Pryde, Goldman, and Fullenbach, as an explanation for an exaggerated confidence in technical solutions, and for failure to introduce appropriate economic levers to control pollution.[24]

The assumption behind these explanations accepts collective management of the environment as a given. The problem is to make it more efficient. This view is also the one endorsed by most Soviet environmental specialists, many of whom argue for more rather than less centralization as the solution.[25] By contrast, John M. Kramer attributes the divergence of environmental theory and practice in communist systems to the mistaken assumption of Marxist theory that "there is such a thing as the 'true inter-

4

ests of society' to which subsystem actors will subordinate their parochial interest."[26]

Kramer's position points to another dimension of the problem. While admittedly there is centralization of political power in communist states, environmental management in these societies is a complex disaggregated process involving inputs from many sources and a plurality of decision-makers.[27] The outputs of environmental policymaking in Moscow, Prague, and Warsaw in fact represent policy trade-offs among the individual subsystem interests, with organizational influence the major factor determining the shape of the "collective decision." As a result, party leaders and planners may not be able to impose their environmental preferences upon the system's subsystem actors, as Bush[28] and Kelley argue they can do, any more efficiently than elected officials can influence the same actors in pluralistic political systems.

The newspaper comments citing failures in environmental management in the USSR and Yugoslavia are extraordinarily similar to accounts of failures in environmental administration in the United States. An observation made by Paul Downing of Florida State University could with some minor alterations be attributed to a Soviet or Yugoslav proenvironmental economist: "We have spent a substantial portion of the nation's resources on controlling emissions. Yet the data . . . show that it is difficult to document significant progress. Furthermore, the rate of progress in air pollution control has not increased and in water pollution control it may, in fact, have been brought to zero. The country does not seem to have benefited greatly from this massive federal effort. One might reasonably ask why not."[29]

East and West share the experience of relatively poor progress in pollution control, a mounting pollution problem, and inefficient environmental administration. The public management of environmental protection has become one of the major policy issues confronting the industrialized and industrializing nations today. There is not a single industrialized country that has not taken a proenvironmental stand, and there is not a single one where pollution has been brought under control. In the industrialized democracies, policy may be proenvironmental, but the machinery to deliver and enforce that policy is dependent upon such factors as the relative strength of the interest groups involved, perceived urgency of national security, public acceptance and mobilization as regards energy use and environmental abuse, and the presence or absence of incentives to ensure policy implementation. In the communist one-party states, lack of citizen access to policymaking, the juncture of interests between government and industry, a too rigidly centralized planning mechanism, and bureaucratic intransigence have been cited as being responsible for emasculated environmental decisions with little enforceable content. When one examines more closely the different reasons advanced for environmental failures in the two kinds of systems, the question becomes, how different are they?

There are also striking parallels in management philosophy and method between the two systems. The similarities were sufficient to suggest to Goldman "convergence": like problems necessitate like functional responses. One may thus expect the "convergence" of all modern societies toward similar economic and political institutions.[30] Environmental management in the United States is not undertaken by private enterprise or in consideration of the operation of market forces. The thrust of American environmental management, as in all the Western industrialized countries, has been regulatory, with a pivotal central regulatory agency (or agencies) responsible for policy implementation. Management has been regulatory because the environment has customarily been treated as a public good rather than a private resource. Anderson and Hill, for example, argue that the late nineteenth-century turnabout in American federal resource disposal policy was not the product of functional environmental demand but the result of the rising influence of the conservation movement. This movement "equated 'exploitation' with private enterprise and private ownership." The authors present a convincing case that general ignorance of the market mechanism, the unwillingness to risk the development of new institutions, and the influence of the European conservation experience urged Congress to adopt policies based on conservation practices developed under European feudalism.[31] Similarly, Marxism has traditionally assigned value only to those objects that have been produced with the help of human labor. Thus, countries with a dominant Marxist ideology have treated natural resources as free goods. To put an end to wasteful exploitation of cost-free resources, communist central planners were forced to introduce regulatory policies as their only option, given their ideological bias.[32]

East and West are experiencing similar bottlenecks in environmental administration, and both are seeking solutions along somewhat similar lines. The Soviets were the first to apply the concept of standard-setting on a national basis. A conclusion about U.S. efforts in pollution control from Kelley, Stunkel, and Wescott's comparative study of environmental management in the United States, the USSR, and Japan could have equally applied to the Soviet Union: "the democratic political system that facilitated the enactment of antipollution legislation paradoxically militates against serious consideration of the more fundamental problem of resource depletion."[33] It thus is a matter of some urgency to study the environmental politics of communist one-party states to determine what difference politicoeconomic systems make in shaping policy formation and implementation in the environmental area.

Methodology

The problem is simply posed but not so simply answered. There is a large and impressive literature on the politics of public administration in the United States, and on the politics of environmental management in particular. There is a smaller but growing literature on Soviet and East European bureaucratic or institutional politics.[34] The debate continues over the applicability of Western social science methodologies and models to the communist experience. A central focus of that debate is the question of the "uniqueness" of communist systems.[35] When Western methodologies are applied to communist societies, the findings tend all too easily to infer similarities between East and West without making any significant additions to our understanding of those aspects in the two systems that the Western observer intuitively knows are *different*.[36]

Despite the difficulties, enough cross-system work has been done to show that the approach can be productive. The theory pioneered by Skilling[37] that some form of pluralism is operative in communist societies has been confirmed many times over by subsequent research.[38] Since the end of the sixties, numerous excellent case studies have expanded our comprehension of the nature of this pluralist activity. Of particular relevance for this study is the work of Jerry Hough, Peter H. Solomon, and John Lowenhardt.[39] From a review of eight cases of decisionmaking in the USSR during the Khrushchev era, Lowenhardt found that state institutions and specialists did influence the decision process in his narrow definition of the term, i.e., that decisionmakers made decisions they otherwise might not have made. His conclusion was that communist decisionmakers respond to outside initiative.[40] In his study of the influence of Soviet criminologists on Soviet criminal policy, Solomon concluded like Hough that the constraints upon the influence of outside specialists were not fundamentally different from those facing outside actors in the West.[41] The evidence is overwhelming that policymaking in every communist state today is a plural rather than a monolithic process, dependent upon inputs from what Tökés has termed the "legitimate" or official interests of society.[42]

In the environmental area, Kelley and Gustafson have described the politics of Soviet environmental policymaking without relating it to systemic differences or common management approach, although Kramer has argued that the environmental record of the Soviet Union and Eastern Europe does not substantiate the theory of convergence. Pryde, Goldman, Kelley, Kramer, and Ziegler, among others, have demonstrated both the complexity of Soviet environmental management and the involvement of different interests in determining solutions, while Enloe, Volgyes, and more recently Kramer[43] have documented the extent of environmental deterioration in Eastern Europe. Pieces of a comparative framework may be found in each of these studies. Similar to the situation in most Western countries, there are an especially large number of organizations and institutions involved in environmental policy in Eastern Europe, embracing the forty-five odd economic ministries of the Soviet central government and the numerous self-management economic organizations of Yugoslavia. Admittedly, some states exhibit greater tendencies toward the autonomous pluralism of the Western industrialized democracies, with Yugoslavia and Hungary at this end of the spectrum. But environmental policymaking in every communist country represents, to a greater or lesser extent, negotiation and consensus among the interests affected by the policy.

The appreciation of "the actor's margin of liberty" in the organizational setting, to use Crozier and Friedberg's terminology,[44] came late to the study of the Soviet system. Ideological differences between East and West during the Cold War and the successful concealment of power struggles from public view under Stalin no doubt prolonged the delay. The first Western social science methodologies applied to the Soviet scene in the sixties were static sociological concepts derived from Parsonian functionalism. They analyzed actors and their behavior in terms of political functions assumed to be given in any organized environment. Hough, for example, determined that the Soviet local party chief performed the function of prefectorial mediator because a local political system required the balancing of disparate interests, and the Soviet system was no exception. As his book so ably demonstrates, the static approach can be a powerful tool in demythologizing our study of Soviet politics and facilitating the recognition of likeness between the Western democratic and Soviet systems. At the same time, the approach tends to seduce the observer into the complacent expectation that all political systems may be reduced to one simple paradigm. The present task is to explain similar environmental outputs in dissimilar political systems possessing, however, certain similarities of environmental philosophy and style. Are the systems' similarities or dissimilarities responsible for the similar environmental failures?

Crozier and Friedberg have outlined an approach that gets at the "uniqueness" problem by focusing on the relation between the actor and the system as a game situation.[45] Environmental management can thus be visualized as a game where organizational structures and regulations provide the constraining framework within which environmental actors mobilize resources and develop strategies to influence the outcome of the game and thereby improve their power position vis-à-vis the other players. Outcomes would include the promulgation of new regulations, the reorganization of existing institutions, or the formation of new ones. In the game situation, organization and regulation are ever-changing and dynamic. On the one hand, they constitute the ordered context within which power relationships unfold: they define the minimum level of predictability of action for each actor and, in so doing, determine both the assets and the risks each brings to the game. On the other hand, organization and regulation are game outcomes, reflecting the temporary equilibrium between the game's players at a given moment in time. An investigation of the dynamic relationship between an environmental actor and the environmental management organization makes it possible to go beyond the sterile attempt to establish the superiority of one system over another in arresting the process of environmental decay to get at the heart of the power relationships that determine environmental management policies.

9

In the game situation, power is inseparably related to organization. Human actors obtain their objectives through their use of power, but power is defined solely in the context of organization. Human beings cannot exercise power over others except in the pursuit of a collective objective described by an organization whose structure determines the substance and process of the power transactions. The analysis of a power relation thus requires answers to two sets of complementary questions: the first regards the resources available to each player, the second involves the determination of the structural constraints underlying the power relation.

Crozier and Friedberg suggest four sources of power that derive from organization and correspond to the different types of uncertainty inherent in an organization's operation: (1) power stemming from the mastery of the technical expertise required by the organization; (2) power deriving from knowledge of or control over the environment in which the organization functions: ability to manipulate groups and institutions that are external to the organization and are essential to the organization's ongoing performance; (3) power stemming from the control of information and communications; and (4) power arising from the knowledge of the internal workings of the organization itself. The success of any actor in a political power relationship depends not only on an objective assessment of his "assets," but also on his subjective ability to utilize those assets within the organizational constraints in such a way as to develop strategies that will maximize his power vis-à-vis the other players.

When this approach is applied to national environmental policymaking, the organization becomes the national sociopolitical structure, and the players become the individuals and institutions involved in the policy process. Environmental legislation and regulation both serve as political constraints defining the players' moves and at the same time reflect the power balance between the various actors at a given moment in the game. We are thus in a position to investigate which of the two organizational features in communist one-party systems plays a greater role in defining the politics of the environmental management actors: the politicoeconomic system or the regulatory principle common to both Eastern and Western environmental management philosophies.

Since diversity has proved to be endemic in the socialist bloc, this study compares two communist states: the USSR and Yugoslavia. Others will be discussed in specific instances where appropriate. The USSR and Yugo-slavia conveniently represent the opposite organizational poles of centrali-zation and decentralization in communist state systems. The choice of Yugoslavia further prevents the temptation to use the Soviet Union as a model for all communist polities. It should not be overlooked, however, that Soviet decisions pertaining to environmental protection exercise deci-sive influence on policy development in other socialist states and also have an impact upon environmental policymaking elsewhere, including the United States. Yugoslavia's claim to a special Yugoslav path to com-munism makes it possible to evaluate the relevance of politicoeconomic structure in the environmental policy process among communist states, while at the same time providing a reference point other than the Soviet experience for comparison with the Western industrialized democracies.

Four elements may be identified in our comparative model of the en-vironmental management process: the regulatory management principle shared by both East and West, the politicoeconomic factors unique to communist systems, the flow of activities in the formation of environmental policy, and the actors in the policymaking process.

The Environmental Regulatory Principle

Ripley and Franklin have conveniently summarized the general charac-teristics of protective regulatory policy. (1) Regulation is *coercive*; it has an *enforcement dimension* that is perceived to be threatening. (2) Regulation implementation is a *hands-on activity* where the regulatory agents must go directly into the field and interact with the regulated clients. These inter-actions set up adversarial relations because the regulated interests receive no rewards. Their actions are restricted, and if they do not comply, they are punished. (3) Regulatory policy is "*activist.*" The regulatory agencies must take positive steps to implement the law. If they do not, the regulated clients will probably take no steps at all, since nonimplementation is eco-nomically preferable in the short run.[46]

These characteristics are embodied in environmental policy in at least seven kinds of regulatory measures.

(1) National standard-setting. Standards are of two kinds: ambient stan-dards and point-source emission standards. Politics is generated by (*a*) the

11

definition of the standards; (*b*) the problem of meshing the two kinds of standards, so that a combination of point-source emissions into the air, for example in a given locality, in fact approximates the appropriate ambient air quality level for that area; and (*c*) the frequent inadequacy of point-source emission standards to solve the pollution problem, as in the case of acid rain or water basin management. Non-point-sources of pollution so far are not regulated in any country.

(2) Technological forcing. An agency may be designated to develop or pass judgment on technology that can be used to meet a given pollution control requirement. In either case, technological development is sought by means of an administrative mechanism rather than through an open, competitive process, and the regulated industries are coerced into developing and/or accepting mandated technology.

(3) "Date certain" principle. In some countries, such as the United States, legal deadlines are set for the regulated interests to meet the promulgated standards. Even in those countries where the law does not specify a deadline, as in the Soviet Union, an industry may be warned and then cited for noncompliance. Political confrontation between the regulating agency and the regulated industry is inevitable. The former's interest lies in securing soonest compliance, while industry desires to delay the deadline as long as possible, particularly if lack of resources (money and technology) makes compliance impracticable.

(4) The delegation of implementation authority to administrative bureaucracies. In the Western countries, delegation is to a separate agency or agencies. In the Soviet Union, delegation can be and frequently is to the same organization that is polluting the resource. In both, the political contest is shaped by the degree of tension between the enforcement agency and the restricted client in meeting implementation goals, and the degree to which the monitoring and control functions are separated from the economic activity of the polluter.

(5) The requirement of regional implementation plans, down to the local level. The politics of this measure is found in the relationship of local and regional authorities to the center.[47]

(6) Land-use planning and regulation as a way to define access to scarce resources. As in (5), there is the politics between center and periphery, particularly that arising between national industrial polluters and local planners.

(7) State subsidy of pollution control costs. In no country does the polluter have to bear the total cost of pollution control. The polluter thus has access to what Fort and Baden term the "treasury commons."[48] This measure may stimulate the sharpest conflict, because the polluter is more than likely making additional demands upon public funds at the same time as other interests are making their own claims.

The principles outlined above may be said to define the parameters of the environmental regulatory process. The politics they delineate is a low-profile, delaying mode for the regulated interests vis-à-vis the regulatory agencies. At the same time, the regulated interests engage in intense political activity to influence the policy preferences of the decisionmakers so as to secure their due share of the public funds. The regulatory agencies may attempt to secure compliance by mobilizing public support; or, if they perceive themselves in a weak political situation, they may strike a compromise with their clients "that all can live with," leading to collusion between the regulator and the regulated.

Politicoeconomic Structure

Four systemic differences between communist and noncommunist states stand out from others that could be mentioned as identifying the aggregate "uniqueness" of the communist polity. The first is the public ownership of the means of production and state ownership of all natural resources. In the Soviet Union and most of Eastern Europe, the state is the major economic producer; in Yugoslavia, a self-management system operates. Goldman suggests that there is a greater danger of collusion in environmental affairs in the Soviet system than in Western societies precisely because the state is both regulator and manufacturer.[49] The total absence of private ownership of natural resources means that the resources of an entire country form a common pool from which the various economic and social interests can draw. Since the resources cost nothing, the demand made upon them exceeds in many areas their capacity to deliver. Water is a prime example. Every communist country, without exception, faces critical problems of water scarcity and water pollution. Unless the rights to scarce resources are carefully defined, demand will continue to exceed supply. Definition of rights to a common resource, however, is a complex political process carried out between water users. Because the process *is* political,

13

definition may never be completed, only revised. Hence, if total public ownership of natural resources makes any difference, it may be expected to increase political controversy and delay environmental solution.

The second difference is the universal adoption by all communist states of some form of central planning mechanism. By contrast, central planning exists in only a few of the Western industrial democracies. As stated earlier, many Western as well as communist specialists are persuaded that central planning is essential if environmental protection and conservation are to become realities. In the words of one Yugoslav expert, "Without planning, you Americans ravaged a wilderness environment in less than 100 years. By planning for environmental protection of our still under-developed country, we Yugoslavs will make haste slowly, it is true. But when we reach your level of development, it will not be at the price of environmental decay. We will have achieved ecological stability."[50] Plans and their realization, however, are two very different things. In all the communist countries, newspaper accounts of unfulfilled plans, particularly in the environmental area, have become a common occurrence. The development and implementation of plans are, once again, political processes. As Benveniste has said, "Even the most powerful Prince cannot always impose decisions on all the minions of his kingdom," particularly when one program is popular among many clients and another is not.[51] We are back to the "parochial interests of subsystem actors" using their "margin of liberty" to shape the planning decision.

The third systemic difference is a mandated ideology and/or the refusal to permit competing ideologies. As was suggested earlier, in the environmental area ideological differences may not be that great. Both East and West appear committed to doing something about the environment and to the idea that the profit motive and environmental protection do not mix. Both ideologies fail to come to grips with the problems of externalities and the real cost of production. The distinguishing elements in the communist ideology as far as the environment is concerned are the retention of the classical Marxist labor theory of value, the public ownership of the means of production, and the concept of the planned solution to environmental problems. The last two have already been identified as separate components of the system. Perhaps the most important function of ideology as it concerns policymaking in communist states is to limit the area of discussion by setting bounds to policy alternatives.[52] National political culture plays its role in conforming the ideology to the individual national environment. In Yugoslavia, one cannot think of policy options outside the self-management system. But while ideology may form the basis for the policy process, the significance of its role in determining policy outcomes is far from clear.

The fourth difference, and the most salient political aspect of communist states, is the monopoly of political power by one party. In the West, environmental debates are conducted within the framework of open decision-making, while in the East, even in Yugoslavia, decisionmaking occurs largely within a closed, single-party context. What impact does political style have on environmental policy outcomes? Can a single party mandate environmental protection? If a one-party system makes a difference, the evidence is that it may be very effective in the formation of a proenvironmental policy, but it is relatively powerless to implement it. One reason is the impossibility of coordinating the individual production targets of the different economic ministries into one program that balances economic growth with environmental and resource conservation. A second reason, which is the focus of this study, is the nature of the dynamics of the power balance between the interests concerned, a power balance that regulatory policy serves to promote. The relevance of one-party dominance to the determination of environmental policy performance may be considerably less than one might expect.

To carry the thought further, there is a widespread popular conviction in the West that without an autonomous environmental lobby and freedom of public participation, neither government nor industry would act. A single-party monopoly clearly cannot coexist with autonomous interest groups. However, paradoxical as it may seem, public pressure and single-party discipline at times can intersect to produce similar results. As Charles Jones has shown in his classic study of air pollution politics, spontaneous public outcry can produce nonimplementable laws[53], just as single-party discipline can father emasculated legislation. The consequence of both actions is a necessary return to the politics of "parochial interests" for legislative or administrative modification.

These four factors taken together constitute the global differences between communist and noncommunist systems. Many of them exist singly or in varying sets of pairs or triads in other countries. But they must occur together to satisfy this study's definition of a communist one-party state. Some might prefer to emphasize other aspects of the system, such as systematic terror, mass mobilization, or communications censorship. However, in the author's view, these aspects may be derived from the first four and are not primary in and of themselves. Moreover, all of them are not present in all communist one-party systems. Systematic terror, for example, has retreated into the background to a substantial degree in Hungary and Yugoslavia.

Typology of Policymaking Activities

The generalized model of the flow of policymaking activities described by Ripley and Franklin assumes four sets of activities in policy formation: agenda-setting, information collecting, compromise and negotiation, and ratification; and four sets in implementation: resource acquisition, interpretation and planning, organizing, and providing benefits and services.[54] The policy formation categories have been repeatedly refined in American policy models, particularly in the area of agenda-setting.[55] With its focus on the actor-organization relationship in policymaking, this study proposes to examine policy formation activities only insofar as they have an impact on the organizational constraints and the mobilizable assets, strategies, and rewards of the relevant actors.[56] In implementation, resources denote equipment, personnel, land, and, most important, money. Interpretation and planning translate legislation into concrete regulations and programs, while organizing involves creating or restructuring bureaucratic units to produce the output, whether it be a product or a desired performance.

All of these activities have been identified in communist policymaking, although they have not been studied as a unified process.[57] A serious obstacle to our understanding of the actor-organization relationship in the policy process in communist states, as Lowenhardt aptly points out,[58] is our frequent ignorance of who the decisionmakers really are. The closed nature of communist decisionmaking makes it particularly difficult to assign responsibility for a major policy decision, unless the issue involves a power struggle between rival contenders for leadership. If the decision is ratified by legislation, one can be sure that in the Soviet Union, the Council of

Ministers accepted responsibility for the decision and that in Yugoslavia, there was consensus in the federal parliament. But since the vote in the Supreme Soviet represents confirmation of a prior decision and there is no vote in the Yugoslav federal parliament, we still remain in ignorance about the specific dynamics of the individual decision. Happily, we can have much more certainty in the area of administrative regulations. In the Soviet Union and most of Eastern Europe, the institutions responsible for issuing these are designated by the Council of Ministers, and if the regulations are particularly important, there will be a joint party-government designation. In Yugoslavia, the designation is contained in the law. The formal organization of environmental administration indicates which agencies are involved in which particular environmental area. It is but one step from there to the identification of "subgovernments" specialized in a particular environmental policy field, a subject that will be taken up later.

A further hindrance to our understanding of public policymaking activity in communist states is our lack of substantive information on policy issues prior to their adoption and/or ratification. Moreover, only a small number of regulations are ever made public. In the Soviet Union, most are handed down within the responsible bureaucracies, and are consequently inaccessible to the researcher. Contracts between self-management institutions in Yugoslavia are considered private and hence not a matter of public information. Censorship in both countries ensures that only those aspects of the issues that are permitted to be made public reach the media, and on many issues there is no public discussion at all. While one may infer that negotiating and bargaining went on, for example, in the seven-year interval between the drafting and passage of the Soviet Air Quality Control Law in 1980, only insiders know the actual content and shape of the negotiations. In the environmental area, discussion in the press has been rather free on conceptual matters, but we know far less about the concrete policy alternatives that are the subjects of legislative or administrative action.

The Actors

The systemic differences between East and West argue against equating the actors in the communist policy process with Western counterparts on a one-to-one basis. The principles of socialist ownership and the monopoly

17

of political power mean there can be no autonomous interest groups or private enterprise, as these operate in the West. In this sense, Kelley's division of Soviet actors in environmental policymaking into Western-style industrial and environmental lobbies is misleading, as is his further distinction between official and semiofficial institutions.[59] One can, however, distinguish between government or state institutions and actors and nongovernmental institutions and actors, including informal environmental groupings. The former may be said to represent the "insiders," the latter, the "outsiders" in the policy process, although the lines can become blurred as we shall see.[60]

The identification of government institutions and responsible public officials is relatively easy because most of these are designated by law or regulation. Nongovernmental organizations, such as expert institutes or the nature protection societies that exist in all the communist states, are also readily identified. It is much more difficult to define an informal group such as an environmental "lobby" because the latter has no legitimate status or formal organization. To borrow Almond's term, it is "nonassociational."[61] In the environmental area, however, there is substantial evidence throughout Eastern Europe and the Soviet Union of the activity of unofficial groups whose members exhibit the shared attitudes and common characteristics that David Truman urged were a group's identifying features. More important, these groups are political in the sense that group members maintain interaction and express a common claim upon the government.[62] The most visible of the informal environmental groups has been the scientists, particularly the natural scientists.[63] But the activity of journalists, lawyers, and economists should not be overlooked.[64]

In the communist environmental management system, then, one may roughly identify two sets of actors: government institutions and officials and nongovernmental organizations, interest groupings, and individuals. The former includes the environmental administrative agencies, the socially owned economic organizations, the Communist party apparat, and the central and republican executives. The second set contains two types of interest groupings: the specialists and researchers working in the environmental area, whom we shall term "the experts," and the "expert" organizations, such as the institutes of the Academy of Sciences, universities, and the lawyers', writers', and journalists' associations; and the public at large functioning as an environmental "lobby" either through the official environmental organizations (such as the Soviet republican societies for the preservation of nature, or the Yugoslav Gorani Movement), or in its capacity to make demands upon the authorities by letters or other approved means to indicate support or the withholding of support on an environmental issue. The actors may be conveniently grouped in the following order:

Environmental administrative agencies

The socially owned economic institutions (the economic ministries in the Soviet Union and the self-management organizations in Yugoslavia)

The central and republican party and government leadership

Experts and expert organizations

The public as individuals or organized in approved mass organizations

Each of these actors will be examined in turn with the aim of determining his "margin of liberty" in the environmental policy process within a four-part framework: (1) the regulatory and structural constraints imposed by the environmental management system, (2) available resources, (3) rewards and costs, and (4) the resulting strategies developed by him to improve his position in the "game." Policy input in this context is viewed not as a given form of activity, but as the product of the interaction of the environmental policy actors with their organizational environment.

It is assumed that the environmental policy process is not zero-sum, as some would see it, where the economy wins and the environment loses, or vice versa. Although pollution costs fall heavily on the economic sector, the jury is still out on whether economic production suffers because of these costs. Czech scientists argue that their economy will experience marked deterioration *unless* pollution controls are taken seriously.[65] The environmental policy game seems a no-win situation. Neither the economic interests nor the environmental advocates can obtain all of their objectives. Because protective regulatory policy benefits the many at a perceived high cost to the few, it is highly controversial,[66] and the adjustment of environmental concerns to economic demands is continuous.

In the politics of this adjustment process in the two states under review, it will be argued that "the experts" have most improved their position vis-à-vis the other actors, because of their exclusive claim to understanding the unknown ecological future (Crozier and Friedberg's first source of organizational power). The public has also become more assertive, although to a much more limited degree, through its status as recipient of the benefits and services of environmental regulation. (Crozier and Friedberg's second source of organizational power.) However, Crozier and Friedberg's third and fourth sources of power continue to make the economic organizations formidable players: control of information and communications and inside knowledge of the internal workings of the policy process. To keep the study's scope within manageable limits, discussion has been restricted to the politics of the three most critical environmental issues in the industrialized world and the countries under review: land and resource use, water, and air pollution.

Chapter 2 is a general description of the environmental policy milieus in the USSR and Yugoslavia. In particular, it will compare their similar regulatory frameworks and also the distinctive structural characteristics of Soviet centralized environmental management with the Yugoslav self-management variant. The next five chapters deal with the actors. For purposes of comparison, the same organizational format is used in each of them. Although some might prefer more emphasis on the natural scientists and geographers in the discussion of experts, I have chosen to stress the economists and legal profession. The objective is a more precise understanding of the role of regulation and the politicoeconomic system in shaping environmental policy inputs and reflecting environmental political outcomes.

Before we turn to the body of the study, a few definitions of terms are in order. Environmental management is commonly understood to refer to two aspects of the process. The first is controlling the effects of pollution: sewage treatment, air pollution control; the second encompasses the notion of preventing future harmful effects, or establishing some kind of equilibrium between man's activities and the ability of the environment to handle them.[67] In the industrialized countries, the main thrust of environmental management so far has been in controlling the effects of environmental damage. This study consequently concentrates on that aspect of the problem, although work is being done in both the USSR and Yugoslavia on the second aspect and will be mentioned where appropriate.

Second, the term environment will be used throughout to refer both to the environment that has been affected by the activity of man, what the Yugoslavs call "the human environment," and to what might be considered untouched nature, in other words, those areas where the impact of man has been minimal.

Finally, a word about sources: the material for this study was primarily assembled during official visits to the USSR and Yugoslavia. Given the reality of censorship, published sources in both countries reflect the present leaderships' fundamentally optimistic view of the environmental problem, and the reader must take this attitude into account when evaluating the published material. This view was also the one most often expressed in the author's formal interviews with environmental officials, heads of environmental mass organizations, and local government representatives. It was much less shared in her private conversations with economists, lawyers, and acquaintances. For each formal interview, permission was sought, and granted, to take notes, and most of the personal citations in the study will be quotations or paraphrasing of these notes. There is no direct attribution of source for the private conversations.

2

The Centipede and the Hydra

The structural differences between the USSR and Yugoslavia in the organization of environmental policy make the sharpest initial impression upon the researcher. This chapter describes these differences and their impact on the common regulatory principle outlined in chapter 1. It will be seen that the opportunities for access to environmental policymaking as well as the rewards and restrictions offered to the individual and institutional actors in each society, are more similar than is immediately apparent. The chief distinction lies in the pattern of political interaction. In the Soviet case, the pattern may be most easily conceptualized as a many-legged centipede, while Yugoslavia's decentralized self-management recalls the creature of Greek mythology, the multiheaded hydra.

Centralized Pluralism

The Soviet environmental management system is complex, with a large number of actors participating in the decisionmaking process.[1] According to the USSR Constitution of 1977, state ownership of the means of production is "the foundation of the USSR's economic system" (Article 10). Further, "the land, its mineral wealth, the waters and the forests are the exclusive property of the state" (Article 11).[2] While state ownership may be unified, the administration and exploitation of environmental resources has had in practice to be distributed over a wide range of state institutions. Figure 2.1 provides a highly simplified diagram of the flow of administrative and planning functions.

Figure 2.1   Flow of Administrative and Planning Functions in the USSR

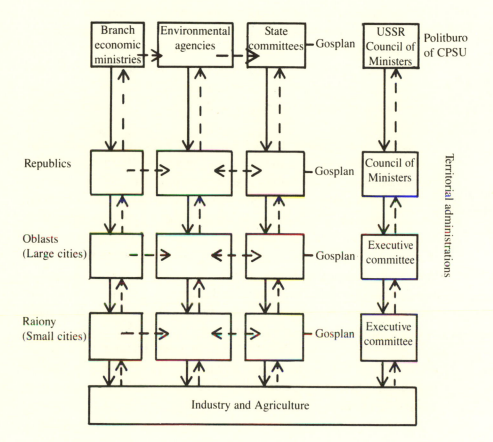

Note. Solid arrows indicate direction of policy and planning decisions. Broken arrows indicate direction of draft policy submission, consultation, and information exchange.

At the top of the system stand the USSR Council of Ministers and the Central Committee (CC) of the Communist Party of the Soviet Union (CPSU). These bodies issue the policy directives. The major policy documents are the five-year guidelines adopted by the CPSU Congress at five-year intervals. From time to time, the Council of Ministers either separately, or jointly with the Central Committee when the matter is especially important, adopts resolutions that turn policy guidelines into specific programs and obligations. The seminal document of the last two decades has been the 1972 Resolution to Strengthen Environmental Protection and the Rational Development of Natural Resources,[3] which first spelled out the overall tasks of each component of the environmental administrative system.

The directives are issued through a process of negotiation between what Soviet jurists call the organs of general competence, or the supervisory state committees,[4] and the specialized organs responsible either for a branch of economic production or a particular element of the environment, such as land, water, or air. The directives are binding upon all parties mentioned in the resolution. There are seven state committees involved in environmental management, ten lead (*golovyie*) agencies responsible for a specific environmental sector, and some twenty-nine branch ministries engaged in administration or exploitation of natural resources. The branch ministries are further divided into all-union institutions, which answer only to Moscow and are organized in a territorial chain of command independent of the republican administrations, and the union-republic ministries, which are responsible to the central government through the republican councils of ministers. Table 2.1 provides a list of the central institutions engaged in environmental management as of 1985.

The all-union ministries administer the sectors of the Soviet economy most vital to national security: defense, the transport building industries, machine building, chemicals, gas and oil, and high technology. Union-republic ministries manage those sectors that tend to have a strong territorial base, such as the coal and oil refining industries, ferrous metallurgy, and the timber and wood processing industries. Agricultural production used to be distributed among several union-republican ministries, but these were replaced in 1985 by a consolidated All-Union State Agro-Industrial Committee. Some observers have considered the differences between the

Table 2.1 Glossary of Central Institutions, USSR (1986)

Institution name	Russian acronym	Union-republic organs	All-union organs
USSR state committees			
State Agro-Industrial Committee[a]	Gosagroprom	X	
State Committee for Construction Affairs	Gosstroi	X	
State Committee on Forestry	Gosleskhoz	X	
State Committee on Hydrometeorology and Environmental Protection	Goskomgidromet		X
State Committee for Material and Technical Supply	Gossnab	X	
State Planning Committee	Gosplan	X	
State Committee on Science and Technology	GKNT		X
State Committee on Standards	Gosstandart		X
USSR branch ministries and organizations			
Automotive industry			X
Chemical industry			X
Chemical and petroleum machine building	Minkhimmash		X
Coal		X	
Construction materials industry		X	
Construction, road, and municipal machine building			X
Ferrous metallurgy		X	
Fish industry	Minrybkhoz	X	
Forest products industry[b]	Minlesprom	X	X
Gas			X
Geology		X	
Health	Minzdrav	X	
Heavy and transport machine building			X
Instrument making, automotive and control systems			X
Internal affairs	MVD	X	
Justice		X	
Land reclamation and water resources	Minvodkhoz	X	
Light industry		X	
Maritime fleet			X
Medium machine building			X
Nonferrous metallurgy		X	
Oil refining and petrochemical industry	Minneftkhimprom	X	
Petroleum			X
Power and electrification		X	

25

Table 2.1 (*Continued*)

Institution name	Russian acronym	Union-republic organs	All-union organs
Power machine building			×
Shipbuilding			×
Tractor and agricultural machine building			×
USSR Academy of Sciences	ANSSSR	×	
Total		20	17

Source: Modified and updated from table facing p. 50, U.S. Congress, Joint Economic Committee, *Soviet Economy in a Time of Change*, vol. 1 (Washington, D.C.: U.S. Government Printing Office, 1979).
a. Replaced the Ministry of Agriculture and related union-republic branch ministries in 1985.
b. In 1981 the Ministry of Pulp and Paper and the Ministry of Timber and Wood Processing were merged into one ministry.

two types of central ministries more formal than real,[5] and there are cases where a ministry may operate along both chains of command. For example, in 1981, the Ministry of Pulp and Paper and the Ministry of Timber and Wood Processing were merged into a union-republic Forest Products Ministry (Minlesprom), which, despite its labeling, retained the direct administrative relationship to Moscow of the old Pulp and Paper Ministry.[6] Subordinate to the Council of Ministers at the republican level are economic activities of lesser importance not included in the table, such as local industry, automotive and river transportation, trade, public catering, and service industries. With the exception of the republican ministry of local industry, these activities are only marginally involved in environmental pollution.

As can be seen from the table, many of the "environmental" agencies, such as the ministries of Health (Minzdrav), Fish Industry (Minrybkhoz), Geology, and Land Reclamation and Water Resources (Minvodkhoz), are union-republic ministries, while the major polluting industries are administered primarily by all-union ministries. The distinction offers the all-union ministries the option of negotiation with the environmental agencies only at the top of the hierarchy. Beneath this network of central institutions are over five thousand territorial units,[7] each with its subdivisions of the central branch and republican organs, all of which are responsible to their superior at the next higher territorial level, and whose decisions, in accordance with the principle of "democratic centralism," may be rescinded by their superiors. As the headquarters of key economic and other operations, the central organs enjoy considerable autonomy in relations with each other and exercise substantial ministerial power over the subordinate bureaucracies. By contrast, the many regional subordinates are highly limited in their autonomy, the expansion of which is restricted by the central institutions.

A characteristic feature of the system is the separation of the administration of natural resources from their exploitation. The State Agro-Industrial Committee administers the state land fund with the exception of land under municipal or state forest designation. The State Committee on Forestry (Gosleskhoz) administers all state forest land, except that found in municipalities, in agricultural areas, or associated with waterways and reservoirs, while Minvodkhoz has jurisdiction over all state waters except the coastal areas. The users of these resources include all the industrial ministries making claims upon them. For example, two-thirds of the logging operations in the USSR are carried out by Minlesprom on land administered by Gosleskhoz.[8] Coal operations also take place on land under Gosleskhoz administration. The separation of resource administration and resource use sets up a relationship between resource exploiter and administrator not unlike that in the United States between a private company with a lease on federal lands and the federal agency that granted the lease. In both cases, the user bears no responsibility for the management of the exploited area and has a direct interest in obtaining the resource as cheaply as possible, while the administrator has only limited means at his disposal to control the user's activities.

The division of labor extends beyond a single set of central agencies. The Oil Ministry may be responsible for oil production, but in order to get the oil out of the ground, the ministry needs the assistance of other ministries responsible for the operations necessary to obtain the oil. The Chemical and Petroleum Machine Building Ministry (Minkhimmash) provides the equipment; the Construction Materials Ministry, the requisite building materials; the Instrument Making, Automation, and Control Systems Ministry, the automated systems; and the Oil Refining and Petrochemical

Industry, the crude petroleum. The administration of the oilfield may be divided between the Ministry of Geology, which is responsible for underground deposits, and the central agency responsible for the administration of the above-ground parcel of land. Each of these organs has limited autonomy in a designated area of specialization. Each also has a monopoly over information and program implementation in that area with specific plan targets and objectives, only one of which may be the oil development project, and not necessarily the principle one at that. Coordination breaks down as the ministries focus on meeting what they perceive to be their priority plan targets, with project delays, nondelivery of requisite equipment, and environmental degradation the inevitable result. As Alex Nove has pointed out, the successful realization of a large development project requires the creation of a supervisory authority with power to force collaboration of the agencies involved.[9] The fragmented structure of Soviet administration hampers the development and operation of such authorities, since they have to operate across institutional boundaries.

One solution to the dispersal of administrative and exploitative functions has been to delegate the coordination of environmental management to the lead agencies. Thus, the lead agency for air pollution control is the State Committee for Hydrometeorology and Environmental Protection (Goskomgidromet). The lead agency for water pollution control is Minvodkhoz; for fish protection, the Ministry of the Fish Industry (Minrybkhoz). However, none of these agencies has exclusive jurisdiction over pollution control or resource management in the designated environmental area. Other agencies may be designated "lead" agencies in subaspects of a particular area, such as the Chemical and Petroleum Machine Building Industry in oil pollution control equipment. Moreover, the sheer number of institutions engaged in both administration and exploitation mandates considerable prior negotiation to achieve minimum coordination of an individual environmental program.

A second solution is to assign a coordinating authority to the state committees with general competence in environmental matters: the State Planning Committee (Gosplan), the State Committee on Science and Technology (GKNT), the State Committee for Construction Affairs (Gosstroi), and the State Committee on Hydrometeorology and Environmental Protection (Goskomgidromet). However, none of these organs so far has been given any authority to take charge of environmental problems, with the result that the environmental management system continues to be disaggregated and dispersed. Table 2.2 gives the current distribution of central institutions engaged in the implementation of environmental policy in the Soviet Union.

The relative autonomy of the central organs encourages the participants in environmental policymaking to develop strategies to increase their autonomy. These include maximizing their area of jurisdiction and/or control, neutralizing or minimizing the expansion of other organs, and delaying or evading responsibility for implementation. A discussion of these strategies occurs in the subsequent chapters on environmental actors. The dispersal of decisionmaking and administrative authority indicates the success of the central organs in resisting further centralization efforts and in protecting and even increasing their "turf."

A second feature of Soviet environmental policymaking is characteristic of all Soviet decisionmaking, namely the focus of political activity on the governmental actors at the national level. The republics were the first to realize the dangers of pollution, and six took the initiative to pass comprehensive environmental legislation in the sixties.[10] Their efforts to impose separate republican controls ran counter to the recentralizing administrative trend of the period. During the Khrushchev era, there was some experimentation with horizontal and territorial economic planning. The experiments ended with the 1965 reforms, which reasserted the principle of vertical branch planning and management. Planning was further centralized in 1973, when the rights of republics in the planning process were severely circumscribed by a resolution restructuring the middle level of management.[11] The return to the branch management principle and the recentralization of planning strengthened the branch industrial ministries at the expense of republican and regional units. Recentralization thus ensured that major input into the formation of a major social or economic decision came from the national level. The result in the environmental area was federal legislation delegating implementation authority to the central branch organs.

In the implementation of environmental policy, financial and material resources as well as organizing authority also come from the top, and local government participates only marginally in questions of allocation and

Table 2.2 Distribution of USSR Central Organs in Environmental Administration

Environmental and management area	State committee ($N = 7$)	Branch ministries and organizations		Lead agency
		Total ($N = 29$)	of which Un. Rep.	
Air				Goskomgidromet
Planning and administration	6	7	4	and
Control	5	10	6	Minkhimmash
Expertise	3	16	9	
Water				Goskomgidromet
Planning and administration	7	6	6	Minvodkhoz,
Major users	1	12	8	and Minrybkhoz
Control	2	10	9	
Expertise	5	21	12	
Land and soil				Goskomgidromet
Planning and administration	3	3	3	and Ministry of
Major users	0	10	8	Agriculture
Control	2	7	7	
Expertise	2	14	8	
Underground				Ministry of
Planning and administration	4	9	7	Geology
Major users	0	5	3	
Control	2	7	7	
Expertise	2	12	8	
Forests				Gosleskhoz
Planning and administration	4	3	3	
Major users	1	8	5	
Control	2	4	4	
Expertise	2	5	5	
Protected Land				Ministry of
Planning and administration	4	2	2	Agriculture
Major users	—	—		
Control	2	4	4	
Expertise	2	4	4	
Wildlife and plants				Minzdrav
Planning and administration	4	2	2	
Major users	—	3	3	
Control	2	4	4	
Expertise	2	4	4	
Human environment				Gosstroi and
Planning and administration	4	0	0	Committee for
Major users	—	—	—	Industrial and

Table 2.2 (*Continued*)

Environmental and management area	State committee ($N = 7$)	Branch ministries and organizations		Lead agency
		Total ($N = 29$)	of which Un. Rep.	
Control	3	3	3	Mining Work
Expertise	3	6	3	Safety

Source: Derived from the CPSU Central Committee and Presidium of the USSR Council of Ministers Joint Resolutions of December 29, 1972, and December 1978.

Note: The ministries and agencies included in the count are those specifically mentioned or otherwise inferred in the resolutions as having responsibilities in the environmental and management areas listed. The count does not include all possible ministries and agencies for each category. N = the total number of organs indicated in the resolutions. The row numbers = the number of organs delegated jurisdiction in that particular area.

distribution. Local government has greater responsibility for the control and production functions of implementation [12] and is primarily responsible for environmental enforcement. But local government has no real powers in the area of funding or acquisition of other resources, or in environmental planning and organization. The localities are thus severely limited in their ability to enforce compliance or assure implementation of policy by local polluters who are likely to be subordinates of a central branch ministry.

Despite these restrictions, the control function offers local officials some opportunities for input. Kramer found that by comparison with delegates to higher level soviets, the delegates to the municipal and district soviets were the most visible in registering complaints about the lack of industrial compliance with environmental regulations. [13] The centralized organization of industrial management means that local factory compliance can only be secured through recourse to the branch ministry headquarters for the appropriate resources and organization. Feedback on the implementation of environmental controls is thus contained within the local area unless political circumstances or national disaster brings a problem to national attention. Exposure in the national media is one input strategy available to local authorities trying to counterbalance the economic clout of the local industrial polluter.

31

Nongovernmental agents (outsiders) have no direct access to environmental policymaking at any level. However, limitation of access does not infer total denial of input. The outsiders have indirect means to exert influence. The average citizen is denied access at all but the local level. But he has the right to take his complaints to his delegate in the local soviet or write in demands (*nakazy*) at election time to which the soviet eventually must respond. Since the beginning of the Brezhnev era, official data have recorded, probably somewhat optimistically, improvement in the deputies' responsiveness to their constituents, and in their performance in reporting back to electors and fulfilling the electors' mandates. Many of these mandates have to do with environmental issues.[14] They do not necessarily reflect specific demands on the part of individuals but rather composites of categories of demands put forward at election meetings between candidates and the public. Analysis of the types of mandates provides an indication of what concerns command public attention at any given time and the strength of the informal "citizen lobbies" whose mandates are sent forward. The author's interviews suggest that Soviet citizens can become as aroused as their American counterparts when new construction threatens community landmarks, or traffic or construction noise levels become intolerable. If citizens fail to receive satisfaction from the local authorities, they may carry their complaints all the way to the top by writing a letter to the CPSU Central Committee at the convening of an all-union party congress, when every citizen has a right to petition the party leadership for redress of grievances. Since these petitions are not published, there is no way to know whether environmental complaints are among them. Like local government officials, citizens may exert particular influence beyond the local level, where the object of citizen concern is a major environmental target, such as Lake Sevan, or water pollution in Alma-Ata.

Citizens have a greater role in implementing environmental policy through the legal delegation of control functions to locally organized groups. However, it must be stressed that mass participation is organized from above and is not spontaneous grass-roots activity. Citizen involvement in the provision of monitoring and control services is written into the annual and five-year plans of the organizations that recruit citizen volunteers. Within these constraints, citizen environmental activists have a margin of liberty that they may exploit depending on the sensitivity of local officials to environmental problems and the militancy of the environmental organization's leadership.

Access to environmental policymaking by nongovernmental actors at the republican and federal levels is primarily the prerogative of the environmental specialists. Perhaps one of the most fascinating developments in the environmental area in the Soviet Union has been relatively open access of environmental experts to the mass media, given the reality of censorship and particularly the censorship of all information involving public health. In the past ten years, publications on the environment have proliferated in the Soviet Union. Bookstores in the large Soviet cities frequented by tourists will almost always have a few environmental publications on hand. It is becoming increasingly rare to pick up a popular Soviet journal and not find some reference to an environmental issue.

Several reasons may be advanced for the increased media coverage. Kramer suggests that the complexity of environmental problems has contributed to indecision among the leadership on how to deal with them.[15] Another may be that it is politically acceptable to promote the environment, and experts find a welcome response in the media for environmental topics. Finally, the material is published in such a wide variety of media throughout the fifteen union republics that the quantity and dispersal of information may make it difficult for the censor to impose a uniform code of conduct. Whatever the reasons, experts help set the environmental agenda by the issues they discuss in the mass media. Through their informational and educational roles, the experts also influence public attitudes. They are featured speakers on television programs dedicated to natural science or environmental issues. They counsel student environmental groups, lead public seminars, and head the local chapters of the republican nature protection associations.

Finally, experts influence "insider" policy through their official expert status. This status is designated by the central government to institutes attached to the branch ministries, environmental agencies, and the prestigious USSR Academy of Sciences. The first two of these are responsible for applied expertise, the last, for "pure" scientific research. Whenever an opinion is required by law, the officially designated "expert" institute is obliged to furnish it. The opportunity in this situation to perform the dual function of expert and environmental lobbyist is obvious. The official designation of "expert" is unique to Soviet-type political systems and is perhaps the single most important factor in the emergence of a proenvironmental lobby based in the scientific institutes engaged in environmental research.

Expert influence extends from the local level through the branch ministries and the republican administrations to the all-union level, where experts routinely give advice on pending legislation and are prominent in determining the shape of environmental rules and regulations. Research in the United States has shown that legislatures tend to rank environmental issues first among the scientific and technological components of the subject at hand.[16] In every country, technological progress presents increasing opportunities for expert contributions to the policy process because of the uncertainty inherent in the application of technology.[17] The Soviet Union is no exception. As a consequence, experts there as elsewhere have acquired a limited power of their own to shape environmental policy.

In summary, centralized pluralism in the context of Soviet environmental policy denotes a politicoeconomic system that focuses on input from a large number of highly dispersed and semiautonomous institutions at the top of the administrative ladder but does not exclude limited input from nongovernmental institutions and actors. Such a top-heavy multilegged figure may best be visualized as a centipede. The horizontal interaction between the semiautonomous government organs at the national level (and to a minimal degree between citizens and their government at the local level) is intersected by the vertical interplay between the various levels of the branch and environmental agencies, supported by expert advice.

Self-Management

In Yugoslavia, self-management has produced a less centralized and less rigidly structured politicoeconomic system. Djilas's exposure of "the new class" came at a time when Tito was locked in a struggle for survival with Stalin. The need to insist on a separate Yugoslav identity directed domestic criticism at the centralization of state power in the Soviet Union and the danger of the state's becoming a power over and above the rest of society.[18] The 1958 Program of the League of Communists of Yugoslavia (LCY)[19] spelled out the principles of self-management. During the 1960s, experimentation with decentralization affected every aspect of social life, including the government administration and party organization. The Croatian events of 1971 brought party indiscipline to an end with Tito's reassertion of the principle of "democratic centralism" and party unity.[20] The 1974 Constitution represents Tito's solution to national diversity by providing for a virtual confederation of the country's six national republics and two autonomous provinces (Chapter 1, Part 3) and the primacy of the LCY as "the leading ideological and political force of the working class" and "the exponent of political activity" (Section 8, Basic Principles). The constitution gives self-management its present legal form,[21] which is described in detail in the 1976 Law on Associated Labor.[22]

Under self-management, social ownership changes its character slightly from the state ownership of the Soviet Union. Article 10 of the 1974 Constitution states that the basis of the Yugoslav economic system is the socially owned means of production and self-management. Article 12 prohibits anyone from acquiring the right of ownership over social resources, including natural resources. No ownership right is permitted in urban areas. However, farmers are guaranteed the right to own arable land up to ten hectares per household and more in marginal hilly and wooded areas. Other citizens may also own agricultural land under certain specified conditions, which include private or vacation homes.

With the exception of land, all natural resources are under social ownership in the Soviet meaning of the term of state ownership. Self-management organizations may acquire the right to exploit them, but they cannot be owned by either a private or public agent. Similarly, business enterprises, known as basic associations of labor (OOUR), may be owned by the workers in that enterprise, but the land on which the enterprise stands is publicly owned by the state.[23] Social ownership in the Yugoslav context thus produces the same relationship between resource exploiter and resource user as in the Soviet Union or on American public lands.

State control of private land in Yugoslavia by definition is indirect. In 1978, 84 percent of the country's arable land belonged to private farmers and yielded around 68 percent of its total agricultural value. By contrast, the socialized sector produced about 32 percent of the total value.[24] In 1976, agricultural land made up 56 percent of the total territory of the Republic, over four-fifths of which was managed by a decreasing and aging agricultural population.[25] Many farms were left without heirs as young people flocked to the cities in one of the most rapid postwar urban migrations in the world.[26] In 1948, the peasants constituted 67.2 percent of the total population; in 1978, only 38 percent. By contrast, the urban population had increased from around 20 percent in 1948 to over 40 percent in 1971.[27] The result has been not only the abandonment of farms and a steady decrease in the amount of land under cultivation, but an increase in erosion to such proportions that in 1978, 54 percent of the land area of the country was designated as moderately to severely eroded.[28]

Since the state cannot intervene directly in the exploitation of private land, remedies for the environmental degradation of agricultural land have been selective and unevenly imposed. To date, there has been no adoption of a national land-use or agricultural policy. With varying degrees of success, towns and republics have tried to pass their own urban and agricultural land-use regulations to deal with rapidly deteriorating local land conditions. The situation has become so critical that in its December 1984 proposals to the Federal Skupština (legislative assembly) for action in 1985, the Federal Council for the Protection and Improvement of the Environment recommended the development of a federal law on the use and transfer of agricultural land.[29]

State control of the rest of Yugoslavia's natural resources is rooted firmly in the self-management principle. The system is confusing to the outside observer and surprisingly difficult for Yugoslavs to explain, although its operation is apparently clear to those who are part of it. The system comprises four administrative levels: the basic level, the commune level, the republic level, and the federal level. At the basic level are the organizations of associated labor (factory subsections or agricultural units in the socialized sector) and the basic local government community, such as a city district or a village. At the commune level are the communes or *opštini*; the work organization or local plant; that distinctly Yugoslav creation, the self-managing community of interest (SIZ); and the primary units of the sociopolitical organizations grouped under the Socialist Alliance with the League of Communists of Yugoslavia (LCY) at its head. At the republican level are the republican government, the republican conferences of the SIZ, and the sociopolitical organizations. At the national level are the federal government of Yugoslavia, the federal conferences of the SIZ, and the sociopolitical organizations. Industry is less structured and tends to be organized territorially by opština and republic. Although encouraged by the constitution, there are few industrial "associations" at the regional level, and those that do exist are relatively ineffectual because of the voluntarism inherent in the self-management principle. All industry, however, is grouped by branch under a republican and then a federal economic chamber. These initiate and participate in branch economic planning and promote and coordinate interbranch cooperation between the republics and with other nations.[30]

The former president of the Federal Skupština, Mjalko Todorović, has characterized self-management as a system where "dependence on the state budget and administration is eliminated, and relations governed by market laws are transcended where these laws have acted in a distorted way."[31] In theory and to a large extent in practice, every enterprise, academic or research organization, and local government unit is a self-supporting autonomous entity. One well-known problem associated with the pay-as-you-go principle has been that richer republics and localities have been able to provide better services and benefits, including environmental protection, than poorer republics. Self-management has had particular difficulty in easing perennial regional disparities in economic development because of the built-in preference for each locality to service its population rather than send money away.

The self-management principle is equally operative in Yugoslavia's nature protection system. The country boasts seven areas under the protection of the United Nations Man and the Biosphere Program (MAB). Each of these areas is required to be self-managing, with the result that only one has been able to maintain a permanent administration: Plitvice Lakes National Park. To achieve its environmental goals, the park must fund its program almost entirely from tourist revenues. There is little money coming from the federal government and only a small amount from the international community.[32] An analogous situation in the United States would be if the Yellowstone National Park Administration were required to generate the financial resources needed to conduct research, manage the wildlife, preserve the flora, and develop and maintain recreational facilities from the proceeds taken in from the annual visitors to the park.

The autonomy of each self-managing organization requires formal agree-

ments, called "compacts," between organizations if there is to be cooperation on a joint project. The local, republican, or federal governments
cannot force cooperation or collaboration. Agreement is and must be
voluntary. The process is thus a delicate one, necessitating large amounts
of time to reach consensus. For example, one of the rivers the Yugoslav
Federal Council for the Protection and Improvement of the Environment
would like to see preserved as a "wild river" (the term is analogous in
meaning to the one used in the United States) is the Una River, which
traverses the republics of Croatia and Bosnia-Herzegovina.[33] An interrepublican environmental protection SIZ has been formed through an interrepublican compact, but for the whole river to be protected, every community along its banks has to agree to the proposal. Agreement entails
spelling out what each commune must contribute financially in goods and
services to ensure the protection of the river and the composition and competencies of the administration to be responsible. The agreement also defines what each community will get out of the compact in terms of tourism
and other benefits. Since the compact would severely restrict industrial
development, commune leaders are naturally concerned lest turning the
entire length of the river into a protected area might adversely affect their
communities economically and result in lower living standards. Discussions have been in progress for several years. Since neither the republican
government nor Belgrade can bring pressure to bear or offer significant
financial assistance, the process of agreement may stretch on indefinitely
before the commune representatives are convinced that the compact will
be in their localities' best interests.

A second feature unique to Yugoslavia and a product of the self-
management system is the SIZ. These function in areas of human activity
outside material production. They are best understood as the providers of
Yugoslavia's social benefits, where there is a public welfare service to be
furnished and consumers to use it. The SIZ are the only institutions not
required to be self-supporting and are maintained by public funds. No
factory or farm can be a SIZ. The 1974 Constitution does not limit the
kinds of SIZ that may be organized, but four types are mandated: education, science, culture, and health and social welfare. The constitution
recommends that other SIZ be established in areas where "their activities
are indispensable," such as pensions, disability, communal activities, power

production, water management, transport, and communications (Articles 52–55). The base of SIZ operations is at the opština level of administration. The SIZ are funded through "contributions" or, as some Yugoslavs bluntly call them, taxes taken out of paychecks and enterprise earnings. At regular intervals, there is discussion on the cost of running local educational programs, scientific research, cultural events, and health and social care. The law specifies the minimum amount that the opštini must pay to each of the mandated SIZ, but they may vote additional amounts or establish other SIZ through a referendum. Opštini have tended to vote for the organization of nonmandated SIZ in the public service areas of water management, power production, and transport and communications.

Under the SIZ system, the provision of social services falls almost entirely upon the wage earner in his local community. In theory, the system lets the worker decide about his health care, community transport, education, and water and power production. In practice, the size of the budget for these services is fixed by law. SIZ employees are professionals in their fields. Limited financial and programmatic decisions are made in the local SIZ assembly, which is composed of delegates elected from the service providers' and service users' organizations.[34] SIZ are organized hierarchically from the opština to the republican level. Delegates to the republican assembly are elected by the opština assembly, with their number determined by the size of the opština. An executive council conducts the day-to-day work of the SIZ at each level. The four SIZ mandated by the constitution and the SIZ for water management also have a federal assembly to which delegates from the republican assembly are elected. The main thrust of SIZ influence is thus at the republican level.

Only those social activities that are included in a SIZ program receive permanent minimum funding. They are assured a certain future, regardless of the opština's financial capabilities, because the federal law provides for a transfer of funds from the wealthy republics to backward republics where wages and enterprise earnings may not be sufficient to cover social welfare activities. Those organizations and services not funded through a SIZ must be self-managing. Up to 1976, research and scientific institutes, like virtually all other organizations, received their funding from the federal government. With the passage of the self-management law in 1976, the majority have had to reshape their research programs in such a way as to be able to finance salaries and other operational costs as well as capital investment from revenue. As might be expected, the change in funding has put a strain on research organizations, particularly those engaged in scientific areas not directly related to economic development. Some small funds are available from the science siz, and there is sharp competition among institutes for partial support from that source.

Environmental protection does not fall under any siz, and so far, only one environmental protection siz has been created, the siz for the protection of the Una River mentioned above. As a consequence, environmental control is not assured any permanent financing or permanent coordinated administrative structure. Contrary to the Soviet Union, the commune is primarily responsible for implementation (resource acquisition, planning and organization, and provision of services) as well as enforcement, and must weigh carefully environmental protection needs against other community priorities.

A third uniquely Yugoslav institution that deserves mention is the socio-political organization. The constitution defines these as political associations "organized on a programmatic socialistically-oriented platform."[35] First and foremost among the sociopolitical institutions is the LCY. The largest organization is the Socialist Alliance of the Working People of Yugoslavia. Organized under the alliance but separate from it are the other mass organizations: the Trade Union Federation, the Veterans Association, the League of Socialist Youth, the women's organization, and all permitted professional and other interest associations, including environmental associations such as the clean air and water associations. As in the Soviet Union, there are no autonomous interest groups, and only those organizations permitted to operate may do so. In keeping with the essentially confederal character of the Yugoslav system, the organizational focus is on the republican units. Local members are elected from delegations to the commune assembly. As with the siz, delegates to the republican assemblies are elected by the commune assembly. Except for the centralized LCY, the republican units are charged with making agreements with one another for a federal program. The federal offices of the major sociopolitical organizations are located in the LCY building in Belgrade, a symbolic confirmation of their dependency upon party authority.

A fourth and final institutional arrangement unique to Yugoslavia is the delegate system. Workers organized in the self-managed factories, basic government units, and sociopolitical organizations elect delegations from which are elected delegates to sit in the three chambers of the opštini assemblies: the chamber of associated work (which is composed of delegates from the work organizations); the chamber of local communities (composed of delegates from the local communities); and the sociopolitical chamber (composed of delegates from the delegations of the primary sociopolitical organizations). Each chamber is balanced in terms of the primary units represented and social composition. Together, the three chambers constitute the opštini assemblies. The chambers in turn elect delegates to their corresponding organs in the republican assemblies. The opština and republican assemblies sitting as a whole elect their respective executive councils.

Under the 1974 Constitution, the self-managing associations of labor, the siz, and the sociopolitical associations are given representation in the Federal Chamber of the national legislature. The chamber is composed of thirty delegates of these organizations from each republic and twenty delegates from the same institutions from each autonomous province (Article 291). The second chamber, the Chamber of Republics and Provinces, is composed of twelve delegates from each republican assembly and eight from each provincial assembly. There is no direct election of delegates. All are elected by the lower legislative units from the pool of delegates contained in the delegations at the basic level. The Yugoslav delegate legislative system is given in figure 2.2.

Yugoslav textbooks make much of the distinctive democratic features of the delegate system,[36] but Yugoslavs admit the system is not working. Delegates are "passive," responding to "bureaucratic pressures"[37] because they are selected and approved by the Socialist Alliance with the LCY at its head. Their constituency is narrow at best and dubious at worst. Management cannot be elected, and, as Granick has shown, management prefers to bypass or ritualize the self-management process to avoid the lengthy round of discussions and meetings it entails.[38] Real decisionmaking thus does not take place within the self-management system, but is imposed upon the system from without by the organized economic and, more particularly, the national political bureaucracies. Given the broad jurisdiction accorded the republican governments in the 1974 Constitution, the system

Figure 2.2 Delegate Legislative System of Yugoslavia

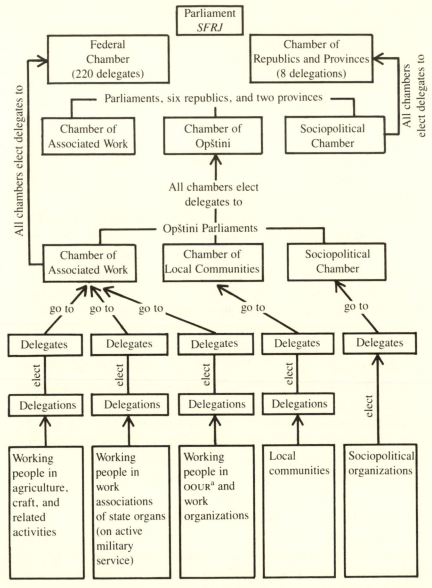

Source: Velimir Zekorić. *Socijalističko samoupravljanje,* 2d ed. (Belgrade: Institute for Textbooks and Instructional Aids, 1978).

[a] Basic Organization of Associated Work.

reinforces republican power, focusing decisionmaking at the republican level and distorting the influence of republican positions on social and economic issues.

Self-management places the federal government in a particularly vulnerable position. On the financial level, the budget for the federal government is not derived directly from the economy as a tax but comes from revenues from tariffs or from contributions from the republics. There is an annual discussion of the size of federal expenditures and the amount required from each republic to meet them. Republican contributions to the federal government are based on the economic output of the republic and derived from republican levies on the republic's economic sector. Since the republican budget must also be financed from the same source, the potential for interrepublican conflict is endemic. In short, the system may be viewed as a hydra, whose many heads vie with each other for funds in the interests of their own republican bureaucratic constituencies.

Legally, the Yugoslav federal government has few powers in the area of environmental regulation. It cannot set standards. There are no federal environmental agencies with the comparable authority and autonomy of the Soviet organs. With its limited budget, the federal government can provide little funding for environmental projects. Its principal areas of jurisdiction are the regulation of interrepublican matters, such as water, and international agreements. Attached to the Federal Executive Council is the Federal Council on the Human Environment and Territorial Management. This council is advisory and educative only. It informs the government on environmental conditions and coordinates joint actions between the republics, particularly in environmental planning. Despite its jurisdictional limitations, the council represents one of the federal government's main strengths in the environmental area.

Federal and republican organs of the sociopolitical organizations also play important initiating and coordinating roles. The coordinating sociopolitical environmental organ is the Yugoslav Council for the Protection and Improvement of the Environment. It has no permanent membership and its main task is to promote public environmental awareness through the simultaneous organization in all of the republics of special education programs and mass *akcije*, or campaigns. The specialized environmental associations in the Socialist Alliance are for scientists, engineers, and other professionals only, and membership is not open to the general public. Their main purpose is to advise the government on policy relating to the association's main concerns (air, water, solid wastes). To a limited extent, they engage in lobbying activities not unlike those of Western environmental groups. One of the most active nonenvironmental sociopolitical organizations in the environmental area is the Permanent Conference of Towns and Opštini of Yugoslavia. Its principal function is to elaborate the general direction of development for its three hundred members and, with the assistance of the executive board, to turn these plans into concrete projects. A permanent committee on environmental protection is attached to the conference. In the flux of self-management, it is probably the coordinating role that offers actors at the federal level the greatest opportunity for maximizing the federal government's position in environmental regulation.

There is little hierarchical relationship between the different levels of Yugoslav government. The main tasks of environmental administration, inventory of pollution sources, and control and monitoring, fall on the opština assemblies. The opština may be aided in its efforts by the republican environmental protection committee, but like its federal counterpart, the republican committee plays only an advisory role. The larger and wealthier communes have more resources to hire professionals to perform the necessary functions, while environmental protection perforce suffers in the poorer districts. Another indicator of an opština's willingness to promote environmental protection is the degree of self-management practiced. In some communes, citizens are involved a great deal in self-management activities; in others, very little. James Seroka found wide differences between localities in the Republic of Serbia in the extent to which the self-management principle had been implemented. The legislative assemblies in those communes that had developed a greater degree of self-management tended to be more involved in deciding policy issues than those where self-management was still primarily an ideal.[39] Thus, one might expect to find a higher incidence of activity with regard to environmental issues in those communes where self-management had become anchored in institutional practices.

The purpose of self-management was to abolish the growth of state power through the decentralization of authority and the dismantling of state bureaucracies. However, the elimination of centralized bureaucratic power may be more symbolic than real. Self-management requires the election of managers and administrative personnel in all Yugoslav organizations. Workers sit on factory workers' councils and janitors participate with scientists and researchers on managerial boards of scientific institutes. Members of executive boards or permanent administrative staffs of organizations told the author they could not be considered "bureaucrats" because they were elected by the workers' councils. In fact, managers are not appointed on the basis of open public competition but are carefully screened by the party authorities before their candidacy is presented to the factory selection committee responsible for making the recommendation to the workers' council for appointment (Article 505 of the Law on Associated Labor). Heads and general secretaries of the sociopolitical organizations speak of being "directed" to their positions, although they are confirmed by approval of the appropriate workers' council. Administrative personnel hold office for four years (Article 512 of the Law on Associated Labor) and then may be reappointed for another term. Reappointment a third time is discouraged, but longer tenures appear more frequent than might be expected under the regulations. The end of service in one administrative position leads directly to a new administrative appointment. If an individual has done well, he will be appointed to a more challenging *dužnost*, or post. If he has done poorly, his next job will be of lesser importance. Administrative personnel thus tend to rotate among the available positions, especially those in the sociopolitical sphere. Since no person occupying a managerial position may be elected to a workers' council or a factory delegation, managers form an administrative stratum set apart from the rank-and-file factory worker. Although in theory the law gives the enterprise director wide discretion, in fact he is answerable horizontally to party and government units. Too much innovation or initiative can focus attention on him and bring political pressure for his removal. As in the Soviet Union, a management position is essentially a political position, and industry must heed the interests of the political bureaucracy.

The principle of electing delegates to higher assemblies of the various self-managing associations by those elected previously to lower assemblies from a selected and approved delegation rules out the spontaneous election of concerned individuals and rewards those with a record of cooperation with the organization. Compliant delegates tend to cede to the interests of their respective organizational hierarchies, further strengthening the bureaucratic element.[40] Because there is no direct election except at the workplace or in the local sociopolitical unit, the interests of the economic and sociopolitical organizations take precedence over the interests of citizens, who have no formal means to express their opinion except at the local level. The constitution guarantees the bureaucracies permanent representation in the government from the local to the federal level. At each level, the organized economic, territorial, and political interests have their own legislative chamber, whose deliberations are carefully monitored by the bureaucracies the delegates represent. Domination by bureaucracy has thus frustrated the devolution of power to local units envisaged by the self-management system by accentuating the localities' unequal capability in resource acquisition and organization.

The conjunction of the centralizing bureaucratic tendency with self-management occurs at the republican level, where the interests of the economic enterprises, the SIZ, the sociopolitical organizations, and local government come together. Whereas in the Soviet Union, where centralization at the top has enhanced the position of the functional branch ministries at the expense of the territorial units, self-management has contributed to augmenting the power of the regional territorial units (the republics and provinces) at the same time as it has confined the enterprises to an essentially territorial mode of organization. Industry tends to operate on a republican basis, and interrepublican expansion or association is small. The result is dispersal and diffusion of both territorial and economic interests at the republican level. A process of intrarepublican accommodation produces common policy positions that are transmitted to the federal level in their economic and social form by the delegates to the Federal Chamber, and in their national and political form by the delegates to the Chamber of Republics and Provinces. When the self-management system is combined with the principle of one-party rule, whereby industrial management, the SIZ, and the sociopolitical organizations are dominated by Communists, it is clear that self-management has failed to eliminate bureaucratic power. On the contrary, the distinctive character taken by the institutionalization of self-management has been a major contributor to the continuing strength of the bureaucratic element in Yugoslav society.

The bureaucratic arrangement of Yugoslav society is the determining factor in the access of nongovernment actors (outsiders) to environmental policymaking. In this respect, self-management appears to provide no more opportunities than the Soviet system. There are no official mass environmental organizations at any level, except the Gorani Movement, which is primarily for schoolchildren. Moreover, the delegate system described above means that a delegate at the republican or federal level is not responsible to a mass constituency but to a particular enterprise association, SIZ, or sociopolitical organization. What public input into the environmental policy process there is occurs only at the local level on specifically local issues.

Nevertheless, self-management does enable and in fact requires citizens to express their opinions more freely than in the Soviet system. Citizens must be consulted by referenda on issues involving additional taxes or bond issues. Citizens can and do express their opinions on whether they want a particular industry or a nuclear power plant in their town, and through pressure they have been able to prevent construction. Citizens can and do complain about excessive pollution, forcing a response from local officials. The opportunities for action on the local level are there. Citizens have difficulty raising issues among a wider public because of the structure of the electoral system, the absence of an official national or federal environmental organization, and the red tape inherent in obtaining approval for the formation of any new organization. Mass participation at the republican level is no longer spontaneous but mobilized primarily through the efforts of the republican environmental protection committees in cooperation with the federal committee through the intermediary of the local commune governments.

Expert input is also dependent upon the bureaucratic structure of Yugoslav society. However, unlike the Soviet Union, expert advice is not delegated by law, but is competitive, won through compacts and agreements. Some institutes, such as the Jaroslav Černi Institute of Hydrology, have a national reputation in their field. Others have primarily a local impact. Thus, some institutes are consulted more frequently and are able to speak with greater authority than others, a phenomenon common to most countries. As elsewhere, experts work as consultants at all levels of government. In addition, as noted earlier, experts have their own specialized organizations where they may indicate their positions on issues by public conference, published statements, letters, individual contacts, and other forms of personal lobbying, not unlike their counterparts in the West.

Finally, the bureaucratic character of Yugoslav self-management places industry firmly among the governmental actors. Yugoslavia has followed the Soviet Union in the formal institutionalization of the presence of industry in the decisionmaking process. In the USSR, the Council of Ministers at the federal and republican levels is composed of the heads of the major industrial sectors. In Yugoslavia, industry participates in the legislative process at each level of government, and at the federal level, one chamber is solely composed of industrial and social administration representatives. In neither country are the environmental agencies party to legislations except in an advisory capacity, although they have an important function in the formulation of regulations. By contrast, in the Western democracies both industry and the environmental agencies are excluded from direct participation in decisionmaking. The arrangements for industry's permanent involvement in decisionmaking in the two communist states place the newer environmental agencies together with the proenvironmental "outsider" public and scientific interests at a permanent structural disadvantage.

At the risk of oversimplification, the differences between the structure of environmental policymaking and administration under centralized pluralism and self-management may be reduced to the locus of political activity. In the Soviet Union, political activity takes place primarily at the top of the federal structure; in Yugoslavia, at the republican and provincial levels. Bureaucratic organization formalized by self-management legislation to a large degree mitigates any differences there might be in the relation of the actors to the system in terms of "insiders" and "outsiders." Although "insiders" in Yugoslavia have a far less controlled range of activity than in the USSR, a similar bureaucratic principle limits spontaneous expressions of public interest outside the government and enhances the role of economic values in decisionmaking.

The incorporation of economic interests into the state administration assures that industry has three of Crozier's four sources of organizational power: ability to manipulate the external environment necessary to the organization's performance, control of information and communications, and knowledge of the internal workings of the organization. By contrast, citizen and expert environmental interests can command only partially two of the four sources: in the case of the experts, mastery of technical expertise, and in both cases, ability to manipulate groups essential to the organization's ongoing performance. The relationship between insiders and outsiders sets up an unequal game, requiring insiders to be coopted to the environmental position for environmental values to prevail. The question then becomes, what benefits accrue to the adoption of a proenvironmental stance where public or scientific pressure can be only selectively exercised and where neither is a determining factor in maintaining or expanding organizational or personal power? The question opens up a whole range of possible strategies and tactics available to the experts, which will be discussed in the appropriate chapter.

The Two Systems and the Common Regulatory Principle

The notion of a common regulatory principle, as described in chapter i, assumes that the *practice* of environmental regulation is essentially the same in all countries where such regulation is in force: regulation by environmental area, national or regional standard-setting, mandated technology, delegation of implementation authority to administrative agencies, the date-certain principle (as defined by the plan), etc. The impact of the Soviet and Yugoslav systems upon this common practice is rooted in the centipede and hydra patterns of political interaction. Because industry is part of government, the antagonism assumed between government and industry in the environmental area in the United States is not strictly operative. Rather, the political weight of the economic interests encourages a utilitarian environmental ideology, generalized legislation without strong enforcement measures, unattainable standards, and planning that mandates compliance within an unrealistic time limit. The details of regulatory practice vary from country to country, within this common framework. A brief description of the similarities and divergences of Soviet and Yugoslav environmental ideology, regulatory mechanisms, and planning procedures will demonstrate the point.

Environmental ideology. In both countries, the principal reason for protecting the environment is to secure man's survival in future generations. Man rules over the environment. It is there for his needs. The dialectic consists in the fact that he can only continue to take from the environment to the extent that he preserves its capacity for regeneration. "Man-Society-Environment" is part of the title of a book on the management of the environment in Yugoslavia, in which the exposition of the man-nature dialectic occupies a prominent place.[41] In the words of a prominent Soviet jurist, "The state's fulfillment of its environmental protection function is the management of environmental quality in such a way as to guarantee the optimal correlation of ecological and economic interests in the process of the ongoing development of socialist society."[42]

The conviction is that essentially there is no contradiction between resource exploitation and a clean, safe environment. One does not have to be sacrificed for the other. Man is dependent upon nature for his continued existence, and as man intrudes, nature is increasingly dependent upon man for her regeneration. As chapter I stated, this philosophy is not very different from its Western democratic counterpart. However, in the West, this view ranges on the conservative side of the environmental spectrum. A more radical environmental position urges "nature for nature's sake." This view supports the continued existence of the snail darter no matter what the cost, and it was the major inspiration behind the U.S. Wilderness Law. By contrast, the official purpose of nature reserves (where human visitation is limited mainly to scientific purposes) in the Soviet Union is that scientists may use their unique ecology to understand more about the man-nature relationship, which is critical to human survival. Protected species serve the same objective. Wild animals are to be protected by the state as state property, subject to exploitation by man under conditions laid down by the state.[43] In Yugoslavia, the attitude may be even more utilitarian. Nature reserves, such as the Plitvice Lakes, are not only areas with a unique ecology; they are also economic enterprises that must pay their own way if they are to be preserved.

Utilitarianism was not always at the forefront of Soviet environmental thinking. During the NEP period in the 1920s the USSR in fact was a pioneer in the concept of protected areas (*zapovedniki*) as unique ecological communities. A leader in the early Soviet conservation movement, zoologist G. A. Kozevnikov, argued that all living things were linked in a "web of life" that in its natural state, unaffected by man, tended toward equilibrium. Any intervention by man adversely affected this balance.

Hence, certain areas where the balance of nature was still intact should be preserved as *etalony*, or reference points, indicating "normal" conditions before man intervened. Scientists could use the *etalony* as standards by which to determine how much environmental degradation had occurred in a despoiled area, how much further degradation it could withstand, and how it might be rehabilitated.[44] The holistic approach to nature went out with the adoption of five-year planning and the emphasis on rapid industrialization under Stalin. The concept survives in its more functional version in the expansion of the *zapovednik* network and in the development of lists of endangered species that now exist in every country in Eastern Europe, including Yugoslavia.

In the man-nature relationship, man is the dominant element. Nature exists for man. Through understanding nature's laws, man can harness nature for his needs. Students in Moscow State University's environmental law course quote Engels on the difference between man and animals: animals only use nature and change it largely by the fact of their presence in it, while man "rules nature by compelling it to serve his aims by changes wrought by him."[45] The transformation of nature occurs through man's work, in which, to quote Marx, "man by his own activity acquires, regulates and controls the exchange of materials between himself and nature."[46]

The key words are "acquires," "regulates," and "controls." If nature is to be used, it must be acquired, regulated, and controlled. In Soviet and Yugoslav environmental ideology, the state performs all these management functions. The state owns the natural resources, and through the instruments of planning and regulation, it can manipulate nature so as to ensure continued economic growth *and* ecological balance. Thus, the second conviction shared by the Soviet Union and Yugoslavia alike is the firm belief that state or social ownership of natural resources is superior to any other method of control. In the author's discussions with Soviet and Yugoslav colleagues, this idea was taken as a given. The argument followed the typical Marxist criticism of capitalism: under capitalism, the interests of the capitalist and the public are irreconcilable. Private owners are only interested in profit, and they destroy nature for the sake of profit. No law can secure the private owner's cooperation in environmental matters when his profits are at stake, particularly since industry can utilize its profits to purchase influence over state environmental policy.

51

The third conviction shared by the Soviets and Yugoslavs follows from the second. If society wants the maximum benefits out of nature without sacrificing ecological equilibrium, the planned approach linked to continuous advances in science and technology is the optimum if not the only solution. Both Soviets and Yugoslavs reject the theory of limits to growth. Science is the answer to the threat of national and global ecological collapse. Through planning, society can project and implement technological development that will save the planet. In his commentary on Soviet achievements in environmental management, the late Academician I. P. Gerasimov, one of the USSR's leading environmental exponents in the Brezhnev era, praised the advantages of the planned socialist economy over capitalism for its "development of the scientific and technological principles and planned implementation of sweeping programmes for the purposive remaking of the environment for the purpose of rational utilisation and reproduction of natural resources, preservation and further improvement of the natural environment."[47]

As was stressed in chapter I, the manipulative, regulatory approach to the relation of man to the environment is not peculiar to communist one-party states. It is an integral component of what Dennis Pirages has termed "the industrial paradigm."[48] The leading interests of virtually every industrialized country share this view. There are few democratic politicians who would advocate limiting growth or curtailing scientific and technological development because of possible environmental damage. At the risk of cynicism, those environmental concerns that have aroused the most public outcry in the United States have been those where the public has perceived a direct threat to human life and not a menace to ecological equilibrium, be it Love Canal, offshore oil exploitation, or nuclear power. In both democratic and communist countries, this approach is used to justify the existing economic and political system as well as continued emphasis on economic growth. But the similarities in viewpoint end there. In the West, thoughtful observers like Pirages can advocate replacement of the "industrial paradigm" with an "ecological paradigm." The industrial paradigm does not represent the official government position, and politicians modify their views to accommodate those of their constituents. In a communist country, these convictions are used to legitimate the institutions of state ownership, regulation, and planning as the only solutions to environmental degradation. Those who would urge a different approach are not heard in the mass media. Environmental ideology thus provides the critical and necessary link between the philosophy of regulation and the politicoeconomic factors unique to communist regimes.

Legislation and regulation. Appendixes 1 and 2 provide tables that indicate the number and kinds of environmental laws passed in the Soviet Union and Yugoslavia over the past two decades. Added to the number of laws in the Soviet Union are the numerous CPSU Central Committee and USSR Council of Ministers' resolutions, only the most widely publicized of which are given in the table. The tables show that both countries observe the virtually worldwide practice of enacting environmental laws by environmental category.

The Soviet pattern is to pass a general or fundamental law (*osnova*) at the federal level followed by the adoption of virtually identical legislation with only slight variations by the union republics. Both the fundamental law and the republican laws represent expressions of principles that define legal norms, the objects upon which the norms operate, and the relations arising from the implementation of the norms.[49] The principles are listed in the same order for all environmental laws.[50]

If the law defines objects, relations, principles, the task of giving the law concrete expression, i.e., identifying responsible organs and establishing procedures and regulations, belongs to the Council of Ministers. These resolutions, particularly those listed in the table, tend to assume a greater importance, since they spell out the obligations of each central ministry, state committee, and union republic in the implementation of a specific law, or in the case of the 1972 and 1978 resolutions, in the realization of stricter and more comprehensive environmental controls.

Both the law and the fundamental resolutions are silent on standards, planning procedures, and the penalties and fines associated with enforcement. Standards and penalties are established by resolutions of the ministry or ministries identified as being the responsible agents in the particular case. Where standards are concerned, more than one agency may be involved, although always a lead organ is designated. Thus, the USSR Council of Ministers Resolution of January 8, 1982, designated that the new norms for the maximum permissible concentration (PDK) of pollutants

53

into the atmosphere were to be drawn up by Gosstroi and other interested ministries and departments and approved by Goskomgidromet and the USSR Minzdrav.[51] Water quality norms are similarly reached through negotiation between Minvodkhoz, Minrybkhoz, and Gosleskhoz. In all cases, standard-setting requires discussion and negotiation of all the ministries responsible for implementing the standard.

Emission levels are the result of complex negotiations at the local level, where the activist and hands-on dimensions of regulatory policy are most visible. The Soviet Union has established PDK in the atmosphere for some two hundred different pollutants.[52] (The U.S. Clean Air Act mandates ambient air standards for only seven.) PDK's designate optimum levels of ambient air quality in a given area and vary from locality to locality, depending on the kind of economic development of the area, its recreational and environmental utility, and similar factors.[53] Emission levels for each enterprise are established on the basis of a locality's mandated PDK for the individual pollutants, the number of enterprises in the area, and the degree to which each contributes to the ambient air level of the pollutant in question, when such information is known.[54]

The determination of required factory emission levels is thus relative and must be reached by consensus among the enterprises, environmental agencies, and government authorities within the individual town. When the inspector from the local Sanitary and Epidemiological Service (SES) of the Ministry of Health cites an enterprise for noncompliance, the enterprise will counter that it cannot make emission levels conform to the mandated PDK for a variety of reasons, primary among which will be lack of financial and technological resources. Where compliance has been given political priority, health inspectors have been able to enforce the law. There has been much publicity over the removal of four hundred noncomplying enterprises out of Moscow, after a Moscow Soviet Executive Committee proclaimed the city "an exemplary communist city"[55] because such events virtually never occur in the West. They are also rare in the East. The tendency is to settle on a *kompromis* where the enterprise gets a reprieve, the norm is lowered to a temporary, intermediate norm, and the enterprise remains open.[56]

Thus, contrary to practice in the United States, where the establishment of primary standards, emission levels, and control technique guidelines have been assigned to one agency, in the Soviet Union the process encompasses a whole array of organs. Standard-setting occurs by negotiation at the national level, the establishment of emission levels is accomplished by negotiation at the local level with reference to national norms, and control technique guidelines are set primarily within the ministry authorized to design and produce the equipment responsible for polluting the environment in the first place.

A second characteristic of Soviet environmental regulation is that the ministerial resource exploiter (and polluter) is commonly delegated the authority to help establish standards, set the fines and penalities for violating the legal norms of use, and develop control technology. The result is standards of such diversity and severity that they cannot be met and penalties for violation that have generally been far too small to deter violators. In this connection, it is interesting that some of the highest fines have been imposed on poachers and persons who illegally cut down trees in the state forest, a resource whose users and administrators are separate legal entities.[57] In addition, ministerial resolutions have tended to provide insufficient differentiation between types of violations and violators and the penalties charged to each, and have permitted industrial charges to be covered by the state budget as part of the planned costs of production.[58] Finally, while some enforcement organs are located in independent agencies, such as SES in Minzdrav and Goskomgidromet's regional inspectorates, the lead control organs for each resource again tend to be located in the ministry that is the principal exploiter or administrator of that resource. Soviet experts have routinely expressed their concern in combining environmental protection and resource use in one organization.[59]

A third and final characteristic of Soviet environmental management is the relegation of enforcement to the local authorities, discussed above. Local soviets have difficulty enforcing the law when their local factories are under a powerful central branch ministry. The *kompromis* that occurs in the setting of emission levels is a key factor in enforcement. Where the hands-on activity described by Ripley and Franklin should be most energetic, the local sections of the environmental agencies and local deputies are unable to take the initiative for lack of independent authority, necessary resources, and organizing capabilities. In the United States, the federal and state environmental agencies represent state power over the private interests of the industrial polluter. While the polluter may try to subvert or coopt the environmental agency, he can only operate from the *periphery* of power. By contrast, as we have argued, in the Soviet Union, the industrial polluter represents the *dominant element* in state power. In the enforcement of environmental decisions, the environmental agencies and local government are constrained to operate at the periphery of state power, and must adjust their demands accordingly.

These features of Soviet environmental regulatory practice make it possible to pass laws expressing the firmest commitment to environmental protection and establishing the highest environmental goals of any country in the world. But unless these principles are transformed into concrete programs and procedures, the law remains a law in name only. It is further possible to pass party and government resolutions, such as the 1972 and 1978 joint resolutions calling for stricter controls over environmental protection, but as long as such resolutions leave major responsibility for realizing such controls to the polluting agencies, the politics of implementation will provide innumerable opportunities for the development and refining of delaying and nonimplementation tactics and strategies to expand bureaucratic turf. Interbranch rivalry can lengthen the process of interbranch consultation as ministries debate the distribution of jurisdictional competence. Seven years elapsed between the first draft of the Air Quality Control Law in 1973 and its final enactment in 1980.

The bureaucratic character of Soviet environmental policymaking has resulted in the passage of environmental laws covering single environmental categories (the legal version of the branch management principle) and in the diffusion of environmental management responsibility. The generality of the law reinforces the centipede by requiring considerable horizontal politicking in the formulation of the necessary enabling resolutions and regulations and by creating a derivative vertical political contest within the branch ministries over policy implementation. Since the majority of ministerial regulations are privileged communications for the eyes of designated personnel only, there is no way to obtain independent verification of whether all the necessary regulations for control of any one environmental area or natural resource have been formulated, not to mention put into practice. In the Soviet system of centralized pluralism, the dilution of the enforcement and activist dimensions of environmental regulation is accomplished to a significant degree through the compartmentalization of environmental legislation, the requirement for accommodation of interest between the regulated industrial sectors and between the industrial sectors and the regulatory environmental agency in the establishment of regulations, and the dispersion and devolution of regulatory authority.

Self-management undercuts the hierarchical structure characteristic of Soviet environmental decisionmaking. After 1965, responsibility for environmental policymaking in Yugoslavia devolved upon the republican governments with the federal government only passing legislation within its areas of competence: protection of the seacoasts and standardization (appendix 2).

The dismantling of the centralized system required greater specificity and precision in the content of the laws, with statements of general principles confined to the initial paragraphs and the body of the text given over to specifics, similar to Western practice. Yugoslav environmental laws name the agency (or agencies) with supervisory or implementation authority in the given environmental area, and carefully define their sphere of jurisdiction. They identify the pollutants to be controlled and mandate the permissible levels of ambient concentration for each pollutant. The laws also describe the penalties for violation and provide definitions of what constitutes nonperformance. The establishment of rules and regulations associated with the laws are the province of the designated regulatory authority, as in the Soviet Union.

Self-management, however, did not create a new regulatory system. In many respects, the Yugoslav system is identical to the Soviet Union's. Environmental legislation is compartmentalized by environmental area with the same fundamental categories of land, air, water, forests, mineral resources, and nature reserves. Regulatory compartmentalization is not simplified by the devolution of power to the republics, for each republic sets its own rules and regulations and, perhaps more important, its own standards. The problems associated with the existence of seven sets of environmental norms and procedures in a country the size of Yugoslavia promoted the passage of the federal law on standardization in 1977 and the agreement to work toward standardization during the 1980–1985 plan period. The lack of a strong enforcement authority at the local level once again dilutes the hands-on initiatives necessary to assure policy implementation. What local official is going to enforce the law if enforcement means the closing of a factory and putting people out of work? The better solution is a compromise so that the factory can remain open. The weakness of the enforcement system is underscored, as in the Soviet case, by the absence of severe penalties.[60]

Self-management also does not fundamentally change the process of negotiation and agreement required in Soviet legislation. Rather it allows for greater flexibility and independence at all levels of government in making the required compacts. It also increases the number of environmental actors and hence the number of possible patterns of interaction. The economic as well as governmental agencies may make self-managing agreements in the environmental area and have concluded almost a hundred in the past decade (see chapter 4). Land-use management poses special difficulties. As appendix 2 shows, by 1976 all the republics had passed laws establishing the principle of territorial planning. The process of developing these plans began early in the seventies, but by 1976, only three republics had approved territorial plans: Serbia, Croatia, and Montenegro. Kosovo had approved a regional territorial plan. Sixteen other regional plans had been ratified into laws, including the plans for the Adriatic, which divided the coast into three sections. Only eleven opštini had plans, all of them in Serbia. In 1981, of cities over two thousand citizens, about one-third had urban plans.[61] Slovenia began its territorial planning process in 1980 and expected to complete the program before 1985.[62] Each administrative unit not only negotiates and approves its own plan but approves whatever sections of other territorial plans that apply to it. Since there is no hierarchical mechanism and agreement is by consensus, the process of adopting a comprehensive territorial plan for one republic by the constituent administrative units is long and time-consuming, with local government providing far more input than in the Soviet case.

Despite the heavy demand on negotiation and interaction, self-management has the ability to pass effective environmental legislation when needed. The most noteworthy example is the Slovenian agricultural land-use law of 1974. Faced with problems of erosion, loss of agricultural land, and low agricultural productivity, the Slovenian government was able to develop the consensus necessary to enact a tough rural land-use program. Under the law, all land in the republic was classified into categories according to its quality. Land that fell into categories 1 and 2, or prime agricultural land, came under a special regime. If the owner wanted to change the use of this land, he had to pay a tax, which was used to improve land of lesser quality. The aim was to inhibit development on fertile land and to reverse agriculture's tendency to shift to the hillsides as bottom land was given over to residential or industrial use. The genius of the law lay in its assigning primary decisions in local land-use regulation to the local self-managing unit, the opština. Although the law generally prohibited all building on agricultural land, it gave the towns power to set aside some agricultural land for building purposes each year, where there was a road and electricity. The town could purchase the land through an authorized agency for a modest fee. Control of rural land use was placed in a local land holding community that became the filter through which every planning and development decision had to go.[63] The law is a good example of the combination of central regulatory guidelines with local regulatory initiative that the self-management system makes possible.

Thus, in both systems the process of regulation requires agreements and negotiations. In the Soviet Union, negotiation occurs primarily at the horizontal federal level, with the lower levels of the hierarchy adopting regulations in conformance with central directives. In Yugoslavia, the hydra system promotes a less structured process with compacts approved at and between all levels of government and interests. The lack of uniformity in environmental standards attests to the dominance of the territorial actors. The federal and republican councils on the human environment and territorial management have criticized Yugoslav environmental regulatory policy on four counts: lack of concrete environmental objectives; regulation by "parcels," resulting in a collection of discrete decisions with little in common between them; lack of a comprehensive environmental perspective on the relation of environmental capabilities to human development needs; and failure of the laws and regulations to reflect the demands of a "self-managed socialist society."[64] Plus ça change!

The planning mechanism. The planning mechanism is the principle vehicle for the designation of institutions, and the allocation of material, technical, and management resources in the implementation of environmental policy. To refer to our image, the Soviet centipede style of organization is reflected in a multilegged form of environmental planning. In Yugoslavia, the hydra self-management system gives the planning actors so much individual discretion that coherent environmental planning is oftentimes hard to find.

The primary Soviet planning mechanism is the national social and economic plan, and the lead organ in the formulation of the plan is the State Planning Committee (Gosplan). Gosplan is guided in its task by the general party guidelines adopted at the party congresses and by the various party and government resolutions addressing specific issues. Up until 1974, environmental measures were not included in the national economic and social plan. In that year, a comprehensive resource use and environmental protection plan was made an integral part of the national economic plan to reflect calculations of need for specific resources over the plan's time period. In consultation with the resource ministries, Gosplan sets forth the concrete directives for resource use together with budget allocations for new investment. Although always subject to the Presidium of the Council of Ministers and the party leadership, Gosplan dominates the planning process and makes the major decisions on the use of each resource and on when and where it is to be used.[65]

The environmental planning process begins when Gosplan presents the overall environmental performance indicators to the environmental lead agencies and relevant branch ministries. The indicators are translated by the lead agencies and branch ministries into specific performance norms at all levels of the hierarchy, each lower level receiving its instructions from its immediate organizational superior. Starting at the lowest level of the organization, the responsible department draws up an environmental plan reflecting the state of environmental protection in that unit and describing ongoing projects or submitting new plans to improve environmental conditions. The plan is discussed and sent on to the unit's superior, who develops a plan based on received information and requests from the lower level. This plan is sent on to the next higher organ, which in turn, forwards its plan upward. The environmental planning process is distinctive in that each branch ministry not only develops its own environmental plan separate from its economic plan, but also is required to send its branch environmental plans for air, water and land use to the designated lead agency for that environmental area. On the basis of these plans, the lead agency develops a comprehensive plan for its environmental area of competence. For example, Minvodkhoz is responsible for developing the comprehensive plan for water use based on the plans received from the ministries but following the Gosplan guidelines.

At the same time as Gosplan transmits environmental performance norms to the branch ministries and lead environmental agencies, it also sends environmental performance norms for every environmental area to the republic planning committees, which transmit them downward through the territorial hierarchy. The territorial units now submit their plans upward. The republics transmit their total plan packages, including a separate, comprehensive environmental section, to the USSR Council of Ministers, which transmits them to Gosplan. The environmental section of Gosplan integrates the three sets of environmental plans from the branch ministries, the environmental lead agencies, and the territorial units into one comprehensive environmental plan and submits this product for Gosplan approval. Gosplan thus stands at the apex of a process, into which the branch ministries, central agencies, and republican governments feed their separate demands based on Gosplan directives.[66]

The complexity and absence of coordination in the Soviet environmental planning process cannot fail to strike the Western observer. Soviet economists fault compartmentalization and the lack of communication between the branches of the economy engaged in similar or associated plan development. The concept of comprehensive (*kompleksnyi*) planning was developed in the seventies to get the environmental planning and administrative *agregaty* (conglomerates) to work toward the attainment of specific goals expressed in standards and norms for particular areas, water basins, and regions. The formation of the environmental planning department within Gosplan was an integral part of this attempt to coordinate interbranch planning of environmental protection.[67]

Another factor contributing to the disjointedness of the planning effort is the lack of correspondence between the environmental plans and other sections of the national plan, which would guarantee, in Soviet officialese, "a social-economic evaluation of planned measures and at the same time assure economic efficiency."[68] Planning guidelines are so constructed that the economic sections of the plan may be assembled in isolation without the need to relate the programs contained therein to their environmental consequences. Projects are thus initiated without proper feasibility studies that would measure their impact on local environmental conditions.

The third factor is that the planning mechanism is insufficiently sensitive to the problem of accommodating long-term economic development to the carrying capacity of individual regions. Since planning remains structured along the branch principle according to industrial sector, ministries design their own development with little or no input from other ministries or agencies on their future plans. One suggestion has been what is termed "the environmental regionalization" (*zonirovania*) of the country, which would divide the USSR into typical regions or zones. A regional typology would identify regional categories possessing common geographic and natural features under which each zone would be classified. Industrial development would then be directed to those regions whose ecological characteristics could best support such development.[69] Work is in progress at the USSR Academy of Science's Central Economic Mathematics Institute (TSEMI) on developing regional programs for the use of mineral resources as well as forecasting and evaluating the status of ecological-economic systems.[70] In the theoretical aspects of environmental-economic modeling, the USSR has perhaps gone farther than any other country. However, practice remains tied to the tried and approved planning mechanism. Only one form of comprehensive regional planning has received official state endorsement: the territorial industrial complex (TIC).[71]

The fragmentation characteristic of Soviet environmental management is reinforced through the planning mechanism. The branch ministries were in existence long before the concepts of comprehensive or regional planning became acceptable. To shift the planning emphasis from the center to an environmentally defined region calls into question the central branch ministries' jurisdiction over planning. It also undermines the rationale for existing administrative areas; in no country is the formation of new administrative units accepted easily. And it gives significant decisionmaking power over plan objectives to a newly created and untested regional authority. Americans do not have a monopoly over incremental decisionmaking, to borrow from Charles Lindblom.[72] The dispersed and disjointed character of the Soviet environmental planning mechanism encourages an incremental mindset. What modifications of the environmental planning process there have been, such as changes in the reward structure, have been much more limited in their objectives as they have been less radical in their effects. Compounding the problem, the 1965 recentralization of planning took from both the territorial and economic lower units most of their ability to control regional environmental planning activities and to coordinate local factory and territorial plans. Nevertheless, republican and local governments have shown considerable ingenuity in drawing upon mass organizations and environmental committees attached to the local soviets to promote horizontal coordination.

Soviet planning, as it has developed over time, has reflected the leadership's commitment to economic development and, with one exception during Khrushchev's administration, its endorsement of the principle of branch ministries as the way to achieve economic progress. The present planning system both reinforces the power of the central economic ministries in Soviet domestic politics and is the result of their exercise of that power in the system. In the planning process as elsewhere, the environmental agencies and nongovernmental actors find themselves in the weaker "outsider" position.

In Yugoslavia, planning has both a centralized and decentralized dimension. The Federal Skupština adopts the General Program for Future Development, which contains guidelines based on both long-term and short-term forecasting of social, economic, and technical needs and the availability of resources to meet these needs. The adoption of the General Program is the beginning of a long process of negotiation. Plans must be adopted by enterprises and adjusted to accommodate the planning goals of their corresponding republican industrial sector and the industry as a whole, as well as the plans of the commune or region in which it is located. The regional plans must harmonize with the republican plans, which in turn must mesh with the industrial sector plans. Negotiations between the republics and industry must use the guidelines of the General Program as a starting point.

Yugoslav economists divide the planning process into two parts. Within the framework of the General Program, industry represents economic needs, or needs of the producer, and the territorial units represent citizen or consumer needs. In this division, the territorial units tend toward a more proenvironmental position, while industry tends to emphasize economic growth. There appears to be no set order for the adoption of plans or negotiations between planning partners. In fact, one of the problems is how to choose the right partners for negotiation and when to bring into the negotiation process those who see little to gain from it. Critical to a negotiation's success is the highly sensitive and difficult calculation of gains and losses for the planning participants.[73]

Environmental protection was incorporated into the planning process in 1979. Since then, enterprise and industry plans must include not only their contribution to local, republican, and federal social and development programs, but projections of how they are to meet the costs of environmental controls.[74] Since the whole cost comes out of industrial profits, industry has cause to argue that the addition of environmental protection requirements reinforces the need for economic growth, at the expense of consumer and ultimately environmental interests.

In the area of territorial planning, localities have been required to include environmental considerations in their plans since 1976.[75] In addition, in the mid-seventies legislation mandating territorial planning at the regional and republican level required urban plans to be revised to meet republican environmental standards. In Macedonia, the central region and all municipalities over 20,000 citizens had already adopted plans. These had now to be revised to reflect the environmental guidelines. As was previously shown, the whole process involves lengthy negotiations between interests at the local level and between the locality, the region, and the republic. As of 1979, few territorial units had approved plans.[76] A recent article in the highly influential Serbian newspaper *Politika* censured Yugoslavia's major cities for their chaotic pattern of urban growth.[77]

The Yugoslav planning mechanism provides for greater liberty of action at the local level, particularly in the urban areas, than in the Soviet Union. Since the national plan represents guidelines establishing a target range for plan objectives, republics, local communities, and industry have greater leeway in setting their own targets. However, the thrust of activity during the policy formation stage is clearly at the republican level, where standards and procedures are adopted to which the localities and industry in principal must conform. Self-management means that industry is in control of its own resources. Since industry primarily operates only within republican boundaries, industrial representatives are in a position to exert the strongest pressure at the republican level against any expensive environmental measures. This pressure is transmitted through their republican representatives to the federal level.

The differences in the Soviet and Yugoslav approach to environmental planning are substantial. The Soviet system works toward coordination by centralization and mandated indicators; the Yugoslav, by decentralization and agreement within a range of indicators. The Soviet system leads to the adoption of unattainable targets, which in turn lead to plan revisions; the Yugoslav, to long delays in adopting any targets, and to neglect or abandonment of plan indicators. The less structured Yugoslav planning system permits greater independence for parties in the negotiating process throughout the system, while the Soviet planning mechanism narrowly limits the options of even the centralized branch and environmental agencies.

Summary

This chapter has pointed out the main structural differences in the Soviet and Yugoslav policymaking systems and their impact upon the environmental regulatory process. The aim was to determine the objective constraints operating upon the environmental policy actors. The Soviet system was portrayed as a centipede with a large number of central organs making decisions to be implemented by their ministerial and agency "legs." The Yugoslav pattern was described as a hydra of competing republics permitting multiple opportunities for "insider" interaction. In both countries, access to decisionmaking is limited, with governmental actors in the strongest position to influence policy. The formal integration of economic interests with state power is a particularly constraining factor for non-governmental actors. Political activity is concentrated at the top of the Soviet system and diffused throughout the Yugoslav system, with most occurring at the republican level. Although the bureaucratic element may be more pronounced in the Soviet context, self-management has by no means eradicated bureaucracy nor given free rein to local popular initiative or local government.

These structural differences were found to have little impact on the general character of regulatory practice, but they did influence specific aspects of regulation. In Yugoslavia, the "parcelization" of environmental lawmaking was rendered more acute by the fact that each republic passed its own set of environmental laws independently of the other republics. Structure had the greatest impact on environmental planning. The Soviet centipede produced discrete environmental branch, area, and territorial plans with their concomitant problems of obtaining and verifying compliance on the part of institutional subordinates. The Yugoslav self-managed hydra required a large commitment of individual planning initiative with no intervening hierarchical authority to force implementation of centrally planned environmental objectives.

In many respects, the centralized and decentralized variants of communist one-party states appear less coordinated and less able to enforce environmental programs than the much criticized American system of environmental regulation. Why? The answer lies in the actors' subjective relationship to the system and its regulatory practice. The next chapters examine this relationship. We will begin with the environmental agencies.

3

The Environmental Agencies

In chapter 1, four factors were identified as critical to a political actor's ability to modify his organizational surroundings and influence policy-making: regulatory and structural constraints; available resources; associated rewards and costs; and the strategies developed to improve his position in the "game." While the first three may be determined objectively, the last is especially important in assessing the actor's subjective perception of his capabilities. With only limited information from the actors themselves, the strategies must be deduced from known policy outcomes, including laws, regulations, and successes or failures of implementation that have been published in the press.

Structural and Regulatory Constraints

Fragmentation of administrative responsibilities. One way to appreciate the fragmentation of Soviet environmental administration is to see how Soviet legal scholars have schematized Soviet environmental management. Oleg Kolbasov of the USSR Academy of Sciences' Institute of State and Law divides administrative competence into six functional categories: issuing of regulations and instructions, research, planning, operational management, control over legal compliance, and prosecution of noncompliance. He further divides administration according to two additional principles: general state and specialized (economic, scientific, and social) branch organs; and the territorial administrative organs at the all-union, republican, and local levels.[1] Jurists S. B. Baisalov and L. E. Il'yashenko make the territorial division and then distinguish between organs of general com-

67

petence, organs of branch competence, and organs of specialized competence.[2] V. V. Petrov of Moscow University's Department of Environmental Law classifies environmental management into the functional categories of planning, use, control, and expertise and the institutional divisions of state committees, specialized branch ministries and organizations, and territorial units.[3] No matter what the classification, it produces a complex, segmented system.

Figure 3.1 gives the distribution of these organs by environmental area and Petrov's functional categories. The figure shows that none of the organs has complete jurisdiction over any area of environmental management. While this situation is understandable and perhaps necessary when it comes to the exploitation of natural resources, multiple and partial administrative authority undermines efficient land-use regulation and monitoring and enforcement activities.

A few concrete examples will indicate the scope of the problem. Gosleskhoz (the State Committee on Forestry) administers all state forest land (*fund*), with the exception of those forest areas located within municipal boundaries, on collective farms, or preserves falling within some other administrative competence. In other words, while Gosleskhoz administers 35 percent of the territory of the USSR and establishes the guidelines for the cutting of timber, fire protection, and reforestation, some eighteen other central and territorial agencies are also legal managers of Soviet forests.[4] Apart from Gosleskhoz, none of these organs engages in commercial lumbering operations. (See chapter 2.) In essence, we are talking about forest administration in terms of one significantly large absentee forest landlord and numerous smaller forest landlords similar to those in the capitalist world, not a unified forest management system. (By way of comparison, the U.S. Forestry Service and the Bureau of Land Management together manage approximately 21 percent of U.S. territory.)[5]

Water management falls under the jurisdiction of Minvodkhoz (the Ministry of Land Reclamation and Water Resources), Gosleskhoz (for water flowing through state forests), the Ministry of Geology (for underground water resources), Minrybkhoz (the Ministry of the Fish Industry) (for the management of water for raising fish stock), the State Agro-Industrial Committee (for water on agricultural land), the Ministry of Power and Electrification (for dam construction and the use of water for hydroelectricity), Minzdrav (the Ministry of Health) (for water affecting public health), and more recently, Goskomgidromet (the State Committee on Hydrometeorology and Environmental Protection), which has authority to monitor water quality but not to make proposals or enforce regulations. The interaction of multiple users and administrators understandably creates conflict in the implementation of water management programs. A major conflict, as Thane Gustafson's research has shown, is the assignment of priority of use between Minvodkhoz and the Ministry of Power and Electrification during peak times, when water is scarce and there is insufficient flow to supply both irrigation and electric power needs.[6]

The State Agro-Industrial Committee administers the land fund, excluding forest land under the management of other agencies, land in cities and settled areas, and land for reclamation bordering reservoirs and other water sources. Among all the central organs, it has the greatest competence in the management of protected reserves, but Gosleskhoz and the USSR Academy of Sciences also exercise jurisdiction. Underground resources are administered by the Ministry of Geology, except where they are located in forested areas under the jurisdiction of other agencies, such as Gosleskhoz, the State Agro-Industrial Committee, the USSR Academy of Sciences, or the municipalities. Multiple management in the Soviet system precludes the possibility of a private owner, who might have a vested interest in the conservation of the resource. All the managers are bureaucrats in partial charge of a resource whose protection is only one facet of their total management activities.

Planning, as was shown in chapter 2, is no more unified. The participation of the many territorial and functional agencies in the centipede system frustrates the development of comprehensive planning methods. Fragmentation affects the organization of control and monitoring. Some twelve central agencies are authorized to monitor water resource use; nine agencies monitor land use and soil conservation; fifteen, air pollution control; and six, forest use. Six agencies supervise protected land (see table 2.2). The designation of lead agencies does not do away with the problem of coordination. The areas of air, water, and land and soil have two or more lead agencies. Moreover, whenever a multiplicity of semiautonomous institutions, each with its own highly specialized jurisdictional sector, attempt to work together, institutional friction is inevitable.

Figure 3.1 Environmental Administration in the USSR

	USSR State committees						Branch ministries			
	GP	GS	GKNT	GKG	GL	GKAP	MIu	MZ	MG	MNNP
Air										
Planning	×	×	×	×	×	×		×		
Use										
Control		×		×		×	×	×		
Expertise		×		×	×			×		×
Water										
Planning	×	×	×	×	×	×		×		×
Use				×	×	×		×		×
Control				×	×	×	×	×		
Expertise		×	×	×	×			×		×
Land and soil										
Planning	×					×				×
Use						×				×
Control					×	×	×	×		
Expertise						×		×		
Underground										
Planning	×		×		×			×	×	×
Use										×
Control			×		×		×	×	×	
Expertise			×		×			×	×	×
Forests										
Planning	×	×			×	×				
Use					×					
Control					×		×			
Expertise		×		×						
Protected land										
Planning		×	×		×	×				
Use										
Control						×	×			
Expertise						×				
Wildlife and plants										
Planning		×			×	×				
Use						×				
Control					×	×	×			
Expertise					×	×				
Human environment										
Planning	×	×	×	×				×		
Use										
Control		×	×	×			×	×		
Expertise		×	×	×				×		

Source: Modified from table made by V. V. Petrov for class presentation at Moscow State University.
Description of column heads: GP = Gosplan; GS = Gosstroi; GKNT = State Committee on Science and Technology; GKG = Goskomgidromet; GL = Gosleskhoz; GKAP = State Agro-Industrial Committee; MIu = Ministry of Justice; MZ = Ministry of Health; MG = Ministry of

and organizations								Territorial administration		
MXM	MEE	MCoal	MRyb	MLDTs	MVD	MMVKH	AN	Re-public	Re-gion	Local
						×	×	×	×	×
×		×		×	×					
×			×			×	×			
	×	×	×	×		×	×	×	×	×
	×	×	×	×		×		×	×	×
	×	×	×	×	×	×				
	×	×	×	×		×	×	×		
						×		×	×	×
	×			×						
					×					
						×		×	×	×
×	×					×		×	×	×
×	×					×		×	×	×
	×	×				×				
×	×	×				×	×	×		
			×					×	×	×
		×	×							
					×			×	×	×
			×				×	×		
							×	×	×	
					×				×	
							×	×	×	
			×					×	×	×
			×					×		
			×		×		×	×		
								×	×	×
									×	
					×			×	×	

Geology; MNNP = Ministry of Oil Refining and Petrochemical Industry; MXM = Ministry of Chemical and Petroleum Machine Building; MEE = Ministry of Power and Electrification; MCoal = Ministry of Coal; MRyb = Ministry of Fish Industry; MLDTs = Ministry of Timber, Woodworking and Pulp and Paper Industry; MVD = Ministry of Internal Affairs; MMVKH = Ministry of Land Reclamation and Water Resources; AN = Academy of Sciences.

Fragmentation is most glaring in the area of expertise. Twenty-six different central organs are charged with the investigation of the protection of water quality alone. The proliferation of expert agencies has produced an overlap of experts, and Soviet scientists have repeatedly criticized ministries responsible for the administration of expert institutes for being "narrowly departmental."[7] The establishment of lead agencies and supra- or intrabranch coordinating committees has been no more successful here than in the environmental management area. The 1972 joint resolution designates GKNT and the USSR Academy of Sciences as the lead agencies in the identification and solution of problems related to resource use and environmental protection. The difficulties GKNT has in carrying out such a mandate are indicated by the 1983 USSR Council of Ministers' resolution citing the committee for failure to be more effective.[8]

The territorial organization of environmental management further fragments jurisdictional authority. For one thing, the territorial subdivision of a central ministry may not necessarily manage the corresponding regional area. The Chief Administration for Nature Protection, Nature Reservations, and Forest and Game Preserves is under the State Agro-Industrial Committee. However, the RSFSR's corresponding republican organ, the Committee for Environmental Protection, Nature Reservations, and Forest and Game Preserves, is attached to the RSFSR Council of Ministers, an organizational arrangement common to many other republics. As a result, the State Agro-Industrial Committee exercises full administrative authority only over the fourteen *zapovedniki* and nature reserves within all-union jurisdiction. This authority is contingent upon the intervention of Gosleskhoz and the Institute of Nature Protection of the Academy of Sciences in areas that come under their jurisdiction.[9] The arrangement undermines the Chief Administration's ability to promote a single nationwide plan for the management of protected areas. When the law on the protection of wild animals came under public discussion in 1980, one writer asked that the duplication and parallelism in the USSR game preserve management system be eliminated and that the three existing game inspectorates be united into one control organ.[10]

Even when the subordinate unit is responsible to the superior ministry, administrative routing frequently leads a subordinate department to different superior departments within the same ministry. For example, river basin administrations that manage interrepublican waterways or water sources of national and international significance, such as Lake Baikal, or the Caspian and Baltic seas, are directly subordinate to the USSR Minvodkhoz. The administrations of river basins located totally within the borders of one republic are indirectly responsible to the USSR Minvodkhoz through the republican ministry.[11] However, the RSFSR river basin administrations are subordinated to one department of the RSFSR Minvodkhoz in matters regarding water use and conservation as far as the economy is concerned, and to other departments where technology and methodology are concerned, the latter departments being more directly linked to their central units in the USSR Minvodkhoz.[12] At the operational level, the system impedes coordination of policy implementation where it is most needed. To take the river basin administrations again as an example: Financing comes out of the single state water resource budget that is developed and allocated by the USSR ministry, but the majority of the administration's decisions may be taken only after securing the agreement of the other interested parties, such as industry, the local SES (Sanitary and Epidemiological Service), and Fish Conservation Service.[13] As these parties must also clear their decisions with their organizational superiors, decisionmaking is thrown back to the ministerial hierarchies in Moscow, which have no direct knowledge of the actual situation in the field. Municipal subdepartments of environmental agencies face a similar problem. Every action must be cleared with the units' bureaucratic superiors after discussion with all relevant local interests. The latter have to clear any proposals they may make with their central organs, which must then agree among themselves. Neither the local environmental agent nor industrial polluter can come to any agreement independently of the central bureaucracies.

The constant referral of problems to the top of the hierarchy cries out for more horizontal communication at the middle and lower levels of Soviet administration, where the issues are best understood. Chapter 5 looks at the ways in which republican and local officials have attempted to coordinate public policy at these levels. However, improved coordination will not do away with the basic problem. A city may pass as many pollution control regulations as it pleases, but with the exception of city enterprises and transport under municipal administration, the city government cannot force the polluters to take action. The polluting factories will only take measures upon orders from their ministerial superiors.

In sum, the fragmentation of Soviet environmental administrative responsibility places the central environmental agencies and their local subordinates in the position of having jurisdiction over segments of environmental policy, part of which they must also share with other agencies competing for the same jurisdictional territory. The location of decision-making at the center undermines the initiative local officials might have in working toward better coordination, since no major pollution control measure may be undertaken without the approval of the central authorities.

In Yugoslavia, the problem is one of gaps in organization. Limited authority does not result from the transferral of decisionmaking to the top, but rather from the subordination of environmental regulation to local and regional economic interests in the face of a weak or nonexistent central environmental authority. The associations of labor (the enterprises), the communes, and sociopolitical organizations are required by law to adhere to environmental conservation principles (Article 236 of the Law on Associated Labor)[14] and to establish environmental protection councils or committees within the enterprise, siz (community of interest), and commune. As was noted in chapter 2, the only centralized environmental agencies are the public health and water organizations, which operate at all levels of government. While the public health structure was never totally decentralized when self-management was adopted, the development of water management from 1965 to the present indicates the difficulties environmental agents faced under the self-management system and a possible path that could be taken in the future development of other environmental management areas.

From 1945 to 1953, all water management was directed by the centralized government authorities. From 1953 to 1965, management continued under centralized direction, but with a slight shift in focus to the republican level. With the introduction of self-management in 1965, water management organizations were put on the same footing as other work organizations and, like these, had to seek their own funding. At that time, water management activities were differentiated into two categories. The first related to water management construction projects such as flood control, river training, erosion, and spring run-off; the second, to water consumption and conservation. The first category was financed with funds from the republican and provincial accounts. Each year the water management authorities negotiated operating costs with republican and provincial representatives. The second category was put on a self-management basis whereby funding had to be obtained from banks or from water consumers. From 1974 on, all water management was turned over to self-management,[15] and in 1975, the SIZ for water management began operation on a republic-by-republic basis. Since that time, water management districts have gradually been defined, with four administrative regions in Croatia, nine in Serbia, and fewer in the remaining republics and provinces. The regional SIZ administrations first formed a republican water management association, and in 1979, the existing republican water organizations formed an umbrella League of SIZ for Water Management (Savez SIZova za vodoprivredu).[16]

These organizational changes have restored a degree of centralization within the self-management framework. The centralized water authority that existed prior to 1975 remains in the form of the secretariat for agriculture, forestry, and water management at the republican and federal levels. The hierarchical SIZ structure and development of the League umbrella organization means that water is subject to more centralized direction than any other resource. However, the jurisdiction of the federal secretariat is severely limited. There is no federal water inspectorate, and water management remains essentially under republican control. Most important, the federal government cannot compel adherence to federal interrepublican environmental laws.

Management of the other natural resources and environmental areas is less bureaucratically organized. While forests are under public ownership and are administered by the federal and republican secretariats for agriculture, forests, and water management, their exploitation is by regional self-managing organizations. A federal law on forests passed in 1965 attempted to mandate a single standardized planning document for forest development throughout the country. Self-management undermined the intent of the law, and since then the republics have passed their own laws (see appendix 2), each establishing their own forest practices.[17] Unlike the SIZ for water management, there is no forest SIZ. However, the forest inspectorates are organized under the republican secretariats, and if problems of erosion and reforestation become severe enough, there is nothing in the law to prevent the development of a SIZ structure for forest management. Revisions in Serbian forestry law [18] have tightened up the qualifications for both forest inspectors and foresters, as well as the regulations on forest practices, indicating an increase in republican support for more efficient forest management.

The SIZ umbrella structure may not be appropriate for all environmental areas. Land-use management in Slovenia has taken a different but equally effective route in its creation of agricultural land associations. A 1979 amendment strengthened the program with the formation of a republican union of agricultural land associations. Each association is made up of agricultural, forestry, and food-processing organizations of associated labor, as well as delegates from the local SIZ, work enterprises, and sociopolitical organizations. The land association assemblies are empowered to make all decisions regarding agricultural land use, manage the communal land fund, and approve all land transactions in the commune.[19] While Slovenia so far is alone in having passed this type of legislation, her example is being studied by the other republics. Common to all the environmental management structures developed in Yugoslavia after 1974 is the need to fill in organizational discontinuities and to centralize existing units under some coordinating organ at the republican level. The biggest gap in the system is the absence of any authoritative interrepublican or federal agency that could integrate the various republican practices and compel compliance to a national standard.

Figure 3.2 gives the general structure of Yugoslav environmental administration.

The figure illustrates two unique features of Yugoslav environmental administration. First, in addition to the usual legislative and governmental bodies engaged in the policy process, the Yugoslavs give not quite equal place to the economic organs, the OUR or organizations of associated labor. The structure of the economic units from the OUR at the commune level to the Assembly for the Social Federation of Work parallels the governmental bodies. In conformity with its Marxist ideology, however, the lowest rung on both the economic and social (governmental) ladders is the basic organization of labor (OOUR). The relation between the economic and governmental bodies was discussed in chapter 2: namely, each economic unit is represented in the local bodies at the commune level and in the chambers of associated work at the opština and republican level.

A second characteristic feature is the environmental council system. As the figure shows, both the OUR and the governmental organs have their hierarchies of environmental councils. Environmental councils are to be found at all levels of government and throughout the economic enterprise and SIZ structures. Agreements made by environmental councils in the enterprise and SIZ at whatever level are "self-managing" and independent of decisions made by the opštini councils. All self-managing agreements, however, are in the form of contracts, and thus legally binding. The kinds of actions that environmental councils in the SIZ and enterprise units may take are indicated in the center of the figure.

The governmental system of environmental councils is to be found in the left side of the diagram. Enterprises and SIZ have their input into these councils through their representation in the chambers of associated work at the opština and republican level, and the election by these chambers of delegates to the Federal Chamber in the SFRY Skupština.

The law requires that there be a committee, department, or council of environmental protection (EP) attached to the executive organs at every level of government. The council is advisory only. Its main purpose is to collect information on the status of the environment within its territory and to make recommendations for action to the responsible governmental organ. At the commune administrative level are the environmental protection organs, and, in the cities, urbanism councils attached to the opština executive. At the republican and provincial level there are the environmental protection and urbanism councils attached to the republican and provincial executive. Interopština and interrepublican coordination takes place at this level. To provide overall direction to this activity a Federal Council on the Human Environment and Territorial Planning was formed in June 1974. Like its republican and local counterparts, its chief purpose is to collect information, to articulate environmental concerns throughout Yugoslavia, and to propose environmental measures for federal legislation.[20] The council has working groups in all areas of environmental concern. It further serves as an interrepublican forum for information exchange and a center for public education on environmental issues.

While every opština should have a council on environmental protection,

Figure 3.2   Administrative Structure of Environmental Management, Yugoslavia

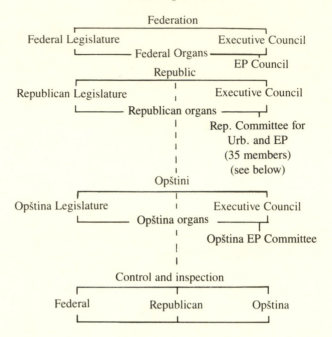

Social Organizations

Federation
Federal Legislature   Executive Council
            Federal Organs
                        EP Council
Republic
Republican Legislature   Executive Council
            Republican organs
                        Rep. Committee for
                        Urb. and EP
                        (35 members)
                        (see below)
Opštini
Opština Legislature   Executive Council
            Opština organs
                        Opština EP Committee

Control and inspection
Federal   Republican   Opština

Republican Committee for Urb. and EP

Delegates	Sections in the committee	Consulting expert bodies
	Nature and Ecology	11 members
	Urban Environment and Development	9 members
35	Working Environment and Development	9 members
	Health and Nutrition	11 members
	Infrastructure	9 members
	Legal Regulations	11 members

Key:

————— Proposals for environmental legislation, regulations, or agreements

— — — — Influence in planning and legislation

Source: Republican Committee for Urbanism and Environmental Protection, Macedonia.

78

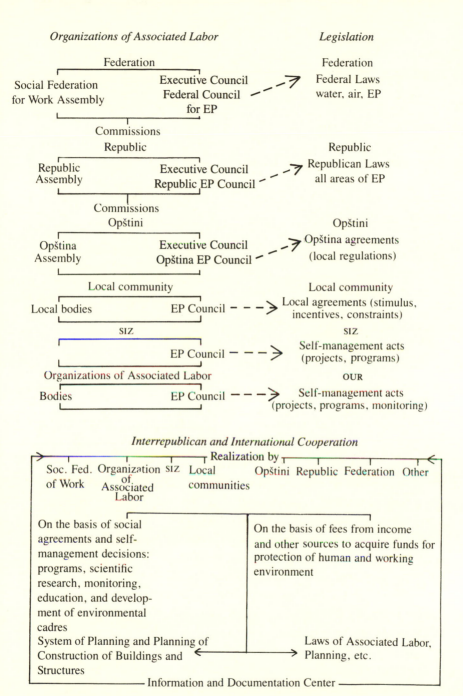

Organizations of Associated Labor   Legislation

Federation   Federation

Social Federation for Work Assembly — Executive Council / Federal Council for EP → Federal Laws water, air, EP

Commissions

Republic   Republic

Republic Assembly — Executive Council / Republic EP Council → Republican Laws all areas of EP

Commissions

Opština   Opština

Opština Assembly — Executive Council / Opština EP Council → Opština agreements (local regulations)

Local community   Local community

Local bodies — EP Council → Local agreements (stimulus, incentives, constraints)

SIZ   SIZ

EP Council → Self-management acts (projects, programs)

Organizations of Associated Labor   OUR

Bodies — EP Council → Self-management acts (projects, programs, monitoring)

Interrepublican and International Cooperation

Realization by

Soc. Fed. of Work   Organization of Associated Labor   SIZ   Local communities   Opštini   Republic   Federation   Other

On the basis of social agreements and self-management decisions: programs, scientific research, monitoring, education, and development of environmental cadres

On the basis of fees from income and other sources to acquire funds for protection of human and working environment

System of Planning and Planning of Construction of Buildings and Structures ← → Laws of Associated Labor, Planning, etc.

Information and Documentation Center

79

Table 3.1 Environmental Bodies and Organs on the Opština Level (Number)

	Year	SFRY	Bosnia-Herzegovina	Croatia
Number of surveyed opštini	1967	399	89	—
	1976	203	107	30
Special council	1967	36	4	5
	1976	59	14	9
Council with related functions	1967	278	50	65
No corresponding council	1967	85	35	9
	1976			
Special administrative organ	1967	43	6	7
	1976	26	14	1
Organ with related functions	1967	139	26	28
	1976	38	32	2
Functions performed by	1967	207	57	44
another organ	1976	139	61	26
No competent organ	1976	10	—	—
	1977			

Source: SFRY, Savezno izvršno veće i izvršna veća republika i pokrajina, Savet za čovekovu sredinu i postorno uredjenje (Federal Executive Council and executive councils of the republics and provinces, Council for the Environment and Territorial Management), *Čovekova sredina i*

communes have been slow in establishing a separate environmental organ, preferring instead to assign the environmental advisory function to an already existing committee. (See table 3.1.) The body that has most commonly assumed this task is the council for urban development. A 1976 survey further confirmed that while inspectorates were organized in the areas of urban development, water, and health in all the republics and provinces, they existed at the commune level only in large cities.[21]

In addition to the organs attached to the government administration, there is a network of expert institutions, some independent, some attached to a SIZ, that play a considerable role in environmental management in the areas of planning and monitoring. These include public health institutes, institutes for urban planning, institutes for the protection of cultural and natural monuments, institutes for urban construction, and the main office of the administration of rural engineering. Table 3.2 indicates the growth

			Serbia			
Macedonia	Montenegro	Slovenia	Total	Serbia proper	Kosovo	Vojvodina
—	18	—	137	—	—	—
—	4	—	—	—	—	—
5	5	11	6	—	—	—
3	1	14	18	12	—	6
20	8	30	104	—	—	—
2	5	8	26	—	—	—
7	7	11	5	—	—	—
2	—	5	4	3	—	1
11	4	31	39	—	—	—
—	—	—	4	1	—	3
8	6	7	75	—	—	—
6	4	6	36	25	1	11
—	1	1	8	—	—	—

prostorno uredjenje u Jugoslaviji: Pregled stanja (The environment and land use in Yugoslavia: An overview of their status) (Belgrade: OOUR Publishing House, 1978), p. 145.

pattern for the institutes most specifically concerned with environmental matters. The institutes with a federal structure, such as the hydrometeorological institutes or the institutes of public health, have specific areas of competence at each administrative level. For example, the Federal Hydrometeorological Service in Belgrade monitors transboundary air and water phenomena, and the corresponding republican institute is responsible for intrarepublican data. When the Sava River flooded in the spring of 1981 and threatened to pollute Belgrade's underground water supply, the Serbian Republican Institute of Public Health published the daily monitoring reports of water quality, while the city health authorities were charged with issuing a water alert should it be necessary.[22]

Table 3.3 indicates that the number of expert environmental institutes has not changed over the past ten years.

What has changed for the majority of them is the need to finance their

Table 3.2 Survey of Environmental Bodies and Organs
at the Republican and Provincial Level

	Body		Administrative organs
	Legislature	Executive council	
SR Bosnia-Herzegovina	Committee for Urbanism and Public Housing	Committee for Territorial Management and the Protection and Improvement of the Environment	Republican Secretariat for Urbanism, Housing, and Public Services
SR Croatia	Committee for Territorial Management, Public Housing Policy, and Environmental Protection	Council for Environmental Protection and Territorial Management	Republican Secretariat for Urbanism, Construction, Housing, and Public Services
SR Macedonia	Committee for Urbanism		Republican Secretariat for Urbanism, Housing, and Public Works
SR Montenegro			Republican Secretariat for the Economy
SR Slovenia	Committee for Territorial Management, Urbanism, and the Environment		Republican Secretariat for Urbanism, Committee for Environmental Protection
SR Serbia	Commission for the Protection and Improvement of the Environment	Committee for Environmental Protection	Republican Secretariat for Urbanism, Housing, and Public Works
SAP Kosovo		Commission for the Environment and Territorial Management	Provincial Secretariat for Urbanism, Housing, and Public Works

Table 3.2 (*Continued*)

	Body		
	Legislature	Executive council	Administrative organs
SAP Vojvodina		Committee for the Protection and Improvement of the Environment	Provincial Secretariat for Urbanism, Housing, and Public Works

Source: P. 146 of source cited in table 3.1.

work by making "self-managing" agreements with interested parties for research and project preparation. As stated in chapter 2, only institutes attached to a SIZ can be assured of funding. The Serbian Republican Institute of Public Health receives 119 million of its 130 million dinar annual budget from the health SIZ.[23] By contrast, the Jaroslav Černi Water Resources Institute in Belgrade, one of the largest and most prestigious in Yugoslavia, obtains only 4–5 percent of its 200 million dinar budget from the Serbian SIZ for Science. The rest of the money comes through work contracts.[24] Since there is no officially designated expert agent in Yugoslavia, a commune may turn to any expert institute it wishes for consultation, and institutes must compete among each other for contracts. Table 3.3 shows that the contract system has encouraged the disparity in environmental practice between the republics, with a concentration of environmental control mechanisms in the more industrialized republics of Serbia, Croatia, and Slovenia. Only the wealthiest communes can afford to sign agreements for monitoring and laboratory expertise. The monitoring of the rural areas is left to the appropriate republican institutes and has been poorly organized. The richer towns are also able to appoint expert inspectors or to organize their own inspectorates in the critical environmental areas.

The USSR has gone much further in the institutionalization of environmental management than has Yugoslavia, whose environmental protection organs are still in the process of formation. Yet greater organization has not eliminated, only changed the character of administrative fragmentation. If the centipede promotes fragmentation by excess structure, the hydra en-

Table 3.3 Institutes for Urbanism, Protection of Cultural Monuments, and Environmental Protection (Number)

	Year	SFRY	Bosnia-Herzegovina	Croatia
Institutes for urbanism	1967	44	7	8
	1970	54	7	8
Institutes for the protection	1967	24	2	7
of cultural monuments	1970	24	2	7
	1976	24	—	9
Institutes for environmental	1967	3	—[a]	1
protection	1970	4	—	1
	1976	5	—	1
Institutes for the protection of	1967	3	—[a]	1
cultural monuments in nature	1970	3	—	1
	1976	7	4	1

a. The functions of environmental protection in Bosnia-Herzegovina and Macedonia were performed by the Institute for the Protection of Cultural Monuments.

courages fragmentation through insufficient structure. The constraints on Soviet environmental agents come from the splintering of administrative responsibility into multiple overlapping segments, setting the environmental agencies at a disadvantage against the monopoly power of the branch ministries. The constraints on the Yugoslav environmental agents derive from the virtual absence of any central coordinating authority. In such a situation, environmental agents are sought after by the wealthier republics and communes but find little support in the more disadvantaged regions.

The weakness of the enforcement system. Chapter 2 commented on the generally low level of fines in the Soviet Union. But all fines are not equally low. Weak enforcement is promoted as much by the arbitrary character of the sums involved as by the actual amount of the fine. For example, the highest fine for illegally catching a river fish is 400 rubles, while for illegally catching any kind of whale the fine is 50,000 rubles.[25] Fines for illegally cutting timber in the first category of protected forests range from a low of eleven rubles for a tree of less than five inches in diameter to over 157 rubles for a tree of over eighteen inches in diameter. The poacher could probably get at least double the amount of the fine if he sold the wood.[26]

			Serbia		
Macedonia	Montenegro	Slovenia	Serbia proper	Kosovo	Vojvodina
4	5	6	11	1	1
5	5	6	19	1	1
5	1	2	5	1	1
5	1	2	5	1	1
5	1	2	5	1	1
—[a]	1	—	1	0	0
—	1	—	1	0	1
—	1	2	1	1	1
—[a]	—	2	—	—	—
—	—	2	—	—	—
—	—	2	—	—	—

Source: P. 147 of source cited in table 3.1.

Suggestions have been made to increase the fine for poaching, as well as to change the poaching regulations. At present, the offender is liable only if he is caught with his dead quarry. Ironically, the game warden may not arrest a man before he shoots, but must wait until the damage has been done.[27]

In addition, the all-union laws specify what should be done to clean up the environment but are not clear on what sanctions should follow upon nonperformance. The determining factor in distinguishing between a minor environmental offense and a crime committed against the environment is the magnitude of the danger brought upon society. The all-union laws leave the decision as to the degree of severity and type of offense that constitutes a criminal violation up to the union republics. During the 1970s, republican criminal codes were updated to include environmental offenses. Under the RSFSR Criminal Code, certain forms of air and water pollution, violations of regulations on exploiting the continental shelf and underground resources, and poaching and the illegal sale or purchase of furs or pelts are criminal offenses. However, the maximum prison sentence for violation in all cases is three years.[28] Administrative sanctions range from moral sanctions and fines administered by a comrade's court to an order closing down the offending enterprise, loss of employment, disciplinary action, and restitution of damage. An order of the Presidium of the USSR Supreme Soviet in 1976 increased personal liability to 10,000 rubles and enterprise liability to 100,000 rubles.[29] While 10,000 rubles may serve as a deterrent to individuals, the penalty for enterprises is very modest, particularly when the fine may be included in operating costs.

A third factor that has contributed to the weakness of enforcement provisions in the environmental area has been the question of damage liability. Technically, restitution for damage comes under Article 88 of the All-Union Fundamentals of Civil Law, but the law is not clear in its definition of what constitutes damage, what are the economic costs incurred, who or what organization(s) are responsible, and who is the legal property owner or user. The determination of damage liability has thus tended to be on a case-by-case basis through court and state arbitration commission decisions. For example, in 1977, the USSR Supreme Soviet ruled that damage caused by mineral resource users on agricultural land could be liquidated by the payment of a sum equal to the calculation of the expenditure necessary to restore the land to its previous level of fertility.[30] As regards damage to land caused by flooding, drying up, salting, or the creation of swamps, a 1978 USSR Council of Ministers resolution determined that restitution of damage would follow the guidelines for damage payments on agricultural land taken out of agricultural use.[31] These regulations solved the question of payment for land that may have been under cultivation but not for damaged land that was not under cultivation. To what level should this land be restored? Should land reclamation go so far as to render the damaged land fertile for every type of agriculture? So far, the regulations handed down in the 1970s have only begun to attack a thorny problem.

Establishing legal responsibility for damage is as problematic as determining damage costs. If a contractor violates the law, is his enterprise liable or the enterprise that employed his services? The 1976 Standards and Rules for Construction forbid builders to allow pollution of agricultural and other valuable lands by production wastes. The practice has been for the contractor to place waste sites on adjacent property and to violate boundary lines. By law the contracting industrial or agricultural enterprise is obliged to make sure the contractor will not damage his land or the adjacent property. In the case of violation, the dispute may be taken to the court or state arbitration commission. But the law is silent on whether the customer or the construction organization is liable for the damage done on the adjacent property.[32]

The fact that liability decisions tend to be determined on a case-by-case basis affords violators ample opportunity to evade the law and creates uncertainty for the environmental inspectors as to whether an individual or an organization is liable or not. A particularly interesting case that came before a state arbitration committee involved a train that hit a deer. The question was whether there was administrative liability, and, if there was, who was the legally accountable person: the locomotive enterprise or the engineer? The decision was that no liability was involved since no sign had been installed warning the driver of a deer crossing. If there had been, the driver, not the railroad, would have been liable for failure to observe the sign, and he would have been charged the value of the killed deer.[33]

A particularly notorious question of criminal liability arose in the pollution of the Kaya River near Irkutsk by industrial discharges from an oil and fat combine. The Baikal Basin Administration fined the director of the combine thirty rubles (!) in 1972, which the director refused to pay, denying his liability in the matter. Instead, he filed suit against the Baikal Administration. In 1979, the case came before the *raion* (district) court, which fined the chief engineer responsible for the operation of the sewage treatment system 100 rubles. The director was never even called to testify. The *Izvestia* reporter of the story demanded that all guilty persons be punished, inferring that the director was as liable as his engineer.[34] The problem of liability was clearly of sufficient dimensions to prompt a prosecutor in the public prosecutor's office in Moscow to ask that the 1980 Air Quality Control Law contain specific statements as to which violations individuals, officials, and enterprises would be held accountable for.[35]

A final negative aspect of Soviet enforcement is the shared jurisdiction of governmental agencies over state land use. In rural areas, the responsibility for planning land use and development is borne jointly by the Senior Raion Land Tenant of the State Agro-Industrial Committee and the Raion Architect representing the USSR Gosstroi. Lacking a clear separation of jurisdictional areas, the division between agricultural and nonagricultural land has become blurred, so that in rural areas there are industrial enterprises on collective and state farm lands, while in urban areas, industrial properties are required to engage in land reclamation, forest belts are planted, and rural lands are reserved by municipal administrations. In the absence of a supervisory body to administer a comprehensive land-use plan, the representatives of the two governmental agencies argue as to what parcels of land come under whose administrative competence. The result of blurred jurisdiction is a continuing problem of industrial encroachment on agricultural land.[36] The problem is aggravated by the fact that the land management service which monitors land use has only the right to stop agrotechnical and forest reclamation operations. In all other instances, the inspectors can only draw up the appropriate papers and send them to the local soviet for action. Before the local authorities have had the time to come to a decision, the polluting enterprise has taken additional numbers of acres out of circulation.[37]

Difficulties in the enforcement of environmental regulations are not by any means unique to the Soviet Union. What is unique is that the polluting agencies are central ministries exercising virtual monopolies in their particular areas. When the delegation of enforcement authority is fragmented and violation entails nominal penalties, the environmental agents are severely limited in their capacity to act. The solution is to "play the game" and compromise.

In Yugoslavia, self-management produces a different set of problems. As in the Soviet Union, penalties are low. For example, the 1981 Serbian Law on Waste Treatment levies fines from 2,000 to 10,000 dinars for a minor violation, and up to 30,000 for a major violation of the law,[38] while the 1975 Serbian Water Quality Law demands fines from 50,000 to 1 million dinars for violations by enterprises and work organizations.[39] The fine for a major infraction of waste treatment regulations amounts to less than a year's pay for the average worker and represents virtually nothing for an enterprise, which may include the charge in its operating expenses as its counterpart may do in the Soviet Union.

Yugoslavs blame weak enforcement on three factors. The first is the legislation itself. As in other countries, the environmental laws passed in the seventies excluded factories built prior to the date of passage from the laws' obligations and penalties. In addition, exceptions and waivers were made for new factories, thereby increasing the already existing pollution. Yugoslav officials insist that money is the primary reason for failure. Pollution control equipment is expensive and must be purchased from abroad, while industries are hard-pressed to invest their earnings in other areas. The second reason for the lack of severity in enforcing environmental standards is a perceptual one. Yugoslavs do not think pollution has reached a crisis point and believe there is plenty of time to do something about it. For example, the average annual emission of SO_2 per inhabitant in Yugoslavia is roughly 40 percent of the United Kingdom's and half that of West Germany.[40] They argue that although still only a developing nation, the country has already taken legal precautions. In areas where a crisis threatened such as the loss of agricultural land in Slovenia, the republic intervened in an efficient manner. Self-management just has to take its course.

The final factor relates to a question of alternatives. Dust from coal furnaces rains down on Belgrade and Zagreb during the winter months, dispelled only when the wind blows strongly enough to clean the air. In the early 1970s, Yugoslavia contracted to build a pipeline from the Hungarian border to Belgrade. Construction was halted when money ran out. The plan was for Belgrade to be heated by Soviet oil or natural gas. But until construction is completed, the city has no other choice but to burn local high-sulphur coal. Energy is a critical factor in Yugoslav industrial development. Macedonia probably has been the most afflicted by an energy shortage, and the republic has been criticized for failure to build energy installations.[41] But the principal problem is the country's reliance on imported crude oil. The federal energy plan up to the year 2000 calls for the accelerated development of domestic energy sources, specifically coal and hydropower. Conservation has already had some effect on oil consumption patterns, but Yugoslavia did not embark on oil conservation measures as rapidly as she might have after 1973.[42] Given the present state of the Yugoslav economy,[43] there can be no question that in current Yugoslav planning, energy has a higher priority than pollution. It is a costly priority. To replace a million tons of imported oil valued at 11 billion dinars with a domestically produced fuel source is estimated to require an investment of 22 billion dinars. Officials believe this amount can be raised by placing a higher tax on all oil, particularly fuel oil, which accounted for 47 percent of consumption in 1980.[44]

The necessity of deciding between unpalatable alternatives presents unsolvable dilemmas. A cement factory outside of Belgrade is coal-fired and has been the object of numerous citizen complaints about smoke and bad air. The citizens are also employees of the factory. With no alternative to coal, the environmental authorities must either close the plant and put the workers out of jobs, accept the continued payment of a fine by the factory, or force relocation.[45] In Kragujevac, the Serbian Detroit, citizens have complained about the fumes from the paint used on the Zastava automobile. According to the company's chief environmental engineer, it has been impossible to take measures because the paint is protected by a U.S. patent and the company is unable to determine the paint's chemical composition without information provided by the U.S. manufacturer. So the company continues to pay the fines, and residents continue to complain.[46] Technological difficulties place the environmental agencies in an untenable situation where administrative sanctions cannot bring about the desired environmental improvement.

Valid as these reasons may be as an explanation of weak enforcement, they do not explain why public drinking water supplies have become contaminated, why the Sava River is described as a "dead" river, or why newspapers are concerned about the danger of disease from the dumping of sewage into waterways.[47] One answer surely lies in the pace of urban growth and the difficulty of developing adequate infrastructures. But, neither is this answer completely satisfying. Kosovo is a region that has experienced only twenty years of development. Millions of dinars from the more advanced regions of Yugoslavia have poured into the area. Yet, in 1979, there was not a single river in the province whose water quality could be classified as first class and safe for drinking. A Belgrade newspaper article cited the opštini in Kosovo for failing to make contractors adhere to regulations requiring the consent of the water authorities for each project. The paper further claimed that waste treatment projects developed in cooperation with the World Health Organization had not been implemented. The report insisted that the fault was not lack of opportunity but a lack of public awareness. Residents, according to the writer, appeared to believe that the proper place for trash was the river![48]

Environmental protection is not yet a priority of local government. Miliroje Todorović, former secretary general of the Council on the Protection and Improvement of the Environment, believes that weak enforcement is primarily a matter of education. But the main problem is that the self-management system is too decentralized to be able to enforce an effective environmental regulatory policy. Faced with difficult choices and convinced that short-term economic gains are more important than long-term environmental objectives, republican and local environmental officials turn a blind eye to industrial violations because industry provides the much needed money to keep government running.

The ambiguity of the environmental mandate. In all stages of environmental policy activity, the environmental agencies in the Soviet Union and Yugoslavia have been given an ambiguous mandate. They are a derivative, not a primary factor, and as such they are in a weak position as regards agenda-building. In the Soviet Union, the environmental department is only one among many departments in GKNT and Gosplan that are responsible respectively for national technological development and national resource planning. In Yugoslavia, similar environmental sections exist in the federal and republican planning boards. In addition, the Federal Council on the Human Environment and Territorial Management is empowered to make suggestions for environmental measures, and to bring environmental issues before the country.[49] However, the eighty delegates are selected from the environmental committees at the republican level and thus represent not their own ideas, but those of their respective republican executive bodies. Any common effort at agenda-building requires referral to the republics before agreement is reached. The republican and local environmental councils may also make legislative recommendations but in an advisory capacity only.

During negotiations on standards, technology, and the delegation of administrative authority, the environmental agencies again are in a secondary position. In the Soviet Union, all parties have to be consulted before a standard is approved; technology is the province of the designated industrial ministries, and the delegation of authority is the product of intense interbranch bargaining. During the seven-year-long negotiations on the Air Quality Control Law, a crucial issue was whether to establish a separate environmental ministry to take charge of air and water pollution control. The final bill that became law was a clear defeat for the environmental agency. Although it upgraded Goskomgidromet's administrative status, it left the old ministerial arrangements in place. In Yugoslavia, the voluntarism of the contract procedure and the lack of a centralized environmental authority undermine any environmental regulatory program. The rich, environmentally aware regions agree to take action, and the poorer tend to do little.

In the implementation stage, the ministerial "legs" of the Soviet centipede segment every environmental policy into as many sets of multiple regulations as there are ministries legally responsible for implementing the policy. In Yugoslavia, the self-management principle fosters regional inequities that compromise comprehensive application of environmental regulations across the country. The severity of the structural and regulatory constraints is an important reason why environmental agencies in the two countries have not become more visible. In a very real sense, the agencies are placed in an untenable position where they may monitor but not enforce within highly restricted areas of competence.

Available Resources

Available resources for the environmental agencies may conveniently be divided into tangible resources, such as financial and organizational resources, and intangible resources, such as the ability to articulate and aggregate the environmental interest. In both countries, the agencies are very weak in tangible resources and are able to compensate for only some of that deficiency with intangible resources.

Tangible resources. The published Soviet and Yugoslav budgets do not provide sufficient information to determine the exact sums of money allocated to the environmental agencies. In the USSR, figures of actual expenditures are secret. In Yugoslavia, there was no national budget category for environmental protection until 1980, when a category for environmental protection was added to the plan indicators. The Yugoslavs are currently examining methodologies that would best determine how to obtain and systematize the relevant data from industry to reflect real expenditures on pollution controls. While the information will be useful in assessing the cost of environmental protection, it says nothing about the amounts allocated to the environmental agencies. Neither of the countries has developed a means to assess regional and sectoral spending on environmental protection. What data are available are sketchy and incomplete, derived from different methods of data collection and different accounting systems.

Some estimate of expenditures on environmental protection in the two countries may be made from official statistics of total amounts spent on pollution control by their federal systems and industrial institutions. These statistics do not include expenditures by the environmental agencies. Unlike the United States, the environmental agencies do not distribute funds for environmental projects. In the case of the Soviet Union, the monies are allocated from the central investment fund directly to the branch ministry or republic; in Yugoslavia, investment is primarily financed through the banks and by small grants from the republics or the federal government. (See chapter 2.)

In the Soviet Union, state investment in measures connected with the protection and rational utilization of natural resources for the 1976–1980 five-year plan averaged 1.5 percent of the total state investment, or 10.8 billion rubles. In the first four years of the Eleventh Five-Year Plan, state investment in environmental protection declined slightly to 1.3 percent of total investment.[50] In the Tenth Five-Year Plan, roughly 77 percent was allocated to water pollution control and about 9 percent to the reduction of air pollution. In the RSFSR, the monies were similarly divided.[51] During the Eleventh Five-Year Plan, the figures go down to 74 percent and 6 percent respectively. Total expenditures from every source on environmental protection during the first four years of the Eleventh Five-Year Plan amounted to 34 billion rubles and include the operational expenses of Gosleskhoz.[52] A brief look at the structure of the balance of Soviet investment will provide a good idea of which institutions received these funds. From 1966 onward, Soviet industry has received on the average 35 percent of total state investment funds, and agriculture has received between 16 and 20 percent. Of the investment to industry in the last two five-year plans, 48 percent went to the petroleum, chemical and petrochemical, and engineering and metalworking industries.[53] A third to 40 percent of this amount on the average went into new construction and only about 20 percent into new equipment.[54] A U.S. Department of Commerce study found that the industrial sectors to benefit most significantly from the investment in new technology were the military-industrial, civilian machine-building, and other heavy industry sectors, which received over half of all new Soviet technology during a ten-year study period.[55] These figures indicate that the principal recipients of the natural resource and environmental protection investment monies over the past fifteen years have been the major polluting industries of the country's strategic industrial sector.

To look at the resources of the environmental agencies from another perspective, table 3.4 provides a breakdown by union republic of total capital investment in agriculture, land reclamation, and environmental protection for 1979.

According to the official figures in the table, union-republic investment in agriculture ranged from a high of 46 percent of total investment in Uzbekistan to a low of 23 percent in the RSFSR. Investment in land reclamation ranged from a high of 22 percent of total investment in Azerbaidzhan to a low of 3.6 percent in the RSFSR, while investment in environmental protection ranged from a high of 8.6 percent in Bielorussia to a low of 1.3 percent in the RSFSR. The table indicates that at least two environmental agencies, the Ministry of Agriculture and Minvodkhoz were substantial recipients of funds targeted for measures relating to environmental protection. On the other hand, much smaller amounts of money were allocated for measures identified specifically for pollution control. If Soviet accounting practices place land reclamation and irrigation under the category of the rational use of natural resources, and pollution control measures under environmental protection, the researcher is not constrained to make this distinction. The data show that those ministries engaged in the direct management and exploitation of natural resources have far greater financial resources at their disposal for environmental protection measures than those with supervisory jurisdiction over pollution control. The environmental agencies' total lack of control over the distribution or monitoring of pollution control monies puts them in a very weak position politically when compared with the wealthy industrial and agricultural polluters, who have a vested interest in deflecting those funds for their own purposes. (See chapter 4.)

Figure 3.3 provides information on the Yugoslav economic and social investments between 1966 and 1975 that had an impact on the environment.

The major investment in recent years in Yugoslavia has been in manufacturing and mining (44 percent of all investment), with investment in

Table 3.4 Total Capital Investment, and Investments in Agriculture, Land Reclamation, and Environmental Protection by Union Republic (1979), Including the Comparison with Investments in 1978 (index)

	Index over previous year	Amount	
RSFSR			
Total capital investment	102	81.6	billion rubles
Investment in agriculture		18.9	" "
Investment in land reclamation		3.0	" "
Investment in environmental protection		1.1	" "
Ukraine			
Total capital investment	96	18.7	" "
Investment in agriculture		5.3	" "
Investment in land reclamation		0.7	" "
Investment in environmental protection		0.5	" "
Bielorussia			
Total capital investment	98	4.2	" "
Investment in agriculture		1.5	" "
Investment in land reclamation		0.361	" "
Investment in environmental protection		n.a.	
Uzbekistan			
Total capital investment	106	5.262	" "
Investment in agriculture		2.4	" "
Investment in land reclamation		n.a.	
Investment in environmental protection		n.a.	
Kazakhstan			
Total capital investment	102.6	8	" "
Investment in agriculture		2.7	" "
Investment in land reclamation		0.520	" "
Investment in environmental protection		n.a.	
Georgia			
Total capital investment	103	1,690	million rubles
Investment in agriculture		445.4	" "
Investment in land reclamation		113.6	" "
Investment in environmental protection		37.9	" "
Azerbaidzhan			
Total capital investment	107	980	" "
Investment in agriculture		504	" "
Investment in land reclamation		215	" "
Investment in environmental protection		28	" "

Table 3.4 (*Continued*)

	Index over previous year	Amount		
Lithuania				
Total capital investment	102	1,645	million	rubles
Investment in agriculture		683.5	"	"
Investment in land reclamation		n.a.		
Investment in environmental protection		n.a.		
Moldavia				
Total capital investment	99	1,520	"	"
Investment in agriculture		663	"	"
Investment in land reclamation		74	"	"
Investment in environmental protection		85.4	"	"
Latvia				
Total capital investment	101.3	1,160	"	"
Investment in agriculture	110	432	"	"
Investment in land reclamation		87	"	"
Investment in environmental protection		80	"	"
Kirgizia				
Total capital investment	98	940	"	"
Investment in agriculture		310	"	"
Investment in land reclamation		82	"	"
Investment in environmental protection		62	"	"
Tadzhikistan				
Total capital investment	102	970	"	"
Investment in agriculture		323.6	"	"
Investment in land reclamation		125.8	"	"
Investment in environmental protection		n.a.		
Armenia				
Total capital investment	110	1,145	"	"
Investment in agriculture		242.4	"	"
Investment in land reclamation		82.9	"	"
Investment in environmental protection		53	"	"
Turkmenistan				
Total capital investment	102	1,230	"	"
Investment in agriculture		415	"	"
Investment in land reclamation		209	"	"
Investment in environmental protection		n.a.		

Table 3.4 (*Continued*)

	Index over previous year	Amount	
Estonia			
Total capital investment	100.9	800	million rubles
Investment in agriculture		n.a.	
Investment in land reclamation		n.a.	
Investment in environmental protection		n.a.	

Note: Land reclamation includes irrigation.
Source: The USSR and the Union Republics in 1979 (Moscow: Statistika, 1980) passim.

Figure 3.3 Share of Construction in Total Investment, Yugoslavia, 1966–75

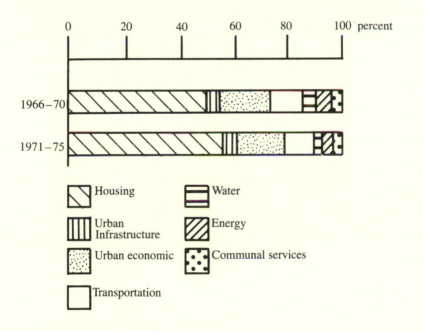

Source: P. 132 of source cited in table 3.1.

Table 3.5 Fund Resources and Taxes in SFRY
(in millions of dinars at current prices)

Period	Taxes from apart- ments	Water fund	Forest fund	Trans- portation fund	Communal activities fund	Fund for under- developed regions
1966–70	41.9	19.7	0.2	68.0	89.7	90.9
1971–75	103.5	44.7	0.5	196.7	290.2	291.8

Source: See source cited in table 3.1.

transportation and housing coming in distant second and third places (16 percent and 12 percent respectively). Investment in agriculture has been far less, and investment in forestry (0.7 percent) and irrigation systems (1.3 percent) has been below that for sociopolitical organizations (2.3 percent). In terms of investment in the infrastructure, housing has come first (50 percent) and economic investments second. By contrast, the environmental categories, water and communal infrastructure, have had the smallest share of investment with the exception of the energy infrastructure.

Table 3.5 provides data on the size of the central funds which, upon agreement with the republics, the federal government is authorized to disburse. The funds are part of the mandated annual local contributions to the SIZ, the local communities, and sociopolitical organizations, and they represent approximately 13 percent of the local community budget.[56]

While the funds for water management and reforestation for both time periods are considerably smaller than the others, the more than doubling of these two "environmental" funds from 1966–1970 to 1971–1975 indicates official awareness of the growing environmental problem. The tripling of the communal activities fund further attests to the perception of the negative impact of rapid urbanization upon the urban environment. In addition to the federal water management fund, the water authorities receive an income from mandated local contributions to the water SIZ at rates fixed in the self-managing agreement by which the particular SIZ came into being. In Croatia, according to Ramet, the rate is approximately 0.77 percent of enterprise income.[57] The environmental agency that probably receives the most amount of money on a permanent basis is the health SIZ, which gets approximately 29 percent of the annual SIZ contributions or 13 percent of the total public funds for the financing of public welfare institutions.[58] While most of the money undoubtedly goes for health insurance and medical purposes, as was noted earlier, public health institutes rely on health SIZ funding for the greater part of their budget.[59]

Although highly sketchy, the available data suggest that financial resources for environmental programs tend to go to institutions with a strong centralized organization, such as the natural resource and industrial ministries in the Soviet Union, and public health in Yugoslavia. In neither country, particularly in Yugoslavia, are the environmental agencies funded on a comparable level with the economic organizations. All environmental monies are distributed directly to the polluter either through central investment, as in the USSR, or through bank loans or tax credits, as in Yugoslavia. Unlike the EPA in the United States, the environmental agencies do not have the authority to determine where, when, and how environmental funds are to be spent. There is thus no way for them to monitor whether the money distributed has been properly spent, since the polluting organizations are not accountable to them for the environmental funds received. As a result, the environmental agents in both countries lack one of the most strategic resources in the bureaucratic game, financial clout. It is as if the U.S. Office of Budget Management handed Union Carbide $2 million with the simple admonition, "Go and pollute no more."

Organization is a more neutral but still negative resource for the environmental agencies. In the Soviet Union, the former Chief Administration for Hydrometeorology (Hydromet) attached to the USSR Council of Ministers was an organ that many Soviet legal experts viewed as the antecedent of a full-fledged environmental ministry.[60] In 1978, it was elevated to the State Committee on Hydrometeorology and Environmental Protection (Goskomgidromet). Despite the limitation of sharing jurisdiction of environmental matters with other agencies and branch institutions, the elevation brought the new state committee an organizational permanence and authority that its status as an administration had not offered. In particular, the committee was able to expand its internal structure and personnel through the establishment of a nationwide monitoring system and its own air and water inspectorates.

All other Soviet institutions involved in environmental protection have resource exploitation as their primary function. While they may bring their

99

organizational forces to bear to assert their environmental protection interests against the resource development interests of competing ministries (see the section on strategy), their dual administrative responsibility inevitably necessitates a choice between the assertion of environmental or resource use priorities. Is it more important for the State Agro-Industrial Committee to control fertilizer run-off or increase agricultural production? The 1985 centralization of agricultural administration is clearly directed toward the latter. Should Minvodkhoz promote water conservation or develop irrigation projects? Soviet planning is geared to the fulfillment of production rather than environmental quotas. Moreover, the expansion of resource use capabilities commonly entails organizational expansion. The legal measures adopted in the seventies to modify their behavior have not changed the preference of central resource use ministries and state committees for implementing production objectives over planned pollution controls.

In Yugoslavia, environmental protection has no permanent organizational status, either in the form of a siz or in the form of a government agency. The federal and regional councils are advisory organs with limited staffing only. While an advisory committee can exercise considerable influence in its expert capacity, it has no funds or benefits to distribute, and no decisionmaking capacity. The lack of an environmental administrative organization at any level of the self-management system, even one similar to the Soviet Goskomgidromet, reinforces the argument that the government and party bureaucracy have yet to perceive environmental protection as a priority.

Intangible resources. The two intangible resources most readily available to the environmental agencies are interest articulation through the mass media and interest aggregation through exchange of information and interaction with other institutions, groups, and individuals engaged in the environmental policy process.

Neither the Soviet nor the Yugoslav environmental agencies have taken full advantage of mass communications to make their case to the public.[61] Soviet environmental officials tend to use the media to present a positive picture of environmental conditions in the USSR, to explain how problems are being solved, or to present new regulations,[62] not to address the serious-

100

ness of the environmental problem. Frequently, the agencies enter press reports as part of their monitoring role or simply as the agents responsible for taking the appropriate measurements. In the press in both countries, the environmental agencies seem faceless. In Yugoslavia, it would be difficult to cite one environmental official in any of the republics who would be familiar to the public. In the Soviet Union, the possible exception may be Iurii Izrael, head of Goskomgidromet. But although Dr. Izrael has written many articles and is quoted fairly frequently in the Soviet press, he is far from being the familiar public figure that the head of EPA is in the United States. Reports naming persons who do something for the environment or bring complaints against violators almost never name individuals in the environmental agencies. The hero commonly is a local party or government official, a representative of a local people's control committee or volunteer attached to one of the environmental inspectorates, a spokesman for the local chapter of the nature protection society, or a scientist. Although often cited for failure to perform it properly, the environmental agent receives little credit for work well done.

There is some evidence that the environmental agencies may be becoming more sensitive to public relations and the need to stress their own role more forcefully. Local inspectorates are beginning to speak out more frankly about the shortcomings of the local soviets and local enterprises in implementing environmental regulations.[63] L. Yufremov, chairman of the prestigious Environmental Department of GKNT has openly criticized delinquent ministries for failure to fulfill planned pollution control quotas.[64] The appearance of environmental officials as active proenvironmental spokesmen is a recent and welcome development.

The most important intangible resource for the environmental agencies is in the area of interest aggregation. Although there is a great deal more evidence of networking among experts, field research in Yugoslavia indicated that a considerable network existed between individuals working in similar environmental fields in the public health departments; the Permanent Conference of Towns and Opštini of Yugoslavia; the sociopolitical organizations; federal, republican, and regional planning councils; local officials; and the federal and republican councils on environmental protection. These officials had been associated with their respective institutions for some time, knew one another personally, and could be called upon for support or to undertake a joint project. During the height of the Sava River pollution scare in the fall of 1984, the secretary general of the Federal Council for the Protection and Improvement of the Environment appeared on television alongside a representative from the Belgrade Institute of Health to discuss the problem. Although environmental officials might be unknown to the public, they seemed to enjoy a good reputation among their colleagues in the related environmental agencies. Much of this contact appeared to be confined to a particular republic. However, exchange of information and experience across republics was beginning to be institutionalized in the subcommittees of the Federal Council for the Human Environment and Territorial Planning, and through membership in the sociopolitical organizations. The interrepublican water SIZ provided another forum for such contacts.

A similar situation must obtain in the USSR. Although the Soviet Union is a much larger geographic area than Yugoslavia, environmental officials within one city and within the smaller republics most certainly know each other. Many of them sit on the environmental committees attached to the local soviets (see chapter 5), and the large number of overlapping jurisdictions suggests that many must meet each other frequently on the job. Moreover, officials who have been educated at the same university retain their relationships with colleagues in related environmental positions in the other republics. Many meet each other at conferences and meetings organized by their superiors. Finally, one can only assume that the environmental "scandals" reported in the national, republican, and local press reflect contact and consensus between the environmental agencies and "friendly" party and government officials. Interagency networks in the communist countries is an area that unfortunately so far is closed to the Western observer. But it is an area that would yield rich returns in our understanding of the communist public policy process.

Rewards and Costs

The rewards won by bureaucrats in the policymaking game, so masterfully described by Bardach,[65] seem eminently relevant to the Soviet and Yugoslav context. Lives there a bureaucrat in any land who lacks ambition or disdains to enhance his reputation and/or power? Like their counterparts elsewhere, Soviet and Yugoslav functionaries are surely interested in improving their organization's position, need some job satisfaction, and desire "the easy life." It is reasonable, then, to assume that the rewards for the environmental actors are the same as those for all bureaucrats, with one substantial difference: the environmental agencies play their game within particularly limiting systemic and regulatory constraints. As a consequence, the rewards for the environmental actors are less substantial than for the other participants in the game.

Take personal ambition first. In the Soviet Union, the environmental agencies are viewed as less prestigious than the more established industrial ministries or state committees with their larger funding and greater share in economic and military development. There is less to administer in an environmental agency and little direct participation in policymaking. In the Soviet Union, Gorbachev's rise was due not so much to his demonstration of agricultural management capabilities within the Ministry of Agriculture as to his contacts within the party and the military.[66] By contrast, Dmitri Ustinov's rise was more directly attributable to his considerable prior experience in the administration of the military-industrial complex. An exception to the rule was the appointment in 1984 of Vicentas J. Normantas as Estonian Minister of Land Reclamation and Water Resources. A man with Normantas's experience in procurement and in agricultural affairs might have been expected to be appointed to a more prestigious post. His selection as environmental minister was apparently the result of Chernenko's concern to improve agricultural production.[67] The appointment confirms the rule. An environmental position becomes important because of the value attached to it by the central leadership or because of prior personal connections. It is not in itself a significant post.

There is little glamour in the job. The environmental bureaucrat has not been portrayed as a hero in the Soviet press. While scientists command public attention and acclaim, the environmental official works in relative obscurity. Author conversations initiated on a random basis with individuals in the street in both the USSR and in Yugoslavia indicated deep veneration for scientists. Scientists, however, were seen as a group separate and distinct from the trained personnel in the environmental agencies. In the Soviet Union, the "real" scientists were the experts in the Academy institutes and, in Yugoslavia, the doctors and professors in the self-management institutes and university centers. An environmental official, on the other hand, was just one more bureaucrat.

It could be argued that being head of the State Committee on Hydrometeorology and Environmental Protection might be enough to satisfy personal ambition and desire for recognition. There is little doubt that Dr. Izrael's work on environmental standards was a factor in his being selected head of what later became the State Committee. But it is not clear that he enjoys a greater reputation as chairman of the committee than he would have had if he had remained a scientist. Nor is it obvious that as state committee chairman, his reputation is any greater in the environmental field than that of the leading environmental academicians, such as the late I. P. Gerasimov or T. S. Khachaturov, or members of Academy institutes, like jurist Oleg Kolbasov and economist Pavel Oldak. Indeed, in becoming head of the State Committee, Izrael might very well have jeopardized his chance for a scholarly reputation without adding any new distinctions to his personal career.

One obvious benefit of being a high-level environmental bureaucrat is the personal power derived from the administration of an expanding agency through control over information and patronage within the organization and access to persons in high places outside it. Yet, although these factors are operative for the head of a state environmental committee, they would seem to hold out fewer rewards to him than to the head of a large and wealthy industrial ministry. There are more opportunities for control over information and patronage in the State Agro-Industrial Committee or Minvodkhoz because the environmental component is only one part of their total mandate. Organizational and personal promotion further accrue through interbranch contacts. The chairman of Goskomgidromet sits on the interbranch Scientific-Technical Council on the Comprehensive Problems of Environmental Protection and Resource Use attached to GKNT, along with representatives from the Academy of Sciences, the GKNT administrative bureaucracy, and the industrial and resource exploiting ministries.[68] Participation in such committees gains one access to the highest decisionmaking bodies of the country and involvement in major policy discussions. On a lower level, interbranch committees can play a definitive role in deciding policy questions related to a specific problem. The Interbranch Committee on Mineral Fertilizers and Toxic Chemicals is restricted to representation from the three lead agencies involved in the evaluation of possibly toxic substances: Minzdrav, the State Agro-Industrial Committee, and Gosleskhoz.[69] Officials sitting on this committee have the major policy input into the use of toxic chemicals.

Job satisfaction may also be more illusory for the Soviet environmental official than for the more production-oriented bureaucrat. At the beginning of an interview, officials tended to wax enthusiastic about the results achieved by their department or organization. But as the interview wore on, the official generally made some comment to the effect that his record of success was probably as good as that of his counterpart in the United States. The hesitant manner in which the statement was offered suggested that the speaker had reservations about the real status of the progress he was reporting. Although positive developments in the environmental area are regularly reported in the papers, the Soviet press appears as ready to cite failure as success, and many progress reports end with a discussion of what is left to be done.[70] Censorship makes it impossible to know the true state of environmental protection in the USSR. The totally negative tone of Boris Komarov's book on the status of the environment in the USSR, *The Destruction of Nature in the Soviet Union*, urges caution in accepting his verdict, but Soviet press reports as well as private conversations with scientists suggest that the truth is sobering. If such is indeed the case, officials responsible for environmental protection must experience considerable job frustration if they are at all serious about their work.

Finally, there is the question of "the easy life." There is little doubt that employment in the Soviet bureaucracy offers privileges and standards of living above that of the factory worker. But while work in the environmental institutions holds out rewards for the environmental official, these do not seem to be commensurate with those available to individuals in other ministries and government agencies. According to Medvedev, the best living and research conditions are to be found in the military and in the Academy of Sciences, in that order.[71] Nor are the attractions of the easy life in the environmental agencies as great as in the more powerful industrial ministries, depending on whether your status in those organizations makes you a member of the *nomenklatura*.[72] The chief attraction may be the possibility of international travel available through the numerous environmental agreements signed between the USSR and other countries.[73]

In Yugoslavia, the rewards for service in the environmental agencies are even less evident. In the absence of any separate environmental organization, there is little to distinguish an environmental researcher or department head in the various health departments from his colleagues in related fields. There is certainly little reward or demand for inspectors, since regional and local environmental committees are not yet organized in most communities. Moreover, as in the Soviet Union, the environment is not viewed as one of the most prestigious areas of endeavor. Energy and science and technology have more priority.[74]

On the positive side, the gaps in bureaucratic organization may be a factor in drawing individuals committed to the environment into service on the communal, regional, and republican committees. Since the 1970s made environmental protection popular, the reputation of a party activist, a local government official, or a scientist has been enhanced by evidence of interest in questions of pollution control. The proof is seen in the formation of the council system and in the incorporation of environmental measures into the planning process. The federal and republican advisory councils on environmental protection offer visible rewards for an administrator with initiative by offering opportunities for a wide range of inter- and intra-republican contacts, as well as a chance to develop and coordinate national projects. There is also considerable reward for personal ambition to be gained from participation in the planning and policy deliberations of the Yugoslav legislatures. As in the Soviet Union, however, all of this activity takes place out of the public limelight behind official doors. While an environmental official makes his few succinct, colorless comments on the relation of the 1984 cold spell to the energy situation during the evening news broadcast, the university professor is granted a more lively and longer appearance regarding the same subject on the weekly TV news analysis program.[75] When all these factors are taken together, a university professorship or an environmental consultantship would seem to offer more job satisfaction and a more attractive lifestyle than employment in the environmental committees' permanent staff or in the health departments or water SIZ. More prestige and social status are attached to the university position; there is more job security because the position is more permanent; and there are more opportunities to travel abroad through exchange professorships and joint research projects. However, if the rewards for the environmental actor in both countries are not as great as for his industrial or academic counterparts, his career is also not as politically sensitive, and there is considerable satisfaction to be working for a cause which is both right and popular.

Strategies

The systemic constraints upon Soviet and Yugoslav environmental officials clearly inhibit their cultivation of aggressive tactics. The environmental agencies have been most successful at incrementalism and accommodation, what Bardach terms "keeping the peace." They have been least successful in developing effective strategies to undercut the power of the economic organizations to decide when, where, and how to comply with the law.[76]

Incrementalism. It is impossible to look at the course of Soviet and Yugoslav environmental legislation and regulation during the past two decades without an appreciation of the steady increase in the regulatory authority of the environmental agencies. Over the past twenty years, the Soviet Union has moved from largely symbolic environmental legislation to increasingly more sophisticated regulation. As environmental rulemaking has become more specific, the environmental regulatory agencies have acquired an increasing role in the monitoring and enforcement of the regulations. The instructions given to Hydromet in the 1972 joint resolution on the strengthening of environmental protection[77] limited the administration to information gathering and monitoring activities in the area of air pollution control. The December 1978 joint resolution[78] entrusted the upgraded Goskomgidromet with a whole range of new responsibilities: the organization and operation of a national state monitoring system; the examination of plans and projects for new development submitted for approval by other ministries to ensure that these meet established air pollution control regulations; on-site inspection of enterprises regardless of their ministerial subordination; and the right to suspend operations if the norms have been violated. Finally, Goskomgidromet, together with Minvodkhoz, the Ministry of Agriculture and the USSR Committee for the Supervision of Safe Working Practices in Industry, was charged with ensuring that industrial enterprises fulfill the environmental protection targets set by the state plans. Under the 1980 Air Pollution Control Law, Goskomgidromet was given sole responsibility for giving authorization for the emission of pollutants into the atmosphere by stationary sources (Article 10). (Regulation of automobile emission standards is the province of the Ministry of Internal Affairs and the Automotive Industry Ministry.)[79] Some of the junior lawyers in the ANSSSR's Institute of State and Law Section on Environmental Protection, which drafted the air quality law, favored giving Goskomgidromet exclusive control over air and water quality pollution measures.[80] Even though they failed in their objective, the new law continued the trend begun in the earlier resolutions to give Goskomgidromet broader and at the same time more specific areas of jurisdiction.

In 1982, the USSR Council of Ministers passed a resolution on air quality that laid down procedures for the elaboration, coordination, approval, and enforcement of the emission and ambient norms for stationary sources mandated by the Air Quality Control Law. Among other things, the resolution stipulated that the norms were to be drawn up by the relevant ministries and union-republic bodies, subject to the approval of Goskomgidromet and Minzdrav. Up until that time, air norms had been subject only to Ministry of Health approval.[81] The resolution further specified that Goskomgidromet would exercise general supervision over the drawing up of the norms for stationery sources in the cities and industrial zones. Increased regulatory powers brought material expansion. As of 1982, the state monitoring system under Goskomgidromet's control officially extended to more than 450 cities, about 1,900 bodies of inland water, bordering seas, and the soil in regions where chemical fertilizers are used.[82]

Minvodkhoz has also expanded its areas of competence in the regulation of water use and water consumption. In the sixties, it emerged from its long battle with the Ministry of Electrification and Power with official support for the need for water resource conservation. In the seventies, the river basin system was created under Minvodkhoz administration, and ambient and point-source emission norms for water quality were established. More recent measures, such as the USSR Council of Ministers' resolution on the comprehensive use of the Volga-Akhtuba floodplain and delta in Astrakhan,[83] have assigned Minvodkhoz additional supervisory authority over irrigation projects. Minvodkhoz also was delegated supervision over the determination of the amounts and kinds of charges to be levied for water consumption in the administration of the water tax that went into effect January 1, 1982.[84] The irony of the water tax is that it extends only to industrial enterprises; agricultural organizations and households are not required to pay it. Moreover, Minvodkhoz apparently has little economic interest in enforcing the regulation since the funding for the ministry's subunits is not dependent upon their efforts to collect the money from the enterprises.[85]

There is also some evidence that the environmental agencies have tightened up their enforcement activities in many of the republics. In 1978, the Armenian Republic prosecutor's office recorded 558 instances of violation of the rules pertaining to the granting of areas for nonagricultural purposes and the illegal seizure of plots of land.[86] The secretary of the Kremerovo regional party committee reported that from 1977 to 1980, inspection agencies suspended operation of more than seventy enterprises. In twenty-six of the cases, evidence was presented to the investigatory organs and over three thousand fines were imposed.[87] In a case near Khaborovsk, the guilty were the chief forest conservation engineer and his son. The two of them had felled some seventy-five old pine trees to obtain several thousand kilograms of the choice pine nuts much favored by discriminating Siberians![88] Legal codes have become more precise in their definition of liability for environmental offenses. In 1980, new fundamental legislation on administrative law violations specifically identified officials who failed to protect nature and to obey regulations, enforcement of which was part of their official duties according to administrative procedures.[89]

These and related regulations indicate that by constantly putting pressure on the weakness of regulation, the environmental regulatory agencies have slowly but surely expanded their areas of jurisdiction and increased their regulatory authority. As Gustafson has argued in his discussion of the emergence of environmental issues on the Soviet political scene, it would be misleading to attribute the agencies' growth to consciously organized influence. Their success is due in no small part to the dynamics of the regulatory principle once it is accepted. After a regulatory agency has been created, or regulatory authority delegated to a branch ministry or committee, it requires little politicking to persuade the decisionmakers that the regulations have not produced the desired result because they are not sufficiently strict, sufficiently comprehensive, or properly enforced. Support will always be forthcoming from those ministries and organizations which see their projects threatened by an aggressive ministerial polluter. While Soviet economists have decried the "lack of political will" to accomplish environmental protection,[90] the environmental agencies have quietly persisted in acquiring more regulatory power.

The use of incrementalism by environmental agents is much less visible and has had much less effect in Yugoslavia. During the seventies there was a proliferation of environmental legislation and some tightening of environmental controls, mainly in the area of incorporating environmental indicators into the planning system. But there has been no comparable strengthening of the hands of the environmental agencies. During the past ten years, several revisions of the air, water, and forestry laws have been made, adding precision to the earlier versions but not tightening up control mechanisms. For example, the Serbian 1977 revision of the air quality law reduced the number of pollutants to be controlled from twelve to eleven.[91] An exception to the pattern might be the 1981 revision of the Serbian forestry law that requires a member of the forest inspection service to be a licensed forestry engineer.[92]

Yugoslav newspapers report cases of agreements not upheld, and dangerously high levels of pollution, but contrary to what one reads in the Soviet press, there are no strident demands for stricter enforcement or greater initiative on the part of the environmental agencies. Since enforcement is almost entirely relegated to the local level, and a great deal of environmental rulemaking is by agreement among self-managing units, the environmental agencies have much less leverage to increase their regulatory power than do their Soviet counterparts.

Accommodation. In both countries environmental agents have shown themselves partial to the strategy of accommodation. The Soviet press is full of instances where environmental agencies are accused of failing to take the appropriate action. Environmental inspectorates are constantly cited for tolerating violations of environmental regulations and nature protection,[93] or for not imposing economic sanctions on delinquent enterprises when it is within their legal competence to do so.[94]

In fairness to the environmental officials, a large part of their seeming indifference to violations of the law is the product of other factors. Sometimes, the damage is of such proportions that a technological solution seems out of reach. So much gravel was dredged annually out of the Tom River that flows through Tomsk in western Siberia that the river's gravel replacement capacity was exceeded. The result was a sharply falling water level and an equally sharp fall in the volume of gravel extracted from the river. As usual, the environmental agencies were faulted for refusing to cite the procurement authorities in violation. The reporter accused the former of having sided with the city executive committee in favor of short-term gain by permitting the uncontrolled exploitation of the gravel bed, rather than pursuing long-term profit through insistence on environmental controls. By 1980, the damage amounted to some 70 million cubic meters of gravel, but no easy way could be found to replace the loss. The problem had become so large that the inspectors were unable to formulate any constructive decision. Since current legislation did not set limits on extracting operations, there was not even a way to determine the size of the violation.[95]

Another factor is the expectation of changes that would make enforcement of regulations under existing circumstances futile. Semipalatinsk health officials were criticized for lack of concern about air pollution. The city had drawn up an air pollution reduction plan in 1976 and by the end of the Tenth Five-Year Plan (1979) had only completed half of it. Investigation by medical authorities showed that the major polluter, a large cement plant, had actually increased the amount of dust it discharged into the atmosphere after installing dust-trapping equipment. The increase was blamed on the plant's effort to boost production, which exceeded the capacity of its furnaces and produced more pollution than its dust traps could handle. Health officials looked the other way because they anticipated the reconstruction of the plant in a few years.[96] Similarly, Minvodkhoz showed itself reluctant to take any measures in 1984 to stop the continuing fall in the water level of the Irtysh River. The ministry's argument was that a comprehensive plan for the conservation and utilization of the river was being drawn up. The implementation of the plan would render all previous measures obsolete, so there was no need to take any action in the immediate future.[97]

The high cost of remediation is another consideration. A good example is the reclaiming of land after mining operations. Common sense dictates in the Soviet Union as elsewhere that no attempt be made to reclaim land that has been severely damaged and covers a large area. Accordingly, land reclamation experts in what was formerly the USSR Ministry of Agriculture have worked out a formula that takes into account the evaluation of the uses to which subsoil and topsoil can be put, and if the cost of reclamation, including transportation, exceeds the benefit, the land is not reclaimed.[98]

While technological problems are an important reason why environmental officials look the other way, the complexity involved in implementing Soviet regulations also exerts a negative influence. In 1981, there were nationally approved PDKs (maximum permissible concentrations) for some 420 pollutants found in drinking or other water designated for human use, for 68 pollutants found in waters designated for fish or other animal life, for 247 inorganic substances, and for 728 organic air-borne pollutants in work places and residential zones. In addition, there were PDKs for 100 pesticides found in food and for 723 radioactive materials.[99] The 1980 Air Quality Control Law requires Goskomgidromet to make an inventory of all stationary point sources of air pollution by location and pollutant, if the pollutant is known. The size of the task is staggering. Yet, without such an inventory, the determination of ambient air and water norms remains essentially based on guesswork.[100]

The norm system itself has become increasingly sophisticated. PDK, established in 1951, is a relative ambient standard that is applied across the USSR on the basis of regional environmental and industrial criteria. In areas that are heavily developed with large concentrations of industry and in recreational or protected zones, PDKs are stricter than in other kinds of regions. The determination of a specific PDK thus requires the introduction of an additional norm, *predel'no dopustimaia ekologicheskaia nagruzka* (the level of permitted ecological load or carrying capacity), or PDN. The concept of PDN was initially promoted by Iurii Izrael in a series of lectures and articles in 1976–1977.[101] Less widely used than PDK because its determination depends on a great many variables, PDN has not yet been given legal recognition. In theory, it is determined by evaluating the economic or recreational potential of a given region in terms of its topographical and climatic characteristics, presence of natural resources, and capacity for self-regeneration.[102]

Since PDK is a regional indicator designating an appropriate ambient air or water quality for a given pollutant, the development of a point-source emission norm logically followed. The norm was first proposed in 1972 by a collective of experts, among them again Dr. Izrael,[103] and was called *predel'no dopustimyie vybrosov* (the maximum allowable emission level), or PDV. Like PDK, PDV is a relative norm. It is determined by calculating the total contribution of all polluting sources to a region's PDK for a given environmental parameter, and then defining a norm for the individual point source in such a way that the sum total of PDV will not exceed the mandated PDK. The 1980 Air Quality Control Law gave legal recognition to PDV.

In every country, the energy and chemical industries are the main pollutors. Soviet industrial spokesmen were quick to point out that a drastic reduction of emissions by these industries, when they were located in heavily industrialized or sensitive areas, in order to bring the region in conformance with PDK norms, would exceed in some cases the limits of existing technology, and in others, the resources available to implement the project. The solution, of course, was what Petrov has called the "ecological *kompromis*." Since many regions and urban areas would not be able to meet the PDV and hence PDK, it was proposed that a progressive time schedule be worked out whereby the industries in a given area would gradually bring their point-source emissions to the level of the standard. The interim standard was called *vremmenoye soglasitel'noye vybrasov* (the temporary agreed-upon emission), or VSV.

VSV is based on a calculation of the cost of control compared to the benefits accruing to the environment and society by reduced pollution, even if the pollution level does not meet the target standard. If VSV was to have any objective validity other than a concession to industry, it was soon seen that "ekotechnology," as the Soviets call it, would also have to be normalized. T. S. Khachaturov of Moscow University's Department of Economics supported the proposal for a new norm, which was given the clumsy label *technicheskoe i sotsial'no-ekonomicheskoe obosnovaniia prinimaemych norm* (the technological and socioeconomic foundation of adopted norms), or TSEDS.[104] The primary function of the norm is a cost-benefit calculation of the required expenses and potential results following the implementation of concrete technological measures to meet PDV or VSV.

The rapid theoretical development of the norm system has left many gray areas where environmental officials find it difficult to oversee legal compliance with any degree of certainty. Both PDV and VSV are the result of discussion and compromise, and at present they are based more on what industry says can be done than on any objective criteria. Thus, while technology must be considered a critical factor in the *kompromis* process, an equally important aspect is the lack of precision in the norm system itself.

Factors of technology and cost affect the performance of environmental officials in Yugoslavia to an even greater degree than in the USSR. Mention has already been made of the problem in the Zastava automobile factory in Kragujevac in identifying the chemical composition of a paint that exuded malodorous fumes. In this case as in many others, the problem is not simply a weakness in technology. Most technology is imported into Yugoslavia. From 1974 to 1978, the share of investment in technology that was attributable to foreign imports averaged approximately 44 percent. In the area of manufacturing, mining, and quarrying, the proportion of investment in foreign technology was as high as 50 percent.[105] Virtually all pollution control equipment must be imported from abroad. The government has attempted to facilitate the import of such equipment by abolishing import duty, but with a foreign debt of over $20 million, the import of pollution control technology is understandably not among the top priorities of the Yugoslav government or industry. And the country does not yet have a sufficiently developed technological base to be able to manufacture such equipment itself.

As in the Soviet Union, the correction of costly major environmental damage tends to be postponed. A particularly catastrophic example of pollution is along the Timok River on the Bulgarian border, the result of the dumping of copper pilings by the Bor Copper Mine, Yugoslavia's largest copper mine and one of its biggest polluters. The concession was developed by the French before World War II, and the mine was subsequently confiscated and exploited by the Germans. After the war, the Soviet embargo of 1948 to 1950 made exports essential. The mine went back into full production under Yugoslav management, and no environmental protection measures were taken for many years. A long-term program is now in effect, but experts estimate it will take from eighty to one hundred years to make the river bottom land, destroyed by uncontrolled dumping over a period of forty years, arable again.[106]

While Yugoslavs cite the technological factor as the major deterrent to environmental enforcement, the norm system must not be overlooked. Not as theoretically elegant as the Soviet Union's, it too encourages the environmental authorities to compromise and look the other way. More than three hundred federal, republican, and provincial laws, in addition to other regulations, govern the environment in Yugoslavia at the present time.[107] Each republic and, to a more limited degree, each commune may pass its own legislation. Standardization proved a sufficiently severe problem during the adoption of environmental planning indicators for the 1970–1975 planning period to prompt the decision to work toward uniform trans-republican environmental norms. In this respect, Yugoslavia may be moving toward a federal arrangement similar to that which obtains in Australia, where an interrepublican committee agrees on common norms for the entire country.[108] Standardization at the republican level, however, may not be able to limit the communes' considerable autonomy in environmental rulemaking. In December 1981, the Republic of Serbia passed noise legislation.[109] The city of Belgrade has been working on its own municipal ordinance for the past several years. Until such legislation is in place, Belgrade industry and motorists are not bound by the Serbian law and may legally make all the noise they please within the Belgrade city limits without fear of violation.[110]

Added to the problems of overproliferation and lack of coordination is the fact that Yugoslav norms in every area are formulated from international and, most frequently, American experience. They thus tend to reflect desired goals rather than possible achievements. The air pollution ambient levels are a case in point. Derived from U.S. standards, the norms cover eleven pollutants and indicate short-term permissible levels of concentration and average daily permissible levels of concentration.[111] The newspapers in the large cities publish daily the concentration levels for sulphur dioxide, ash, and carbon dioxide. During the winter months, the levels can rise to a danger point, causing the health officials to call an alert. But the levels in January and February alone are often well above the legal permissible levels with no public health official making any particular com-

115

ment. During a visit to the municipal public health institute in Belgrade, the author visited a monitoring station, which was registering high levels of sulphur dioxide concentration. The health official could only shrug his shoulders in sympathy. Norms were one thing. Practice another.

Influence over client groups, and strategies to break monopoly control. The foregoing discussion suggests that the relation between environmental agency officials and industry is asymmetrical. Industrial organizations exert greater pressure on environmental officials than the other way around. Nevertheless, the environmental inspectors do not submit all the time.

The Soviet press contains numerous instances where environmental officials have denied permission to build a facility, given warnings, or attempted to close an installation. Three cases concern Lake Pleshcheyevo for noncompliance, Lake Ladoga, and air pollution in Togliatti.

The first case involved the use of groundwater by a chemical plant in the town of Pereslavl'-Zaleskii on Lake Pleshcheyevo, fifty miles northeast of Moscow. The first section of the plant was built in the early sixties. In 1967, the Ministry of Geology refused to give its approval for further development because an evaluation of the groundwater below the lake showed that the level was low and that the water, which contained hydrogen sulfide, fed directly into the lake. In 1970, the RSFSR Minvodkhoz opposed the construction of a second section of the plant, which, however, was built. Studies of the groundwater in 1975 confirmed not only that the lake was directly connected to the underground water sources, but that city wells were drawing directly from the lake. Yet, in 1981, a third section of the plant was started. The situation was the more serious since the lake formed part of the watershed of the Moscow basin. In this situation there was no question that the environmental authorities did their job, and that the industrial ministry overrode their opposition.

The story given above is intriguing not only for its depiction of the power of an industrial ministry but also for its silence on the source of information. The story was reported in an article in *Literaturnaia gazieta*, the organ of the USSR Writers' Union, in June 1981.[112] The union is known for its proenvironmental activism. The report was the second to have appeared on the same subject. Evidently someone first reported the story in 1979 to no avail, and when the third section of the plant was started in 1981, went back to the journal again. The article does not, of course, say who the informant was. Given the reference to the environmental agencies, one may assume that either the environmental officials themselves or someone associated with them provided the information regarding the agencies' position on the groundwater level. The story thus is a good example of the kinds of action the environmental agencies may take when faced with a serious problem.

The story of pollution in Lake Ladoga near Leningrad is similar. The polluter this time was a pulp and paper mill, constructed again in the late fifties or early sixties. No treatment facilities were built. The mill consumed a thousand tons of water to produce one ton of pulp. A body of water that emptied into Lake Ladoga and was used initially as a settling tank for the mill was soon contaminated. The environmental authorities strongly expressed their concern about the situation in 1970. In 1976 and 1980, the Leningrad Provincial Executive Committee cited the mill for inadequate treatment facilities. The provincial People's Control Committee did the same in 1979, and the chief sanitation inspector wrote to the superior USSR ministry thirteen times asking that something be done. In 1979, the public prosecutor's office finally became involved. The source for the story is once more *Literaturnaia gazieta*.[113] In reading the article, one gets a sense of frustration and powerlessness on the part of the environmental agencies. Publicity can be a poor weapon against the monopoly power of a branch ministry.

The final illustration relates to air pollution in the city of Togliatti near Kuibyshev in the Urals. A conference held in 1982, attended by the polluting branch ministries and the responsible environmental agencies, found the status of environmental protection in the city "very unsatisfactory." The conference participants drew up a list of necessary measures to redress the situation. No action was taken, except that the authorities were able to shut down two units of the Togliatti Nitrogen Association because of excessive pollution. The problem facing the environmental authorities was that no money is allocated for environmental protection measures when a plant is undergoing reconstruction. Funds are given for this purpose only when new construction is involved. So the city was unable to obtain funds from the ministry for the installation of the proper air pollution equipment. Problems of retrofitting are similar in every country. The irony of this particular situation was that although industrial expansion had been forbidden in the city because of the seriousness of air pollution, local plant managers were able to obtain investment monies of 400 million rubles for new construction for the 1980–1984 five-year plan.[114] After such reports as this, it is easier to understand why environmental officials prefer to keep the peace.

Yugoslav self-management does not provide any better opportunities for the environmental agencies to take direct action against industrial intransigence. The regional organization of Yugoslav industry, when contrasted to the central power of Soviet industry, might seem to impose fewer constraints upon the environmental agents in their exercise of the law. This is not the case. Once an industry has decided to move into an area, construction may be prevented only through rejection by the local authorities or through popular local initiative (see chapter 7). The environmental inspectorates are unable to deal on an equal footing with industry, which provides jobs and money for the community: witness the dilemma of the cement factory outside of Belgrade. When the project reaches interrepublican proportions, as it did when the federal government approved the building of a dam that would flood the Tara River Canyon in 1984, an inspectorate is powerless to stop construction. Revision of a decision at this level necessitates the combined pressure of Yugoslavia's most distinguished scientists operating through their professional environmental and other sociopolitical organizations (see chapter 6).

Despite the hurdles, the environmental agent can make his position prevail. A notable example is the resolution of the Croatian Republican Committee for Health and Social Security, passed in May 1985, to uphold the decision of the Health Inspectorate of Kaštel Sućurac opština near Split to close the Jugovinil Company's operation "Klor." The plant had been dumping fifteen kilograms of mercury daily (five tons yearly) into Kaštel Bay on the Dalmatian coast. The resolution marked the end of a protracted battle, lasting several months, between the industry and the inspector in the field, Dr. Igor Jelović, and represented a solid victory for the latter. Evidently anticipating an adverse judgment by Zagreb, "Klor" closed down its production of chlorine in advance of the final decision. The decision sets a precedent for proceeding against the other operations in Yugoslavia that produce chlorine using the mercury electrode method.[115]

The closing of the Kaštel plant represents a significant step forward for the environmental agencies in asserting the needs of the environment over the preferences of industry within the self-management system. However, the agencies' success must be put in perspective. The closing involved the lay-off of 115 workers. The Institute for Medical Research and Medical Work in Zagreb, which provided the expert advice in this case, was against the shut-down and in favor of the installation of "clean," safer technology. However, the cost of the new equipment was estimated at 5 billion dinars, or over $83 million. The republican committee wisely decided that in view of the amount of mercury being released into the Adriatic, suspension of production was necessary, pending the raising of the necessary funds for retrofitting. The importance of chlorine to the chemical industry makes it unlikely that prosecution will proceed with the same results against the other chlorine plants using similar production techniques. Nor is it likely that the country can afford to invest in clean technology for all of them.

A third factor inhibiting the environmental agent's performance is the fact that, as in other areas of Yugoslav life, every pollution control installation must be implemented through the agreement of all parties concerned. The environmental official is not likely to be party to the compact discussion, although he may have defined the conditions. To a large extent, he is external to the whole process. A case in point concerns the Sava River Compact. Yugoslavia's most serious problem at the present time is water. In 1980, a pollution control compact was signed between the opštini along the river. A report on a conference on water quality held in Ohrid in 1982 stated that the signing of the contract had brought no concrete results. The conference further criticized the responsible SIZ and water management associations for insufficient thoroughness in data collection and analysis, thereby preventing the implementation of "concrete" (*stvarna*) social action programs to protect and improve water quality.[116] There was no mention of input by environmental organs at all.

Continued oil spillage into the Sava River during 1984 illustrates another way in which the environmental agent remains external to the process of environmental decisionmaking. The federal water law establishing federal jurisdiction over interrepublican waterways was specifically written with control of the Sava River in mind. As mentioned earlier, the law makes no provision for a federal water inspectorate to monitor water quality, but leaves inspection to be organized by the republics. Belgrade residents in the winter of 1984–1985 were jokingly toasting visitors with "water mixed with oil" in place of their usual *rakija*. While Belgrade newspapers were more diplomatic, the average Belgradian blamed the condition of Belgrade drinking water on industries located upstream in Croatia. The Croatian position was that the source of contamination had so far not been established. In the absence of a federal water inspectorate, there is no way the Serbian government can determine the source of pollution on its own, as long as the Croatian government insists on its right of inspection of point sources along the length of the river that flows through Croatian territory. The politics of the problem provides no independent role for the Croatian inspectors, but makes them party to the Croatian position. By January 1985, the situation had deteriorated so far that delegates to the Federal Skupština initiated a movement to amend the water law.

Finally, self-management encourages republican and local interests at the expense of the common interest. The authority of environmental officials is undercut by parochial demands. While the Sava River exemplifies the interrepublican dimension of the problem, the failure to reach agreement on the management of Kornati National Park is typical of opština politics. The original proposal was to establish the headquarters in the town of Murter and to create two work associations, one at Murter and one at neighboring Salima. The Zadar opština felt bypassed; local officials objected, and the proposal went down.[117] In order to break the local impasse, the law governing the creation of national parks would have had to be changed.

Conclusion

The implementation of the environmental regulatory principle delegates environmental management functions to existing organizations or generates a new set of bureaucracies. There is a temptation to see in new institutions the creation of new structure. This chapter demonstrates that in terms of the four features presented in chapter 1 as characteristic of communist sociopolitical systems, the formation of new bureaucracies has produced no fundamental structural change in either country. What has occurred is the addition or modification of bureaucracies, not a transformation of structural relations. It is inevitable that no matter what the politicoeconomic system, those institutions that exerted political power before the regulations went into effect will continue to do so afterward. Since the regulations set up a negotiating situation, it is also inevitable that the stronger negotiator will be able to make his position prevail, whether it be central economic institutions as in the Soviet Union, or regional or local industry and/or government as in Yugoslavia. The politicoeconomic structure of both countries has been seen to hamper the adoption by the regulatory agencies of direct, aggressive strategies of confrontation. The Soviet centipede merges the environmental agent with the polluter and makes the central ministry responsible for determining when and if pollution control measures will be taken by its subordinates. In the Yugoslav hydra, mutually supportive economic and political interests at the local and republican levels vitiate the implementation of regulations.

If the regulatory principle limits their options, it also has provided opportunities for the environmental agencies to increase their power. Whether the regulations are enforced or not, they assure the permanency and even expansion of the regulatory organs. While their power may lack the clout of the industrial institutions, the insistence on the regulatory principle in both countries enables the younger bureaucracies to carve out a new power domain. The process once begun is irreversible unless the regulatory system is abandoned. Since abandonment of the system would threaten the operation of other established bureaucracies, the environmental agencies have won a firm position for themselves in the bureaucratic politics of both countries.

4

The Economic Enterprises

Industry and agriculture are the prime targets of environmental policy-making. Their compliance or noncompliance with regulations determines the effectiveness of environmental management programs. In communist one-party states, the economic enterprises enjoy a privileged relationship vis-à-vis the centers of political power. Whereas the other participants in the environmental policy game have an inferior structural position, and must rely on the expansion of the regulatory principle to advance their interests, industry, in particular, may exploit both sets of constraints to its continuing advantage. The unique power of the economic enterprises has contributed more than any other single factor to the continuing vitiation of environmental protection goals in the two countries.

Structural and Regulatory Constraints

Industry's special relationship with the party and government. Industry's position in the Soviet Union[1] and Yugoslavia[2] may be considered under two aspects. The first aspect is one that the author has touched on before,[3] and that has generated regular comment elsewhere in the literature. Alex Nove has described the relationship between industry and power in these terms: "the Party cannot simply seek to 'maximize its power,' . . . It *also* desires results [italics mine]."[4] Voslensky expresses the same thought in reverse: "The fundamental economic law of 'socialist realism' obliges the Nomenklatura . . . to guarantee by economic measures the security and maximum extention of its own power."[5]

In all communist one-party states, including Yugoslavia, the economic units are neither totally engaged in profitmaking nor totally subservient to the power interests of the one-party leadership. Rather, they perform two functions: the first is to produce for profit; the second is to maintain the power of the ruling group through the use of economic levers, what the leadership calls "building socialism."[6] Nove balances the two functions nicely. The leadership wants economic growth not only because the military machine requires it, although that may be a major factor, but also because its rationale for holding power is that it is better able to provide conditions for economic development that are more equitable, less prone to violent swings, and more goal-directed than the capitalist economies. The whole concept of the leading role of the party rests on the premise that the party knows best how to increase material abundance in preparation for the eventual advent of communism. Andropov insisted the most effective way to convince Third World countries of the virtues of socialism (i.e., to expand Soviet influence) was to demonstrate the capacity of the socialist system for superior economic performance.[7]

The problem is that at the same time that economic performance is needed in the Soviet Union's competitive relations with the "capitalist" countries in the first and third worlds, the economy is needed at home to perform its function of security and control. The fear is that at some time some economic interest may escape from the ruling group's control, gain political autonomy, and initiate the leadership's downfall. The need for the two functions constitutes an ongoing crisis foreign to the periodic swings in free-market economies. In its concern for economic growth, the party in several communist states has attempted economic reform, either through increased centralization as with the cartels in Czechoslovakia and East Germany and the *obedinenia* in the Soviet Union; or through decentralization such as the reforms in Hungary and China and self-management in Yugoslavia. When the liberal reforms produce strains and cracks in the party's control over society, as they started to do during the "thaw" in the Soviet Union, in Yugoslavia in the seventies, or in China in 1987, the economy's control function takes over to the detriment of production. In the case of Yugoslavia, liberal-minded managers were replaced by personnel considered more "reliable" in regard to their commitment to Yugoslav communist orthodoxy.[8]

The necessity for the economy to perform the two functions means that the relationship between industry and power is more interdependent than that which obtains in a free-market system. In the latter, industry's drive for profit urges it to political action to procure the passage of government policies that will protect and promote industry's profit-making capabilities. In this context, economic interest fuels the impulse to power. In communist one-party states, the reverse occurs. The impulse to power fuels the economic machine. The economy is required to be both a productive organism and a vehicle by which the ruling group assures its dominant position in society.[9]

This point has been demonstrated many times over: in Poland, Hungary, Czechoslovakia, and Yugoslavia. The Yugoslav economy has been in permanent crisis since the end of the 1970s. The external debt is expected to rise to $40 billion by 1990. Inflation may be as high as 100 percent and unemployment continues to rise. The reform faction of the Yugoslav party advocates far-reaching measures that would permit greater autonomy for enterprises, the introduction of a market-oriented pricing system, and greater emphasis on the private sector.[10] Of critical importance to the successful implementation of the current "stabilization" program (the austerity measures to rehabilitate the economy)[11] is allowing nonproductive enterprises to fail, in other words, introducing competition. However, the problem in Yugoslavia is the same as in every communist one-party state, namely, that no serious economic changes can be successful without radical changes in the political system. Economic competition generates political competition. And political competition jeopardizes the monopoly position of the ruling group. One change demanded by Solidarity in Poland has been proposed in Yugoslavia: to hold party leaders responsible for economic failures and to make them face the appropriate legal penalties. While there has been some evidence of movement in this direction from the replacement of Macedonian party leaders,[12] no similar purge of party leaders for economic failures appears to be in progress in the more industrialized republics.

The interdependence of the economy and power is more than a matter of personal relationships, patron-patronee networks, or leadership fascination with industrialization. It is a fundamental condition of the communist one-party state. The party leadership needs industry, particularly energy

124

and heavy industry, to maintain its power in terms of internal and external security. Agriculture and light industry are of lesser consequence because the satisfaction of popular demand is not a key factor in regime stability. Environmental conditions are also not so critical that the nonapplication of environmental regulations threatens the leadership's power position with ecological disaster. The control and production functions of the economy are primary; the control function of the environmental agencies is derivative. The party leadership's monopoly over the economy and the economy's guarantee of party power ensures that industry dominates every policy discussion concerning the environment and the economy.

The special relationship also ensures that if it is a question of a trade-off between the economy and the environment, in the absence of an environmental emergency, the economy will be the beneficiary. Industry's game position is rooted in the Soviet politicoeconomic structure, whereas the environmental agencies' position is linked to the regulatory principle. The asymmetrical opposition of the two augurs poorly for the future of environmental protection in both countries. For the degree of centralization or decentralization of the economy has an impact on the economic monopoly of the party leadership only as regards extent and size (in Yugoslavia, the monopoly is regional and republican, rather than national and federal), *not* on the economy's performance of its two functions. The communist leaderships' concern for the environment has been primarily shaped by a growing realization that environmental protection and the rational use of natural resources are bound together. Since it is impossible to have one without the other, regulation is necessary. However, industry's special relationship with the party and government leadership means that the economic units are directly involved in both the regulatory decision and its implementation. They are thus in an optimum position to make the case for production prevail in environmental deliberations.

It may be argued that U.S. companies are similarly well placed to make the ease for production prevail. In the congressional hearings regarding the catalytic converter, General Motors threatened to close down plants and fire workers if the timetable for meeting standards were not changed. The final decision was the product of political, not technological considerations. But there is a fundamental difference in the relationship between General Motors and the U.S. political leadership and that of the Soviet and Yugo-

125

slav industrial organizations and their government. While an important economic element in American society and undoubtedly a factor in the election of some congressmen and U.S. presidents, General Motors does not perform the second function of maintaining the leadership in power. The company may object to expenditures on environmental controls that cut into its profits and contribute to unemployment. But since it does not serve as a vehicle of control, its interests as an industry can be separated from the interests of the state. As a result, the government environmental authorities can use state power as an instrument external to the company to force compliance with state environmental regulations.

The second aspect of industry's special position is its organization into specialized noncompetitive components. The 1965 Soviet ministerial reforms abolished Khrushchev's experiment in the territorial principle of management and reestablished the centralized branch system of economic management.[13] Industries considered of strategic value were placed under the direct control of Moscow, while those of lesser importance or confined to a specific region or territory were made union-republic ministries. The reform placed industrial development in the hands of centralized conglomerates, outside republican local soviet control. Only the direct intervention of a central party or government authority can now force a powerful central ministry to adhere to environmental regulations that it prefers to ignore. The "lunar landscape" of the coastal areas of northeastern Estonia is one tragic consequence of recentralized power. The region has been devastated by massive mineral resource extracting operations under the jurisdiction of the All-Union Ministry for Mineral Fertilizer Production.[14]

The formation, dissolution, or reorganization of an industrial ministry is a formal act of government. So is the merging of small enterprises into larger units,[15] the creation of subordinate research institutes, or the reorganization of research, development, and innovation (RDI) institutions to link innovation more closely to the work of the industrial enterprises.[16] Without a free market, every part of a state-owned economy must be created by administrative fiat. In principle, each unit in the system ought to be making products designed to fulfill the demand of other units, which in turn produce to meet the requirements of still other industries, with no production overlap or duplication. In practice, as Nove describes, subdivi-

126

sions in a whole array of different ministries manufacture the same product, and the administrative boundary lines between ministries can be rather fuzzy.[17] Many ministries prefer to produce their own equipment rather than risk the uncertainty of delivery from another ministry.[18] The attempt by a ministry or ministerial subsection to secure its own sources of supply reinforces the monopoly character of the branch principle of specialization. With all facets of production under its control, the same ministry or ministerial subsection is in an optimum position to monopolize a specialized market as sole supplier to planned ministerial consumers.

Ministerial and ministerial subsection outputs are essential for the realization of planned production norms not only for the ministry and its subsections but also for enterprises outside the ministry that depend on it to realize their quotas. The fulfillment of planned norms is crucial to both management and workers if they want to reap the rewards attendant upon successful completion of the plan. A series of dependencies is set up whereby if one link is broken (a factory closed), plan fulfillment for a whole chain of enterprises is thrown into jeopardy. Industry's monopoly position helps explain why environmental agencies can issue negative reports over periods as long as ten years with no response from the delinquent enterprise. To close a factory or move its location means replanning a whole string of contingent variables to compensate for the change. Factories cannot be peremptorily closed. The closure must be programmed into the plan, and a major change would entail long-term forecasting and integration into a five-year planning period. An illustration may be found in Czechoslovakia, where the author was able to study the long-term plan for Prague. The plan proposes reduction in air pollution over a twenty-year period, based among other factors on projections of local investment by the central industrial ministries (particularly the construction ministry), the size of the labor force, the planned shift from gas-fueled public transport to electric, and the movement of some industries out of the Prague area.[19] Since the city controls virtually none of the industries within its boundaries and few of its services, the realization of the long-term forecast is clearly dependent upon whether the central industrial ministries decide at some future time to modify the plan indicators or choose to adhere to the plan. In a planned economy, everything has its target date. The likelihood is that in both the long and short term, industry in the Prague area will assign greater priority to the fulfillment of production norms upon which other industries depend than in reducing air pollution in the city.

Yugoslavia has no industrial monopolies of the size and extent of the branch ministries in the USSR because of the decentralization of industrial organization and the absence of a central plan. Stojanović, indeed, faults Yugoslav industrial management for the slow progress of industrial integration.[20] The privileged position of Yugoslav industry is found in its territorially based character, whereby an industrial enterprise locates in a particular area to the exclusion of all competitors.

The procedure for forming an organization of associated labor (OUR) is set forth in the 1974 Constitution (Articles 90 and 110). Much more is required to start a business in Yugoslavia than a group of interested workers. The founders of the new organization are obliged by law to consider not only the economic but *social* feasibility of the operation and to consult local interests. The local interests have official recourse if the founder rejects their views. In addition, the founders must follow specific regulations as regards the establishment and start-up of the business. It goes without saying that a rival industry in the area will give a negative opinion of a proposed enterprise if it considers that enterprise to be in competition with it. The founder must further consult with the industrial branch section of the republican economic chamber responsible for coordinating and planning republican industrial production, one of whose functions is to prevent duplication and overlap.[21] In short, the establishment of an enterprise expresses the convergence of local and republican political interests and branch economic interests.

Once the enterprise is in operation, these interests again come into play to keep it going, regardless of whether it is profitable or not. The enterprise guarantees employment to a certain number of workers who are unlikely to find it in their interest to vote for the closing of the plant. Local officials also gain from the income generated by the plant and are reluctant to see it go under. The politics of the situation undermines the need for aggressive competition on the part of plant management. Wishing to protect their positions, the workers will favor borrowing for the purchase of expensive plant equipment to improve work productivity rather than voting for higher work norms or the hiring of additional, less expensive outside labor. Banks can be persuaded by politicians to grant loans to enterprises that do not meet the official requirements. Borrowing shores up an inefficient operation. Debts accumulate and the plant remains open, protected by a political and economic network extending at a minimum to the republican level.[22]

The regional character of industry is further strengthened by the difficulties inherent in expansion into another republic. Once again, the constitutional procedure has to be followed for opening a new work organization, and local officials must be convinced of the benefit of allowing a firm from another republic to establish itself. Even if permission is granted, there is no security that the new plant will not at some time petition to become an independent self-management organization, taking into the reorganized unit all of the parent plant's capital investment. Moreover, self-management in the banking and financial world inhibits the free movement of capital. A firm desiring to expand into another republic may encounter difficulties finding the capital for expansion.[23] These problems tend to keep industry tied to the political interests within a single republic, inhibiting their adoption of a more independent economic stance.

The Yugoslav delegate and assembly system is the final contributor to industry's privileged position. Industrial interests are permanently represented in the opština and republican assemblies, while each industrial sector has its special economic chamber to promote its particular interests at all levels of government. Federal delegates from the regional industrial sectors who bring back benefits to their regions are highly valued and reelected many times over. A prime example is Nataljia Grzečić, long-time manager of the Hotel Libertas in Dubrovnik. For over fifteen years, Mrs. Grzečić represented Dubrovnik and the hotel industry in federal economic fora, promoting tourism and making the political contacts invaluable to local economic, party, and government interests.[24] The economic development of a region depends upon delegate performance like hers.

Republican industrial sectors may also exercise pressure from outside the delegate system to bring about desired legislation. A case in point is the adoption of the federal law on power development on the Drina and Neretva rivers in May 1984. The Republics of Macedonia and Bosnia and Herzegovina are very poor in energy. During the winter of 1984, electric output fell short of demand and the electric power companies were forced to cut off the power at specified times of day. Although not overly supplied with electric energy, Serbia was not in the same predicament. However, as a sympathy measure, the Serbian company also cut off electricity to residents in Belgrade for several hours during the day. The action of the three companies aroused public fears and generated great concern in the federal assembly about the future of electric power generation in the three republics. The result was the passage of a bill providing for the building of new power stations along the Drina and Neretva rivers. One of these, located on the Tara River, would cause the flooding of the Tara Canyon, one of the great natural wonders of Yugoslavia. The national concern created by the electric power stoppages obscured the agreements being made between the three republics on the construction of power stations, and the bill was voted before any action could be mobilized to stop it.[25]

As in the Soviet case, the structural constraints of the Yugoslav system operate to the permanent advantage of industry. What local assembly would insist on environmental controls to the possible detriment of production? By law, industry must help finance all local social welfare programs and contribute to the local sociopolitical organizations, including the League of Communists of Yugoslavia. Industry also pays for the party and government at the republican level and decides on transfers of aid from the more industrialized to the less developed republics. At the inter-republican level, industry can use its close relationship with government to promote its own projects, as was the case with the energy agreement on the development of the Drina and Neretva rivers. The result is that where environmental controls promote business, such as in Dubrovnik and along the Adriatic, there is stricter observance of the regulations. Where they seem separated from industrial interest, as in Kosovo noted earlier, or the Tara River Canyon, industry prefers to ignore them.

Thus, in the two countries, the special relationship of industry to the government gives industry a permanently dominant position in any discussion with an environmental agency. In the Soviet Union, industrial pressure is exercised vertically through the central branch economic ministries. In Yugoslavia, it is exercised horizontally at the community and republican levels. Each head of the hydra seeks to protect its own industry at the potential expense of the others, and at the expense of the environment. Until industry in both countries can be convinced that environmental protection promotes rather than thwarts economic progress, it is unlikely that the production orientation will change.

The bureaucratic structure of industrial environmental control. A second structural element favoring the staying power of the industrial enterprises is the organization of environmental protection within industry itself.

The environmental obligations for the industrial ministries in the Soviet Union were spelled out in a series of resolutions of the USSR Council of Ministers, starting in 1965. The impetus for the organization of environmental councils in the ministries and their subordinate units came from the 1972 resolution on the strengthening of environmental protection and a 1974 decree on industrial enterprises that mandated the creation of environmental sections in the enterprises.[26] A 1978 joint CC CPSU and USSR Council of Ministers resolution required that bonuses and rewards for workers and managements be made contingent upon a plant's fulfillment of all sections of its plan, including the environmental section, not just the production norms. The resolutions assign the individual enterprise a large number of environmental "rights." These include the right to plan its environmental targets, to create environmental sections, to improve its environmental technology, to undertake capital construction in the area of environmental protection, to design a bonus and reward system to stimulate the observance of environmental norms, to provide environmental education, and to account to the responsible ministry for the fulfillment of its environmental norms.

In fact, it is doubtful that at this writing every factory has its environmental section. The bureaucratic protocol required to implement the all-union resolutions is long and cumbersome. Prior to the formation of a factory council, the ministries supervising must draw up guidelines (*tipovyi akty*) setting forth the procedure for the formation of the environmental sections. Some industrial ministries were fairly fast in establishing guidelines. The Ministry of Oil Refining and Petrochemical Industry, for example, promulgated its guidelines in 1976. However, the Ministry of Chemical and Petroleum Machine Building (Minkhimmash) did not issue its policy until 1979.[27] In 1978, a USSR Council of Ministers' resolution adopted the twin standards of PDV (maximum allowable emission level) and VCV (temporary agreed-upon emission level.[28] The new standards made the work of the environmental sections easier, but required ministries whose guidelines antedated their adoption to update their regulations, thereby causing further delays in the establishment of a factory environmental section on a permanent basis. While the branch ministries were developing guidelines for enterprises to use in implementing the new responsibilities, the local factories were required to reach an agreement with the towns in which they were located on how the environmental regulations were to be implemented in that particular area. In 1977, the city of Sverdlovsk signed a four-part agreement with the local enterprises. The agreement set forth what each factory had to do to meet the PDK set for the town, and when and how the factories would proceed to implement the agreement.[29]

Finally, each factory must pass its own set of rules that integrate the ministerial guidelines with the regional agreement in a form that will enable the factory to act. Some factory *akty* contain only a statement about the environmental section, while others regulate all environmental protection operations in the enterprise. Given the complexity of the process described, it is probable that many Soviet enterprises and organizations are still without their interenterprise regulations, and of those that have them, a substantial number may have only just begun to organize an environmental section.[30]

The creation of a factory environmental section is no guarantee that the factory will henceforth perform its environmental obligations more punctually. In smaller factories, there are neither sufficient personnel nor funds to create a separate section, so the environmental functions are given to other factory sections, most often the technical safety division, the main technology section of the factory. All these sections have production as their primary concern production. Most are extremely busy seeing that production runs smoothly and consequently have little time or interest to look out for the environment. In addition, assignments to environmental control duties tend to be rather arbitrary. The chief of the energy section may be charged with water conservation, while the chief of the section for technical safety may be in charge of air pollution control. Given the hierarchical factory organization, and the absence of interfactory communication, the likelihood is that there will be little or no cooperation between the two sections in the implementation of the planned environmental measures.

An environmental section that has been established in larger factories may be assigned only monitoring and statistical recording duties, such as checking and recording daily emission levels. The section appears to be given no authority to order a change in technology or to stop production in that section or shop where environmental norms are being violated. More often than not, the environmental section is under the supervision of the chief engineer and is accountable to him. The chief engineer is responsible for the plant's technological production and development. In this capacity, he should consider choosing technology that allows for rational resource use based on environmental restraints. However, his main job is tied to production, and while environmental matters may come under his long-term planning concerns, they are secondary to the day-to-day running of the plant. The result again is that environmental regulations are shunted aside. In his doctoral study on the topic, Viktor Kruglov provides an informative account of the different types of organizations and varied assignment of functions by which industries in Sverdlovsk oblast have chosen to implement the environmental section mandate.[31]

Soviet experts interviewed by the author differed as to how to make the environmental section more efficient. A Leningrad economist was in favor of putting it under the immediate control of the factory director. Colleagues in the Department of Environmental Law at Moscow State University (MGU) proposed keeping the section under the factory chief engineer, but suggested the creation of an environmental subdepartment of the technological section. Others urged that each ministry develop position descriptions (*tipovoe polozhenie*) that specified the exact qualifications and duties of the person in charge of environmental protection to ensure the appointment of qualified personnel to the position. Still others, citing the guidelines for the creation of an environmental section developed by Minkhimmash, urged the statewide standardization of the responsibilities of the environmental sections.[32] The discussion of the organization of environmental protection in industry indicates how much leeway the industrial enterprises have in the matter. The initial ministerial decree specified a very simple obligation, the formation of an environmental section in every factory and organization. The absence of any supervisory control over their actions, the hierarchical chain of command, and the necessity for agreement with local authorities enabled the branch ministries to transform the regulations into a bureaucratic headache, thereby deferring the day of compliance until such time as the ministry deemed appropriate.

In Yugoslavia, environmental councils are also mandated for every enterprise.[33] As in the Soviet Union, the councils may be separate entities in conformance with the legal regulations, or they may be distributed among the technical departments of the factory. Once again, organization structure undercuts the ability of the councils to act.

First Engineer Jelena Vuković, chief planner for ecology and environmental protection at the Zastava Automobile Plant in Kragujevac, provided a thorough description of the kind of work she and her associates performed. The most serious problems, in her view, were the reduction of noise levels in the pressing shop, the wastewater treatment system, and the protection of workers from paint fumes in the paint shop. The reduction of noise levels was difficult because it was almost impossible to make noisy motors less noisy. The solution was the purchase of new quiet motors at a tremendous expense, since noise-insulated products are more expensive than noisy ones. The third problem (see chapter 3) was currently irresolvable since the American paint company from which the paint was purchased refused to divulge the patented chemical formula that would enable her and her colleagues to develop measures to protect the workers. The success story was the completion of a system, financed entirely by the factory, for the collection and treatment of industrial wastewater. She took us to the treatment center to show us how all the plant's water was collected in one spot and purified to the level prescribed by law before being dumped into the city's wastewater system.

According to Engineer Vuković, the plant was constantly visited by the city inspectors even though its pollution was closely monitored by the factory's internal environmental section. If a worker thought he was being affected by some pollutant, he was obliged to contact the plant inspector first and then the city inspector. If, however, he thought the problem was serious enough, he might go directly to the city inspector. The environmental section had no jurisdiction over the protection of workers at work; that was the responsibility of the factory committee for work safety. Vuković said that there had been many complaints from one district regarding the paint fumes. The opština environmental protection committee was pressing the factory to resolve the problem. But the factory, opština, and district knew the problem could not be solved easily, so they temporized by deciding to pool resources and undertake their own research to determine the composition of the paint.

On first acquaintance, the Zastava plant appeared to have organized a model environmental section, conscious of its obligations to its workers and its community. But further discussion indicated that there were difficulties. The plant, of course, is self-managed, and there is a workers' council, as required by law. The hard decisions come when the workers are called upon to decide where they are going to put that small part of the factory profits not assigned to community welfare, fixed investments, or wages. Understandably, the council's preference was either to return some part of the profit to the workers as a bonus, or to increase the amount allocated to investment so as to increase income. Vuković insisted that Zastava workers were very conscious of safety and the environment. Nevertheless, when pressed, she admitted that conflicts over the allocation of remaining profits tended to be decided in favor of production or bonuses for the workers.[34]

In securing protection from industrial pollution, the community plays a critical role in Yugoslavia. In the preceding chapter mention was made of a polluting cement factory near Belgrade, where workers had complained of cement dust in their residential area. The complaints had led to the cooperation of the environmental protection council of the opština in which the plant was located, the opština town council, the regional planning council, and the environmental section of the two-year-old cement factory in an investigation of a solution. To assist them, they had hired the environmental protection department of the Institute for Technology of Nuclear and Other Raw Materials as consultants. The opština did not want to lose jobs or income from the closing or moving of the plant and so insisted on exploring options for improving the cement-making process.[35]

The above suggests that the implementation of environmental regulations in Yugoslav industry depends primarily on four factors: the support of plant management and the workers' council of the factory environmental council, the willingness of the plant and its community to undertake environmental investments, the intensity of worker and/or public complaints, and the diligence of the city environmental inspectors. The Yugoslavs point out that under their system, environmental control is external to the industrial structure, and hence the inspectors have no vested interest in overlooking violations. The paint and cement factory cases indicate otherwise. If the pollution problem involves a great deal of expense and research, the plant's environmental council will probably be powerless to persuade plant management to take action. The impetus for action comes from either the workers or the public and must be sufficiently vocal to arouse the concern of the opština authorities. Self-management means that either the plant must then take action on its own or share expenses with the opština. A rich, prosperous community with committed public officials and an aroused public may vote the funds. A poor or disinterested community might not. The local inspectors in the first community may be very active; those in the second may prefer to remain largely invisible.

It thus makes little difference whether the structure of industrial environmental control is vertical and hierarchical, or horizontal. Without economic incentive or resources to do otherwise, industrial enterprises in both systems will prefer to pursue production goals and will circumvent environmental controls, the existence of enterprise environmental committees notwithstanding.

The impact of planning regulations on the fulfillment of environmental protection criteria. The compartmentalization of the Soviet planning process is especially visible in the environmental planning of the branch ministries. In the first place, the environmental section of each ministerial plan is separated from the economic sector. In addition, each ministry prepares its own environmental plan in isolation from the other economic and resource ministries as well as environmental agencies. Local enterprises forward their plans to the responsible ministries without consultation with other local institutions. The only agreement at the local level is the one with local government on measures the plant will take to bring its emissions to a level where the area will meet the mandated PDK (maximum permissible concentration). The problems inherent in the lack of coordination are not such as to encourage a plant director to persevere in his environmental obligations. Large construction projects such as the building of a sewage treatment plant, the installation of appropriate air pollution equipment, or the building of a waste disposal site require the cooperation of the many supervising ministries that specialize in the component parts of the construction project. Each ministry must weigh this project against other priorities. The contracting plant cannot effectively supervise construction because the firms participating in the project are subordinated each to its own responsible ministry, which alone decides on whether and when to provide materials and workers to its subordinate. Such conditions do not encourage a plant director to start a substantial environmental project.

The problem of interbranch coordination is particularly critical for plan implementation in the development of TICs (territorial industrial complexes).[36] While TICs are officially approved planning entities, they are far from fully realized in practice. The major cause of the delay is that they cross traditional administrative boundaries. A territorial commission of Gosplan has been created for the West Siberian Petroleum and Gas Complex, but what is needed is the formation of a TIC administration with powers to reallocate money and to order departments across ministerial boundaries.[37] Until an appropriate administrative system is worked out, the comprehensive features of TIC planning risk being distorted by interministerial rivalries. Unfortunately, environmental protection does not constitute one of the comprehensive elements, but continues to be a secondary planning issue separate from the economic plan indicators. In a book describing the development of computer models for optimizing the formation of TICs, none of the models, including that involving the composition of initial information, contains an environmental impact category. Evidently, not even the large and excellent literature on Siberia's fragile ecology has been able to influence the planners to reform traditional planning categories.[38]

A second difficulty with fulfilling plan criteria lies in the bonus system. The 1978 linking of the bonus system to environmental performance represented a concrete step toward providing economic incentives for environmental protection, but it cannot be considered a viable long-term solution. First, as scholars have consistently pointed out,[39] the bonus system does not stimulate managers to fulfill the objectives desired by the leadership, but rather to keep plan targets as low as possible in order to be able to meet them and qualify for the bonus. Thus, as far as fulfilling environmental targets is concerned, reform of the reward system must be considered only a modest modification of the rules of the game. When environmental indicators were first introduced, the enterprise manager could easily ignore

137

them in favor of the production norms with their attendant rewards. When the implementation of environmental controls was tied to the bonus, the factory manager's interest shifted to the planning of incremental improvements rather than major environmental measures. An example was given in the previous chapter in the case of air pollution over Irkutsk, where the management of the polluting plant put off the installation of expensive air pollution controls pending a planned reconstruction of the plant.

V. V. Petrov, among others, has argued that tying environmental controls to the bonus system is not enough. The factory manager will only do what is necessary when his planned profits are attacked. Petrov recommends that fines levied for noncompliance be increased so as to make a difference in the factory pocketbook, and that contrary to current practice, the fines be counted against the planned factory profits. Managers would thus be obliged to fulfill their environmental obligations if they wanted the bonus.

A third way in which the planning process has an impact on the fulfillment of environmental criteria lies in the rigid and task-oriented formulas handed down by the ministerial hierarchy to the enterprises for the drafting of environmental plan proposals. A factory developing a plan for the control of water pollution must give account of the 420 pollutants listed in "The General Requirements for the Composition and Water Properties of Water Objects at Points of Economic-drinking and Cultural-residential Water Use."[40] The factory must state the level of actual pollution for each pollutant, the projected level of pollution at the end of the plan period, and a summary of measures to be undertaken to meet the projection. There are similar forms for reporting point-source emissions of a long list of air pollutants from different kinds of smokestacks. It is a question whether most plants have the measuring equipment or the specialists capable of doing the job. Even if they do, the task is enormously time-consuming. It is understandable why the manager might take his time in completing the form or simply falsify the records, as was apparently done at thermal and electric power plants in Ekibastuz in Kazakhstan.[41] In the event that all the required information is obtained and a plan drawn up, the manager knows that the plan can always be revised if it cannot be accomplished.

Finally, there is the question of relating environmental plans to the actual costs of implementation. Soviet critics of the failure of enterprises to fulfill their planned environmental norms tend to underrate the problem of funding and materials,[42] while managers complain frequently that these are lacking. The critics reply that when the order for certain environmental control measures is sent down to the factory through the planning channels, funding and materials follow the order. But this is often not the case. Funding for environmental projects comes out of the central and republican investment monies and is distributed through the central ministries (factories are not obliged to use their profits for environmental measures). With their production orientation, ministries are not enthusiastic about allocating funds for environmental controls. It took the city of Saratov ten years to wring 200,000 rubles out of the USSR Ministry of Light Industry to reconstruct the water treatment plant of a major Saratov tannery.[43] Similar ministerial reluctance was shown in Bratsk. The city was suffering severely from air pollution created by the USSR's largest pulp and aluminum mills. The gas from the aluminum mill apparently had formed a film on the mill's electrolysis bath, raising the danger that workers might be burned. The USSR Ministry of Nonferrous Metallurgy promised to provide the plant with ventilators, but as of 1982, none were in operation.[44]

Even when funds are allocated, enterprise directors frequently do not use these monies to implement the environmental plan, but shunt them off into the production fund or do not use them at all and return them to their ministerial superiors. Exact figures on the amount of environmentally designated monies returned to the central ministerial funds are unavailable in the USSR. Some idea of the sums involved, however, may be obtained from information released in Poland in January 1980 during the heyday of the Solidarity period. According to the Warsaw periodical *Perspektywy*, during the 1976–1980 plan, 55 billion zlotys were earmarked for environmental protection outlays, of which only 38.8 million (75 percent) were actually used. Although this figure represented an improvement over the utilization of environmental funds during the previous five-year planning period (65 percent),[45] environmental protection programs were not benefitting from all the money allocated to them. Similar information on a local level found in the Soviet press suggests that the Soviet record may be considerably less impressive. In 1976, the town of Penza, southeast of Moscow, approved the construction of a water treatment and sewage plant at an estimated cost of 17.6 million rubles. By 1981, only 2 million rubles of that had been spent.[46] According to Dr. Antonin Kerner of the Law Faculty at Charles University, Prague, the most important thing for an environmental project was to get the first monies allocated in the five-year plan. Allocation, however, did not mean the project was carried out, just that the funds were available. Difficulties in obtaining requisite equipment was one explanation, he said, for delay in the initiation of environmental projects; managerial shunting of environmental funds to meet short-term needs was another.

In Yugoslavia, major legislation has tried to make planning a positive factor in the realization of environmental protection since 1974. Three documents guide the elaboration of the environmental component of the economic and social plans across the country. The first is the constitution, which requires every enterprise and citizen to practice environmental protection (Articles 192 and 193). The 1976 Associated Labor Act imposes the responsibility for environmental protection upon the worker and his work organization, stipulating that a factory may not decide on the disposition of its disposable income without first setting aside a sum for environmental protection, as it does for the SIZ (Articles 110 and 111). The 1976–1980 five-year plan first mentioned the need for environmental controls and the 1981–1985 plan finally mandated environmental measures.

Section 41 of the 1981–1985 plan obliges the republics to set common standards and methodology for environmental control by 1985.[47] Goal 10 of the Basic Plan obliges all factories and enterprises to include environmental protection in their investment planning, changing a recommendation in the 1976–1980 plan into a legal obligation. Yugoslav and international banks may not extend credit for a construction project unless environmental measures are included in the development plans. The Slovenes reportedly strongly supported this stipulation, demanding its strict enforcement, because of the fragile, mountainous character of their terrain. Again by law, a group of specialists must be formed to review each investment project. Some of the republics, like Macedonia, have yet to create such a group or to establish a procedure on project review, but all were required to have a system in place by 1985.[48] However, 1985 has come and gone, and few of the plan's environmental provisions have been implemented. Agreement on the overall plan was particularly drawn out. A draft federal compact on energy production for 1981–1985 was reached only in February 1982, two years into the planning period.[49]

Once the federal plan has been agreed upon, it is returned to the planning institutes of the republican governments where talks ensue over the production and consumption norms needed to fulfill the federal guidelines. Representatives from the republican councils for environmental protection and territorial planning participate at these meetings along with delegates from industry, the SIZ, the sociopolitical organizations, and local government. While the republics are drawing up their plans, the factories and enterprises, as well as the cities and communes, are formulating theirs. There seems to be no particular pressure to come to agreement. Typically, many organizations do not have their five-year plans in place until well into the third year of the federal plan. To achieve their environmental objectives, industry may enter into "self-managing contracts" with other industries or with local government. In 1985 the Federal Council for the Protection and Improvement of the Human Environment recorded ninety work organizations that had entered into such agreements.[50]

Because the federal plan provides guidelines only, resistance to them may come at any level. The republics may not be able to write a plan in agreement with the federal guidelines, because republican industries will resist guidelines they consider impractical and delay agreement until late into the planning period. Local factory opposition may hinder the adoption of local opština plans. Moreover, the mandated expert project review committees are republican appointees, and thus subject to republican political pressures. Resistance is less a matter of a deliberate refusal to fulfill plan quotas, for there are no rigid norms, as the neglect or changing of plan guidelines to fit the industry's perceived circumstances. In the absence of any well-defined hierarchical authority, the industrial bureaucracy, in consultation with other local or regional bureaucratic interests, may so modify the guidelines as to vitiate the achievement of planned national environmental and economic goals.

Assets

Tangible. As was shown in chapter 3, in comparison to the other environmental actors, the industrial organizations in both countries are clearly the best off as far as financial assets are concerned.[51] Through direct central distribution of monies and favorable tax and lending policies, the state subsidizes their pollution control efforts without comparable state monitoring of where or how the funds are used. In both countries, the chief beneficiary is heavy industry. However, industry is limited in borrowing power and what it can do with its profits.

In the Soviet Union, the financing of an individual project may be realized through an allocation from the state budget, through the centralized resources of the branch ministries, or through the decentralized resources available to the enterprise. Both ministerial and enterprise resources come from industry's planned profits. Prior to 1965, the ministry retained the substantial portion of these monies.[52] Since the 1965 reforms in the Soviet Union, enterprises have returned a proportionately smaller share of their planned profits to the central budget, but they have been highly circumscribed in what they can do with the retained money. Important to the environmental question is that industry's right to retain profits either centrally or decentrally has given the branch ministries new bargaining power with the planners over what projects should be financed.

In 1977, the share of capital investment in ministerial funds was approximately 9.4 percent. This figure (88 billion rubles) represented 72 percent of all capital investment for that year. In using these monies, ministries have shown the most interest in retooling existing enterprises. In the Tenth Five-Year Plan (1976–1980), the share of investment in this area averaged 67 percent over industry as a whole. While some of this investment undoubtedly went into environmental controls, leading Soviet economist V. G. Lebedev points out that the main thrust of reconstruction was to increase plant operating efficiency to reduce repair and maintenance costs. At the same time, the increased share of capital investment in equipment as against construction testified to greater management attention to technological improvements. The proportion of industrial expenditures on scientific-research institutions, including payment of salaries and other items, also increased. In 1977, it averaged 59 percent across industry as a whole and reached 71 percent in the transport and communications industries.[53] These figures indicate that branch ministerial priorities are heavily weighted toward the development of production-oriented technologies. The more independent bargaining stance brought about by the reforms, has, not surprisingly, been primarily exploited for economic goals.

While the reforms strengthened the autonomy of the branch ministries, the enterprises' discretion in the utilization of retained profits is not very large. With the money at their disposal, enterprises may undertake only small investment projects. Larger programs require funding from the ministry or the state budget. Even if the enterprise should wish to invest in environmental controls, the likelihood is that the expense would be more than it could generate from its decentralized resources. The ministry thus stands at the pivotal point in the implementation of environmental protection goals. The party leadership and government may write resolutions, but the ministry holds a large portion of the financial solution.

In Yugoslavia, the local enterprise also does not have much power to decide on its investments. However, the power to make that decision is found not in the industrial hierarchy but in negotiations between the party, government, and economic authorities at the local and republican levels. The law and local agreement stipulate what share of local industrial profits must go to support the various sizova, the political organizations, and local government. In principle, the factory workers' council decides what to do with the remainder. The current five-year plan requires that some part of it be set aside for environmental expenditures. However, similar to the Soviet case, the factory's own resources will not be sufficient to undertake any but a small project. In the Zastava plant, the worker's council was reluctant to put more money into the environmental fund if such an action took away from investment in production or workers' wages. The case of the cement factory cited in the previous chapter indicates that the development and funding of a major environmental project requires at the very minimum commune assistance. This assistance in turn necessitates consultation with the financial and political interests in the area.

The cement factory case further suggests that industry can exploit a weak financial position with local party and opština officials to produce a collective decision favorable to production. If the commune did not want the cement factory closed or relocated, the options narrowed down to one: namely, to install the cheapest possible environmental controls to do the job. The position of the polluting factory in this instance was nearer to the position of a polluting factory in the West, where loss of jobs or industrial relocation urge local officials to compromise on meeting environmental norms. The bargaining power of the Yugoslav firm lies in the tacit threat of economic disaster if its position is not adopted.

Intangible. The first intangible asset enjoyed by the economic organizations is control over information. In the United States, most of the information on environmental conditions comes from self-reporting by industry. The propensity of private industry for information monopoly was decisively demonstrated in 1973 with the revelation of the large oil companies' virtually exclusive possession of data on oil reserves.[54] The reliance of the EPA on the chemical industry for accurate reporting of critical toxic waste data in 1982 was a major factor in the scandal surrounding the agency's chief administrator.

Environmental data collection is also the product of industrial self-reporting in the Soviet Union and Yugoslavia. Since Gosplan was authorized in 1972 to develop the methodology for including an environmental protection section in the planning process,[55] the Soviet industrial ministries have been required to issue to their subordinate departments and enterprises detailed instructions on the collection of pollution data based on Gosplan and environmental lead agency directives. The requisite data are developed at the enterprise level by the plant environmental section and forwarded up the ministerial hierarchy. Data on each environmental area are sent to the lead agency responsible for that area before their eventual transmission to Gosplan. Only the ministry has complete environmental information for the enterprises under its jurisdiction. The 1980 Air Quality Control Law gave Goskomgidromet monitoring authority that included entering a factory without being requested, and taking measurements. However, the lead environmental agencies are not sufficiently staffed to be able to take every necessary measurement, and they must rely on the branch ministries' data. As in every country, self-reporting raises the possibility that the data provided by the ministry may be false, misleading, or superficial. Furthermore, because planning is based on the branch principle, information is also transmitted according to the branch principle with the environmental part of the plan kept separate from the production sections.[56] The environmental information generated for the planning agency is thus locked into the economic branch planning process and hence only utilizable for limited decisions. The result is that Soviet planners do not get environmental information in a form that would enable them to plan for optimal environmental management and resource use. The ministry retains its secrets.

Another important source of ministerial power in information control is that access to all data is on a need-to-know basis for authorized persons only. The information collected remains in the hands of the ministry that collected it for viewing by the party and government leadership or by other persons to whom the ministry will give authorization. Information may be restricted to one bureaucracy and oftentimes to one department, and it is released only at the discretion of the heads of that bureaucracy. It is thus virtually impossible for anyone outside the inner circle of a given ministry to know all the facts on a particular environmental situation or to relate those facts to a similar problem in another ministry. It is even difficult for a research department in the same ministry to get the facts from another department that will enable the experts to carry on their authorized research.[57] Official censorship also comes into play. Although more environmental information is published now than even ten years ago, the release of environmental data remains a sensitive issue, especially information concerning public health and welfare.[58] The branch ministries have little incentive to give freely of the environmental information they have collected. The compartmentalized control of information by the branch ministries is a major source of power in environmental decisionmaking. One way the party and government leadership may have tried to circumvent this source was to locate a monitoring and inspection system under Goskomgidromet.

In Yugoslavia, environmental data collection is in its infancy.[59] The 1980–1985 federal environmental guidelines cannot be translated into action until some standardized reporting system is set up. The general monitoring provided by the institutes of health and hydrometeorology, although improving steadily, is insufficient in itself, and scientists attached to these organizations have not earned a good reputation. The Sava River scandal indicates that there can be strong local and regional pressure on data-reporting by regional inspectorates. At the present time, the Yugoslav governments have to rely on the still crude self-reports of industry, with all their inherent distortions. If the Federal Skupština (assembly) manages to establish a federal water inspectorate, there is some chance for the formation of an independent federal data collection system.

The economic organizations' second intangible asset complements the first: Industry is particularly well placed to control its organizational environment. The logic of the situation produces two interdependent behaviors. On the one hand, the ministerial bureaucracies attempt to expand their areas of jurisdiction to undermine the power that their fellow ministries derive from the exercise of their administrative monopolies. On the other hand, each ministry withdraws behind its ministerial "walls" to reconstitute the monopoly threatened by interministerial competition by trying to ensure that the total production process remains under its sole jurisdiction. The stability of the system derives both from the ministry's control of its internal suppliers and the closed-circle relationship established between the ministry and its external suppliers. In the absence of competition, all parties to the production circle have an interest in maintaining the status quo, because it affords to each actor the greatest opportunities for action vis-à-vis the other members of the circle with the least possibility of interference from the outside. There is no way to judge the economic performance of the members except by the plan indicators, which may be easily manipulated because of each member's monopoly of information. The process just described is what Crozier has called the "autonomization of systems of relationship." The more the system assures stability and balance, the more autonomous it becomes, and the more difficult to change from the outside.[60]

The branch ministries derive a major portion of their power from their ability to maintain and increase their administrative autonomy. Resistance to novelty is built into the tendency of organizations to survive.[61] In the Soviet case, it matters little whether a proposed reform has economic or environmental objectives. Ministerial autonomy means that the party and government leaders have limited leverage to move a ministerial bureaucracy in the direction they desire. If the number of reports on ministerial failures to assume environmental obligations seems to be increasing in the Soviet Union, one reason may be a rising perception on the part of certain segments of the Soviet leadership of the difficulty of changing ministerial behavior without some mobilization of public opinion.

In Yugoslavia, industrial "autonomization" differs only in the greater decentralization of its economic sectors. One of the major reasons for the perpetuation of unprofitable enterprises in Yugoslavia is that enterprises have borrowed from each other and from financial institutions to keep going, for the collapse of one business threatens to bring down a series of interdependent concerns, in a domino effect. To stave off this eventuality, the Yugoslav government has preferred to let the total economy absorb the loss by permitting continued overdrafts and price increases to such an extent that an enormous debt has been built up in the system.[62] Through self-managing agreements, Yugoslav enterprises create in their own way an autonomous production circle where vested interests combine to keep the circle going rather than change industrial behavior. The horizontal and vertical interdependence of industry, government, and the sociopolitical organizations within each republic urges the three to close ranks in order to find ways to keep the unprofitable industry open rather than risk the uncertainties of economic and political reform.

Hence, whether it is centralized or "self-managed," industry in both countries has sufficient autonomy and control of its production environment so that the economic organizations can, in effect, "sabotage" an environmental policy decision, despite the best intentions of the party and government authorities. The policy decisions provide the legal ground rules by which the "sabotage" is carried out. While industry may attempt to acquire similar control of its production setting in the United States, it is limited by the fact of competition. The setting of environmental standards and compliance dates are far more highly politicized in the United States than in either the Soviet Union or Yugoslavia, precisely because industry in the latter countries is secure in its autonomous production circle and safe from the sharp eyes of environmental inspectors and a suspicious public.

Costs and Benefits

The foregoing suggests that the immediate benefits accruing to the industrial organizations from the implementation of environmental regulations at the present time are marginal. Naturally there are managers in both countries who are sincerely concerned about the environment and anxious to do their share. But neither the system nor the regulations are structured to offer many tangible rewards. Tying factory bonuses to fulfillment of the

147

environmental plan speaks to personal ambition and the desire for the easy life. However, since the terms of the plan are negotiable and can be readily manipulated, plant personnel may receive their bonuses without having to assume their full share of environmental obligations. In Yugoslavia, an incentive to fulfilling environmental obligations can be seen in the stipulation that all investment projects must contain an environmental component or else the money is not forthcoming. But again, if unprofitable industries can obtain refinancing without being forced to change their behavior, solid concerns will certainly be able to find developmental financing through the hydra network without having to follow through on the environmental component of the project.

On the cost side of the ledger, there is little data available to suggest how much industry has to pay for environmental controls, particularly in Yugoslavia. However, a few individual examples may provide some idea of the dimensions of the problem. In the Soviet Union, most environmental investment comes out of the state budget, since investment from a ministry's or an enterprise's own funds tends to go toward factory renovation and retooling. Hence, the actual cost of a major environmental protection project, such as a sewage treatment system or air pollution control equipment, is not generally borne by the factory or the ministry at all. The observance of environmental controls on a daily operational basis is another matter. According to officials at Gosleskhoz (the State Committee on Forestry), in 1980 it cost approximately 8 rubles 17 kopeks to clear-cut a hectare of woodlot, while selective cutting costs ran upward of 25 rubles. Clear-cutting was thus the general rule, even though there might be differences of opinion regarding the environmental hazard of the method. Fire protection and pest control ran anywhere from 5 percent to 10 percent of the Gosleskhoz's annual budget.[63] The widespread use of clear-cutting has been cited as the cause for much of the country's erosion problems, as well as the death of entire forest stands. The first deputy minister of forestry of the Kazak SSR described the problem succinctly: "Most forestry enterprises utilize only clear-cutting. This has resulted in a complete stripping of trees from whole regions, from mountains and along rivers. . . . Tree cutters do nothing whatever to promote tree growth. As a result, bare earth is left behind in forested areas and any growth is crushed beneath tractors."[64] There is no way of determining the cost of such destruction to the Soviet economy. A recent report on Siberian forestry practices stated that 40 percent of potentially usable timber was left by the lumberers because it took too much time and was thus too costly to cut it up and load it on trucks![65]

A second example of the problem of determining environmental costs concerns land reclamation. According to M. F. Grishaev,[66] former deputy chief of the State Administration for Land Development (*zemlieustroistvo*) of the USSR Ministry of Agriculture, more than 100,000 hectares are reclaimed each year. Land damaged after the passage of the Land Act (1968) must be reclaimed at the Ministry of Mining's expense, while the reclamation of land destroyed prior to the act is at the state's expense. Areas that have experienced severe degradation are not scheduled for reclamation because the state determined it was not cost-effective. Mr. Grishaev indicated that by 1980, most ministries had finished reclaiming reclaimable old land, and the process was expected to be completed within the current five-year plan.[67]

The deputy chief was unable to provide the author with figures on the cost of land reclamation other than those found in the annual yearbook. He said the figure was generally based on costs incurred to bring new soil to the reclaimed site and to transport the site subsoils to a disposal area, and on the comparative cost of developing new, hitherto undeveloped land. For instance, if the cost of transporting soil to a reclaimed site was less than the cost of development of a new parcel of land, the area would be reclaimed; if it was not, the area would be left alone. Mr. Grishaev roughly assessed the average cost of new land cultivation at between 5,000 to 10,000 rubles per hectare depending on soil conditions in the raion or oblast. Translated into comparable transportation fees, this sum would cover the cost of transporting the necessary material for land reclamation fifteen to twenty kilometers. Another way he expressed the cost was to estimate 15,000 rubles per hundred tons of topsoil per hectare of improved land.

T. C. Khachaturov of the USSR's Academy of Sciences' Institute of Economics and the Faculty of Economics at Moscow University has estimated the total cost of controlling pollution during the Tenth Five-Year Plan (1976–1980) at 25 billion rubles. Of this sum, 75 percent was spent on water pollution control alone.[68] In addition, he estimated the cost of air pollution control equipment to vary between 10 to 30 percent of an enterprise's investment fund, and in the case of the gas industry, it could rise to

Table 4.1 Structure of Expenses for the Protection and Rational Use of Water Resources by Production Branch, USSR, 1977 (percentage)

	Protection and rational use of water resources	Sewage treatment	Biological treatment
National economy, USSR	100.0	72.3	33.4
Industry	93.0	67.0	30.5
Electrical energy	10.1	4.2	0.9
Fuel	7.0	6.0	2.6
Ferrous metallurgy	12.4	5.6	1.6
Nonferrous metallurgy	9.9	6.2	1.2
Chemical and petrochemical	23.9	18.1	8.7
Mechanical engineering and metalworking	15.3	13.5	5.8
Timber, woodworking, and pulp and paper	5.0	4.9	4.2
Construction materials	1.0	0.8	0.4
Light	3.2	3.2	1.9
Food	5.2	4.5	3.2
Agriculture	1.0	0.8	0.3
Transportation	2.0	1.4	0.6
Construction	1.6	1.5	0.8
Other	2.4	1.6	1.2

Source: T. S. Khachaturov, ed.-in-chief, *Environmental Protection and its Social-Economic Effectiveness*, Academy of Sciences, USSR, Institute of Economics (Moscow: "Nauka," 1980), p. 133.

as much as 50 percent.[69] An example of a specific cost to the chemical industry is the USSR Ministry of the Chemical Industry's allocation of 2 million rubles for a "sanitary-protection zone" in the city of Vinnitsa to protect residents living near a chemical factory from the fumes escaping from the plant.[70] Not all environmental investments, however, bring a negative return. A proposed installation of pollution control equipment was estimated to give the Khartsysk pipe plant in Donetsk Oblast an annual economic benefit of some 385,000 rubles through the secondary production of carbolic acid.[71] Khachaturov has prepared a breakdown of the proportional cost borne by different industries for water pollution control (see table 4.1).

Physical-chemical treatment	Mechanical treatment	Other forms of treatment	Recycled water supply	Other[a]
11.6	17.5	9.8	20.9	6.8
11.3	16.5	8.7	20.4	5.6
0.9	1.1	1.3	5.5	0.4
0.7	1.9	0.8	0.4	0.6
0.8	1.8	1.4	5.6	1.2
2.0	2.8	0.2	3.6	0.1
2.2	4.4	2.8	3.6	2.2
4.2	2.0	1.5	0.9	0.9
0.1	0.5	0.1	0.1	—
0.1	0.3	—	0.2	—
0.2	1.0	0.1	—	—
0.1	0.7	0.5	0.5	0.2
0.1	—	0.4	—	0.2
0.1	0.1	0.6	—	0.6
0.1	0.5	0.1	0.1	—
—	0.4	—	0.4	0.4

a. Utilization of water for extraction of valuable substances, use of sewage effluent in agriculture, water reservoir zones.

The table confirms the expected. As elsewhere, the cost of pollution control is unequally shared. By far the largest expenses are borne by the chemical and petrochemical industries, with machine building and metal-working industries and ferrous metallurgy coming in second and third place. Per 100 rubles of net production, the cost of environmental protection in the chemical and petrochemical industries is 2.8 times higher than the average for industry as a whole, 1.9 times higher than the average for the electric energy industry, and 1.2 times higher than the average for the woodworking and paper industries. In other words, the industrial branches, which produce 10.9 percent of gross production, are responsible for 23 percent of all expenditures on environmental protection. By contrast, the

Table 4.2 Estimated Cost of Water Regulation and Transfer in the USSR

Region	River	Kopeck/m^3
Northwest	Northern Dvina	0.22
Eastern Siberia	Yenesei	0.27
Western Siberia	Ob	1.10
Far East	Amur	0.72
Central Region	Volga	2.36
	Moscow	13.90
Central-Black Earth	Don	8.91
Baltic	Western Dvina	2.36
Southwest	Dnieper	6.24
Donetsk-Dnieper Region	Dnieper-Donbass Canal	22.10
Kazakhstan	Irtysh-Karagan Canal	21.40
Central Asia	Karakum Canal	20.20

Source: T. C. Khachaturov, principal editor, *Environmental Protection and Its Social-Economic Effectiveness* (Moscow: "Nauka," 1980), p. 142.

construction, metalworking, and metallurgy industries, which produce 42 percent of gross production, are responsible for less than 7 percent.[72]

Another way of looking at the cost of environmental protection to industry is on a unit basis. Once again, Professor Khachaturov provides some interesting data regarding per unit costs of water treatment and regulation. According to his figures, the inclusion of a cubic kilometer of water into a recycled water system costs 20 million rubles or two kopeks per m^3. The capital investment required to regulate waterways and transfer water to the main canals is shown in table 4.2.

Khachaturov estimates an outlay within the next five to ten years of 205 billion rubles for water development, if all the problems are to be handled. Of this amount, he estimates 115 billion for water resource improvement, 12 billion for water supply to cities and industry, 25 billion for hydroelectric development, 4 billion for the development of water transportation systems, and 7 billion for flood control, antierosion measures, and other programs.[73] Both the scope of the problem and the size of the required budget indicate that the cost will more than likely be borne by the Soviet state.

Research so far has turned up no comparable data for Yugoslavia. A general idea of the cost of pollution to the economy as a whole may be gathered from tables 4.3 and 4.4, which show documented negative effects on the environment and attempts by the constituent parts of the country to correct them in the area of forestry and protected reserves. Unfortunately, the data are not expressed in monetary terms.

One hard figure on costs was given recently by Andelko Kalpić, president of the Federal Council for the Protection and Improvement of the Environment. According to his estimates, the processing of all wastewater would cost industry 300 dinars monthly per employee, or the cost of a pack of cigarettes a day.[74] The absence of more precise monetary data on pollution costs reflects the fact that up to the present writing, Yugoslav industry and agriculture have had no accepted method of accounting for pollution damage. With the incorporation of a pollution cost accounting category in the 1980–85 five-year plan, figures will certainly be forthcoming. Although the newspapers publish data from time to time on the economic cost of pollution, they are not extensive enough to merit citing.

Both the Soviet Union and Yugoslavia are clearly moving in the direction of ascertaining the real costs of pollution control for industry and the economy as a whole. Even on the basis of very incomplete Soviet data, it is understandable why the largest industrial contributors to pollution should seek to delay installing pollution control equipment, and why they are reluctant to pay the operating costs to keep the inadequate pollution control devices functioning. However, it should be remembered that the industrial polluters include pollution control costs under their operating expenses, before the planned profit is figured. Thus, the expense is not quite as severe as it might seem initially. Still, the costs to the high polluting industries are sufficiently severe to serve as a disincentive to fulfill factories' environmental obligations. They cannot appear any less onerous to Yugoslav industrial organizations, when the prevailing attitude is that environmental protection is a luxury only the "rich" countries can afford.

Strategies

Because of their special position in the socioeconomic system, the economic organizations in the Soviet Union and Yugoslavia participate directly in the total flow of policymaking activities to an extent not experienced by the other environmental actors.

153

Table 4.3 Negative Influences on the Environment, SFRY

	Year	SFRY	Bosnia-Herzegovina	Croatia
Illegal cutting of forests	1971	674	213	65
(in m³)	1976	438	187	52
Index	1976/71	65	88	80
Waste water from energy industry (in m³/sec)	1976	171	23	28

Source: P. 133 of source cited in table 3.1.

Table 4.4 Social Correction of Negative Influences, SFRY

	Year	SFRY	Bosnia-Herzegovina	Croatia
Reforestation (in hundreds	1961	312	23	89
of hectares)	1971	162	18	32
	1976	246	67	48
Index	1976/61	79	291	54
Protected nature areas	1951	31	—	9
	1961	113	29	19
	1971	255	43	99
Number	1976	291	43	113
Index	1976/51	258	148	594
Hectares	1976	4,610	273	919
Protected historical entities				
Number	1976	1,646	4	420

Source: P. 133 of source cited in table 3.1.

Policy input stage. Industrial representatives sit in the legislative assemblies of both countries. In Yugoslavia, they have their own chamber at the local and republican assemblies. At the federal level, the constitution mandates a quota of industrial delegates to the Federal Chamber elected from the economic organizations in every opština of each constituent republic and autonomous province (Article 291). In the Soviet Union, managerial-technical personnel represent around 10 percent of the delegates to the Supreme Soviet, while their ministerial superiors together with other members of the state apparatus represent around 15 percent.[75] More important, heads

			Serbia		
Macedonia	Montenegro	Slovenia	Serbia proper	Kosovo	Vojvodina
115	23	3	115	13	127
35	22	1	65	3	73
30	96	33	57	23	57
9	2	22	74	3	10

			Serbia		
Macedonia	Montenegro	Slovenia	Serbia proper	Kosovo	Vojvodina
15	7	16	88	2	72
15	4	25	49	8	11
71	4	14	21	10	11
473	57	87	24	500	15
1	—	8	9	1	3
3	3	9	26	7	17
6	11	14	52	7	23
6	11	14	67	8	29
200	366	156	258	114	171
1,092	397	86	1,009	5	829
40	0	1,057	121	0	4

of ministries and managers of enterprises and related organizations form a substantial portion of the membership of the drafting subcommissions of the Legislative Proposals Committee of the Supreme Soviet, which have been responsible for drafting some key environmental legislation. For example, heads of ministries and managers of enterprises and organizations composed 32 percent of the membership of the drafting subcommissions for the 1968 Fundamental Land Law, 31 percent of the membership on the drafting subcommission for the 1970 Water Management Law, and 21 percent and 25 percent of the membership on drafting subcommissions responsible for the forest and mineral wealth legislation of the 1960s.[76] The subcommissions' discussions may usefully be compared to the legislative committee hearings in the United States. Contrary to U.S. practice, however, according to which only legislators are members of the committee, in the Soviet Union the interested branch ministries are represented on the subcommissions. In addition, subcommission members may coopt experts from their own ministries into the commission, and they may also go out into the provinces to discuss *sur place* with experts and enterprise directors employed in their branch organization.

In the Soviet Union, the drafting process begins with a policy decision by the Council of Ministers that is approved by the party. The drafting subcommissions must conduct their negotiations within the constraints of the policy guidelines, which makes the process time-consuming. First, there are negotiations and consultations within the drafting subcommission and between the branch ministries over the draft to be submitted for review to the Supreme Soviet. Then the draft is published, and written and oral comments are solicited from the relevant ministries and the public at large, followed by subcommission amendment of the draft leading to its eventual adoption as law by the Supreme Soviet. Soliciting views of the ministries is critical in order to avoid amendment later. A ministry may thus become party to a draft not only by having members on the drafting subcommission but also by being subsequently consulted either directly or through a subordinate enterprise or organization. The drafting commission refers to the comments of these groups during its conduct of a lengthy and apparently quite open discussion of the draft at hand. According to one Soviet source, a rough draft of the 1970 Fundamentals of Water Law was sent out to some 130 different institutions for comment. The same Soviet source commented on the divergency of opinion between the water polluters—those interested in felling timber and floating timber downriver—and the water purists—those concerned with reforestation and the maintenance of water quality to raise fish.

If agreement cannot be reached, a ministerial conference may be called, where representatives argue their respective positions until a compromise is reached. In the case of timber floating, the lumber industry secured its goal of maintaining the practice in the remoter roadless sections of Siberia, while the Ministry of the Fish Industry obtained its objective of having the protection of spawning grounds written into law.[77] Ministerial agreement is essential because the ministries are responsible for developing the regulations that flow from the law and seeing that the law is carried out.

Despite differences in opinion, relations between the concerned ministries in the drafting process are not adversarial, even as regards relations between the economic organizations and the environmental agencies. They may be competitive but they must be accommodating, because the guidelines are known and the law must be written. The length of time between the resolution to draft a law and the adoption of the law is a sure indication of the strength of the different viewpoints, but all know that agreement has to come. The eight-year lapse between the call for a draft and the passage of the 1980 Air Quality Control Law indicated substantial controversy over the role of Goskomgidromet in the implementation of the law. As might be expected given industry's strong structural position, the final law retained former branch ministerial control over major aspects of air quality management. While Goskomgidromet became a lead agency in implementing the law, the state committee had to share its authority with the State Inspectorate for the Control of Gas-cleaning and Dust-catching Equipment of the Ministry of Chemical and Petroleum Machine Building.

In Yugoslavia, decentralization has not meant less industrial involvement. It cannot be sufficiently emphasized that no law can be passed that does not have the support of industry in that particular area. As was seen in the cases of the cement factory pollution and paint fumes problem, there is an interdependence between local government and local industry. Under self-management the money to solve a problem must be raised locally or borrowed with local approval. As a result, in Yugoslavia as in the Soviet Union, the relationship between government and industry cannot be adversarial as it tends to be in the United States. As in the USSR, both sides in Yugoslavia participate in the formation of the decision and in its ratification. However, a distinction must be made with regard to the relative autonomy of industry's participation in Yugoslavia and in the Soviet Union. In Yugoslavia, official guidelines are found in the federal plan and in party resolutions. In addition, the party uses the sociopolitical organizations to indicate directions in which it would like to see particular issues move. Thus, for example, the Federal Committee for the Protection and Improvement of the Environment was involved in trying to persuade the concerned

157

parties of the validity of making the Una River a wild river. However, in contrast to the Soviet case, if the parties cannot agree, accommodation is not forced upon the negotiators and there is no way the party can impose its views. Thus, whether industry is a signer of the compact (*sporazum*, or legal agreement) or an interested participant in the negotiations, its views tend to prevail. The Una River wilderness agreement was abandoned because the communes could not be convinced of economic benefit.[78] In the negotiations preceding the adoption of the Sava and Neretva River Compacts, all the communes along each river had to agree to the provisions of their compact, knowing they would eventually share the cost of clean-up. Given the necessity of voluntary agreement, it is not surprising that many compacts are so general in nature as to lack all legal teeth. The Sava and Neretva River Compacts are cases in point.

The ability of Yugoslav industry to manipulate the public agenda directly is clearly exemplified by the way in which the electric energy companies of Serbia, Montenegro, and Bosnia and Herzegovina exploited the 1984 winter heating crisis. By focusing public and official attention on the energy shortage, the companies were able to head off the organization of environmental concern long enough to get their large-scale hydroelectric development project through the federal assembly. Environmental expert opinion was not fully consulted until after the passage of legislation. By that time, the underlying principles and the general spatial design of the project were unchallengeable since they had already become law. The ensuing controversy was thus confined to the issue of the site for the Tara River Dam; it could not tackle the basic question of whether the Tara should be dammed at all.

The weight of Yugoslav industry in the decisionmaking process and its interdependent relationship with the territorial political interests explains why much of Yugoslav environmental regulation, including the self-management compacts, appears to be largely symbolic. Domestic politics and an eye for world opinion were probably responsible for the passage of the Yugoslav environmental laws during the 1970s. The Stockholm Conference, the internationalization of the American environmental movement, and the first domestic concern over environmental degradation on the Adriatic made the adoption of environmental legislation good political strategy. Industry was a party to the legislative decisions in every republic, and the legislation reflected its interests. Perhaps the clearest example of industrial manipulation is the federal water law, which failed to provide for a federal inspectorate independent of republican control to protect republican industry.[79] The decentralized character of the Yugoslav legislative process urges industry first and foremost to seek accommodation with its local and republican party and government supporters.

Policy output stage. The ability of the Soviet and Yugoslav economic organizations to frustrate environmental policy goals brings fresh support to widespread scholarly pessimism in the United States regarding the capability of government to implement any policy, particularly environmental policy.[80] Since the ground rules to frustrate policy implementation are not written into structural constraints but into the fine print of regulation, we shall return once more to Bardach and see how the implementation games played in the United States[81] can surface in new variations abroad.

In implementing environmental policy, both countries, like most of the industrialized world, have adopted the principle that the polluter should pay. The principle means that industry cannot enjoy environmental values as "free riders" like the concerned scientist and average citizen.[82] Environmental enthusiasts press for optimum pollution controls because they believe that such controls cost them little or nothing. But industry is forced to relate the marginal benefits of control to marginal costs. In communist one-party states, by virtue of its second function, industry must also ensure that nothing that is undertaken destabilizes the power of the ruling elite. Hence, although the one-party system is clearly able to produce consensus about environmental goals (witness the impressive Soviet and Yugoslav corpora of environmental legislation), when achievement of these goals conflicts with production and control objectives, the implementation games begin.

The most common game played by Soviet economic ministries in the environmental area is tokenism. A good example is the history of the establishment of environmental sections in the factories. The first Council of Ministers' resolution was handed down in 1965, the second and third, in 1974 and 1978. A Moscow doctoral candidate found that as of 1980, a large number of Soviet enterprises were without the required intraenterprise regulations, and of those that had established environmental sections, many had relied on existing chains of command, thereby depriving the new section of the necessary autonomy to perform its functions competently.[83] In adhering to the letter of the law, industry had emptied it of content. The sheer size of the Soviet bureaucracy presents many opportunities for such token action. Tokenism may also be found in the Yugoslav system. There was much publicity about the signing of the Sava and Neretva River Compacts in 1980. However, the Conference on Environmental Protection that met at Ohrid in 1982 to commemorate the tenth anniversary of the Stockholm Conference found that so far "there had been no positive results. That means that we are prepared for everything except concrete work."[84] The ninety self-managing compacts signed by industrial enterprises for environmental protection may also be largely symbolic. The report did not indicate whether concrete pollution controls had resulted from the agreements.

Procrastination is a second game familiar to Soviet bureaucracy. Earlier in this chapter there was the example of the ten-year delay in providing ventilators to the aluminum factory. The major polluting ministries are frequently urged in the press "to expedite in all ways" the necessary technological processes, while industrial managers are cited for "insufficent attention" to environmental problems.[85] Aside from the chemical, thermoelectric, and metallurgy ministries, the USSR Ministry of Food Industry and the USSR Ministry of the Meat and Dairy Industry come under the heaviest criticism for "being slow to introduce" the required technologies and controls.[86] The steady stream of USSR Council of Ministers' resolutions on strengthening environmental protection in the Soviet Union confirms industry's predilection for a strategy of procrastination. The council may resolve, but industry stubbornly adheres to the same old habits.

Yugoslavia provides similar examples: the inaction following the river agreements, industrial procrastination in complying with the 1980 wastewater treatment law,[87] and the continuing threat to the Adriatic posed by oil and other sewage outflows from factories and towns along the Yugoslav coast, despite the existence of three Adriatic agreements.[88] A report on rising pollution in Serbia in 1980 noted that few labor organizations have provided the necessary machinery for purification, and of the existing systems, few are well maintained and operated,[89] although they are mandated by law. Much procrastination is hidden behind ineffective monitoring services and demands for more research and closer cooperation with scientists. While research certainly must be undertaken to demonstrate the extent of a pollution problem and suggest alternative solutions, it is not clear the degree to which industries such as the Zastava plant in Kragujevac or the cement factory near Belgrade hide behind research investigations to put off concrete action. In the case of the cement factory, the basic technology options are already known. But commissioning, writing, and presenting a report and weighing solutions upon which the factory and the town can agree constitute a long process that clearly prevents the factory from doing anything for quite some time. In the meantime, the residents continue to suffer.

Tenacity is a third game. In the preceding chapter, it was seen how an enterprise like the mill on Lake Ladoga or the nitrogen plant in Togliatti can continue to function for years and even expand its productive capacity despite negative recommendations from the environmental agencies. It was also seen in Semipalatinsk how an enterprise that had complied with regulations by installing an air-filtering system deliberately overworked its equipment to fulfill production norms, thus precipitating the breakdown of the filtering system. A particularly interesting example of tenacity is provided by the Siberian city of Chita. The local power industry sent a proposal to build a new central heating plant to the USSR Ministry of Power and Electrification. In conformance with regulations, the ministry's appropriate expert institute returned a report recommending that a system of boiler houses be built rather than a central plant. The recommendation was based solely on cost. Objections were raised that the initial cost of the central plant might be more but the savings in terms of environmental harm would be enormous. The report was returned to the expert institute for reevaluation. Procrastination set in. The power industry continued to argue in favor of the boiler system, as a temporary solution, and the central plant was not built.[90] The case exemplifies the principle that if one says something enough times, it becomes true.

Tenacity is a common practice in Yugoslavia as well. The report cited above on environmental conditions in Serbia notes that violations of environmental regulations in the republic are increasing because enterprises, thinking they are saving money, are buying outdated and dirty technology. The report attributes these purchases to "ignorance," but goes on to say that enterprises are convinced that investment in environmental protection is an expense with no positive economic effect.[91] Enterprises in Yugoslavia are deliberately purchasing environmentally inadequate technology for short-term economic goals. When Andelko Kalpić, president of the Federal Council for the Protection and Improvement of the Environment, was asked in a journal interview how it could happen that "things have been permitted" that went against environmental protection measures adopted for the Adriatic, his response begged the question. Heavy industry, he said, was permitted in some areas of the Adriatic coast. Few areas had developed solid environmental protection plans. More negotiations were necessary where "certain locations" were the issue. The sense of his talk was that industry simply went ahead and built where it wished with the tacit agreement of local authorities.[92] A reporter covering pollution of the Adriatic concluded that almost none of the industries cared about what the law said. The question was, "who will do what, when and how?"[93]

A fourth game is the Eastern variant of Bardach's "territory," or "not our problem." In the Soviet Union, this game is rooted in the twin problems noted earlier of bureaucratic compartmentalization combined with the proliferation of overlapping responsibilities. Examples of this game are plentiful. The reader may recall from the previous chapter the criminal case involving the environmental engineer of an Irkutsk oil and fat combine in the pollution of the Kaya River. The plant director not only refused to pay a fine levied against him, but turned around and sued the Baikal Basin Administration. The substance of his written statement was that he was not responsible for the problem.[94] In a second example, experts reported that environmental constraints "drastically" limited the amount of coal that could be utilized as fuel from the Kansk-Achinsk coalfield. The government authorized the organization of an institute to investigate a coal-conversion process. The responsibility for organization was given to the Ministry of Coal Industry. For three years the ministry did nothing. A scientist commenting on the situation suggested that if and when the ministry did set up the institute, it would be a "narrow departmental organization" concerned solely with the problem of coal mining."[95] A third example of "not our problem" comes from the Maardu phosphorite lode near Tallinn in Estonia, where inefficient open-pit mining techniques have caused severe air and groundwater pollution. The problem is getting worse because the mine is subordinate to the USSR Ministry of Fertilizer Production and hence outside the direct control of Estonian environmental agencies.[96]

In the first case, the director refused to take responsibility for pollution conditions in his plant. In the second, the organizing authority to establish an institute for environmental research was assigned to a ministry with a vested interest in the continued production of a product whose environmental impact it was asked to investigate. The reporting scientist suggests that given the circumstances, the institute will more than likely consider the environmental issues "not our problem." In the third, the mine management obviously believes that the implementation of Estonian environmental regulations is not its concern. The Soviet leadership is well aware of the territorial problem and is constantly demanding more comprehensive planning and program development. But structural and regulatory constraints combine to make "territory" more effective in bureaucratic competition than cooperation.

A particularly Soviet component of the game of "territory" is the bureaucracy's traditional preoccupation with secrecy. Information does not pass from one ministerial department to another without official authorization. If it is a characteristic of bureaucracies to prefer confidentiality as a way to enhance their administrative bargaining positions, the Soviet insistence on secrecy shuts each ministry behind a communications wall, frustrating the leadership's goals of comprehensive solutions to environmental and economic issues.

Recourse by industry to the game of "not our problem" in the environmental area is harder to identify in Yugoslavia, but it is suggested in reporters' statements, such as the one cited above, that the main question for the labor organizations is, who will have to do the cleanup?[97] The game is manifested in several different ways. The first derives from the examples of the Zastava Automobile Plant and the cement factory outside of Belgrade, where "not our problem" has become "not our problem alone." Not bureaucratic indifference but economic and technical factors urge industries to look for outside support in handling their environmental problems. Indeed, industry may have successfully promoted the view that environmental problems are of such a nature that they can only be solved with the aid of much research and the application of science and expensive tech-

163

nology. In other words, the problem is beyond one enterprise's capabilities and cannot be accomplished without recourse to other industrial organizations and government institutions.

Another manifestation may be found in the polemics surrounding the cleanup of the Sava River oil leak. Downriver from the pollution source, the city of Belgrade fears contamination of its water supply and has requested that the polluter be found and made to adhere to the law. Croatia refuses to allow any other inspectorate to search for the pollution source on the basis of republican autonomy. While the republics argue about jurisdiction, the polluter continues to pollute. Until the jurisdictional dispute is solved, it is not the polluter's problem to clean up the source of the oil spill. This case recalls the strip-mining devastation in Estonia.

Finally, "not our problem" surfaces because of contrary economic and/ or regulatory stimuli. The electroenergy companies planned a dam that would flood the Tara River Canyon because economically it was a good location, and there was no law against it. Potential irreparable environmental damage did not enter the calculation. Similarly, industry urged the building of a nuclear power plant on Vir Island in the Northern Adriatic out of economic expediency and the absence of contraindicated regulations (see chapter 7). A third instance may be found in the erosion and degradation of agricultural land that has been occurring over the past decades. The law provides for only small private holdings, which do not provide a sufficient income for a family. Migration to the city occurs. The farm is either left to deteriorate, farmed by the old people left behind, or sold to city people eager to build their vacation home. The family has no economic interest in preserving the farm by practicing conservation methods. And while the law regulates farm sales, it does not forbid them. Erosion is not the problem of the former farmer or the new vacation lot owner. The result is that some 20,000 hectares of land a year permanently leave the agricultural sector, and erosion has reached crisis proportions.[98]

The response "it's not our problem" to a gap in environmental regulation is one reason for the constant study recommendations and amendments that are made to environmental legislation in all countries. To solve the degradation and disappearance of agricultural land, the Federal Council for the Protection and Improvement of the Environment has urged that an investigation be made by the federal government during 1985–1986 with a view to making new legislation. Similarly, the federal water law is now under review in the attempt to eliminate the legal loophole found by republican rivalry. In the Soviet Union, the change in the factory reward system was one attempt to turn environmental protection into the factory's problem. The difficulty is that no matter what regulation is passed, it is possible to find a loophole in it that will make it possible to play "not our problem." Therein lies the dilemma of the regulatory principle, particularly in countries where the economy and the leadership are in a symbiotic relationship.

The strategies described above do not exhaust the list, but appear to be the most common in the two countries under review. The reader may immediately associate them with actions by industry in the United States. In the Soviet case, industry delays until it can bargain for funds and materials out of the central till. In the Yugoslav case, industry tries to cast its burden upon its self-management partners. While the structural constraints in the two systems dictate slight modifications in the strategies in terms of focus, the two countries amply confirm Ripley's description of the regulated interests' response to regulation given in chapter 1. Industry passively resists and at the same time engages in intense political activity behind the scenes to modify the regulations. The fact that in the communist countries the economic organizations are both regulatory decisionmakers and implementers only reinforces this behavior pattern.

Conclusion

A great deal of attention has been devoted in this chapter to discussing the particular position of the economic organizations vis-à-vis the party and state bureaucracies in the USSR and Yugoslavia in an effort to explain the systemic foundation of the failure of environmental implementation in the two countries. The second function inherent in the structure of an administered economy gives the industrial organizations a higher degree of autonomy in their relations with the party and state leaders than all other social and environmental agencies. Industry knows it is the mainstay of the political regime. The more autonomous the organization, the more it can afford to bypass party and state directives. In this connection, it is significant that the Soviet Ministry of Defense organized an environmental section only in 1983.[99] Each type of industrial organization uses the environmental regulations as a rule book by which to wage its battles in the competitive bureaucratic arena without regard for the real object of the regulations. The impasse produced when negotiations with industry break down or when industry displays procrastination, indifference, or obstinacy in pursuing its own course cannot be broken by the party short of asserting the entire weight of its moral and political authority. The Soviet centipede and the Yugoslav hydra are no different in this respect, except that self-management promotes situations where industrial compliance is even less likely, since it cannot be coerced by any hierarchical superior. Political gamesmanship suggests that authority loses its credibility if employed too often for small causes. There is a real danger that the incremental strategy utilized by the environmental agencies, while expanding their jurisdictional territory, may in the long run work to the detriment of the environment and to the advantage of the industrial organizations. For industrial behavior may only be modified by determined party intervention. There is little likelihood of the party's risking its dominant position for an environmental issue short of ecological catastrophe.

166

5

The Party and Territorial Administrations

The existence of communist sociopolitical systems is dependent upon the maintenance of the Communist party's leading role. The party's position is embedded in their constitutions and permeates every facet of life. The party leadership determines all policy, decides the structure of the governmental administration and economic organizations, allocates all resources, and controls key appointments. The party educates. The party appeared so all-powerful to one Soviet environmentalist that he insisted the failures in environmental protection had little to do with lack of money or lack of sufficient public education on the subject. The real problem was "lack of will" on the part of those having "real" power. The party's leading role has a public and a hidden dimension. The party holds publicized congresses and meetings and makes pronouncements and resolutions. Party leaders are quoted in defense of a desired policy by industry, scientists, or the environmental agencies. And yet, in discussions with Soviet and Yugoslav experts on environmental policy, the party's role was a topic that was never raised voluntarily. However, whenever asked, the officials being interviewed were invariably found to be Communist party members.

Officially the party is moderately proenvironmental. In the document issued by the Twenty-sixth Congress of the Soviet Communist Party on the basic direction of Soviet economic and social development for 1981– 1985, an entire chapter (albeit the shortest in the document) is devoted to the "protection of nature." However, the Third Party Program drafted in 1985 says not one word about the environment, although it does mention the necessity of resource conservation.[1] The brief chapter on environmental protection and natural resource use in the Guidelines for the Twelfth Five-Year Plan focuses on improvements in water resource and soil conservation, air pollution control, the state monitoring system, and overall environmental management.[2] The Social Plan for Yugoslavia for 1976–1980 also contains a short section on environmental protection, with frequent references to environmental needs in related chapters on investment, industry, and import tariffs.[3] Yet implementation of party resolutions and party-approved environmental laws by ministers and organizations confirmed by the party is, as we have seen, frequently more symbolic than real. Is the party as proenvironmental as it claims to be? Or does the fault lie with the failure of the territorial administrations to do their part in executing approved environmental programs?

Structural and Regulatory Constraints

A partial answer lies in the structural constraints imposed on the party apparatus and territorial administrations by virtue of the role the economy must play in maintaining the leadership in power.

The environmental-economic trade-off in the formulation of party policy. In both countries, continued low economic performance has kept the issue of economic reform in the forefront. Efficiency in production means setting managerial skills ahead of political loyalty in the appointment of economic personnel. In communist one-party states, the preference for reliability over ability is a built-in characteristic of the economy in its performance of the second function. Nevertheless, if the party wants to maintain its leading position in society, with all the attendant domestic and international ramifications, it must demonstrate ongoing economic progress. Gorbachev's sweeping reappointments are proof of the new leadership's need to match reliability with some minimum criterion of efficiency in bringing new blood into the leading strata of Soviet society.

Does this mean that the Soviet and Yugoslav leaders are insincere in their statements of concern for the environment? By no means. Rather, environmental matters cannot achieve priority consideration unless there is an unambiguous link between the environmental and the economic goal. The shifts and turns in leadership thinking on environmental issues over the past two decades confirm that such issues are relevant to Party policy only insofar as they have an impact on economic growth.

The landmarks of Soviet environmental legislation were written during the Brezhnev era, when environmentalism achieved legitimacy because of its economic thrust. Gustafson has documented the shift in the leadership's earlier fascination with big dam construction to a recognition under Brezhnev that improvement in agricultural production was inexorably linked with water conservation and irrigation.[4] The Brezhnev leadership showed itself particularly supportive of an environmental approach in the development of Siberia. The first Soviets to promote environmentalism publicly came from the institutes of geography and Siberian institutes of the USSR Academy of Sciences that were assigned the task of investigating the resource exploitation and development of Siberia. Indeed, it was the proposed economic development of Siberian Lake Baikal that spawned the first concerted "lobbying" effort in the area of nature conservation, resulting in the first major Soviet conservation plan. This change in official thinking did not reflect a decrease in the traditional Soviet enthusiasm for gigantic projects and large earth-moving schemes. Construction on BAM began under Brezhnev, and the Siberian and Volga river diversion projects became official party policy during his tenure. But the leadership's receptivity to environmental issues encouraged the participants in public debate over the project to give due weight to the relation between the perceived economic benefits and the associated environmental risks.[5] Under Brezhnev, environmental protection became institutionalized. In 1973, it was officially incorporated into the plan. In 1975, recognition of plan fulfillment was made contingent upon fulfillment of the environmental component. New laws regulating air quality and the protection of wild animals were written. The government required inventories of water quality, air pollution, land use, resource exploitation, and endangered species of animals and plants. On balance, the Brezhnev era must be seen as one of the most productive periods for environmental protection in Soviet history.

Chernenko and Andropov continued the focus on environmental protection in the agricultural area.[6] It may still be too early for an accurate assessment of Gorbachev's position. However, despite his efforts to earn a reputation as a pro-environmentalist, the Soviet leader may, in fact, be more traditionally production-oriented than his immediate predecessors.

An encouraging sign was the dropping of the river diversion project from the 1985–90 guidelines, but there is no indication whether its abandonment was permanent, or whether it was for financial, political, or environmental reasons. Most probably it was a combination of the three. His main accent has been on a renewal of the flagging economy, symbolized best perhaps by the creation of the new State Agro-Industrial Committee through the merging of the former USSR Ministry of Agriculture and the union-republic food industry ministries.[7] During the summer of 1985, the Supreme Soviet in Moscow lamented the country's failure to observe environmental regulations,[8] while a conference on Siberia in Novosibirsk stressed the need for accelerated regional development with but a small nod to the attending environmental risks.[9] The nuclear disaster at Chernobyl in April 1986 called into question not only the strictness and efficacy of Soviet nuclear power safety measures, but also the lack of severity of all the central bureaucracies in realizing their mandated pollution controls. Moreover, Soviet silence on giving the international community the relevant data so that it might take its own precautions confirmed once again that secrecy in the interests of an overly sensitive perception of national security remained the number one Soviet priority, no matter what the size of the catastrophe.

The shifts in the Yugoslav leadership's consideration of environmental impact over the past fifteen years has also reflected the changing economic situation. As in the Soviet Union, the environment achieved official legitimacy in the seventies, when water pollution, erosion, and urban blight became visible problems impinging on economic and social progress. But the deepening economic crisis has blunted the original environmental enthusiasm. The Sava River and Tara Canyon controversies indicate a movement back to a production-as-usual mentality. In the former, industrial output was put ahead of clean water; in the latter, energy was given priority over nature conservation. Only when the Serbian health authorities stressed the imminent danger of contamination of Belgrade drinking water could the issue of water quality inspection rights be brought into the Federal Skupština (assembly).[10]

The two controversies bring out another preoccupation of the Yugoslav party leadership, which in the long run may prove most harmful to the country's environment: increasing interrepublican rivalry over the char-

170

acter of economic development. To combat Yugoslavia's paralyzing economic crisis, a long-term program of economic "stabilization" was adopted in July 1983.[11] The plan called for an austerity program to cut back public and private consumption, an increase in exports to finance the country's $20 billion foreign debt, and the promotion of market principles, including the promotion of private enterprise. Two years later, the republics had done little to implement the plan. Part of the reason was the intensification of the reform debate within the LCY (League of Communists of Yugoslavia) in the last half of 1984. The debate exacerbated the already fissiparous nationalist tendencies within the party.[12] The leaders in each republic took adversarial positions committed to improving economic conditions in their own territory and to promoting their view of reform by supporting like economic and political interests in the other republics and provinces. Thus, the leaders of Serbia, Bosnia and Herzegovina, and Montenegro agreed on the Drina and Moraca electric power project. And Slovenia supported Croatia against Serbia in her position regarding the pollution of the Sava. In both cases, potential or actual environmental degradation was never the initial issue. Rather, each of the republican players strove to exploit both "functions" of the economy to maximum advantage in the political struggle for national ascendency within the party.

Enmeshed in the economic and republican differences is the generational issue, which has played its part in the downgrading of environmental protection in the 1980s. Most Yugoslavs interviewed believed that the continuation in leadership of the veteran communists of World War II was not only a principal source of the country's economic problems but also the main reason for the lack of serious party attention to environmental problems. Party control of the electoral process and all administrative and managerial appointments had maintained an elite in power that, because of its age, had had little experience of environmental degradation and consequently no interest in solving or preventing it. With Yugoslavia's underdevelopment and rural lifestyle their main childhood memories, their whole interest was concentrated on the most rapid economic development possible. To many Yugoslavs, the environment will not be taken seriously until a new generation replaces the wartime veterans bent, in their view, on maintaining their privileges and insouciant of the future.

As argued in chapter 4, the link between the party and the economy is

171

fundamental. When the economy fails, as in Poland and Czechoslovakia, the party must resort to force if it is to remain in power.[13] Since the leadership's concern for the environment is structurally dependent upon the country's relative economic performance, we may expect swings in the intensity of their commitment to an environmental program based on the degree to which environmental problems are seen to impede or promote economic progress. In all honesty, Western political leaders tend to react to environmental issues in the same way—until that time when their election hinges on a different response. When, as in 1968 in the United States or 1982 in Germany, the public calls for environmental protection, then it ill-behooves a politician to try to buck that demand. When he does, as Reagan did in 1981, a well-organized campaign by the environmental lobby has the ability to turn the most obstinate proindustrialist into an ardent environmental spokesman. In communist one-party states, a leader may seriously believe in preserving the environment. But his position depends on his ability to retain control of at least a minimally performing economy. So long as there is no public confrontation of views on alternative economic and environmental solutions and no mechanism for an automatic change in leadership (elections), communist societies will necessarily focus less on the spread and consequences of environmental degradation than do pluralist democratic societies.[14]

The relation of the territorial administrations to the center. In the Soviet Union, the economic reforms of the sixties shrank the rights of the republics in planning economic development in their own territory. The 1973 resolution on the restructuring of middle-level management further diminished republican rights by delegating to the central ministries the decision-making authority in planning as far as plan targets and resource distribution were concerned. One consequence of the reorganization has been the loss of republican control over environmental matters.

In the late 1950s and 1960s, during the period of relative decentralization, the republics led the way in passing environmental protection legislation. Many passed comprehensive environmental laws. Estonia was the first to pass a nature protection act in 1957. The Ukraine, Bielorussia, Azerbaidzhan, Georgia, Moldavia, Lithuania, and the RSFSR all passed their own laws. All but the RSFSR set up republican committees for environmental protection to coordinate the republics' environmental regulatory and control functions. The Ukrainian, Moldavian, and Georgian committees tried to exercise general management through the individual special environmental control organs organized under the centralized branch ministries. The Bielorussian, Azerbaidzhani, and Lithuanian committees combined the general management function with the direct administration of the exploitation and protection of important environmental resources. For example, the Bielorussian committee had jurisdiction over both the use and conservation of water resources and nature reserves. The Azerbaidzhani committee had jurisdiction over nature reserves and the animal world, while the Lithuanian committee regulated the animal world, marine resources, and monuments of nature.[15]

The subsequent economic reforms made the attempts of the republics to impose their individual environmental controls largely ineffectual. The late sixties and seventies saw the passage of the fundamental environmental laws (*osnovy*) at the all-union level. The 1972 Party and USSR Council of Ministers' resolution confirmed a deteriorating environmental situation. The major polluters, as well as the environmental and resource ministries, were all centralized institutions in which employees answered only to their superiors up the ministerial ladder. While local enterprises were unquestionably subject to local laws, the enterprises involved with resources and heavy industry that were subordinate to a central ministry complied with federal and local regulations only with the approval of their superiors. Without federal legislation, the republics had little legal power to control ministerial actions. Even with the legislation, the central ministries could still bypass republican regulatory authority.

The environmental degradation resulting from the extraction of oil shale in northeast Estonia provides a graphic illustration of the problems encountered by a republic in controlling pollution caused by a branch ministry within its territory. The two central ministries involved in oil-shale extraction in Estonia are the USSR Ministry of Coal Industry and the USSR Ministry for Mineral Fertilizer Production. Estonia's 1957 environmental law makes the pollution of the environment a crime, but the law does not apply to industries under the control of Moscow. In addition, planning the development of a production process is the prerogative of the central ministry and is thus likewise outside of Estonian control.[16]

173

The 1975 All-Union Fundamental Law on the Protection of Underground Resources establishes liability for breaking the rules and requirements for extraction that are determined by geological survey and other research.[17] However, the federal *osnovy* only set up general practices. The only law that is enforceable and provides for criminal or civil liability is at the republican level. But republican law is not necessarily binding upon organizations outside republican jurisdiction. Thus, the impressive corpus of environmental *osnovy* cannot be considered an adequate solution to the problem. The regulatory impasse at the republican level is one reason for the proliferation of council of ministers' environmental resolutions at both the all-union and republican level over the years, because the council of ministers is the legal superior to the branch ministries. In Estonia, the environmental situation in the northeastern part of the republic became so critical that it was the main topic of a regular session of the Presidium of the ESSR Council of Ministers at the end of 1984. The Presidium took the only action it could: it passed another resolution decreeing that "additional remedies" were to be applied, with a view to creating "optimal circumstances" by the year 2000.[18]

Estonia is not alone in its frustration. In Armenia, there is worry over air pollution and the degradation of Lake Sevan.[19] In Georgia, there are reports of unacceptably high emissions from iron and steel works, chemical plants, and building materials complexes, all of which enterprises fall under a central ministry.[20] Air pollution in Alma-Ata reached such dangerously high levels that the Kazakhstan minister of power and electrification was forced to give a public response in the Kazak press on the measures the ministry was taking to reduce pollution. The power industry's headquarters is the USSR Ministry of Power and Electrification in Moscow.

In Kirgizia, extensive irrigation has drained water from the national scenic landmark, Lake Issyk-Kul'. The shoreline has retreated and it is expected that it may retreat yet another kilometer. Irrigation construction is the province of the republican minvodkhoz (ministry of land reclamation and water resources) whose superior is the USSR Minvodkhoz in Moscow.[21] The proposed solution to the disappearance of Lake Issyk-Kul' is to divert water from a nearby river into the lake, as part of a larger plan to build up reserves of electric energy through the construction of hydroelectric stations. This project is under the USSR Ministry of Power and Electrification, whose sway over Soviet rivers was challenged under Brezhnev by the Minvodkhoz proponents of irrigation![22] The building of the dams and the tunnel to divert the water has not allayed republican fears that when everything is in operation, the water that is diverted will not be used to maintain the water level of Lake Issyk-Kul' but will go for irrigation purposes.

Kirgizia's concern was summarily dismissed by M. Muzakeyev, the chief of the Laboratory of Hydrology and Climatology of the Institute of Geology of the Kirgiz SSR Academy of Sciences. Referring to "well thought-out recommendations" by "leading scientists in the country" made at a section meeting of the newly formed Scientific Council on the Complex Utilization and Protection of Water Resources attached to GKNT (State Committee on Science and Technology), Muzakeyev flatly stated that "the all-union interest in Issyk-Kul' . . . places special responsibility on the Party, Soviet and economic organs of the republic." To soften the message, the scientist presented a project developed by an all-union research organization designed to maintain the lake's water level. And as further reassurance, he pointed to the amendment to the draft plan for the Economic and Social Development of the USSR adopted by the Twenty-sixth CPSU Congress, modifying the formulation about the use of Issyk-Kul's resources.[23] But he made clear that the future of the lake was out of republican hands and under the direction of the interested central agencies.

A proponent of the establishment of a committee on environmental protection in the RSFSR went straight to the core of the republics' concern: "Many all-union departments are working in the republic. Their participation in the territorial system of environmental protection is practically not coordinated."[24] The republics' dilemma may be summed up in the words of the secretary of the Division of Chemistry and Biological Sciences of the Lithuanian Academy of Sciences: "It is necessary to overcome negative phenomena caused by branch administration, when the separation of certain departments and planning organizations from the real environment in the field and their striving to solve only their own problems are felt all the more. It is necessary decisively and everywhere to bring the use of natural resources into accord with the requirements of ecology. . . . These problems must be solved by starting, not just from the need of any single department, but comprehensively."[25]

175

Republican ability to implement appropriate pollution control measures is especially weakened when a central decision sets up a triangular relationship between a central ministry and two or more republics, and provides different outcomes for each. The most obvious example is the now-abandoned proposal for the diversion southward of the Ob River in western Siberia. The project was probably the largest river diversion plan in history. It was pushed forward by the USSR Minvodkhoz and supported by the Central Asian republics, notably Uzbekistan and Kazakhstan. The project must certainly have been attractive to Minvodkhoz. It was Promethean in scope, with the first stage alone calling for the removal of some 5.5 billion cubic meters of earth. The Central Asian republics desired the project as they faced increasing water shortages in the years ahead, while Siberia was concerned about the dangers to its ecology and economics if the scheme were realized. The ministry and republican supporters argued the economic viability of the scheme, saying that the canal would pay for itself within ten years, and total cost would be only around 10 billion rubles. The Siberian detractors argued the economic irrationality of diversion, presenting real cost estimates of 20 billion rubles and expressing skepticism that the canal would pay off in thirty years. From their point of view, national food production could be raised more economically by increasing grain yields in Western Siberia, where natural rainfall would supplement irrigation.[26] The fall of the first secretary of Uzbekistan, Sharaf Rashidov, lost Central Asia its most powerful spokesman. With the help of the Siberian environmental lobby, Great Russian interests reasserted themselves. The project was abandoned.

The republics thus find themselves in a situation where whatever territorial environmental management schemes they may adopt may be jeopardized by new construction and development projects coming from the central ministries in Moscow, some of which may economically advantage one republic at the environmental expense of another. The Siberian river diversion debate had a fortunate outcome because of the ascendancy of Great Russian interests and Gorbachev's desire to bring the Central Asian republics back under closer tutelage to Moscow. But the result was less happy in little Estonia. Republican capability to implement republican environmental concerns thus finds itself dependent on party politics at the center, where environmental issues become secondary to the political issue, and on the strength of central support to republican-based branch ministry enterprises, which can argue in the all-union interest.

In Yugoslavia, the problem is the reverse. The republics have too much power to determine environmental policy within their territory, and the environment can become a political football between them. As indicated in chapter 2, self-management in essence gives the republics and provinces the major voice in deciding their internal affairs, assigning the federal government a very limited set of powers. In his classic defense of the system, Edward Kardelj posited the viability of single-party rule over the limited "democratic pluralism of self-managing interests." But as Cohen has argued, the systemic instability resulting from the devolution of administrative competence upon the republics and communes is probably the main source of the country's difficulties in virtually every area of governance.[27]

According to the constitution, basic economic policy is decided in the Federal Skupština. In reality, the Skupština decisionmaking process gives the representatives of republics and provinces decisive policymaking power, while relegating the details and day-to-day economic issues to the republican and provincial assemblies. Of the two chambers, by far the most politically important is the Chamber of Republics and Provinces. Deputies to this chamber do not sit as individuals but as delegations representing their republic or province. Before the chamber reaches consensus on any bill, the chamber delegations must have secured the agreement of their corresponding republican and autonomous provincial assemblies for the proposed legislation. In case of conflict, the chamber has worked out a process of *uglasavanje* (harmonization of positions) based on intense and extended negotiations between delegations.[28]

The 1974 Constitution assigns the critical policy decisions to the Chamber of Republics and Provinces. The chamber adopts the social plan of Yugoslavia; formulates policies and passes federal laws regarding monetary affairs, prices, labor, credit, and trade; and determines which goods shall be taxed and how much. It further determines the amount of the annual federal budget and the way in which this money shall be raised. The Federal Chamber, representing the opštini and work and sociopolitical organizations, votes only on federal statutes and on issues of a federal character. In addition, the Chamber of Republics and Provinces decides independently of the Federal Chamber on questions relating to the contraction

177

of credits for national defense, the supervision of federal administration agencies, and the formulation of enforcement policies for the implementation of federal statutes.[29] These last two provisions give the republics jurisdiction over whatever federal environmental enforcement organs may be established in addition to their own enforcement agencies.

While not the cause, the broad constitutional powers given to the republics and provinces in the 1974 Constitution assuredly hastened the split within the LCY along republican lines, with the Serbs advocating integration and unity at the federal level, and the Croatians and Slovenes urging greater republican autonomy.[30] The widening differences between the nationalities have increased distrust and suspicion. In the Republic of Serbia, Vojvodina and Kosovo have become virtually autonomous in their own right. Many Serbs blame Slovenian Stane Dolanc, federal minister for internal affairs, for encouraging the provinces' independence by opposing Serbia's efforts to bring them more strictly under Serbian control. Nationality differences were apparently behind the trial of the Belgrade Six in 1984, some Serbs saying that the "conservative" Croatian leadership forced the more "progressive" Serbian government to make the arrests.[31] The accusations and counteraccusations have revived fears of Great Serbianism among the smaller republics, especially in Slovenia, just as Serbia is demanding integrative constitutional reforms.[32]

The Sava River and Tara Canyon controversies must be placed against this background. The 1974 Federal Law on Interrepublican and Interstate Waters required republican agreement on new construction and automatically made a republic delinquent if it failed to secure such an agreement. It further stated which materials and/or pollutants could not be discharged into the water and held the enterprise responsible. And it stipulated that the Federal Hydrometeorological Institute and the Federal Institute of Health should test the quantity and quality of water in the river. But it did not provide for an independent control of discharges into the river. Moreover, all the monitoring, testing, dissemination of information, and issuing of warnings regarding water quality are organized through agreements with the responsible organs of the interested republics.[33] Serbians will tell you that no federal agency was given independent monitoring authority, because none of the republics would consent to such a provision. The only way to get the law passed was to give the republics the upper hand in the regulation of water quality, a power that was reinforced through their constitutional right to supervise federal agencies.

The actual compact on the Sava River signed in February 1980 is not an agreement between republics but between the communes bordering the river. While the compact contains articles urging communities to exchange information, mesh plans, and enter into further agreements to finance water system improvements, it is silent on substantive issues, including monitoring.[34] It sets no dates for cooperation to begin, contains no enforcement measures if cooperation does not occur, and is so general in tone that it is no wonder that environmentalists have condemned the signers for inactivity (see chapter 3).

The first major challenge to both the federal water law and the Sava River Compact was the 1984 oil leakage. In the controversy that ensued, Croatia stood on her prerogative to issue the information and warnings about pollution within her borders, while Serbia became increasingly frustrated at her inability to prevent contamination of Belgrade drinking water. At a meeting of the Serbian Republican Section of the General Conference of the Socialist Alliance in December 1984, Milivoje Todorović attacked the Sava River agreements as being inadequate. Others said that eight hundred approved regulations had resulted in nothing, while still others faulted the LCY for not having taken a firm enough stand. The result of the meeting was a decision to press for a change in the federal water law, create an independent inspectorate, develop an inventory of pollution sources along the river, and increase fines for noncompliance.[35] At the end of December, the Belgrade-based *Politika* reported an increase in concentrations of oil in the river.[36] In early January 1985, the first meeting of the Republican Committee of Inquiry for Investigating Pollution on the Sava and Iber rivers met to formulate research plans.[37] Under increasing Serbian pressure, the Committee for the Health of Workers and Social Policy of the Federal Chamber "categorically" demanded that the Federal Executive Committee pass a law as quickly as possible on a fundamental water management policy for rivers with two or more interested republics. Belgrade papers predicted an early passage within the first trimester of 1985.[38]

As of this writing, no new law or amendment to the 1974 law has yet come into effect. Much depends on the way in which the national irritations aroused during the controversy are soothed. The Sava may be a test case for effective interrepublican environmental management. Yugoslavia cannot afford to sacrifice its major water system to republican conflicts. The question is whether the protagonists can set the common interest over their historic national rivalries.

The Tara River conflict is an example of interrepublican cooperation in what was presented as the common interest. The Tara River is one of the few unspoiled rivers in Yugoslavia. It rises in the mountains of Montenegro and flows northward into the Drina River near the town of Foca. In its passage to the Drina, the river twists and turns between limestone walls. Its most dramatic section is a thirty-five-mile long canyon at the foot of some of Yugoslavia's most spectacular mountains, the Durmitor Range. The unique beauty of Durmitor and the Tara Canyon caused Yugoslavia to have them designated nature reserves under the protection of UNESCO's Man and the Biosphere Program.[39] One would have thought that a scenic landmark with international recognition would have been inviolate. However, the Tara forms an important part of the Drina River system. Montenegro is energy-poor, and has only two rivers where hydropower can be obtained, the Tara-Drina system, and the Moraca. The Moraca is a much shorter river that falls precipitously from the mountains into Skadar Lake on the Adriatic. After the electric power shortage during the winter of 1983, Montenegro, Bosnia and Herzegovina, and Serbia sought federal approval for a hydroelectric project that would involve the construction of a whole chain of dams on the Drina and Moraca river systems. The enabling law was passed on May 28, 1984,[40] despite the protests of experts and environmentalists. Indeed, it is doubtful whether their criticisms were ever seriously entertained by the project designers.

The benefits of approval for each of the republics were substantial. In return for a one-time-only nonreturnable investment, Montenegro obtained the construction of a series of dams to increase her power supply, most of which were funded by outside agencies. Because of the federal water law regulating the exploitation of interrepublican rivers, the other two republics needed Montenegro's agreement in order to build dams on their part of the river system. The uniting of the three republics behind a common purpose gave them increased political strength, enabling them to suppress information in the press, manipulate public opinion, and ram a law of their choosing through the Federal Skupština. Although expert opposition was successfully mobilized after the law had been passed, it succeeded only in obtaining the relocation of the dam. Dam construction had become a dead issue.

The two examples indicate the danger of republican power for the Yugoslav environment, whether that power manifests itself in interrepublican rivalry or cooperation.[41] It is easy to postulate that once the constituent republics realize they have a vested interest in preserving the environment, they will cooperate for an environmental goal as closely as they did for an economic objective. By that time, Yugoslav environmentalists say, it may be too late.

The limited scope of the lower territorial units. In normal Soviet planning procedure, Gosplan guidelines come down through the central bureaucracies and plans are submitted up through the same bureaucracies, with copies of the plan required to be submitted to the territorial organ at the level of each planning unit. Since very few economic endeavors are under the direct jurisdiction of local government, a local soviet executive committee may learn of a proposed branch ministry development project within its boundaries on the eve of the commencement of construction. To counteract the problem, the larger municipalities in particular have tried to set up coordinating regulatory mechanisms. At the municipal or *kraj* level, most local governments of any size have a committee for environmental protection. While the functions and responsibilities of these committees may vary, they all are advisory only with no administrative power.[42]

The functions of the environmental committee, as illustrated by the Leningrad committee, fall into four categories: to coordinate the activities of the organizations directing the city's environmental work, to prepare recommendations for the municipal executive committee on matters of environmental protection and natural resource use, to evaluate applications for construction and development permits, and to exercise control over the enterprises and organizations in their compliance with environmental regulations. The composition of the Leningrad committee as formed in 1979 tells us a great deal about its ability to carry out its mandate. All were public officials prominently engaged in environmental protection and pollution control in the city. The chairman was deputy chairman of the Leningrad City Executive Committee (Gorispolkom), and the deputy chairman was the head of the environmental section of the planning commission. Members of the committee included environmental officials, an Academy of Sciences representative, and a professor from Leningrad State University, but not a single representative of industry.[43]

To accomplish its mandate, the committee is divided into five subcommittees according to environmental objective. Subcommittee chairmen insist that no construction project, whether it be the expansion of the Leningrad Metro or the relaying and enlarging of the sewage system, can go forward without first being submitted to one of the subcomittees. Subcommittee disapproval means the project is returned to the project sponsors for modifications. The subcommittees also have the right to request an explanation from the management of noncomplying enterprises and organizations. When the committee so requests, administrators of suspected delinquent factories are required to submit data on the status of pollution control and resource use in their plant. If on the recommendation of the subcommittee, the environmental committee sitting as a whole finds the enterprise delinquent, the names of the enterprise and its director are forwarded to the Leningrad Gorispolkom for further action. At various times during the year, these names are published in the Leningrad Gorispolkom *Bulletin.*[44]

The functions and composition of the Leningrad committee appear to be typical. Deputy chairman of the Moscow Gorispolkom Environmental Committee, Dr. Margerita Shesterina, stressed the professional qualifications of subcommittee members and further emphasized the importance of volunteers to aid the subcommittees in individual investigations. A distinctive feature of the Moscow committee's activities is the custom of selecting one environmental area to investigate each year.[45] The results of the investigation are presented at a special meeting of the Moscow Gorispolkom for full discussion and executive action. Frequently, the investigation centers on a "voter's mandate," the complaint made by voters to the city executive committee at election time.

The role of the environmental committee and the Gorispolkom in achieving local environmental results should not be lightly dismissed. Dr. Shesterina cited her committee's success in getting a brick and flour milling factory closed in Moscow. In Leningrad, the environmental committee was able to generate the momentum to have some sixty factories moved out of the city. In the United States, local zoning boards may also only determine that violations have occurred; it is the town board's responsibility to take action against violators. In Soviet communities where there is a far-sighted governmental administration, an active environmental protection committee, and some political influence, the environmental protection committee can provide limited coordination and supervision. Moscow and Leningrad are clearly in this category, but Tallinn, Tashkent, Alma-Ata, and other Soviet cities also have records of environmental achievement.

Nevertheless, the top-heavy character of the Soviet administration suggests caution in the evaluation of committee performance. The need for central funding and the branch ministerial chain of command set definite limits to the control exercised by these committees over resource use within city boundaries. In 1977, the city of Leningrad allocated about half its budget (449 million rubles) to social needs. These monies had to be spread over six critical social welfare budget categories, including environmental protection. It is not surprising, therefore, that the city required some 51 million rubles from the all-union investment fund to achieve its air and water pollution control objectives.[46]

To obtain such funding, especially when large sums are at issue, requires strong political influence at the highest echelons of the Soviet party and government. One of Leningrad's oldest and most cherished environmental programs has been the construction of a dam across the Gulf of Finland to prevent the recurrent flooding caused by the backsweep of waters from the gulf into the city's waterways. For a long time, the flood control project encountered persistent opposition from various central agencies. The city fathers had decided to attempt construction at local expense, when in December 1982 Grigorii Romanov, who was then chairman of the Leningrad party organization, announced that Andropov had given his support to the plan. Central leadership endorsement was visible proof of the political ascendency of the Leningrad party chief at that time. In the Soviet Union, as elsewhere, pork barrel politics can have a salutary as well as deleterious effect.[47]

Because environmental control and monitoring take place primarily at the local level, the self-managing Yugoslav opština must perform a wide range of administrative functions in the area of environmental management. Its assembly is responsible for identifying and taking inventory of the sources of pollution in its territory; making decisions regarding the protection of water, air, land, and food and supervising the implementation of these decisions by the appropriate opština organs. The assembly also must prepare a program of measures and actions for the protection and improvement of the environment that includes concrete obligations, deadlines, and material resources for the program's realization, and appoint the inspection organs to monitor compliance. As mentioned earlier, since the inspection services are composed of trained technicians in a particular field, the larger and wealthier communes can afford to hire more qualified personnel than the smaller, poorer ones. To supplement their own resources, communes may make a compact to pool funds and resources for the creation of a common service or laboratory, or for a common pollution control project. They may also sign joint self-management agreements with an existing service or laboratory for consulting or monitoring work.[48]

As it does in the Soviet Union, money remains the main obstacle to environmental action at the opština level in Yugoslavia, but for a different reason. There are very few federal funds that can be distributed for environmental purposes (see table 3.8), and the amount of money in each is small. The only local SIZ with an environmental interest is the water SIZ. Limited resources necessarily place curbs on the environmental decisions a community is able to implement, and it is not surprising that local government in the rural areas has fallen behind the wealthier municipal governments in the adoption of air and water pollution measures and land-use regulations. One way a commune can raise funds is to hold a referendum demanding the community to give a designated percent of its wages to an environmental purpose. Organization is a second obstacle. Chapter 3 indicated that many opštini still have not designated an environmental committee, and of those that have, the authorized committee more often than not tends to have its main responsibilities elsewhere, such as in urban problems or infrastructure. Inspectorates exist mainly in the large cities, and the republican inspector has to cover the rest of the territory.

Because the economic and social plan primarily establishes guidelines, it does not represent the same kind of impediment to local initiative in economic development as in the Soviet Union. However, the self-management system obliges agreement, not coercion. The process of reaching agreement is time-consuming and uncertain. It may stretch out over two or three years, or fall apart. Now that environmental indicators have been included into the economic and social plan, there is the additional problem that a delay in a plan's adoption postpones the coming into force of all directives relating to a mandated environmental objective until well into the period covered by the plan. Realizing the objective is delayed that much more, since that process cannot even start until the directive comes into force.

Revisions and changes in territorial planning laws have also slowed the adoption of mandated regional and local land-use plans. The failure to develop adequate urban plans is a major reason for the chaotic growth of Yugoslav cities, which has been the object of considerable censure by the press.[49] The industrialization and urbanization of post-World War II Yugoslavia occurred so quickly that local administrations are only now beginning to assess the environmental damage. Between 1961 and 1971, over 1 million Yugoslavs moved.[50] In 1948, there were 83 urban centers with populations above 10,000. In 1971, there were 148. While the more established industrial centers grew three to five times, the more recently industrialized cities like Niš and Split expanded over sixteen times. The result was that in 1978, over 70 percent of the population lived in cities, compared to only 20 percent in 1946. Deforestation and erosion worsened as peasants abandoned their farms to the care of older relatives or left them altogether. The migration to the cities overwhelmed existing infrastructures. Municipal housing construction could not keep up with the influx of newcomers, and squatter shanties mushroomed around the edges of cities. Between 1950 and 1975, industry grew over six times to employ over 40 percent of the labor force. Where there was only one paved road in 1945, there was an entire network in 1975.[51] Overwhelmed by the pace of economic development in the period of expansion, the town and cities paid little attention to the growing evidence of air and water pollution or ground contamination by solid and toxic wastes. Now that the country is in an economic slump, municipal planning in the environmental area threatens to be even more neglected, despite calls in the press for action.

In the face of these difficulties, a few communities have been remarkably successful in the planning and execution of pollution control measures. One such success is the draining and cleaning of Lake Palić, where the rich and royal of nineteenth-century Austro-Hungary used to spend their summer vacations. Since local citizens initiated the project, the story of the lake will be left to chapter 7. A second success is the development, approval, and implementation of the first stage of the territorial plan for Lake Ohrid in southwestern Yugoslavia. The story deserves to be told in some detail as it highlights the impact of institutional constraints upon environmental management at the local government level.

Ohrid lies between Yugoslavia and Albania. It is a preserve for rare flora and fauna and, with Lake Baikal in the Soviet Union, it shares the distinction of being one of the two lakes in the world where plant and animal life from prehistoric eras have survived. It is thus one of the world's oldest lakes, and it is of such ecological interest that it has been designated a nature reserve under the protection of the UNESCO's Man and the Biosphere Program.

Ohrid is also a cultural monument. During Greek and Roman times, it was at the crossroads between Byzantium and the Peloponnisos, and Byzantium and Rome. The Via Appia ran across its waters. The tenth century saw the founding of Christian churches of the Slavonic rite, which were to provide the cultural foundations for the Serbian and Macedonian languages, as well as a level of art and learning unequaled anywhere in the Christian world at that time.[52] Many of the old churches still stand on the lakeshore, their interiors resplendent with the brilliant colors of the original frescos. Ohrid Village is like a Mediterranean village with its small houses climbing up steep hillsides along narrow alleys and streets that are shaded by overhanging eaves and balconies. And with its Mediterranean climate, Ohrid Lake is a tourist's paradise.

After World War II and up until 1970, tourism was encouraged. Hotels, campsites, and private summer homes crowded the lakeshore with little thought to their environmental impact. Lake Baikal was the catalyst for the decision to establish an environmental management plan for Ohrid.[53] UNESCO provided both information and some funding, and the Yugoslav federal government also helped finance the plan development. While the momentum for conservation came from the outside, it was realized from the beginning that plan goals could not be achieved by the simple passage of a local ordinance. Social action was necessary to convince the inhabitants of the three communities involved that environmental controls would reap benefits for them.

After extensive preliminary studies,[54] the plan was ready in 1973. The plan gave priority to the development of a sewage system for the Yugoslav side of the lake, and the first step was to determine the cost of the system and to identify organizations that would contribute the necessary monies. When the proposal for the water treatment system was finally released in 1979,[55] the cost of the construction of a system to cover the northern and most densely settled end of the lake was estimated at 1.3 billion dinars (at that time about $3.5 million). Twenty percent of the money was to come from the local opštini, 40 percent from the World Bank, and 40 percent from federal sources: the Fund for the Underdeveloped Opštini, the Fund for the Developed Opštini, and the Economic Bank. Of the money to be raised locally, 58 percent was to come from the Ohrid Opština, as it was the largest township, and 42 percent from neighboring Struga. Money from local sources would come from local taxes, the monies from the tax on water consumption, and other SIZ contributions. In addition, a 5 percent charge on personal incomes would be levied for a specified period of time as approved by public referendum and imposed by the associations for associated labor (OUR).[56] In preparation for the referendum, experts visited all the Yugoslav villages to inform the public about the need for the plan and, particularly, the sewage system. The collection of the local money was put to a vote and was approved by a wide margin.

At the present time, the entire Yugoslav coastline of Ohrid is protected to a depth of 600 meters from the lakeshore edge. Certain areas are under strict protection, and no buildings may be built near the sites of some of the more famous monasteries until after the year 2000. Private building may not be expanded beyond the areas now set aside, and the opštini may decide what hotels and other accommodations may be built in their communities only within the areas zoned for tourists. The tourist areas are separated by green belts, where nothing may be built, to keep the natural look of the lake. Eventually, transportation is to be removed from the lakeside and the roads set back from the shore where they cannot be seen. But no dates or financing have been approved. Industry is not prohibited, but only "clean" industry that operates on closed air and water systems will be permitted after submission of construction plans to a review process.[57]

The adoption of the Lake Ohrid environmental protection plan demonstrates that a local community has only a limited ability to undertake a pollution control project of any scope and must turn to external agencies should it decide to do so. The local opštini did not initiate the proposal for development of an environmental protection plan. Most of the momentum came from concerned individuals and groups from outside the area. Lake Ohrid enjoyed such a worldwide reputation that the Republic of Macedonia was able to generate international as well as national support. International and national consultants were called in to design the water treatment system, and international and federal funds were required to initiate the first stage of the plan. With the hydra system permitting no decision at the federal level without consent of the republics, an opština is not going to assume any substantial environmental commitment without some assurance that the republic will support it. Equally important, the citizens of the two opštini targeted to implement the sewage system had to agree to give up additional income to the opština to pay their share of the cost. Assuredly, outside pressure and the certainty of outside funding influenced their vote.

The dispute over the location of Kornati National Park headquarters mentioned in chapter 3 is an example of the importance of external pressure in the case of opštini disagreement over an environmental compact. In this instance, the disputed items had nothing to do with environmental protection. Interopštini rivalry was simply stronger than the desire to cooperate. Since the proposed area did not have Ohrid's international acclaim, the external pressure on the opštini to agree was markedly less than it was at Ohrid. Domestic external pressure, however, was not absent. Supporters of the park moved to solve the disagreement by changing the law to take the issue of park headquarters out of opština hands. Up until 1984, there was very little of such external pressure on the signatory opštini of the Sava and Neretva Compacts, and up to that date there was virtually no movement to clean up the rivers. External constraints would thus appear to play a critical role in interopština environmental cooperation.

In sum, while self-management legally and organizationally gives local authorities considerable freedom in undertaking environmental programs, in practice, material, financial, and above all political realities determine local government's choices. Opština willingness to embark on some aspect of pollution prevention would seem to depend most on the course of republican and interrepublican environmental politics. Unfortunately, at this level, constitutional arrangements have encouraged as much discord as the cooperation they were expected to promote.

Figure 5.1 State Capital Investment in Environmental Protection in the USSR and the RSFSR, 1973–86 (millions of rubles)

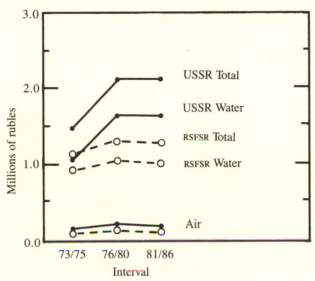

Source: Same as for table 5.1.

Assets

Control of public spending. In the Soviet Union, the central government monopolizes control over both the collection and allocation of financial and material resources.[58] In Yugoslavia, the federal budget is subject to republican dispensation with individual republican approval required on all fiscal and taxation policy before it can become law. The republics thus have the largest input into the distribution of the national income. In both countries, local government has the fewest financial assets. Each is subject to a set of national and republican constraints that largely determines their options in the allocation of the income coming to them from taxation.

Figure 5.1 and table 5.1 review the figures on state capital investment in environmental protection in the USSR and the RSFSR from 1973, the year the environmental category was added to the national social and economic plan, to 1986.

The slightly lower priority assigned to environmental protection in the

Table 5.1 State Capital Investment in Environment Protection in the USSR and the RSFSR, 1971–84 (millions of rubles)

	Years	Annual average	Years	Annual average	Years	Annual average
USSR[a]	1971–75		1976–80		1981–84	
Total investment in environmental protection	7,291	1,458	10,824	2,165	8,634	2,285
Water	5,411	1,082	8,338	1,668	6,404	1,601
Air	725	145	950	190	665	166
RSFSR	1973–75		1976–80		1981–84	
Total investment in environmental protection	3,367	1,122	6,457	1,291	5,050	1,263
Water	2,789	930	5,112	1,022	3,841	960
Air	274	92	609	122	433	108

Source: *Narodnoe khozaistvo SSSR v 1984g* (Moscow: "Financy i statistiki," 1985), p. 405, and *Narodnoe khozaistvo RSFSRv 1984 g* (Moscow: "Financy i statistiki," 1985), p. 241.

Note: These figures should be taken as indicative only. When compared to the figures given in 1979 for the period 1971–79, there are substantial differences. For example, in the 1979 statistics, data for the USSR as a whole are given only from 1973 on, the date environmental protection became a mandatory part of the plan. Thus, a total expenditure of 4,755 million rubles is given for the period 1973–75. The RSFSR figure for the same period is 2,903 million rubles as compared with the 3,367 statistic given in 1984, a difference of 16 percent. Discrepancies of the same magnitude occur with the other data. See *The USSR in Figures 1979* (Moscow: Statistika, 1980), p. 200; and *The RSFSR in Figures 1979* (Moscow: Statistica, 1980), p. 98. The figures demonstrate, however, the preponderant attention given to water pollution over the past fifteen years.

a. Total expenses on environmental protection in the USSR between 1981 and 1984 were 34 billion rubles, of which 9 billion was spent in 1984. Industrial funds for environmental protection in the RSFSR during the same period were 46.7 billion rubles, of which 13 billion were available in 1984.

Eleventh Five-Year Plan (1981–1985) substantiates the present policy swing toward greater emphasis on industrial production.[59] While in all three periods, the major investment is in water, the figure indicates that during the time period under review, investment in air pollution control increased at a slightly faster rate for the Union as a whole, and at a substantially higher rate in the RSFSR. The reader is referred to table 3.4 for the breakdown of republican investment in environmentally related areas for 1979. Chapter 3 also presented relevant data on the allocation of central investment to the industrial sectors. From 1976 to 1984, the USSR officially allocated an average of 27 percent of its total capital investment to agriculture.[60] About 14 percent of this amount went to agriculturally related environmental conservation and preservation measures, such as irrigation projects, erosion control, soil conservation, land reclamation, and pollution control.[61] Table 3.5 indicates that agricultural investment in the republics has been quite logically based on the republic's relative size and wealth and the national strategic importance of agricultural development in that republic. The substantial agricultural investment in environmentally related measures confirms official party recognition of the interrelationship of environmental protection and food and crop production. Nevertheless, the steady rate of state investment in heavy industry attests to the built-in pressures from the branch ministries to divert those funds for military and industrial production objectives.[62] The continuing defense buildup, in particular, is sober proof of the preponderant influence of the military-industrial complex over party leadership decisions.[63]

Access to funds at the republican and local levels depends on the decision at the center. Since the 1965 reforms made the all-union ministries the sole holder of funds allocated to enterprises in both the all-union and union-republic ministries,[64] the republics and local government must negotiate with the branch ministries for their share of the ministerial purse. During the preparation of the budget, the enterprise administrator must follow the guidelines and schedule of his hierarchical superior, the central ministry. In the press of planning deadlines, the republican organ of a union-republic ministry may choose not to keep to the timetable for submitting its plan to the responsible republican gosplan but submit it at the same time as it forwards the completed plan to the ministry in Moscow. As a result, the republican planning unit may have no time to study and comment upon the republican ministry's program. Even in the management of the funds that the republic or local government is allowed to keep for regional objectives, the central plan controls the investment choice and the amount allocated to each category of recipient. A republic or municipality may modify these guidelines only by further negotiation at the top.[65]

The direction of all capital investment and resource distribution through the branch ministries and central agencies thus discourages the local generation of income and the allocation of centralized capital investment for

Table 5.2 Budgetary Expenditure of Yugoslav Sociopolitical Communities, 1978–79 (thousands of dinars)

	Federation	Republics and provinces	Towns and regions	Communities
Total expenditures				
1977	93,449.2	46,125.3	4,054.0	22,204.1
1978	82,088.3	54,741.9	5,654.0	26,003.6
Social activities [a]				
1977	13,684.3	7,479.9	543.2	2,403.8
1978	16,418.8	11,292.9	436.7	3,441.3
National defense				
1977	38,130.9	146.7	44.6	444.2
1978	42,594.7	162.7	55.6	566.2
Administrative agencies				
1977	5,274.4	7,450.5	2,318.9	14,633.5
1978	7,218.3	9,904.5	3,342.8	16,811.4
Contributions to budgets (ceded resources)				
1977		18,786.9		293.0
1978		16,245.7	10.9	316.6
Additional resources [b]				
1977	6,139.0	2,792.1		47.3
1978	7,028.2	2,913.9		51.8
Investments in noneconomic activities				
1977	1,562.5	1,979.7	458.1	1,525.7
1978	1,888.0	2,560.3	672.2	1,388.7
Interventions and investments in economic activities				
1977	22,257.3	6,270.7	612.2	346.5
1978	511.4	9,871.5	955.6	598.7
Liabilities and reserves				
1977	6,400.6	1,220.1	77.0	2,510.2
1978	6,429.1	1,790.2	2,828.8	

Source: *Statistical Pocket Book of Yugoslavia, 1980* (Belgrade: Federal Statistical Office, 1980), p. 61.
a. Including pension and disablement insurance.
b. Additional resources for the economically underdeveloped republics and the autonomous province of Kosovo.

environmental purposes to provincial cities and towns.[66] Kushnirsky, indeed, asserts that municipalities received almost no central investment funds of any kind during both the Ninth and Tenth Five-Year Plans. Cities may complain about deteriorating sewage and water treatment systems and other environmental infrastructures, but without the central funds or approval provided by plan guidelines to spend locally generated income, such projects rest as deadletters.[67]

The thrust of public spending in Yugoslavia is indicated in table 5.2. According to the table, in 1978, 52 percent of the federal budget was spent on national defense; 18 percent on social services, including the payment of pensions and disability insurance; 9 percent on administration; 8.5 percent on assistance to the economically backward regions of Yugoslavia; and 3 percent on noneconomic activities. The republics spent minimally on defense, 21 percent on social services, 18 percent on administration, 5 percent on aid to the underdeveloped regions, and less than 5 percent on investments in noneconomic activities. Investment in economic activities was 18 percent. That same year, the republics gave a healthy 29.6 percent of their budget to the federal government for aid to the underdeveloped regions (41 percent in 1977). Administrative expenses figured most prominently in local commune budgets, where they represented 64.5 percent of the total expenditure. By contrast, the communes spent 13 percent on social services and 5 percent on noneconomic investments. If one compares the 1978 budgets of all levels of the Yugoslav government, an average of 19 percent was spent on social services, 22 percent on administration, and less than 4 percent on noneconomic activities. When the enormous SIZ (community of interest) budget is added to the government's social services budget, it turns out that the public priorities in Yugoslavia are social welfare and government administration. Substantially less money goes for noneconomic activities, among which are included environmental protection measures. Moreover, so much of the republican and commune budgets has been designated for essential administrative and public services, including aid to the underdeveloped republics and provinces, that there is little left over for the communes to allocate independently.

Self-management then does not leave the lower government administrations much more leeway in determining how locally generated funds are to be allocated than does the Soviet centralized allocation system. Virtually the entire commune budget is predetermined by the republics through federal and republican regulations regarding commune distribution of local money to the siz[68] and essential administrative and social services and to priorities set at the federal level through republican agreement, such as assistance to the backward regions. Under these circumstances, commune interest in undertaking a major environmental project is understandably low, unless the community can find funding from the outside. Table 5.2 shows that obtaining republican or federal funds for such initiatives is doubtful since republican preference clearly lies in other areas.

It thus appears to make no difference in environmental terms whether the financial decision is centralized or decentralized, as long as the control of public spending is in the hands of a single party. If the decisionmaking unit does not consider the environment a priority, the money will be allocated elsewhere. Despite the mechanism of local referenda, self-management has added little to local government's financial autonomy.

Environmental and economic visibility. A positive asset for the territorial units in each country is the national and international visibility of their environmental or economic resources. Both Lake Baikal and Lake Ohrid are known to ecologists the world over. The Adriatic coast is a vacation symbol to millions of foreign tourists. The Tara River Canyon is less known abroad but a national landmark to Yugoslav scientists. In the environmentally conscious world after the Stockholm Conference, no politician can afford to appear to be unwilling to preserve internationally or nationally recognized scenic wonders. Siberia demonstrates the international visibility of natural resources. The whole world is watching to see how the Soviet leadership manages the critical environmental component of the development of the earth's last frontier. Many Soviet scientists share Boris Komarov's concern that the leadership is not sensitive enough to Siberia's unique environmental conditions.[69] Nevertheless, international discussion of the critical issues in Siberian development has most certainly been a factor in encouraging Soviet central decisionmakers to give increasing consideration to environmental risks and their economic ramifications, at least in questions of water management.[70]

At the domestic level, a republic's national or regional sensitivities to the value of a particular resource are also probably a positive asset to territorial administrations desiring to undertake environmental action. Neither state is secure in its multinational identity. And neither country's leadership can afford to disregard national preferences. As we have seen, landmarks in the USSR that have a special significance for a republic, such as Lake Sevan in Armenia and Lake Issyk-Kul' in Kirgizia, merit special funding and special notice in the party program and planning guidelines. In inter-basin water transfers, the central government must consider the views of the donor as well as recipient republics, as the Siberian river diversion controversy made clear. However, republican nationalism may also have a negative impact on resource conservation. As Leslie Dienes points out, the peripheral republics are much weaker politically than the Russian Republic.[71] Estonia's difficulty in preventing its northeast from becoming an ecological disaster is a case in point. However, when the question is not one of strategic resources, the Great Russian members in the CPSU Politburo may be reluctant to hasten the development of a politically unreliable region and thus welcome the opportunity to soothe national consciousness with assistance in preserving a republican landmark. Siberian development, for example, presents far fewer political imponderables than the development of Central Asia. The possibility cannot be excluded that Kirgizia may see the water level of Lake Issyk-Kul' preserved while the extensive exploitation of Siberian resources may render that area an ecological wasteland, despite the best efforts of Soviet planning and research.[72]

In Yugoslavia, the visibility of an environmental or economic resource may also be an asset. Lake Ohrid has both international and national recognition. Within Yugoslavia, it is viewed as a focal point in both Macedonian and Serbian history and thus commands special attention from each republic's political leadership. Slovenia, the most industrialized republic, prides itself on having the best-administered environmental management system, and it pioneered in agricultural land-use regulation. Serbia points to Kragujevac, the Yugoslav Detroit, as an example of industrial-communal cooperation in the construction of water treatment systems. While the agreement on the development of hydropower on the Drina and Moraca river systems and the controversy over the Sava River might seem to illustrate the negative aspects of resource visibility from the environmental point of view, the outcome of the two controversies suggests that national recognition of environmental value may be one of the most important factors in developing republican awareness of the need for environmental management. The decision on the Tara Dam was modified, and most certainly a negotiated solution will end the further pollution of the Sava. After all the publicity, it is more than likely that money will be found to facilitate the clean-up and that the water law will be revised to provide for a more independent monitoring system. The Sava is too valuable a resource to be let go.

The party network. The third asset of the republics and lower territorial administrations is the horizontal and vertical party network that can intervene at its own discretion in regional and local affairs. While the organization of industry is totally vertical, the party organization operates horizontally as well, with a comparable party unit at each level of administration. The party committee has the right to intervene in administrative matters, and party demands require execution before the target schedules of the plan.[73] Thus a community in need of an environmental improvement may be able to obtain its goal through the intermediary of the party. The best example is the city of Leningrad.

The Leningrad Gorispolkom (executive committee) had mobilized its scientists and approved a construction plan for building a dam and eliminating pollution in the Gulf of Finland,[74] but the implementation of the plan had to await the intervention of the chief party executive at the highest echelon of the Soviet party to obtain the necessary funding. Similarly, the intervention of former CPSU CC Politburo member and first secretary of the Kazakhstan Communist party, D. A. Kunyaev, certainly played a critical role in bringing Alma-Ata's air pollution problems before the Soviet public, thereby forcing an "explanation" from the Kazakh Ministry of Power and Electrification.[75]

Party connections can obviously be used both to promote and impede an environmental cause. It was not until S. R. Rashidov, first secretary of the Uzbek Communist party, died (possibly by suicide) that Siberian environmental interests could come to the fore and effectively speak for the abandonment of the Siberian river diversion project.

In Yugoslavia, party intervention functions more obliquely. One of the most important vehicles for party influence is the Socialist Alliance. Through the Socialist Alliance, the party assures that communists occupy all key posts, both elected and appointed, including those in the socio-political organizations grouped under the Alliance and in the delegate system.[76] When a national issue needs support, scientists in their professional associations can contact influential communists in their organization. These communists know like-minded colleagues in the other sociopolitical organizations, and through these contacts can mobilize a sizable "lobbying" effort. The Tara River Canyon represents the best example in the environmental area of the ability of like-minded party members to coordinate their actions within the organizations of the Alliance. The "Save-the-Canyon" movement eventually involved the leadership of the Socialist Alliance in a protest letter to the federal government and the passage of an Alliance resolution against the construction of the dam at the proposed site.

In the Sava River controversy, proenvironmental Serbian party members in their function as heads of the Serbian sociopolitical organizations played an important role in generating political support in the Serbian Assembly for a clean-up program. The result of such pressure was the establishment of a Committee of Inquiry for the Investigation of Pollution on the Iber and Sava rivers in January 1985. Although the LCY has been generally criticized for its lack of interest in the environment,[77] the evidence suggests that there is a growing core of proenvironmental members willing to politick for a worthwhile environmental cause.

Political salience. The success of Leningrad and Moscow in securing capital investment funds for environmental protection that are denied other municipalities is directly related to their political salience. Both cities not only have domestic political importance, but also are the points of entry for the large majority of foreign visitors to the Soviet Union. According to official statistics, expenditures on the reconstruction of Leningrad's sewage and water treatment system, which had been virtually destroyed during World War II, totaled 906 million rubles between the mid-1950s and 1980.[78] In Moscow, between 1976 and 1978, 161 million rubles were spent on environmental protection out of the city's total planned expenditure for the five-year period of 235 million rubles. Virtually all of the city's capital investment monies came from central investment funds.[79] A much publicized achievement of the Tenth Five-Year Plan (1976–1980) was the clean-up of the Moscow River and the return of fish life to its waters. Considerable expense was also incurred to improve both water and air quality prior to the Summer Olympics of 1980.[80] Investment in pollution control in the Soviet capital for the Twelfth Five-Year Plan is 126 percent higher than during the previous five years. While this represents a slowing down from environmental investment in the seventies,[81] it is still significant. From the ecological point of view, being the first city of communism has definite advantages. Areas of less political prominence, such as Chita, Semipalatinsk, or Togliatti, which have severe pollution problems, have not been so fortunate.

Political value may be even more critical at the republican level, as Estonia and Kirgizia bear witness. Politically, the Central Asian republics weigh more on the nationality scales than little Estonia. The rapid demographic growth of these republics as compared with the rest of the Soviet Union has created such a potentially explosive situation that some trade-off to satisfy national demands is essential. The logic of Great Russian supremacy militates against the intensive industrialization of Central Asia, or the concentration of economic effort in the Ukraine.[82] The environment doubtless represents the least threatening trade-off for the maintenance of a modest economic profile. On the other hand, as the abandonment of the Siberian river diversion project indicated, Great Russian hegemony can operate to secure environmental protection within the Russian Republic borders while at the same time practicing a pseudo-colonial policy of forcing environmentally destructive economic development vital to national security on the peripheral republics (Estonia).

In Yugoslavia, political salience is particularly important at the local level. Environmental protection is clearly a matter of greater urgency for a republican capital than for less politically visible areas, and the larger cities are able to find funds for pollution control projects. The contamination of Belgrade's water supply is a national and international scandal. The pollution of Kosovo's rivers is not.

Specific Yugoslav assets. As semiautonomous entities, the Yugoslav republics exercise far more control over information and organizational milieu than their Soviet counterparts. Their control over information is well illustrated by the Sava River controversy. Each of the riparian republics, Slovenia, Croatia, and Serbia, alone possesses the relevant data identifying polluters within its territory. Only the republics have developed comprehensive inspection systems in the areas of urban development, construction, water, and public health. At the local and municipal level, expanded networks are found solely in the major cities.[83] Most of the republics have yet to complete a full pollution inventory, but global figures are now available on waste treatment, water quality, sewage discharge in the main river systems, and air quality in the main urban areas.[84] Croatia, Serbia, and Slovenia are probably the most advanced in compiling pollution data. The J. Černi Water Resources Institute, for example, has completed an authoritative survey of Serbian water quality and catalogued the entire Serbian river system.[85] This kind of systematic monitoring of air and water quality has now spread to virtually all the republics.[86] The republic releases this information at its own discretion and in consultation with the inspectorates of the larger cities when a crisis occurs. Only the republic knows the full extent of ambient pollution within its boundaries, and can identify the point sources exceeding the legal emission levels. A republic may use this information to crack down on polluters or to cover up the extent of a pollution problem, but the information is made public only with its approval. Information control should not be understood to be inclusive. Republican officials will be the first to say that they have little data on the actual cost of pollution control to industrial and agricultural polluters, the cost of retrofitting pollution control devices, or the share of construction costs necessary to budget when building a new project. They hope to acquire much of this information through the recent requirement that factory management inventory pollution conditions within the plant. But at present, the republics are the largest repository of information on environmental conditions in Yugoslavia.

The republican leaderships dominate the lower territorial units through the practice of democratic centralism within the LCY and the selection of delegate candidates through the Socialist Alliance. A major source of the republics' control over their organizational environment is their power over the public purse. If a republican leadership is concerned about pollution within its territory, it has far easier access to external sources of funding than the locality, for it can pressure the federal government to donate from the two republican funds and can designate money from within its own resources to help finance a project. The Serbian inventory of water quality and the Ohrid water treatment system are good examples, as is the long-term project for cleaning up the land devastated by the copper tailings from the Bor Copper Mine mentioned in chapter 3. The present negative state of the Yugoslav economy may not make the funding of environmental measures attractive at this time. However, in the seventies, many republics were active in antierosion measures, reforestation, and national park development. The land-use plan for the Adriatic coast was agreed upon at that time. The republics can use their organizational control for positive or negative environmental purposes. The danger is that perceived republican economic needs (the Tara River) or republican political rivalries (the Sava) will divert attention from the implementation of the necessary environmental measures.

Costs and Benefits

So far, there is no systematic information available in most communist countries on the costs of pollution to local communities, regions, or the country as a whole either in terms of environmental degradation or public health. In the Soviet Union, the release of this information remains a matter of national security, although a great deal more material is now in the public domain. In Yugoslavia, a considerable part of the data has yet to be collected and, as we saw earlier, the republics release what information they have when they choose to do so. As elsewhere in the industrialized world, the relationship between health and environmental conditions is clearly recognized. More will be said on the relation between pollution and disease in chapter 7, but a few comments on national and regional effects are appropriate here.

One seminal Soviet study edited by economist A. D. Lebedev makes strong inferences about the extent of environmentally induced health problems in the USSR, although no figures are given.[87] In another important study, Soviet economist L. G. Mel'nik has estimated that the economic loss attributable to the increase in illness among the population accounts for one half of the total economic loss due to air pollution.[88] In his study, *The Demographic Factors of Health*, well-known demographer M. S. Bednyi has amply documented the important link between public health costs and demographic and geographic factors such as population density, migration flow, environment, and climate.[89]

On the regional level, a *Novy mir* roundtable discussion on Siberia held in the spring of 1982 provided a particularly revealing glimpse of the impact of pollution on the population that had migrated to Siberia. "[There are some regions] where we can claim the highest per capita availability of medical care in the world, but still the morbidity rate is extremely high, the death-rate rising, and the incidence of chronic illness growing. . . . It is apparent that our existing health-care model does not always work, especially in the eastern territories, where there is a tremendous migration flow, vast economic projects that have not been cleared for ecological soundness are under way, and the environmental impact of economic activity is especially vivid."[90]

At that same conference, Vlail Kaznacheyev, head of the Institute of Clinical and Experimental Medicine of the Siberian Branch of the USSR Academy of Sciences, reported in an extraordinarily frank moment that the rapid development of Siberia's natural resources had brought a serious upsurge in genetic defects in newborn babies. His colleague, V. Bessonenko from Kuznetsk, cited the effects of acid rain and warned of the development of a "vicious circle" that was straining medical facilities in the heavily industrialized Siberian regions (the Kuzbass, the Southern Krasnoyarsk region, the Norilsk area in Northern Siberia).[91]

These comments are substantiated by official statistics on the accelerated postwar economic growth of the regions east of the Urals. Between 1940 and 1975, the overall volume of industrial production increased thirty-one times in the West Siberian economic region as compared to a national average of seventeen times. The Kuzbass TIC (territorial industrial complex) alone produces 33 percent of the region's entire output, although occupying only 4 percent of the area. Its population density of thirty-one persons per square kilometer is twice as high as the all-union level. In the heavily mined southwestern section of the Kemerovo oblast, the fertile layer of topsoil that could be used to restore the thousands of acres of coalfields to agricultural production has been largely destroyed, and experts estimate that 38 percent of the fields will require a long period of recultivation.[92] The Novosibirsk Science Research Sanitation Institute has estimated that the accumulation of dust, soot, and gas in the air over Novokuznetsk has reduced flow of solar radiation by 40 percent or more.[93] The combination of demographic and industrial pressures has strained an already fragile ecological support system, and scientists have stressed the need to deter-

mine the damage inflicted on the environment on the basis of losses resulting from "the incapacitation of the population due to unsatisfactory
ecological and hygienic conditions."[94]

The Ukraine has been a special victim of environmental degradation.
Scientists have warned of the dangers of pesticides as regards human health
and agricultural run-off.[95] In 1984, one of the worst ecological disasters in
the history of the republic occurred when a dike containing 4.5 million
cubic meters of potassium waste ruptured near Lvov and poured a mass of
liquid for a distance of five hundred kilometers into the Dniester River.
Large portions of the population had to be evacuated, while fish and
vegetation were destroyed and water systems polluted.[96] In 1986 came the
Chernobyl nuclear catastrophe with its tragic and unknown consequences
for human and animal life, water, vegetation, and soil.

In Yugoslavia, systematic information gathering on the cost of pollution
to cities and regions is only just beginning. However, some basic facts are
known. Eighty percent of the agricultural land is eroded, and 7 percent
"excessively" eroded. Croatia hosts about 56.5 million tourists annually,
most of these crowded onto the Adriatic coast, creating a temporary
population density similar to that of the United Kingdom or West Germany. Most of Yugoslavia's river systems classify below three on the six
basic pollutant measures, and all but one have one pollutant classified as
"beyond classification."[97] Too rapid urbanization is destroying the quality
of life in the large cities. Dr. Srečan Mitrović of the Federal Social Planning
Board estimates that 10 percent of the population in the five largest cities
of Yugoslavia suffer from bronchitis and require treatment. Using the 1971
census as his basis for calculation, Dr. Mitrović interprets this figure to
mean that some 210,400 individuals receive medical care for some respiratory illness at a minimum cost of 16,000 dinars per person, or an annual
cost to the state of almost 3.4 billion dinars. One of the causes of respiratory illness is the automobile. Dr. Mitrović equates five hundred personal
cars to the carrying capacity of ten buses or one metro. Reasoning in these
terms, Dr. Mitrović believes that the immediate high costs of urban environmental protection can be offset at least partially by a short-run decrease
in yearly payments to health care (in 1980, 13 percent of the national
income was spent on public services) and in the long term by an increasingly smaller share of contributions to health care and improvements in
the quality of life.[98]

The social benefits resulting from reduced pollution are of course directly related to the costs: less environmental degradation, lower health care costs, less crowding of medical facilities, improved urban environments, and better nutrition through less toxic food. In this area as well, Soviet and Yugoslav experts have been active. Soviet researchers are working on models to calculate the incremental benefits resulting from incremental increases in pollution control. One of the most sophisticated of these was developed by R. L. Raiatskas and V. P. Sutkaitis.[99] (See chapter 6.) Such research is indicative of the importance party and government leaders are beginning to attach to the cost-benefit factor in the environment-economic-social equation.

The individual benefits accruing to regional officials from environmental vigilance are less obvious. Clearly, economic success promotes personal and regional prestige the most. Negotiations over regional plan targets focus on economic projects and new investments, not pollution control. In the USSR, there is severe interrepublican competition for central investment funds for resource and industrial development: for Siberian coal versus Donbas coal, for agricultural development in Siberia or in Central Asia, for investment in old industrial regions with aging plants as opposed to new plants in Central Asia with its large population. Should development be directed toward easily transportable energy sources and materials requiring no processing that can be immediately used in the west, or toward the creation of a more independent economic entity in the east?[100] There is little in this competition that speaks of environmental protection. In Yugoslavia, the selection of plan priorities is a highly sensitive bargaining process between the republics and industry.[101] Industries are not interested in investing in unprofitable ventures, including environmental projects. Bonuses and recognition in both countries come from showing economic growth at home.

The environmental factor in regional and municipal thinking would seem to become critical only when it becomes visible in social costs or becomes a weapon in the competition for national ascendency. An Armenian republican official may appropriately show solidarity with his nation by deploring the classification of the republic on an all-union scale as a "zone of high potential for atmospheric pollution."[102] There is an even greater personal (political) benefit to be derived from the promotion of environmental issues associated with the national culture: witness Kunyaev's stance in Alma-

Ata. The list of the peripheral republics' demands for environmental protection for their national landmarks is ever increasing: Lake Sevan in Armenia, Lake Issyk-Kul' in Kirgizia, Kissyl Kum Desert in Kazakhstan, the Kara Deg Volcano in the Ukraine.[103] In Yugoslavia, Serbia's indignation over the level of pollution in the Sava River illustrates how an environmental grievance in the hydra can be used to promote public solidarity with a republican leadership. In each system, officials evidently believe they stand to gain more than they lose in personal prestige when they can transform an environmental matter into a national crusade.

In both countries, the relation of local officials to environmental issues is more direct than that of their republican superiors. Since local officials are required by law to bring polluters to punishment and to improve their community's quality of life, the community has the right to make demands in these areas. We may only imagine the demands made on local officials in those communities affected by radioactive fallout from Chernobyl. In Bratsk, air pollution from the city's giant pulp and aluminum mills, the largest in the USSR, forced the city to resettle two entire residential areas at a cost of 50 million rubles per resettlement.[104] A *Pravda* correspondent gave a lurid description of a "thick black plume" hanging over the highway between Ulan-ude and Irkutsk in central Siberia and cited 1,600 uncontrolled sources of air pollution in Chita Province alone. Motor vehicle emission was described as the second major contributor to a situation which the windless Arctic weather for many months of the year had made that much worse.[105] At election time, voters may send mandates to the deputies requesting action on problems that concern them. A review of published mandates in Leningrad from 1970 to 1980 found that a surprising number of them addressed environmental matters: the improvement of a park, the planting of flowers, the preservation of trees. In Yugoslavia, residents in Subotica and Sarajevo and on Vir Island pressured their local governments to take proenvironmental action. Health officers in Zagreb, Ljubljana, and Belgrade have had to answer innumerable complaints about air pollution, data on which are published daily in the newspapers.

Even though neither the Soviet nor Yugoslav local officials are freely elected, they nonetheless represent a constituency. They alone see the consequences of pollution, yet must deal realistically with local polluting enterprises. They must also be practical in interpreting the financial limitations imposed upon them. Caught between these two millstones, local leaders in both countries must be prudent in their response to a local environmental problem. To clash with industry is to threaten economic development, and their own careers. To fail to prosecute or to insist on a necessary environmental action can result in a public health catastrophe that might also prove fatal to their future.

Strategies

Given the severe structural restraints, the Soviet territorial administrations, like the environmental agencies, have chosen strategies based on the regulatory principle. The lower organs have attempted to modify existing regulations by manipulating the political and communication networks. In Yugoslavia, the more independent position of the territorial administrations has encouraged the development of strategies appropriate between equals.

Policy input. Since the 1965 recentralization of economic decisionmaking, the Soviet republics are no longer direct participants in the basic environmental decisions. Their changed circumstances have led them to develop strategies to retain control over their internal organization through the tightening up of internal controls and the manipulation of their external environment.

During the seventies and early eighties, many of the republics adopted stricter and/or more comprehensive regulations in those environmental areas that were most critical to them. In 1979, Estonia decided to put 10 percent of its land area into its state nature conservation program, more than doubling the size of the land area in the program at the beginning of the decade.[106] Armenia,[107] Lithuania,[108] Kazakhstan,[109] Latvia,[110] and Georgia[111] all passed "additional measures" aimed at tightening up the enforcement of regulations. Latvia, for example, changed the wording of its Criminal Code regarding criminal liability for water and air pollution. Formerly, an enterprise or organization was liable if pollution had occurred under specific conditions such as dumping or runoff of untreated water. The current wording stipulates criminal liability if it can be shown that pollution could or has occurred through any action of the polluter, regardless of the pollution source.

Another strategy has been the use of republican environmental committees to coordinate and supervise the implementation of republican environmental regulations. More republics appear to be turning to the committee system, and the RSFSR is now considering following the example of the peripheral republics and setting up a committee of its own. The Russian Republic is further weighing the advantages of drawing up one republican-wide environmental protection plan to counteract the lack of coordination in republican environmental planning caused by the branch ministries' control of the planning process.[112]

The republics may also turn to the mass media to attract national attention. Lake Issyk-Kul' is one example. In Kazakhstan, the press has been particularly energetic in publicizing pollution problems within the republic, particularly air pollution over Alma-Ata and the mining district of Ekibastuz and the degradation of Kazak rivers. Not that press reports reveal all the details. Ekibastuz and the Donbas coal region may well be the most polluted areas of the Soviet Union.[113] One article cited the Ekibastuz Territorial Industrial Complex as the major polluter. According to the writer, 45 percent of the burned fuel escaping from the Complex's stacks entered the atmosphere as dust and "poisonous fumes, creating a considerable local health hazard."[114] However, the reader is not told the nature of the health hazard, its extent, or the number of persons affected. The republics can also use the press to hide the extent of pollution. An article on Ekibastuz published in the same paper a month and a half earlier makes no mention of air pollution and praises the miners for their high productivity.[115] But the prime case is Estonia, where officials of the government have utilized press interviews and public speeches deliberately to cover up the republic's environmental difficulties.[116] When the Estonian vice-minister for the environment was interviewed by the Swedish press in 1980, he did not deny the problem caused by phosphorus and oil shale mining, but chose to gloss over it and concentrate on the republic's record in the area of wild animal and fish conservation![117]

Perhaps the most effective input strategy is to activate the party network. Once again, Kazakhstan is a case in point. One could argue that the republic's relatively frank publication of negative environmental information may be directly linked to republican party influence at the top echelons of the Soviet leadership. To give added political clout to an environmental regulation, the republican councils of ministers, like the Georgian and Armenian councils in 1979,[118] secure the participation of the republican party central committee and pass a joint resolution. As this chapter has argued, the party's horizontal intervention either to help or hinder a specific republican environmental action may be vital to the success of a republic's environmental protection effort.

Local leaders obtain their most important environmental objectives through recourse to the same strategies. This study has presented ample evidence of an increasing tendency for local officials, like their republican counterparts, to use the press to publicize local environmental problems: auto and air pollution in Erevan, air pollution in Alma-Ata, pollution of rivers in the Urals, or air pollution in Siberian cities. Just as in the republics, the information disseminated may be both positive or negative, depending upon the desired objective. Leningrad was successful in exploiting its party connections to obtain the necessary funding to build the dam in the Gulf of Finland. Significantly, approval of the dam project was in the form of a joint decree by the CPSU CC and the USSR Council of Ministers.[119] The input of the environmental committees in reviewing development projects should also not be overlooked. That the work of the local environmental committees in the Baikal area was recently singled out for national recognition suggests that someone in the central leadership may be following the performance of these organs closely. The *Izvestiia* report particularly stressed the "support" given to the committee in its promotion of environmental goals by local party organs and officials, especially the district party committee (*raikom*) first secretary.[120]

The relation between an environmental issue, the publication of information about it, and the politics leading to publication is an area where much research has yet to be done. This chapter insists that the relation is critical to effective environmental action at both the republican and local levels, that the territorial administrations recognize it as such, and that they have deliberately designed strategies to exploit it for their own goals, whether these be proenvironmental or not. Given party control over the mass media, one can only assume that extensive media exposure of a pollution problem in a given locality reflects party intervention. The culprit is not always the central ministry. We have cited numerous examples where local officials were also publicly exposed. The party may choose to intervene against the local administration, or, as in Estonia, not to intervene at all. An accurate assessment of republican and local input into environmental decisionmaking requires more knowledge than we now have about the conditions of party intervention in a local environmental issue and the politics behind the airing of the issue in the press.

In Yugoslavia, the republics *are* the legislators. Each passes laws in the areas of greatest importance to it or agrees to abide by corresponding federal or, in the case of the autonomous provinces, republican legislation. In the Yugoslav hydra, the collective decisionmaking process seems to enhance the propensity of semiautonomous bureaucracies to dissipate energies and deflect goals.[121] Each republic jealously guards its exclusive jurisdictional prerogatives at the expense of standardization of methodology and cooperation in environmental problem-solving. We have described one attempt to surmount legislative compartmentalization in the formation of the League of siz-a for Water Management. However, the establishment of an organization and its ability to carry out concrete activities are two very different operations. One example will suffice.

In 1977, a federal law on standardization in the areas of planning and construction was passed. The 1980–1985 Social Plan called for implementation of the law through the development of nationwide standards in environmental methodology and permissible levels of pollution. At the present writing, these standards are only in the discussion stage. The slowness in the adoption of environmental standards may stem from republican caution. Economics is a prime consideration. Slovenia has been a leader in urging stricter standards, particularly as regards extending credit to new industrial development without including adequate pollution control measures in the project design.[122] Many republics prefer less costly development with a minimum of environmental controls. In the process of its development, Kosovo has exercised virtually no control over pollution in the development of its waterways. Given the requirement for consensus, standardization is likely to tend toward a minimum rather than a maximum value. The higher value will rouse the opposition of the poorer republics against the rich, which can "afford the luxury" of environmental controls. On their part, the richer republics have shown increasing reluctance to contribute more money to the development of the poorer republics, which as was shown above constitutes a substantial portion of their contributions to the federal budget and from which, if Kosovo is any example, they believe they have derived little benefit. Under the existing conditions of self-management, the collective effort to standardize environmental methodology, technology, and norms has become transformed from an objective technological problem into a highly volatile political issue.[123]

Second, collective decisionmaking by autonomous political entities engenders a marked reluctance to commit one's own resources for an uncertain venture. The Sava and Neretva river agreements are examples where common interest in principle exists, but where the uncertainty of the implementation process discourages the signatory republics from venturing the resources necessary to carry out the agreement. It is far easier to commit oneself to a symbolic proposal than to put into operation a program demanding the contribution of financial and material means from one's own pocket. The Una River agreement is a case where negotiations broke down because of the actors' refusal to venture an uncertain future.

Third, the risks involved in collective decisionmaking by semiautonomous units encourage the deflection of goals from the main purpose. Once again, the Sava River agreement is instructive. No doubt the Serbian press played up the pollution of Belgrade's water supply and the fact that the source of pollution manifestly lay upstream. But the real issue was political, not environmental. The ease with which the republics have entered into some environmental agreements and the slowness with which these have been implemented should not be taken as a criticism of self-management per se. As Bardach notes, agreeing first and implementing later constitute standard administrative behavior.[124] Stojanović stresses the importance of timing and picking one's partners during negotiations on the five-year plan.[125] Because each republic is in control of its own resources, it must adopt a strategy of caution and remain the "odd man out" until it can be assured that commitment will benefit all its interests: political, economic, and social, as well as environmental.

Communes must also commit their own resources. However, since they are secondary rather than primary decisionmakers, they must adjust their strategies to conform to both vertical and horizontal realities. As the adoption of the Ohrid land-use plan illustrates, one strategy to reduce future uncertainty is to mobilize and commit external resources: republican, federal, and, where possible, international. A second specifies the extent of local resource commitment. Given the intensity of outside pressure, the towns around the lake knew that they would eventually have to agree. To avoid overcommitment, they had the amount of resources demanded of them spelled out. The Ohrid plan, however, also bears the "symbolic" regulatory aspects of the Sava and Neretva agreements. The first stage alone has been initiated, while the others have merely been approved in principle. Even the land-use plan may turn out to be without real substance. The towns have already begun to "revise" it by permitting subdivisions of land into smaller parcels than were originally stipulated for second home development.

Finally, successful opštini projects, like the draining of Lake Palić and the construction of the water treatment system at Sarajevo prior to the 1984 Winter Olympics, indicate that towns may prefer one-shot *akcije* (actions) to long-term schemes. Commitment is easier to secure when its termination date is known. The Una River agreement compelled the opštini to make a permanent and hence indefinite commitment with regard to their economic future. Furthermore, unlike the Ohrid plan, there was no second or third agreement stage in which negotiation, bargaining, and changes would be possible. A "wild river" ruled out economic development, and it was not clear that tourism could provide the requisite opstini income. In short, when making an environmental decision, both the republican and local governments prefer regulations which relativize commitment and leave them alternative options or loopholes.

The implementation phase. In both countries, the strategies of implementation carry over from those of the policy input phase. In the Soviet Union, we have seen how republics (Kirgizia), regions (Siberia), and municipalities (Leningrad and Moscow) play on the exclusivity of their particular resources to attract implementation funds. The lower territorial units may also utilize party contacts (Romanov and Kunyaev) for the same purpose. When they wish to, they may publicize the failures of industry to comply with the law or upbraid environmental officials for their laxity in enforcing the law. They may publish glowing pictures of model regions as did the local party apparat of Kemerovo oblast.[126] Or they may fault their own citizens for improper use of environmental resources, as the Central Asian republics have faulted the way in which local farmers and herdmen have used the irrigation system.[127] Since implementation is the continuation of interbureaucracy negotiation, the "party card," natural resource assets, nationalism,[128] and mass media access may be traded off against demands for enforcement or laxity in carrying out the regulatory mandate. But nationalism, as we have seen, is an uncertain strategy, which pays off for some republics (Kirgizia) and not for others (Armenia, Estonia). In Georgia, the enterprises under the central branch ministries continue to pour raw sewage into the Black Sea, in defiance of all regulations and official protest.[129]

In Yugoslavia, implementation is a continuation of the negotiation process initiated by legislation or original compact. The strategies of implementation are virtually identical to those of the policy input stage except that regulation is no longer a matter of principle, but the commitment of real resources. Under these conditions, delaying strategies become particularly important. Local communities may pass more regulations: witness the 800 regulations governing pollution of the Sava, air pollution regulations in Skopje, and the multiple regulations protecting the Adriatic. Or they may put off having to make an unpalatable decision by calling for more consultants and more studies, as did the town outside of Belgrade with the polluting cement plant. Finally, a local administration may adopt a strategy of nonaction, as appears to be the case in Rijeka, which continues to pour its untreated sewage into the Adriatic. The application of republican, federal, or international pressure to force the communities to the appropriate environmental action has only been partially successful. Ohrid is one example; the agreement on the protection of the Adriatic, another. Although the coastal communities have adopted an environmental protection plan that divides the Adriatic coast into three administrative zones and provides for a host of pollution control measures, local communities vary in the severity with which they choose to adhere to the regulations, and pollution increases.[130]

Conclusion

In the Soviet Union, territorial administrations become the victims of the branch decisionmaking taking place at the top of the hierarchy where the special relationship between the party leadership and industry assigns environmental considerations a backseat. To overcome their disadvantage, the lower territorial units attempt to manipulate that part of the regulatory process under their jurisdiction. Their success has been relative to their ability to exploit indigenous economic, environmental, and political assets. In Yugoslavia, by contrast, the republican and opstini administrations are their own environmental victims. While the Yugoslav territorial administrations have a somewhat greater margin of liberty in resource allocation than their Soviet counterparts, this chapter has shown that there is a marked reluctance on the part of the republics and opstini to undertake environmental objectives, because economic decisions are central to the maintenance of party supremacy.

In the last analysis, the overriding structural constraint on the ability of the territorial administrations in both countries to develop and implement effective environmental policies is the special relationship of the single party with the economy. In the centipede, the territorial administrations become secondary institutions like the environmental agencies, deriving their freedom of action from the regulatory principle, which they can only manipulate within the constraints of central party and ministerial dominance. In the hydra, the republics exploit the regulatory principle to strengthen and expand their already substantial structural independence. There is a temptation to believe that Yugoslav environmental regulation is more symbolic than real. Under current conditions of self-management, the existence of autonomous territorial entities must be considered more of an environmental liability than the domination of the Soviet environmental policy process by the central party and ministerial organs. If the choice is to control pollution by regulation and not by economic incentive, some standardization in terms of regulation and enforcement is necessary, as a way of compelling the various Yugoslav territorial units to uphold their own laws and agreements.

6

The Experts

With the specialized elites[1] we come to the first group of those labeled "outsiders" in chapter 1. In one sense, this label is misleading. The relationship of the specialists to the policymakers in communist one-party systems differs little from that of Western professionals to their governments. Both have won their privileged advisory position through the application of the regulatory principle. In no country do experts actually make the environmental policy decisions, but in every country they play a key role in the formulation of policy options. In this advisory capacity, experts are at one and the same time "outsiders" privy to the councils of the decisionmakers and "insiders" responsible for providing the scientific and technical knowhow without which environmental policy cannot be made.

Structural and Regulatory Constraints

Soviet and Yugoslav experts share the same structural relation to policymaking as their Western colleagues in that virtually all are employees working through large bureaucracies. The constraints on Soviet and Yugoslav experts, therefore, may be expected to be similar to those on Western environmental specialists. In a provocative article, Schnaiberg identifies the chief among these: the necessity for expertise in environmental solutions, the continued fragmented social organization of science resulting in a division between scientific labor and power, and the control of access to communication.[2] These constraints are magnified by the structural characteristics of the centipede and hydra one-party systems.

The necessity for expertise in environmental solutions. Experts play a role in policymaking in direct proportion to a society's level of modernization.[3] Expertise alone is able to reduce the uncertainty generated by the acceleration of the rate of social and economic change when technology is applied to society.[4] Wolchik's research substantiates the ever-increasing importance Soviet and East European scholars attribute to the harnessing of what the Soviets have termed the "scientific-technological revolution" (STR) to economic development.[5] The interdisciplinary team appointed in the early 1960s by the Czechoslovak Communist party to study the relation of the STR to Czechoslovakia's economic future concluded that expert knowledge was essential for rational policymaking and called for measures to promote the development of specialized expert cadres.[6] From the Brezhnev era to the present, the economic strategy of the Soviet leadership has been to combine the theoretically superior advantages of the Soviet centralized planning system with the best aspects of the STR.[7] In the words of Mijet Suković, the vice-president of Yugoslavia's Federal Chamber, "Without science, Yugoslavia has no future."[8]

The utility of experts in environmental problem-solving appears to have greater acceptance among decisionmakers everywhere than in other issue areas,[9] possibly because environmental issues are such newcomers to the political scene. Articles 16 and 17 of the 1977 Soviet Constitution make specific reference to the role of science in environmental control. In both the Soviet Union and Yugoslavia, the succession of legal and administrative attempts to improve environmental protection suggests that the leaders are less dogmatic and more open in their approach to environmental management options than in their approach to purely economic questions where official orthodoxy has ruled. During the last two decades the Soviet Union has created a core of environmental scientists and experts in related fields to administer and advise on environmental topics. Nolting and Feshbach estimate the percent of Soviet environmental natural scientists relative to the total number of scientists employed in research and development to be 3.1 percent, or slightly higher than the share of American environmental scientists among the total number.[10] In Yugoslavia, graduated scientists in natural science and mathematics employed in the economy made up almost 16 percent of the total number of employed scientists in 1980, while natural science and mathematic research organizations represented close to 12 percent of the total. Between 1954 and 1980 Yugoslavia's specialized schools graduated a total of 37,324 specialists in agriculture, forestry, animal husbandry, and food production.[11] While these figures do not indicate how many were actually employed in environmentally related research, it should be noted that research workers in the natural sciences and mathematics constitute the largest proportion of research workers outside of those in the technical sciences (which represented over 50 percent of all research scientists). Both countries, therefore, share the Western experience of having created a nucleus of specialists to provide expertise in a subject matter where twenty years ago a scientific discipline per se hardly existed and where few social scientists were working.

Finally, as elsewhere in the industrialized world, the last two decades have seen the environment move onto the public agenda, largely as a result of the findings of scientists. In the Soviet Union, the seminal environmental debate in the mass media over the future of Lake Baikal was generated and carried forward by scientists.[12] At about the same time, scientific concern over the mounting evidence of pollution, specialist participation at the Stockholm Conference, and the growth of the American environmental movement created a political climate in Yugoslavia favorable to the consideration of environmental problems. The mid-seventies saw the establishment of the environmental advisory committees attached to the executive at all levels of government. In 1976, the Federal Council for the Protection and the Improvement of the Environment brought out the first issue of *Čovek i životna sredina* (Man and the Environment), a scientific journal devoted exclusively to environmental issues. As in the West, environmental issues became the focus in both countries of public discussion on the relationship between science, public policy, and the quality of life.

At the present time, then, Soviet and Yugoslav environmental experts find themselves in a particularly advantageous position to influence the politics of environmental management. They do so from the vantage points of specialized institutes set up for the purpose of investigating specific environmental issues, whence they are called upon for advice and consultation concerning policy proposals and for research and analysis during policy implementation.

The fragmented organization of environmental expertise. The fragmented

215

social organization of scientific study is not unique to one-party systems. In the United States, the compartmentalization of science has been reinforced by the flow of funding to technology production research in scientific areas that have specific industrial applications.[13] The Soviet Union and Yugoslavia are experiencing similar and perhaps more severe difficulties due to the distinctive organization of science in the two countries.

In the Soviet Union, environmental expertise is organized under specific central institutions and performed by specially authorized organs (see chapter 3). Expertise in drafting long-term directives for environmental protection and rational resource use and annual economic and social plans is located in the lead environmental control organs: Goskomgidromet, Minvodkhoz, the State Agro-Industrial Committee, and the Ministry of Geology. Expertise in environmental planning on a territorial basis is vested in Gosplan and its regional subdivisions, the republican council of ministers, and the planning committees of the local soviets and local environmental agents in the cities and large industrial centers.[14]

Expertise in urban planning and construction design for cities and other large population centers is provided by the planning and construction design research organs of Gosstroi and the relevant research institutes of air, water, and other health-related problems of the USSR and union republics' ministries of health. Where the design involves a particular piece of equipment, the expertise is provided by the designated expert agency of the appropriate ministry. Expertise for large-scale economic projects that result in considerable transformation of the environment and have substantial environmental impact is the province of GKNT and, in particular, its interbranch Scientific Technical Council for Comprehensive Problems on Environmental Protection and Rational Resource Use. The 1972 joint resolution on strengthening environmental protection requires that both these organs work closely with the USSR Academy of Sciences and its research institutes.[15]

The Ministry of Public Health provides expertise comparable to the United States Food and Drug Administration and Consumer Products Safety Administration. The ministry is responsible for testing new types of raw materials, chemicals to be used in industry, and all consumer products. The testing of chemicals, including fertilizers, pesticides, and material to be used in agriculture and forestry is the function of Minzdrav, the State

Agro-Industrial Committee, and Gosleskhoz. To speed up the process of evaluating test results, the three agencies have set up a special expert inter-branch committee that decides on whether a product is to be used.[16] Expertise on air pollution control equipment is delegated to the State Institute of Scrubber Installations of Minkhimmash, while the Ministry of Health, Minvodkhoz, and Minrybkhoz provide the expertise on water pollution control. The last two ministries are also the designated experts on hydraulic engineering. Agricultural research is now organized under the State Agro-Industrial Committee and its institutes at the all-union and union-republic level. The Committee likewise administers the All-Union Scientific Research Institute for Nature Protection and Conservation.

The above review suggests three fundamental characteristics of the centipede variant of science fragmentation. The first is the proliferation of expert organizations. The 1972 and 1978 resolutions on improving and strengthening environmental protection in the Soviet Union identify sixteen central ministries and agencies responsible for expertise in air pollution control, twenty-one in water pollution control, fourteen in land use and soil conservation, five for forests, and four for protected land (see table 2.2). The second characteristic is that the organs identified are the authorized experts in that particular field. For example, the All-Union Scientific Research Institute for Nature Protection and Conservation prepared the draft of the 1980 law on the protection of wild animals and made the decisions on which animals would receive legal protection. Expert institutes tend to be highly specialized and narrow, with interdisciplinary expertise rare except at the higher levels of government in committees such as the environmental protection and resource use committee attached to GKNT.

The third characteristic is the essential rigidity of expert organizations. All research and the rendering of expert opinion are performed according to plan. It is difficult officially to develop or obtain an expert opinion on a given problem if that answer must be given immediately. Experts, like everyone else, have their quotas. A particular problem must be fitted into their general plan of work, which in turn must be approved by the supervisor. An expert may have his plan of work amended, but amendment also requires approval, and unless the inserted project has priority, as the author discovered, its chances of getting accomplished are less likely than those of the original plan. When the only mechanism for changing equipment, methodology, or inquiry midstream is a modification of the plan, expert results can be slow, or, as has been repeatedly pointed out in the Soviet press, entirely inappropriate to the needs of the agency that is the institute's superior or principal contractor.

The system has its advantages and disadvantages in terms of the seriousness with which expert opinion is taken by the decisionmakers. On the one hand, the opinion of the legally designated institute represents *the* expert opinion. Formal channels for competing opinions are limited, although there may be other expert sources in the universities and the Academy of Sciences. In 1965, a reform of research and development (R&D) aimed to do away with research overlap by putting GKNT in charge of all R&D, thereby reducing the potential for expert competition.[17] The assignment of official status coupled with the traditional Russian respect for science probably cloaks the Soviet expert with more authority than his counterpart in the United States, where expert competition is a way of life. Moreover, because the policymaking system is largely bureaucratic, the Soviet expert does not have to consider public opinion in the framing of his advice. Most important, in legitimizing an institute's research, the enabling regulation authorizes the institute's superior to allocate the resources necessary for the conduct of the research program. In effect, the regulatory principle makes the Soviet expert's research realizable.

The disadvantage is that the separation of scientific work and power is reinforced. The 1965 reform made control over the direction of scientific research the legal monopoly of the central party and government organs and concentrated this control in the hands of the most powerful of these institutions: the military-industrial ministries and the high technology and energy sectors. The reform further encouraged each ministry or agency to set up its own research organs to provide the expertise for its immediate particular needs. Since every expert organ is responsible for a specific scientific or technological area within a particular ministry or organization, its research strategy is to investigate the problem under consideration from the narrow viewpoint of its superior agency. Five years after the Ministry of Coal Industry was authorized to establish an institute to investigate a clean coal-conversion process, it still had not started research. Academy scientists feared that what research it finally produced would be oriented purely toward the interests of the coal ministry.[18] Attempts to apply pure research gains to production by cross-fertilization from the Academy of Sciences into the branch ministries have also run aground. Ministries have persisted in trying to subordinate the Academy design bureaus to ministerial jurisdiction.[19] In the view of the well-known economist Pavel Oldak, the distribution of problems among many institutions has resulted "in short-sighted answers that lack comprehensive solutions."[20] Under the eyes of his bureaucratic superior, the expert is obliged to concern himself with a narrow subject matter at the expense of a more global approach.

Opportunities for cross-disciplinary fertilization, however, do exist. Primary among these are the *aktivs*, conferences or roundtable discussions organized by the Academy of Sciences, central and republican ministries and agencies, or the periodicals. These meetings serve to bring together the expert *obshchestvennost'* (community) in a particular field to discuss policy issues and offer policy recommendations.[21] The seminal environmental meeting of this kind was the *Voprosy filosofii* roundtable discussion in 1971 prior to the Stockholm Conference, which in effect legitimized public debate on environmental degradation in the Soviet Union and opened the way for discussion of suitable remedies. Another important environmental conference organized by the organ of the Soviet writers' organization, *Novy mir*, in 1982 brought together the community of writers and scientists particularly interested in Siberia and raised important ecological questions relative to Siberian development (see chapter 5). In 1980, the author was in Leningrad during a conference organized by the USSR Ministry of Education on teaching about the environment in higher education. The conference followed an earlier all-union conference held in Tbilisi on the general organization of environmental education in the Soviet school system.

These conferences are often neither party-sponsored nor generated and thus represent meetings of colleagues on a policy issue of common interest.[22] However, the meetings are managed by the higher administration of the organizing agency, which determines the tone and direction of the conference, and attendance is by invitation only. As a result, the deliberations of the conference tend to represent the concerns and opinions of the leaders in a particular field rather than the free-ranging speculations of all members of that scientific community. The Soviet conference system thus reinforces the hierarchical bias of Soviet bureaucratic organization, thereby

Table 6.1 Survey of Research Themes and Projects, SFRY

Project Themes	Total	Bosnia-Herzegovina	Croatia	Macedonia
Population, process of urbanization	43	6	19	
Production and industrial processes	22	1	8	
Land use and regional development	18		2	
National defense	3	1		
Agricultural land	13	2	1	
Forests, plants, animal world	21	3	8	
Water	49	1	20	2
Air	30	8	13	
Secondary raw materials and waste	10	1	2	
Nature areas and wonders	18		5	
Historical entities and monuments	7		3	
Urban and rural settlements	22	1	3	1
Economic areas and objects	2		2	
Housing	7			
Urban infrastructure	8	1	1	
Recreation and leisure	6		1	
Infrastructure	11	1	3	
Monitoring of condition of information system	12		4	
Legislation	9		2	
Planning	11		1	1
Investment, economic measures	5		1	
Education	1		1	
Total	328	26	100	4

Source: P. 138 of source cited in table 3.1.

enhancing the authority of the lead expert, with its interdisciplinary character going only so far as the organizing bureaucracy sees fit. The separation of scientific labor and power noted by Schnaiberg in the U.S. organization of science thus appears structurally more fundamental to the Soviet system, where resource allocation and determination of research orientation are controlled by the center and distributed through the ministerial legs of the centipede.

In Yugoslavia, the main constraints upon expert influence derive from the country's decentralized administrative structure and self-management organization. Expertise is located in the federal, republican, and municipal

| Montenegro | Slovenia | Serbia | | | | Federal organs |
		total	proper	Kosovo	Vojvodina	
	12	6	4	1	1	
	8	5	2	3		
	13	2	2			1
	2	2	2			
1	2	7	5	1	1	
	5	5	4		1	
2	13	11	10		1	
1	6	2	2			
1	6					
1	7	4	3		1	1
	2	2	1		1	
	7	10	10			
		6	3	3		
	3	3	3			
	3	1	1			1
	6	1	1			
	3	2			2	3
		6	6			1
	7	2	2			
	2	2	2			
6	105	79	63	8	8	7

institutes attached to a government department, such as the institutes of public health, the institutes funded through the SIZ, particularly the SIZ for science, or the self-management institutes like the Jaroslav Černi Water Resources Institute and the institutes for urbanism, planning, and environmental protection. In both instances, there is a direct relation between the provision of environmental expertise and specific community or industrial requests. The distribution of environmental research by subject matter and republic given in table 6.1 provides a good demonstration of this relationship. Not surprisingly, by far the largest number of research projects are in those areas where environmental degradation has been most visible, such as urban development, water, and air, and these projects have been undertaken in the most industrialized republics. In 1978, there were twenty investigations relating to water pollution in progress in Croatia, thirteen in Slovenia, and eleven in Serbia. There were thirteen studies on air pollution in Croatia, six in Slovenia, and two in Serbia. By contrast, Serbia and Slovenia had funded more research on urban and rural settlements and agricultural land development than had Croatia. Macedonia was engaged in only two research projects on water and none on air, while Bosnia-Herzegovina had eight ongoing studies of air pollution and only one on water. It is to be expected that research on construction design and industrial processes would hold a significant place in the country's research effort, but it is noteworthy that research on forests, plants, and the animal world occupies a strong secondary position.

The distribution of projects reflects the fact that scientific enterprises, like their economic counterparts, must earn money to pay operating expenses and salaries. As has been seen, local funds from industrial and income taxes go only to the support of basic public services administered by the responsible SIZ. While many environmental questions are health-related and fall under the health SIZ, most are excluded from the possibility of public funding except as the project might come under the SIZ for science and/or education. The federal water and forest funds derived from taxes and fines (see chapter 5) are expended on necessary public works projects, such as reforestation, not on research. Thus, what public monies are received by expert institutes must be supplemented by the sale of their services to industry, agriculture, or the local economy. The resulting "job-oriented" research approach contrasts sharply with the more elaborate structure of theoretical and applied research programs produced by the consultation of GKNT with the central ministries in the USSR. In Yugoslavia, there is a direct link between the research institute that sells its services and the client, which may be an enterprise or government institution. The budget for the year is drawn up on the basis of monies paid in from the sale of services. A few examples will provide an illustration of this relationship.

The Republican Institute for Environmental Protection of Serbia is a government agency divided into two organizations. The first is concerned with nature conservation, the second with the human environment.[23] Its function as mandated by law is to serve as consultant to local government in the latter's development of economic and territorial land-use plans. The institute is also under contract from the government of Serbia for the development of a territorial plan for the whole of Serbia.[24] The Belgrade Municipal Institute of Public Health works mainly for the city of Belgrade in such areas as hygiene in schools,[25] applied research in environmental noise, and worker hygiene in the food industry. However, individual enterprises and factories do come to them with projects, which the institute will contract to do and for which it will be paid.[26] The Institute of Hygiene and Epidemiology of the Council for the Human Environment and Territorial Management of the Executive Council of the Government of Serbia is under contract with the Serbian SIZ for Social Insurance to develop noise norms and measurement standards for the whole of Serbia. It is also under contract with the Serbian government for an ongoing study of the daily consumption of pesticides in food, a topic that has become a major environmental concern.[27]

Among the self-managing institutes, the Jaroslav Černi Institute has gained the reputation of being among the most competent in the area of water resource management. The institute contracts primarily for applied research in water resource engineering, particularly as it relates to a regional or local water resource problem. Such research is at the request of the interested local government.[28] Another successful self-managing institute that receives no public financing is the Federal Institute for Urban Planning and Construction. While most of its income is derived from domestic contracts, it is expanding the number of its contracts abroad. In 1980, it completed a lengthy study of the urbanization of Libya under contract with the Libyan government.[29] SMELT of Ljubljana advertises its services as an engineering consulting firm. With offices in Belgrade, Pristina, Tripoli, and Libya, its 1980 reference list contained the names of 562 clients from every kind of industry from all over Yugoslavia, and ten clients from abroad, including Libya, India, Nepal, and Iran. All of the work performed was applied research.[30]

Of course, not all expertise is job-oriented. One has only to read the papers published by Energoprojekt and other institutes in *Čovek i životna sredina* to see the fruit of more theoretical investigation. But financial decentralization has made contracted research attractive and necessary, and it has thus encouraged applied studies as a more profitable venture. The direction of research is thus determined by the flow of funding from industry and government to projects addressing their particular concerns. Since both are controlled by the party, the ultimate determination of research priorities lies in the hands of the republican party leaders.

The advantage of the self-managed institute is that it is free to seek clients where they can be found and is not constrained to work under a hierarchical superior. The expert thus has a larger measure of professional independence than his Soviet counterpart. Greater professional autonomy, however, has not resulted in a higher degree of acceptance by party and government officials of expert opinion, because of the inherent disadvantages self-management places upon the research institute.

The primary disadvantage is money. The funding problem created and sustained by the self-management system sets limits to the areas of research that can be profitably supported and encourages borrowing of ideas and methodology from countries that are more able to afford a more comprehensive research program. While funding problems exist in all areas of Yugoslav research, they are particularly severe in the environmental area, in large part because of the systemic bias toward industry and economic development. The present economic crisis with its massive debt and domestic austerity program contributes to undermining research efforts in all but what are perceived to be the critical economic and social areas, as funds for research activities are pared down to a minimum.

In their search for funding, the institutes contract to do narrow, specific jobs for specific organizations and localities. The Yugoslav press has repeatedly faulted environmental researchers for not undertaking the kinds of research activities that will provide, for example, a comprehensive strategy for the cleanup of the Sava River basin, or a development program for the future growth of Belgrade that considers all the environmental factors.[31] In short, research in Yugoslavia appears to be as fragmented as in the Soviet Union, with the researcher concentrating on the narrow and specialized question that the contract demands to the neglect of the global problem. Perhaps even more important, the practical orientation of self-management provides few opportunities for the expansion of pure science research.

The Republic of Serbia has recognized the negative aspects of fragmentation. One solution has been the promotion of a multidisciplinary approach to environmental problem-solving. A pilot project was set up at the University of Belgrade. In existence since the mid-seventies, the Center for Multidisciplinary Studies combines pure science, applied science, and social science in a two-year graduate program. The program is organized around the investigation of twenty-one environmental subject areas and is divided about equally between subjects of general knowledge and subjects of specialized knowledge. In addition to the customary prerequisites for admission,[32] the applicant must be employed and have a recommendation from his or her institute or workplace, because the work organization helps pay the student's way. The recommendation must indicate the student's individual interest, the organization's interest in having the student apply (what specific environmental problem does it want investigated?), and the social interest the student's admission will serve when he or she works at the center on the problem of concern to the work organization. If the work organization cannot pay for the student's entire course of study, additional financing may be obtained from the Program for Scientific Investigation of the Serbian Council for Environmental Protection and Territorial Management. The work organizations are expected to provide physical facilities, equipment, and materials to enable the student to study the problem that brought him to the center.

The aim of the center's administration is to change the prevailing narrow professional view of young scientists to a broader approach. The instructional method is multidisciplinary, intended to demonstrate that nature is a unit. Traditional subjects like physics, chemistry, or engineering are not taught individually, but are applied together to the study of one environmental area, such as air or water. During the last year of study, the students are divided into research teams and assigned to investigate a problem selected from the list of those proposed by the sponsoring institutions. A biologist, physicist, and chemist may find themselves working with a hydraulic engineer and an economist on the problem of obtaining an adequate drinking water supply for the city of Belgrade. The hope is that students will take the comprehensive method and team approach back to their work organizations, and that, if a team cannot be formed, they will ask advice from appropriate experts in the disciplines related to their projects when tackling the next work assignments.[33]

Innovative as the center's method is, it still does not solve the basic structural problems posed by self-management. In effect, the research institutes determine the research program. Equally important, the method may contribute to what is perhaps the experts' most serious problem in Yugoslavia, the party's distrust of intellectuals. Because of the direct relation between the program and needs of the sponsoring institutions, the center risks becoming the consulting partner to these organizations. While the center retains its academic autonomy in designing the general curriculum of instruction, the specialized curriculum represents the sponsors' concerns. Speculative or non-task-oriented questions are neglected in preference to solving the sponsor's problem. The center's approach thus indirectly reinforces the general tendency of party and government officials toward overreliance on and overvaluation of scientific research from outside the country, with a concomitant downgrading of domestic research achievements. Director of the Institute for Socioeconomic Research in Titograd, Dr. Bosko Gluscević, expressed the matter plainly. The country's economic crisis, he said, "was anticipated by many experts who repeatedly warned of far-reaching consequences and dangers unless an adequate policy was pursued. Such proposals were rejected or, to put it mildly, simply ignored. . . . Even now, we have deeply rooted opinion in the party apparatus that we do not need any wise people, but only obedient ones."[34]

Borrowing knowledge from abroad may seem very rational, particularly in a small country with limited resources. The experts are eager for international contacts, and examples proliferate of scientific cooperation between Yugoslavia and other countries. In 1985, there were twenty-seven environmental research projects across the country that were being undertaken jointly with the UN, OECD, and other international organizations, while the Department of Environmental Protection of the Institute for Technology of Nuclear and Other Raw Materials was carrying out a study of radioactive and other polluting emissions under a grant from the U.S. government.[35] However, Yugoslavia is a communist state. The expert's recourse to the outside for fundamental knowledge makes him susceptible to the charge of "contamination" by foreign or "capitalist" influences. At the same time, there are insufficient domestic means to produce a "socialist" science that could provide a "loyal expertise" that the party could unreservedly accept. The tension between the party and the expert community highlights the Yugoslav variant of the separation of knowledge and power. Decentralization and self-management notwithstanding, as the principal political force in the country, the party leadership in all the republics wants scientific answers to the questions it poses in terms that will reinforce its commanding position in Yugoslav society.

The two communist systems thus exhibit a somewhat different emphasis in the fragmentation of scientific labor and its separation from the sources of power. The Soviet researcher is more confined in his research organization, but his opinion appears to carry considerable weight if his institute is the officially designated expert organ for a particular problem area. The Yugoslav researcher is much freer in his research ventures. However, the need to contract out for research jobs gives a practically oriented entrepreneurial character to research that undermines the researcher's credibility with party officials, already suspicious of the intellectual's good faith and loyalty to socialism. Nevertheless, in both societies, the scientist is constrained to study what his employers deem important. And his employers demand not comprehensive solutions to environmental and economic problems but quick fixes in technological production to spur rapid economic growth.

Control over communications access. While the structure of Soviet expertise acts favorably upon the Soviet specialist's opportunities to influence environmental decisionmaking, his access to information is severely limited. In Yugoslavia, the reverse is true: the organization of expertise weakens the expert's position, but he has much less restricted access to information than his Soviet counterpart.

In the Soviet Union, data collection is delegated to specific ministries, agencies, or research organizations by central or republican government regulation and directives. The legal authorization for data collection in the environmental field is found in the fundamental health, land, water, forest, air, and wildlife management laws, and the 1972 and 1978 joint CC CPSU and USSR Council of Ministers resolutions on strengthening environmental protection. As a rule, the chief data collectors are the lead agencies in the particular environmental area: Goskomgidromet collects data on air pollution; until recently, the Ministry of Agriculture, collected soil data; and Gosleskhoz, data on environmental degradation in forests.

In practice, the division of labor is not as clear cut as it might appear in the regulations, and there is considerable overlap. As it did prior to the air pollution law, Minzdrav still collects most air pollution data, and the local section of the Ministry's Sanitary and Epidemiological Service (SES) is still relied upon as the most appropriate source for urban air pollution information.[36] Minzdrav also collects data in areas under the jurisdiction of other ministries, such as water (under the lead jurisdiction of Minvodkhoz), and pesticides (under tripartite ministerial jurisdiction, as was discussed earlier). The 1978 resolution further authorizes GKNT and the USSR Academy of Sciences to be the lead agencies in the identification of technical problems relating to pollution control. The overlap in responsibilities means the same information is stored away in all the various cubbyholes of the designated ministerial and agency bureaucracies.

As shown in chapter 4, the ministries control the flow of information in the planning process as well. Since planning takes place by the branch principle, the information generated is the basic data requested by the central planners and sent forward piecemeal by industrial sector in a form and content satisfactory to the responsible sector superiors. In 1966, the Soviets attempted to rationalize information processing by establishing an All-Union Scientific and Technical Information Center to consolidate all scientific and technical information under one roof.[37] But consolidation did not affect the bureaucracies' monopoly of the release of industrial data.

The information system imposes severe constraints upon the expert. Access to all data is on a need-to-know basis for authorized persons only, and only partial data are collected by any given economic or environmental agency. Moreover, researchers in institutes attached to ministries or other state agencies do not necessarily have access to the information collected by other subdepartments of their supervisory organizations. Public documents from one ministry are not freely available to scientists in a research organization under another ministry, and the information must be requested formally. The authorities at the top of the bureaucracies are in a position to decide what data to make public, what data to distribute among scientists, and what data to keep secret. Planning and environmental data are especially sensitive.[38] Since the international outcry over Lake Baikal, the Soviet government has preferred to restrict severely the release of environmental data, especially that pertaining to the impact of pollution on human health.[39] Even more important, much of the requisite environmental information is in the form of ministerial documents, which are not public information at all.

The problems that information censorship makes for the researcher are obvious. An inside expert in one ministry would find it difficult, if not impossible, to put together a global picture of even a localized environmental problem from the information he could obtain by virtue of his official employment position alone. In 1981 and 1983, Charter 77 dissidents in Czechoslovakia charged that little progress was being made on pollution control in that country precisely because of government restrictions on data dissemination.[40] This is not to say that no data comes into the public domain. On the contrary, over the past ten years there has been a marked increase in environmental reporting in the USSR, as the sources for this study testify. Much of the published scientific work comes from specialists in the "environmental institutes" of the Academy of Sciences or researchers attached to the universities. But these works must be read within the context of the scientist's limited access to information and the subjection of his printed work to censorship.[41]

Deprived of hard data, the Soviet scientist must focus on theory building, the application of which may never occur. In the area of environmental-economic modeling, the theoretical work has been particularly innovative. In 1972, Leontiev and Ford published a pioneer article proposing an inter-branch environmental-economic model of the impact of industry upon the environment.[42] The article set a precedent for the inclusion of environmental factors in input-output economic analysis. Since then, environmental modeling has been taken up at TSEMI by M. Ia. Lemeshev, K. G. Gofman, and their associates.[43] Probably the most comprehensive set of models of economic and environmental variables (excluding social factors) is that developed for Estonia by R. L. Raiatskas and V. P. Sutkaitis. The authors consider environmental quality as a form of capital. Reduction in the amount of environmental capital requires a comparable input of conventional capital to produce the same level of output, defined as the gross output of useful commodities and the output of pollution by-products. The level of pollution at any one time is expressed as the difference between the sum total of pollution created in the production process and an environmental factor expressing the environment's regenerative capacity. The model demonstrates that the higher the level of pollution, the less the total output, since pollution speeds up the rate at which fixed capital goes out of service, accelerating write-offs through obsolescence, corrosion, and loss of quality. The environment thus is understood to have a regulatory impact on production through the damage done to the economy by pollution.[44]

In Yugoslavia, the researcher experiences far fewer limitations on data collection. Access to Western and other publications is easy, if the institute or research organization has the hard currency to order them. As mentioned earlier, environmental data collection is just beginning in industry and in the environmental institutes. While permission is required from the responsible state authority for access to data in a state institute, the system is not as rigid as in the Soviet Union, since most institutes are organized at the republican or opstina level. Nevertheless, the very existence of a permission process indicates that the republic holds the final decision on data release and publication. The main problem for the expert is not inaccessibility of data as much as lack of sufficient data. The joint publication by the federal and republican councils on the human environment and territorial management of an overview of the status of the environment in 1979 was a pioneer effort in comparing environmental conditions between republics. While the book contains much demographic and traditional statistical yearbook data, it is short on substantive information on environmental degradation, an indication of the state of the art at that time. Its successor document, the *National Report on Environmental Conditions and Policies in Yugoslavia* published in 1985, provides more detail on water, air, and soil pollution, and a new section on noise pollution. As the statistics accumulate in the eighties, the fuzzy image becomes clearer, but there is still a long way to go.

In summary, the Soviet expert benefits from the authority vested in him through the official designation of expert institutions but is constrained in the relevance and comprehensiveness of the advice he can give by compartmentalization of information. By contrast, the Yugoslav expert is relatively unconstrained by information censorship but finds his influence limited by the self-management requirement that institutions be self-supporting and by the distrust of party officials regarding his advice.

Assets

Financial. Funding is a problem in both countries. Improvement in environmental protection depends on scientific and technological research to develop environmentally safer forms of production. Much of this research in all industrial societies has been oriented toward uncovering the harmful side effects ("externalities") of production upon the natural and human environment. The Soviet Union and Yugoslavia are no exception. Along with other industrialized countries, they exhibit what Schnaiberg calls "a dialectical relationship" between environmental protection and industrial expansion, which sets up a conflict between the scientific investigator and the sources of capital.[45]

In the Soviet Union, research and development has been under some form of direct political control since Stalin's time. The 1965 R&D reforms brought them explicitly under centralized political direction, and since 1968, the all-union R&D plan has been an integral part of the long-term and five-year national plans.[46] Nolting estimates that the central planning of R&D projects may approach 40 percent to 50 percent of all R&D, with central ministerial planning amounting to another 30 percent.[47] Where do the leadership's priorities in research and development lie? In chapter 4, we saw that the industrial bureaucracies were having the most difficulty in the implementation of their technological programs except in the military and heavy industrial sectors. In 1979, the Soviet Union devoted around 22 percent of its trade with the West to the purchase of energy-related technology, most of which was designated for the Siberian pipeline.[48] Technological innovation promises to be a continuing problem for the USSR. Comparative indicators of technological change between the USSR and the Western countries indicate a Soviet tendency to underperform relative to the West at a similar stage of economic development.[49]

Soviet statistics bear out the low priority assigned to environmentally related research and technological development. In 1979, total expenditures from all sources in all areas of science and technology, excluding the educational institutions, were officially given as 20.2 billion rubles or somewhat under 5 percent of the gross national income.[50] In 1980, the figure was slightly less, 19.4 billion rubles or 4 percent of the GNI.[51] Between 1980 and 1984, state investment in science and technology averaged 4.6 billion rubles annually and constituted 2.6 percent of all state investment. During the same planning period, state investment in all measures connected with the protection and rational utilization of natural resources, in which we must include environmental research, averaged 1.3 percent of total state investment.[52] Given the symbiotic relationship between the party and industry, the party leadership has a vested interest in research contributing to industrial expansion, and the prognosis for increased funding for environmental research except as it might contribute to growth in production is poor.

In Yugoslavia, R&D reflects the self-management principle and is only loosely guided by a central policy in the national social plan. As in the Soviet Union, planning guidelines focus on industrial expansion. "The policy of expanded reproduction is based on the faster rise in resources for investment in fixed assets . . . in order to ensure . . . in particular the realization of agreed targets of activities which are of especial importance for . . . the overall development of the country." According to the plan, the estimated volume of productive investment in these target activities should amount to 65 percent of all investment, of which 36 percent should be in industrial groupings of "special significance," 11 percent in agriculture, and 4 percent in tourism. The special industries include energy, basic metals, and chemicals.[53]

The structuring of investment decisions according to social plan is only one factor in the orientation of research toward economic growth. As was seen in chapters 4 and 5, while self-management may apply to the generation of income, a large share of industrial income distribution has already been determined by law, including setting a certain portion aside for environmental controls. Faced with the choice of what to do with the remainder, enterprises are not particularly eager to invest their own limited resources in environmental research. Interviews at various environmental research institutes in Yugoslavia suggested that research contracts with enterprises were the exception, except in the case of SMELT. As a consequence, environmental research is almost totally dependent upon public monies.

The main sources of public funding for the environmental research institutes have been the health and culture SIZ-a. Until 1975, two-thirds of the financing for the Republican Institute for Environmental Protection of

Serbia came from the republican SIZ for culture, and one-third from the Republican Secretariat for Urbanism and Planning. With the introduction of self-management in 1975, the institute has been receiving an ever-decreasing amount from the SIZ for culture. Since all research organizations risk the eventual cut-off of public funds, some institute staff interviewed by the author questioned how long they could survive unless they totally reoriented their work, which they perceived as being essential in the long run but not economically necessary to any industry or public body in the short run.[54] From 1975 to 1980, the budget of the Republican Institute for Public Health of Serbia was cut 300 million dinars. Prior to that time, the institute had a pure science department of three hundred workers. In 1981, the same department employed only one hundred workers. Priority had gone to clinical medicine. The total institute budget for 1981 was around 130 million dinars, over 90 percent of which came from the Serbian SIZ for health. The balance came from ongoing or new projects contracted with local or republican governments.[55] Thirty percent of the funds for the Belgrade Municipal Institute of Public Health comes from the city health service, 60 percent from the Republican SIZ for Public Health SR Serbia and 10 percent from contracts with enterprises. Funding from these sources is for applied clinical work only.

Pure science research is funded through the annual competitions sponsored by the SIZ for science.[56] Total contributions to the SIZ not involved in social welfare services, including the science SIZ, are very small. In 1979, they represented 7 percent of all SIZ contributions. Clearly, the science SIZ cannot possibly meet the demands made upon it. Experts said that competition for science SIZ grants was high and that money was generally given on an annual basis only. A long-term research project had to be resubmitted every year of the project's duration, and it was not at all certain that it would survive new competition and be refunded.[57]

With public money in short supply, the Yugoslav environmental researcher is forced to seek international funding. In the construction of the sewage system for Lake Ohrid, the Yugoslav federal government's share, although substantial, was not the most important. The main contributions came from UNESCO, private Western philanthropic enterprises, and Western governments. Joint international projects such as those undertaken in cooperation with the UNEP, OECD, or the U.S. government are enthusiastically welcomed by the money-poor investigator. One reason that Yugoslavia may have created so many "biospheres" is that an area set aside for all mankind is a more likely candidate for world funds than a regional or national preserve. Yugoslav national parks receive virtually no republican or federal funding. The director's assurances notwithstanding, the enforced economic development of the Plitvice Lakes could very well be a time bomb for the lakes' ecosystem. In like manner, the intensive economic and tourist development along the Adriatic may result in the destruction of the very resources that attract industry and visitor alike. The establishment at Split of the UN-sponsored research center on the Mediterranean assures at least some ongoing scientific research that otherwise might have suffered serious setbacks for lack of funds.

Communications. As was shown above, the Soviet specialist is formally more restricted in his channels of information than his Yugoslav or Western counterpart.[58] He is restricted in access to rapid publishing and library resources; in ability to attend national and international conferences, for which funding and participation are at the discretion of his bureaucratic superiors; and in contacts with scientists in his field outside his work organization. All his research must pass through a censorship review before it may be accepted for publication. A typical department or work section may have only one outside phone in the chief administrator's office, and permission has to be sought to use it. Whether the specialist chooses contact by phone or by letter, the response from an unknown colleague will probably have been discussed with the latter's superior. Access to libraries, documents, and other research materials in the specialist's own and other agencies depends on his research and organizational status, while formal requests for information from other bureaucracies go through a maze of hierarchical channels before reaching their destination.

Scientific communication would be seriously impeded if only formal channels and norms existed in the Soviet Union. However, there is increasing evidence that informal channels and norms do exist, and that these grease the communication wheels of Soviet expertise in ways similar to informal information networks in Western countries.

In the United States, a large literature[59] attests to the existence among American specialists of "invisible colleges," or networks of scientists who maintain a constant exchange of information about their particular area of research. These groups tend to form around a nucleus of highly productive and visible scientists. Linkage is organized through the most influential members, while attraction of new members to a group is primarily through the work of the key figures. In the USSR, Soviet sociologists like I. I. Leiman have also identified "invisible colleges."[60] In a stimulating study, I. V. Sergeeva confirms Leiman's description of "scientific collectives" outside the formal institutional structure as a common form of professional association in Soviet scientific institutes,[61] while G. G. Diumenton has described external links between Soviet scientists. In a 1970 study of communication between scientists outside their institutes, he found definite patterns of interaction. The main pattern was between institutes of the Academy of Sciences, and within cities. Communication between Academy institutes in Moscow was highest and fell off proportionally with distance.[62]

The author's field research found evidence of substantial communication among environmental experts in the Moscow area and considerable external ties with other Soviet and East European cities. Members of the Department of Environmental Law at Moscow State University (MGU) were familiar with the work of the environmental section of the Academy Institute of State and Law and knew the members personally. Many institute members had received degrees from MGU. Leading Academy of Sciences personnel as well as MGU graduates who were now working in the republican capitals were invited to attend university conferences and to give lectures, while the head of the Environmental Law Department received similar invitations to Leningrad and other universities. The environmental specialists at MGU and the Academy Institute of State and Law formed two distinct groups, organized around different key members advocating slightly different approaches. The Academy institute group urged greater centralization of environmental management decisions, while the MGU group emphasized the importance of responsibility and liability in the legal process. As might be expected of the more prestigious organization, the influence of the Academy institute seemed to be stronger, extending to the corresponding institutes of Eastern Europe. In Prague, members of the environmental section of the Czech Institute of State and Law knew the work of the leading researchers in environmental law at the institute in Moscow, particularly that of Oleg Kolbasov, head of the environmental department, and they regularly participated in conferences organized by the Soviet institute.

Environmental specialists in other areas also appear to be organized in groups. Among the economists, there are those who support the views of economist M. Ia. Lemeshev and/or are engaged in studying mathematical environmental models at TSEMI and elsewhere, and those who work on optimization models at Leningrad University and Leningrad Institute of Economic Engineering. Vidmer has documented the existence of at least four schools of Soviet management science, each with its set of member institutes, journals, key figures and geographic distribution.[63] The natural scientists and geographers also have their networks, as the fight over Lake Baikal and the discussions on Siberia testify. While these "invisible colleges" seem largely confined to one bureaucracy (the Ministry of Education, the Academy of Sciences) or discipline, they can be both interdisciplinary and interbranch. For example, the professors in the faculty of biology at MGU were well acquainted with the work of colleagues in the faculties of geography and economics. In Leningrad, the "invisible college" of proenvironmental professors has been formalized into an all-university committee to advise on environmental education for all departments. Moreover, since academicians are often appointed university professors and vice versa, those who hold both positions provide a link between the two main academic bureaucracies.[64] Zhores Medvedev's success in piecing together the story of the nuclear disaster in the Urals was due largely to his recomposition of the "invisible college" of his contemporaries. Many of the names of his university friends disappeared from the scientific literature in the fifties. They resurfaced in 1966 and 1967, thanks to the existence of an interdisciplinary network of scientists working in the bionuclear field, who were looking for ways to get around censorship restrictions on the publication of research findings on radiation.[65]

Paradoxically, centralized planning may contribute to the formation of these informal groupings. As with other specialties, only so many environmental experts are graduated and placed each year. The relatively small number of environmental researchers in each field would seem to encourage contact. Job security is relatively stable. Contacts once established persist and indeed may strengthen over the years, resulting in perhaps a greater feeling of solidarity than may occur within scientific communities in the United States.

The key figures in each group may readily be equated with the "technological gatekeeper" posited by Allen and Cohen[66] with only slight modifications. According to these authors, the American "gatekeeper" who developed and maintained contacts outside the laboratory and was the channel of information flow was usually the primary researcher but, very infrequently, the department head. Sergeeva, on the other hand, found that the Soviet "gatekeeper" and department head were the same person 50 percent of the time. The finding is to be anticipated, given the more rigid, hierarchical system; the circumscribed publishing opportunities; and the need for the political authorities to control information flow through the centipede. In a university setting, the department head dominates, and leading scholars tend to be in this position. At MGU, they appeared to have more links outside the department and the university than junior faculty members. They were also the ones who were invited to scholarly conferences or who arranged that junior colleagues went along. And they were far more likely to be sent abroad. Indeed, junior staff perception of foreign travel opportunities was that travel, especially to the "capitalist" countries, was reserved for senior personnel. In a department head's dealings with department faculty or students, hierarchy prevailed. Colleagues were deferential, while students generally came upon invitation. Given the "gatekeeper's" commanding position over information flow, it is vital for the aspiring *kandidat nauk* or researcher to cultivate his section chief. Similarly, visiting Western scholars make every effort to get to know the key figure in their research area in the hope that this person through his informal network will provide the necessary introductions to other scientists working on the same problem.

There is one other type of social information network that has some parallels with the old boy network of the West, but that has been identified as a specific response to the rigidity of the Soviet bureaucratic system. Crozier calls it "the primary group,"[67] while Dawisha prefers the term, "family group."[68] It is an informal group of friends who support and reinforce each other, who are willing to use their influence or any other means to promote the members of the group, and who are ready to cover up the discrepancies between plan requirements and reality for the benefit of each other. Clearly, these types of groups are critical to maintaining information channels between different bureaucratic organizations and different levels of the bureaucracy.

In the published literature, the same persons keep being named as participants in this or that conference with an environmental subject matter, and their professions range from philosophers and journalists to geographers, scientists, and educators. Gustafson has argued that "receptiveness at the top" gave Lake Baikal's defenders the access to media coverage and lead policymaking circles.[69] The links between D. A. Kunyaev,[70] and the protectors of Lake Issyk-Kul', and between G. V. Romanov and the supporters of the dam on the Gulf of Finland, offer other examples of the extension of these groups to influential party leaders. On the less visible level, the author noted that the senior members of MGU's Biology Department had contacts in Gosplan and GKNT and were informed on matters pertaining to their professional interest. With the traditional veneration given to science and scientists and the importance of science and technology for Soviet economic development, there are obvious reasons for a mutual cultivation of relationships between the scientific community and the party and government apparat.

On the other hand, the failure of the Lake Baikal supporters to prevent industrial development, like the failure of Issyk-Kul's defenders to prevent the construction of the dams, indicates a corresponding failure by environmental scientists to penetrate existing "family groups" or to solidify new ones to offset the close ties between the industrial interests and the Communist party. A partial explanation may lie in the relative newness of environmental expertise. In view of the present emphasis on environmental education for all students at all educational levels, the formation of pro-environmental primary groups may be expected to increase. There is little doubt that they are a major asset for the environmental expert in his efforts to dilute the overwhelming industrial influence in policymaking circles.

In Yugoslavia, informal associations akin to the "invisible colleges" and "family groups" also exist. However, their function is somewhat different. In the Soviet Union, the regime's preoccupation with secrecy poses problems in the transmission of information up, down, and across the closed bureaucratic hierarchies. In Yugoslavia, where information is more open, the groups' functions are more similar to that of analogous Western groups: to sift and coordinate information from multiple sources. Since there is far less restriction of information, information itself is not a scarce commodity. What is scarce is the knowledge of which piece of information is of relevance to decisionmaking at a given moment in time.

As a guest of the Yugoslav Federal Council for the Protection and Improvement of the Environment in 1981, the author was introduced to specialists in many different fields, all of them associated with environmental matters. Most of these specialists knew each other and were aware of each other's work. Many were good friends. If they were not acquainted, they felt themselves loosely associated in a common endeavor because each knew the secretary general of the council. Although the hydra system favors the concentration of networks in one republic, the author observed communication between Serbian environmental specialists and colleagues from Macedonia, Bosnia, Slovenia, and the Vojvodina. "Invisible colleges" appeared to form most easily between research institutes with similar subject matter and organized in a similar way, such as exists in the chain of institutes under the health system or the institutes attached to the federal and republican councils for environmental protection and territorial planning. Cross-disciplinary communication appeared to be weakest within the state institutes and strongest within the sociopolitical organizations. As one environmental department head put it, "The institutes are government bureaucracies. In the sociopolitical organizations, we are all colleagues and friends."

An indication of the growing strength of the Yugoslav scientific networks is the successful mobilization of the environmental expert community across disciplines within the professional associations and within the larger organization of the Socialist Alliance to put pressure on the Federal Skupština (assembly) to change the legislation on the building of the dam in the Tara Canyon. Not only were the scientists organized among themselves, but they were able to use their nonscientific contacts in the other professional associations to mobilize individuals in the social sciences and other fields. Two organizational factors appear to have been important to the scientists' success. The first, noted in chapter 5, is the solidarity between the Communist chairmen of the professional organizations, who are bound together by the ties of party association. The second is the location of the

Yugoslav scientific "gatekeeper." The author's field research suggested two kinds of information flow in Yugoslavia, one leading to public policy decisions, the other channeled toward research. The "gatekeepers" of *policy* information flow as opposed to *research* information flow were more apt to be the heads of the professional associations. Since the former are responsible for the implementation of party and government decisions within their organizations, they can alert association members of pending policy decisions and receive feedback on that decision. However, the Tara Canyon events demonstrate that neither individual specialist networks nor the environmental associations through their chairmen had sufficient connections with industrial interests to be able to break the party-industrial tie. On the contrary, prior to the initial decision, expert representations against the building of the dam were repeatedly ignored, and reports of these speeches were deliberately kept out of the press.

A similar failure of primary group networking may be noted in the Sava River controversy. Assuredly, environmental scientists in all four of the republics along the river were concerned about the increasing pollution of the river. Yet, the group that formed to take stock of pollution in the Serbian portion of the river was composed only of Serbian experts. And the Serbian newspapers made no mention of expert cooperation across the republics, if any indeed took place. The evidence thus suggests that the "invisible college" and the "primary group," particularly in their interrepublican dimensions, have yet to become commonplace in the environmental policy arena. The general party distrust of the specialist noted earlier and the nonintellectual background of most of the party leadership offer only partial explanations. The most critical may be the failure of the expert community itself to realize the importance of interdisciplinary and interrepublican communication.

Costs and Benefits

The costs and benefits of expert involvement in environmental research are similar to those for their involvement in other areas, although the negative and positive peaks are probably not as sharp as in the more strategic research sectors.

The costs that the specialist incurs in assuming a position that is contrary to the official line or violates the confidence laid upon him may be divided into two categories. The first relates to social and economic pressures similar to those identified by Schnaiberg as operating on American scientists. These include attacks on reputation, criticism for being non-objective or nonscientific, loss of job or demotion, loss of access to information or publication possibilities.[71] The similarity in position between the Western and the Eastern specialist in this respect is close. Soviet scientists are very sensitive to the dangers of taking an officially unacceptable view or of violating the rules of conduct or secrecy. The year 1980 was a low point in U.S.-Soviet relations, and the author found Soviet colleagues most circumspect in their dealings with her. While Yugoslav scientists may appear somewhat less vulnerable, they too know that there are limits to a stubborn adherence to a policy unpopular with the leadership. Yugoslav experts told the author that the organization of the opposition to the location of the Tara River dam required considerable courage since the decision to build the dam at the contested spot had already been taken. Normally one did not challenge the government after a decision had been made.

The most important personal economic pressure on the Yugoslav scientist, to which his Soviet counterpart is less subject, is the absence of multiple opportunities for pure scientific or nonapplied research in his home country. Junior researchers in the environmental area expressed concern over the lack of institutes and funding for environmental research and wanted to go abroad, particularly to the United States, where the opportunities to work in their chosen speciality were so much greater. The absence of job possibilities and the scientific community's attraction to work abroad help explain the lack of leading environmental scientists in the public domain of the stature of a Gerasimov, Lemeshev, or Khatchaturov. It is unfortunate that poor countries must bear the cost of losing national talent for want of money to fund comprehensive R&D programs.

In both countries, the costs can go into a second category, although the risks are noticeably higher in the Soviet Union. A man of Sakharov's stature can be publicly persecuted and imprisoned. A less strategically important scientist can lose not only his job, but his apartment, publishing outlets, trips abroad, access to Western goods and information, and many other privileges that his high-status position as a scientist affords him. He can be ousted from his professional organization and his career closed. The fear of losing everything must be considered a major factor in keeping the Soviet expert oriented toward his narrow specialty within his ministerial or Academy institute at the expense of broader and more controversial issues. This fear in turn reinforces the political power of the supervising ministries, the continuation of secrecy, and the compartmentalization of information.

In Yugoslavia, there is considerably greater freedom of expression. However, the Belgrade Trial in 1984 and 1985 served to alert the intellectual community that arbitrary symbolic arrests and punishment had not disappeared from the Yugoslav scene. Although the immediate result of the trial was to increase public discussion over the future of Yugoslavia, the sentencing of three intellectuals demonstrated that those who come out in defense of individuals or ideas in disfavor with the leadership still run significant risks.[72]

In the Soviet Union, the benefits of not becoming involved in controversial issues and of picking the "right" research area are clear. According to Zhores Medvedev, military research institutes along with the Academy of Sciences are considered first-category research organizations of special national importance. Salaries, research facilities, and living conditions within the military are higher than elsewhere, encouraging scientists to want to work there, notwithstanding the severe restrictions on the publication of scientific papers and on private life.[73] Next in terms of benefits comes the Academy of Sciences, then the universities and the research institutes of the branch organizations. Despite the growing number of environmental scientists, the weight of expert research and advice in the Soviet Union is concentrated in those areas related to military, industrial, and energy production. According to Nolting and Feshbach's figures, in 1973 43 percent of all scientific workers worked in the branch scientific institutes as compared with 9 percent in the Academy of Sciences, and 80 percent of all experts employed in the branch ministries and agencies at that time were working in the critical energy and industrial areas.[74]

The aspiring scientist is not likely to want to lose his perks for an uncertain environmental cause. Those who publicly come out and disagree, as in the case of Lake Baikal,[75] tend to be senior scientists of known reputation. The political arm-twisting that can occur even at this level of the scientific hierarchy is seen in the final report of the Academy of Sciences' Lake Baikal Commission appointed by GKNT in 1977 to review the lake's status. Allegedly, the commission submitted three negative reports before a more positive fourth was found "acceptable" to the government leadership.[76] The risks involved in straying too far from the accepted party line reinforce the Soviet expert's commitment to a narrow specialty area. Here he may give his technical opinion freely and in the process try to exert influence in his own limited area of expertise.

In Yugoslavia, the opportunities to work, consume, and travel abroad are distributed more evenly among the population, and the scientist's privileges are not as marked as in the Soviet Union. Yugoslavia has yet to commit itself to an investment in science that might yield the Yugoslav specialist the status now enjoyed by his Soviet counterpart. The principal benefit is financial, in the form of higher pay. Since the main sources of funding come from government and industrial contracts, the Yugoslav specialist is under pressure both to do research and to publish findings acceptable to those two groups. In this aspect, he is more susceptible to the kind of pressure identified in category one. The locus of this pressure encourages specialists to select their causes carefully and to band together on those issues capable of arousing both domestic and international public opinion. The international dimension seems to be particularly important in encouraging proenvironmental scientific action. If scientists are not tireless champions of the environment in Yugoslavia, it may be that the prevailing political climate of distrust of scientific advice dissuades specialists from expending their rather limited political capital on small causes. It is far more cost-effective to devote one's effort to a representative issue symbolic of the general environmental problem, such as the Tara dam.

A second benefit is the special kinds of rewards derived from the experts' obvious control over sources of information: the prestige of involvement and the power that an expert acquires from becoming adviser to the power holders. The two are interconnected. Kolbasov's Department of Environmental Law was asked to draft the air pollution law. The Yugoslav Federal Council for the Protection and Improvement of the Environment annually evaluates the most serious environmental problems facing the country and submits recommendations for legislation to the Federal Skupština. To be an adviser to the centers of power enhances the specialist's reputation in his field, and he is much sought after by those seeking to rise in his profession. Service in one area brings nomination for a higher service in another or appointment to a choice administrative post. And the expert has the inner satisfaction of knowing his advice counts when important policy decisions in his field are being made.

The experience of expert power is heightened in the Soviet Union where knowledge is privileged. The practice of gift giving is concrete evidence that the "gatekeeper" has access to information that no one else may have, and his favor must be sought to obtain it. Information scarcity enables the Soviet expert to play, to a much greater degree than in the West, the role of information broker. In Yugoslavia, a specialist plays a similar role through his inside knowledge of party attitudes toward developments in his special area. In both countries, the absence of any real competition over information means that an expert who advises the decisionmakers has a monopoly on the information required in his field to make that decision. This monopoly becomes more solid in direct proportion to the growth of his knowledge of privileged information and influence with the decisionmakers. In the Soviet Union, his position is reinforced by the legal delegation of expertise. The benefits derived from the practice of expert power obviously encourage accommodation to the prevailing political line. There are few in any society who would give up the sense of "making things happen" for the support of a politically unpopular environmental issue.[77]

Finally, there is the personal satisfaction of trying to build a better world in which to live. This factor should not be underestimated in understanding why experts engage in environmental politics. While that satisfaction must be traded off against the possibility of severe costs, the costs have clearly not been perceived as so prohibitive as to prevent the environmental specialists from entering the political arena. Both societies offer tangible material and psychological rewards for those interested in the pursuit of science, and the increasing number of environmental experts indicates the attractiveness of the environmental field. In addition to these more personal considerations, public awareness of environmental degradation in the Soviet Union and Yugoslavia is increasing, and with it the opportunities to advance a cause that socialism is deemed to solve best and that has few political enemies. The balance sheet of costs and benefits for the engagement of the environmental specialist in environmental politics would seem to favor engagement.

Strategies

The strategies of environmental experts may be divided into five groups, all of which are directed toward maximizing the regulatory principle to build power and influence. Because experts are involved in all phases of policymaking, the division of strategies between policy input and implementation is not appropriate to the discussion and will not be used here.

Broadening the scope of the planning and legislative process. As in the Western countries, Soviet and Yugoslav environmental experts are present at all stages of the legislative process. But it is important to note the differences. In the Soviet Union, top party officials and key ministers formulate a general policy in response to demands from the ministries and other agencies, and they delegate the responsibility of concretizing the policy to state organs essentially of their own choosing. In Yugoslavia, policy is initiated at the federal level by the Federal Executive Council and at the republican level by the republican executive council.[78] Policy proposals at the federal level are the result of negotiation and bargaining between the republican party and government leaders at the federal level. At the republican level, policy proposals are negotiated between republican party officials and government leaders in response to demands from the sociopolitical organizations and industrial groups. In both the Soviet and Yugoslav cases, the legislature does not make policy. Rather, the laws are the embodiment of policy that has been previously determined. By consequence, the participation of experts tends to be delegated and co-opted; nonstructured participation is rare.

In the USSR, the delegation of legislative and planning tasks to the bureaucracies favors the narrow in-house expert with detailed knowledge of his particular area as it relates to his organization's functions and objectives. Middle-level specialists may participate in drafting legislation, as did those at the Institute of State and Law in drafting the 1980 Air Quality Control Law, but it is carried forward and supported by senior-level

245

bureaucrats. One-party dominance and control through "democratic centralism" concentrates the discussion within those groups who have the jurisdiction to decide, while delegation ensures that as a rule, only those experts are co-opted into the decisionmaking circle who have official standing as representatives of the interested bureaucratic parties and have competence to advise on the scientific technicalities of the decision.

Vanneman's research indicates a high level of expert participation in the drafting subcommissions of the Supreme Soviet's Legislative Proposals Committee (LPC). In the subcommissions that drafted the fundamental legislation on water resources and the fundamental forestry law, 20 percent and 37.5 percent of the memberships respectively were "scientific workers."[79] While assuredly specialists support their bureaucratic superiors in the event of controversy, their very presence is an indication of influence. When views cannot be reconciled, as happened when talks stalled over regulations regarding the elimination of timber-floating down the Siberian rivers,[80] a conference may be called where experts argue the technical aspects of their chiefs' positions. Experts in the administrative or legislative drafting committees may have special influence on the final legislative product. During the discussion of the draft of the 1980 air pollution law, specialists at the Institute of State and Law achieved two of their primary objectives. Goskomgidromet was made the chief, if not sole, environmental monitoring agency, and noise was included as an air pollutant in the final act.[81]

The delegation and co-opting of expertise in the policy input stage make it virtually impossible for other experts who might have an interest in the policy to become involved. Even if secrecy were not a Soviet preoccupation, the non-co-opted expert would not have the same access to the information utilized in making the policy as his co-opted colleague, and the timelag in acquiring it would eliminate his chance of mounting a counterattack. The delegated institutions monopolize the decisionmaking process in the delegated area to the exclusion of all other parties.[82] The practice encourages consensus and accommodation among the participating experts while eliminating critics. The participants are eager to continue their involvement in policy decisions, as it enhances their personal prestige, and they are understandably reluctant to raise issues opposed to the policy at hand. The critics will never be heard. Through the 1972 and 1978 joint resolutions on strengthening the environment, the USSR Academy of Sciences is the only institution party to virtually every policy decision associated with the environment. Given this unique position, it is not surprising that the Academy institutes have emerged as the strongest champions of the environment. Not employed by a ministry interested in exploiting or managing a natural resource, specialists in the Academy institutes can take a longer, less instrumental view of environmental protection than can their colleagues in the resource ministries whose jobs depend on validating resource development.

In the Soviet Union, the delegation of expert authority tends to replace the Western politics of expert bargaining with the politics of institutional and self-promotion. When the specialist's recommendation is given official approval, in effect it becomes the policy. While the party and government leadership has the option to adopt or not to adopt a given solution, the institute director or his superior organization also has the option of trying to persuade the leadership that its solution is appropriate. As the successful sponsor of objective pollution norms, Iurii Izrael is now head of the lead agency responsible for the monitoring and enforcement of the standards he promoted. As one bureaucracy advances up the promotional ladder, there are others ready to take over should an institution falter. The rise and partial fall of the Ministry of Power and Electrification is a case in point. From the decade-long struggle between the Power Ministry, Minrybkhoz (the Ministry of the Fishing Industry), and Minvodkhoz (the Ministry of Land Reclamation and Water Resources) over jurisdictional turf in water management, Minvodkhoz emerged as the officially designated lead organ.[83]

In Yugoslavia, decentralization makes it difficult for experts to acquire the same degree of far-reaching influence and status as some of their Soviet colleagues, since their expertise is confined to a small territory. Nevertheless, expert "monopolism" exists. Experts provide input at critical stages of the policy process. The first is during the setting of the legislative agenda. The primary sponsors of the legislative program are the federal and republican executive councils. However, in drawing up their program of work, the councils not only consider the program and previous position of the party and government organs, but also the "action" statements of the sociopolitical organizations, including the professional associations. Each asso-

247

ciation is required to present a program, generally at the end of the year. As these programs give the professional association's opinion on legislative action needed in the association's particular field of expertise, membership in these associations enables the specialists to have a direct input into setting the public policy agenda. A case in point is the 1984 action program of the Federal Council for the Protection and Improvement of the Environment, which urged that appropriate measures be taken in 1985 in the areas of water quality, the chemical pollution of food, and conservation of agricultural land.

The second opportunity for input is in the drafting stage. Yugoslavia has adopted a two-track drafting system. The first track, which is highly political, consists of bargaining between the interested industrial and territorial parties. The second track is the process whereby specific institutes or groups of institutes sign contracts to develop long-term plans or concrete legislative and planning proposals and form special internal commissions for drafting texts. As Burg notes, these groups always work under political supervision and maintain contact with the appropriate responsible party and state organs. The draft proposal constitutes the basis for the subsequent bartering and negotiation in the assembly by which agreement is reached to pass a law. In addition, experts are co-opted to participate in the work of both chambers' permanent committees as nonvoting members.[84] As in the Soviet Union, the expert has become a necessary adjunct of the legislative process.

Expert participation at the local opština level differs little from that at the federal or republican levels. Through their professional associations, experts advise on needed legislation. A consulting institute contracts to draft the required legislation, such as a regional territorial plan. It presents the draft to the assembly, where it is referred to a subcommittee for study. Interestingly, the draft of a territorial plan is not usually made public for the community to study, nor is there a referendum on its adoption. Since all the local organizations are technically represented through the delegate system in the assembly, all the relevant interests are legally considered to have been consulted.[85] The assembly votes on the final document.

The ability of the Yugoslav system of contracted expertise to enhance the power of certain specialists and to exclude others in individual policy decisions is well demonstrated in the controversy over the Tara River dam.

Conservation experts were not among the consultants under contract with the Federal Council of the Republics and Provinces to draft the original hydrodevelopment plan. Excluded from the drafting process, the environmental specialists tried unsuccessfully to exert influence by taking their case to the public before the enabling legislation was passed. The contracting agency held the inside monopoly position. Once the draft became law, the environmentalists could no longer question the basic plan, although they could and did generate enough pressure to force the Federal Council to modify its decision.

The Tara River dam was a setback to the environmental specialists, but it does not detract from their progress in utilizing the legislative and planning process to expand their influence. In both countries, the regulations requiring expert consultation or monitoring by environmental specialists have proliferated. In the Soviet Union, one may cite the 1972 and 1978 joint resolutions, the 1978 granting of greater authority to GKNT and the Academy of Sciences in overall identification of environmental problems, and the 1980 Soviet air quality law. In Yugoslavia, there are the monitoring regulations in the air and water laws and the planning requirement that industries engaged in new development and seeking loans must plan the necessary environmental controls. Even the Sava River controversy may result in a more permanent official organization of expert involvement in water management, if the establishment of an independent water monitoring agency becomes federal law. The danger in this expanded influence is the absorption of expert influence in legislative and planning technicalities at the expense of the global environmental policy issues.

"Knowledge is power." The second strategy is based on the specialists' recognition of their control over new information. Decisionmakers cannot afford not to consult expert opinion, even when they plan to disregard it. In the environmental area, Soviet experts appear to have utilized this strategy to better advantage than their Yugoslav counterparts, partly because environmental management is better organized in the USSR and partly because their role in it is more clearly defined.

Soviet specialists have been effective in many areas. To the natural scientists and the geographers goes the credit of placing the environment on the public agenda by describing the seriousness of the country's ecological problems and advising the leadership of the limits of unscrupulous economic exploitation. Their efforts produced the change in leadership attitudes toward conservation and resource use in the seventies and won a permanent place for these issues in policymaking circles. Foremost among the early environmental activists were Gerasimov, Lebedev, and Preobrazhenskii of the Academy's Institute of Geography and Vorob'iev and Belov of the Institute of the Geography of Siberia and the Far East. The Institute of Geography in fact was the pioneer in environmental research through a program started in 1962 to investigate the interrelationship of human disease with the human environment.[86]

The social and natural scientists together were responsible for providing the Soviet Union with an impressive edifice of environmental standards, ranging from the common and widely used ambient and emission norms to the more sophisticated standard proposed by Pavel Oldak, the ecological quality of technology. In the development of the norm system, the environmental professionals have become the arbiters of how "clean" the environment should be. Because of the lack of real legislative activity in policy proposal and adoption, the battle over norm levels typical of the U.S. Congress is totally absent from the Soviet scene. With no strong political opposition from industry, Soviet specialists have been able to set optimum norms, but under current conditions these have proved impossible to meet. To avoid compromising their optimum goal, they have had to recognize the principle of an intermediary temporary norm. One may argue that optimum goals are useless. Basically, the decision is one of costs versus benefits in terms of the amount one is willing to pay for a certain level of pollution.[87] But Soviet environmental management is regulatory and delegated. In their official role as specialists without the intervention of conflicting expert views from industry, Soviet scientists have, in effect, sold the decisionmakers the concept of optimum standards. As one young researcher proudly told the author, Soviet norms are more numerous and higher than anywhere else in the world. In Yugoslavia, by contrast, self-management automatically imposes concerns about cost, and Yugoslav specialists have recommended adoption of pollution levels within the range of those deemed obtainable in Western Europe and the United States.

Environmental economists may feel that their influence over the planning and legislative process is debatable. The fact remains that they are setting the parameters of the discussion. They have brought onto the public agenda the fundamental issues of the assignment of economic value to "externalities" and the correlation of environmental conditions with "the human factor" in the economy. What is more, they have shown great ingenuity in proposing highly innovative solutions. Although all have been framed within the constraints of the ideology, they attempt to produce environmental improvements through economic autoregulation rather than through the existing clumsy system of administrative rulemaking. Khachaturov, Gofman, and Gusev have proposed different strategies for integrating the environmental component into the evaluation of the effectiveness of capital investment, Khachaturov by distinguishing between "losses prevented" and "residual damage," and the latter two by applying coefficients of damage per unit of effluent. Gofman and Gusev jointly have also devised a formula for measuring environmental investment inputs by determining the economic and social costs of not applying environmental controls and comparing these with the expense of installing the requisite environmental technology. N. N. Loiter has attempted to evaluate the social effectiveness of the costs of individual environmental controls by measuring the growth of labor productivity, decrease in illness, and various demographic indicators. At the first U.S./USSR Environmental Economics Symposium (1978), O. F. Balatskii of Kharkov Polytechnical Institute proposed a methodology for determining economic damage resulting from environmental degradation and for measuring the interconnection between expenditures for environmental protection and the level of pollution, using a model describing four types of damage (*ushcherb*).[88]

The assignment of a value to natural resources is a controversial issue that has had its defenders and opponents, but the number of defenders is on the increase. M. T. Meleshkin has argued that the concept of free gifts from nature can only obtain in a situation of unlimited natural resources.[89] But while there may be general agreement that value should be assigned, there is no agreement on whether resource users should pay for every measured unit of resource used. Gofman, among others, has been a strong advocate of pollution payments.[90] He has also proposed that enterprises be charged a resource user fee giving them the right to deplete specific natural resources. The enterprise would further pay for holding resource use within specified parameters in the form of a resource conservation fee. By manipu-

lating the ratio between the payments for resource use and resource conservation, the state would have an economic means of controlling the rate
at which resources were being depleted or regenerated, while at the same
time providing an economic instrument to encourage conservation.[91] The
Soviet government has taken a first step in the direction proposed by Gofman by introducing the water fee mentioned in chapter 3. In the early
1970s, two Soviet economists proposed a methodology for determining the
economic loss of a resource reserve based on a concept of marginal profitability (differential rent). That concept was incorporated into the Standard
Methodological Instructions, which were approved by the State Mining
Technical Inspectorate of the USSR in March 1972.[92]

Last but not least, Soviet economists may not yet have obtained the
adoption of their mathematical environmental-economic models as legal
planning instruments, but they have succeeded in getting the concept accepted in Soviet thinking about planning and development. Brezhnev's
multipurpose (*kompleksnyi* as opposed to single-purpose) development
strategy borrowed from the ideas of Leontiev, Lemeshev, and Gusev.
Again, Leontiev and Ford's concept of comprehensive planning[93] was the
seminal idea behind the idea of the territorial-industrial complex (TIC)
elaborated by economic geographers G. M. Krizhanovsky and I. G. Alexandrov. The Institute of Economics and Industrial Organization of the
Siberian Branch of the USSR Academy of Sciences has been mainly responsible for the mathematical elaboration of the concept in collaboration
with the Siberian divisions of the All-Union Academy of Agricultural
Sciences and the USSR Academy of Medicine. The outcome of the work
was the completion of Siberia Program, a comprehensive program for the
development of Siberia through its division into three regions, each with
their network of TICs. Unfortunately, however, Leontiev's proposed balancing of ecological and economic needs does not seem to have become an
integral part of either TIC planning or research.[94]

The fourth area where Soviet environmental experts have made a contribution is in addressing the problems posed by the implementation of
environmental policy. The legal profession has been particularly strong in
this area. In part, the environmental regulations and legal amendments of
the late 1970s were a response to the jurists' complaint that the laws were
not tough or precise enough. For example, the legal literature contains

numerous studies on the problem of evaluating environmental damage and assigning an appropriate monetary sum for damage restitution.[95] A Supreme Court decision in 1977 ruled that damage caused by mineral resource users on agricultural land could be liquidated by the payment of a sum equal to a calculation of all necessary expenses that would be involved in the restoration of the land's previous level of fertility.[96] The Ukrainian jurist Shemshuchenko has contributed to defining environmental criminal liability and accountability and is an advocate of heavy fines to deter crime.[97]

These examples are sufficient to indicate the scope of the Soviet environmental experts' contributions in environmental policymaking. There can be little question that they have had an impact in gathering the crucial scientific data, in strengthening and rationalizing legislation, and in formulating economic instruments for the planning process. Where their control of knowledge has exerted less influence over decisions has been in areas that challenge existing economic and administrative arrangements. Nevertheless, the record of environmental legislation and regulation during the seventies indicates a progressive shift toward more precise and less arbitrary environmental legislation and more procedural requirements for expert consultation. The provision of expert advice has become formally institutionalized. Knowledge has proved to be, if not a guaranteed power builder, at least a handy tool for influence.

There is little evidence that "knowledge is power" has been as effective in increasing expert input into Yugoslav environmental policymaking. With theoretical solutions and pollution control devices coming from the West, the experts have yet to find a home market for their ideas. More important, economic issues have been and remain the leadership's primary concern. Expertise in energy or economic development is clearly more in demand than environmental specialists. Few Yugoslav economists do research in environmentally related economic issues.

There are signs that the situation may be changing. The two reports on the status of the environment in Yugoslavia that have been cited throughout this study are one indication. The mobilization of expert opinion for the preservation of the Tara River Canyon is another. The research findings being published in *Čovek i životna sredina* are a third. Proenvironmental experts may also be beginning to make greater use of public occasions to address environmental issues. In June 1985, Milivoje Todorović, the newly elected secretary general of the Union of Engineers and Technicians of Yugoslavia, called for a graduated pollution charge at a conference on "The Meaning of Environmental Health in General and for National Defense in Particular" attended by party leaders and senior military officers. Todorović proposed that the charge be integrated into product and service pricing. The more a firm polluted, the higher the pollution charge. A firm that installed pollution controls would pay no charge, and thus its products would be more competitive in price than those of its polluting rival. Todorović further suggested that the charge on the single polluter be extended into a system of charges to cover an entire ecological system, such as the Sava River basin. If every polluter on the river cleaned up his pollution, he argued, Belgrade would not have to install the multibillion-dinar water treatment plant it now must build to provide safe drinking water for the city.[98] Initiatives such as these suggest a growing awareness among experts that knowledge can and in fact should be used to build influence.

At the implementation level, "knowledge is power" becomes virtually institutionalized in both countries. The application of norms or pollution control technologies, land-use development, and regional planning require experts to implement them. More research is needed before we can answer with any degree of certainty whether such expert advice is routinely accepted by local governments and responsible administrators, but there is no reason to believe that advice required by law would be systematically flouted. In the Soviet Union, there is a great deal of evidence to the contrary in the planning of cities, the adoption of centralized heating systems, the shift from coal to oil in the major urban centers, and the diffusion of environmental standards and procedures. In Yugoslavia, there has been no charge that specialist advice has been neglected. Rather, the critics accuse the experts of failing to give the advice that would enable communities to take the proper action.[99] Where that advice has been relevant to the problem at hand, as at Lake Palić, or Lake Ohrid, it has been utilized. In both countries, experts are using their control of knowledge to demand that expert advice be more comprehensive in its approach to a particular problem, whether through team consultation as taught at Belgrade's Center for Multidisciplinary Studies or through more interbranch and interinstitute cooperation as advocated in the Soviet Union. Pavel Oldak ruefully commented that "there is not one research institute in (our) country that could handle a major economic and ecological problem on its own."[100]

"Don't rock the boat." Once again, the Soviet experts have been more successful with this strategy than their Yugoslav colleagues. In all countries, bureaucrats appear to prefer expert advice that does not challenge their bureaucratic position. Rich has found that information that serves this function is limited in scope and provided by experts with a reputation for credibility and professionalism who have established a good informal working relationship with the decisionmakers.[101] The insistence on a single ideology makes heavy demands on professional credibility and strong work ties. Because of its greater centralization, the centipede more clearly defines the boundaries of political acceptibility, and environmental experts have been able to utilize those limits to maximize the strategic value of their advice. In Yugoslavia, the political conflict between the republics gives experts much wider latitude in formulating expert proposals. But this greater freedom has prevented the focusing of specialist advice on the narrow type of problem-solving most welcomed by bureaucrats and conducive to building confidence. The Yugoslav experts' willingness to "rock the boat" would seem to be a key factor in their lower level of influence.

Soviet environmental experts have been most effective when they have confined themselves to narrow, easily applicable advice that does not threaten existing power structures. Their main success has been the regime's overall recognition of the need for environmental protection, discussed earlier. Brezhnev consulted both agricultural and environmental experts in his efforts to solve the USSR's long-standing agricultural problems. Water experts have been able to make a case for leadership consideration of the environmental aspects of the Siberian and Northern Volga River diversion projects.[102] Environmental factors are routinely evaluated in Siberian natural resource development projects. There are probably few areas of economic activity in the Soviet Union today where environment protection is not a mandated concern.

The jurists have had particular impact in streamlining and strengthening judicial procedure and in encouraging economic self-interest on the part of enterprises to fulfill their environmental obligations. The jurists' decision to classify environmental lawbreaking under the traditional legal categories made it possible to identify certain environmental infractions as violations of the criminal code and hence to use the militia to search out violators.[103] During the 1970s, the recommendation by Soviet jurists that criminal responsibility for environmental infractions be increased resulted in a more stringent reformulation of the RSFSR statute on responsibility for air and water pollution. Certain actions were made specific objects of criminal liability, including violations of regulations on the exploitation of the continental shelf, poaching and the illegal sale of pelts, and violations of regulations on underground resources.[104] The lawyers' demands for stricter fines and stricter interpretation of the rules for closing a polluting factory have also borne fruit. In particular, Kolbasov and his colleagues were able to persuade the authorities that Goskomgidromet should be given administrative authority to close factories, and this provision was included in the 1980 air pollution control law (Article 24).

The economists' concept of marginal profitability was given qualified acceptance in the area of resource exploitation, although it failed to be linked to resource conservation, as noted above.[105] Their proposal for a water tax similar to that imposed by France, the Netherlands, West Germany, and Czechoslovakia,[106] has now gone into effect. Industrial objection has so far prevented the imposition of a pollution tax,[107] but that may be coming. Both the legal and economic experts might claim success in their drive to deprive both management and workers of their annual bonuses unless they fulfilled the environmental sector of the plan when the USSR Council of Ministers passed a resolution to that effect in 1978. The same resolution required workers to be fined if they did not report infractions of environmental regulations.[108] One may argue that the leadership's acceptance of expert recommendations is too limited and does not address the heart of the environmental problem. Nevertheless, there is little doubt that over the past two decades, the leadership has slowly gained confidence that the experts' suggestions will neither erode the ideology nor their power base. In return, the strategy of not rocking the boat has substantially increased expert influence and status as the leadership has come to depend on specialized input. And the evidence suggests an ever-increasing dependence. What other than expert advice could have persuaded the Twenty-seventh CPSU Congress to abandon, at least temporarily, the Siberian river project, which had been approved by every party congress over the previous fifteen years?

In Yugoslavia, the deteriorating economic situation has politicized policy options as the competing heads of the hydra have sought to improve their power positions. Many experts have entered the political fray on the side of greater economic liberalization. The adoption of what is essentially a partisan position has substantially undermined their effectiveness as providers of "objective" expertise, as the political implications of their proposals have become more visible. The traditional distrust of the expert by Yugoslav party leaders has thus received new reinforcement. A meeting in February 1985 of the Serbian Academy of Arts and Sciences went so far as to compare current problems in Yugoslavia with the church-state issue of Renaissance and Reformation times.[109] Academics have cited the 1974 Constitution as Yugoslavia's chief impediment to change.[110] The republican party leadership, understandably fearful of any change that might risk its power, receives the arguments of the country's most distinguished scholars with mixed emotions. For many republican bureaucrats, the problem is not simply economic growth and development but the preservation of regional autonomy. Expert advice that does not take the hydra into account becomes suspect to those desiring the maintenance of republican independence. Because it does infringe upon a very sensitive political area, Yugoslav expert advice tends to be perceived as more politicized than it may in fact be, to the extent that it strengthens the arguments of one or the other parties in the political power struggle. In this highly charged political climate, a strategy of not rocking the boat has little chance of being appreciated.

Linkage of environmental with economic issues. This strategy has been referred to in the course of this chapter and does not need elaboration. Experts in both countries have oriented the majority of their arguments toward showing that environmental precautions taken in time will save money and pay off their investment in the long term.

In the USSR, the promotion of environmental-economic modeling and the cost-benefit discussions of the conversion of the Siberian rivers speak to the concern of the specialists to persuade the decisionmakers that environmental protection is economically sound. Officials in Yugoslavia, such as Dr. Srečan Mitrović in the environmental planning section of the Federal Planning Committee, assert categorically that once republican and industrial administrations realize the positive economic impact of environ-

257

mental protection, there will be no more problems in the implementation of environmental regulations. The growing evidence of the negative economic effects caused by pollution and the knowledge that capital investment is becoming increasingly limited argue in favor of the possibility that party and government leaders in both countries will give an increasingly sympathetic ear to models, natural resource pricing theories, and social cost evaluation systems. In an article setting forth the problems and dangers of the chemical pollution of food, Radojic Kljajić of the faculty of agriculture of Belgrade University stresses the fact that biological and chemical agents reduce the planned return on agricultural products by 30 to 40 percent.[111] The problem is to mediate bureaucratic reluctance to change: to break down the closed bureaucratic boundaries in the centipede that suprabranch agencies like GKNT and Gosstandart (the State Committee on Standards) seem unable to transcend[112] and to persuade regional organizations in Yugoslavia to work together. Soviet and Yugoslav environmental specialists both admit that their leaderships have yet to accept the economic argument in all its earnestness. But personal conversations confirmed the impression that the economic argument was a long-term strategy aimed at convincing enough decisionmakers to turn regulation into action before it was too late.

Networking. A final strategy is the building of networks of communication like the "invisible colleges" and "family groups" described above. This strategy has been particularly effective in the Soviet Union in fostering expert participation in agenda-setting. The restrictions on the exchange of information in the Soviet Union and the limits to organized public expression of opinion in both countries make the experts in a very real sense the only persons capable of bringing an issue to the attention of the decisionmakers. Although the ad hoc group that formed around Lake Baikal was not able to stop the construction of the pulp and paper mill, it did succeed in making the government adopt landmark pollution control and environmental planning measures for the lake, which has been considerably upgraded.[113] Since then, groups of scientists have protested the deterioration of water quality in Lakes Sevan and Issyk-Kul', and scientists, particularly those of the Siberian Division of the USSR Academy of Sciences, have represented most strongly the ecological problems associated with the development of Siberia and the Siberian river diversion project.[114]

Soviet specialists regularly utilize popular journals to sensitize the public to environmental problems. *Priroda* has a circulation of over 1 million. The organ of the Soviet Writers' Union, *Literaturnaia gazeta* has become known for its proenvironmental position. Since the party program is pro-environment, professional journals in all the disciplines regularly publish articles on environmental issues. The number of scholarly works on environmental questions proliferated in the 1970s, with each expert author using the occasion to promote his environmental view. As perhaps in no other issue area, the Soviet mass media has been remarkably open in its consideration of environmental issues. Finally, experts are active leaders in the environmental mass organizations, the republican societies for the protection of nature, which they also use as a channel to inform the public of critical environmental questions (see chapter 7).

So visible have the proenvironmental specialists become that permanent informal proenvironmental groupings may now be identified as associated with specific institutions, such as the Academy of Sciences Institutes of Geography and State and Law, TSEMI, and the Soviet Writers' Union, not to mention the ad hoc groups. On the republican level, scientists of the constituent Soviet nationalities have joined together to promote the preservation of a particular national or cultural landmark such as the Kara Deg volcano in the Crimea.[115] What has developed has gone beyond a collection of well-placed individual defenders of the environment but stops short of being a Western-style interest group. The same institutes and organizations where scientists work as experts are providing the institutional base for an emerging "environmental lobby." Bureaucratic backing coupled with official standing places the Soviet specialist in the optimum position to play the dual role of environmental spokesman in the public interest and "objective" specialist. As expert, the specialist represents his institute; as "lobbyist" he is connected through the informal networks with the growing group of Soviet professionals concerned with ensuring the environment a permanent place on the public agenda.

In Yugoslavia, the environmental expert has shown himself to be more effective in exercising influence through his participation in the professional organizations. Yugoslavs say that these play a more important role in policymaking than the specialized institutes because of their direct connection with the party through the Socialist Alliance. Inclusion in the Alliance enables the professional organizations to transcend their republican origins and to provide their memberships with concrete opportunities for inter-republican and international action. The Alliance in turn provides the framework for interpenetration between the party and mass organizations within which experts may exploit their informal groups to "lobby" for the environment.[116] We have seen the strategic importance of the head of the professional organization as "gatekeeper" of policy information flow.

Collaboration between environmentalists in the party and specialists in the professional organizations saved the Tara River Canyon. The same collaboration is found in the organization of national and international environmental conferences. Many are sponsored by the Federal Council for the Protection and Improvement of the Environment with federal and republican funding. Others are promoted by specialized environmental organizations like the Clean Air Association, frequently in cooperation with a foreign or international institution. Conferences enable scientists to speak out "objectively" without fear of association with partisan interests and to be assured of some publicity for their views. Professional conferences, however, are more than a forum for individual statements. They enable a whole group of specialists to take a public position on an issue. In such manner, specialized conferences condemned the proposed dam site on the Tara River, criticized the way specialists performed their research tasks, and faulted pollution control of the Sava and Neretva rivers. The party connection once again makes it possible for members of the professional organizations to develop contacts abroad through attendance at and sponsorship of international conferences. Specialists use these opportunities to integrate their domestic networks into the international "invisible colleges" to generate funding and research exchanges.

Summary and Conclusion

Because experts are hired professionals, the constraints upon expert influence in both Yugoslavia and the Soviet Union are similar to those existing in Western societies. The degree to which the hiring agency is part of a centralized or decentralized system makes a difference in a one-party state mainly in the availability of competing information channels and in the extent to which expertise is openly partisan or formally restricted to a more "objective" expression of professional judgment. In the Soviet Union, the institute provides the base for the environmental "lobbying" effort, while in Yugoslavia, the greater opportunity for competing views made possible by the hydra system promotes expert utilization of the sociopolitical professional organizations for policy input. Unlike the environmental agencies, the expert institutions or professional associations do not administer any section of the environment and tend to be single-purpose. Thus, the expert is not caught in the double bind of resource user and environmentalist and can more unequivocally promote the environmental cause.

Like the environmental agencies, the Soviet and Yugoslav specialists' increasing activity in policymaking is made possible by the regulatory principle, and they have sought to expand their participation by maximizing the principle. They have been more successful in this objective than the environmental agencies, primarily because of the requirement for expert advice at all levels of policymaking and specialists' control over new scientific and technological information. The leaderships of both countries want to promote economic development as rapidly as possible without risking the ultimate catastrophe. Since neither country has a predetermined idea of what the "correct" environmental policy should be to achieve this objective, the environmental expert is freer in the framing of his advice than his colleagues in other areas. This unique constellation of factors has enabled the experts in both countries to become the most visible spokesmen for the environment and to acquire a considerable role in setting the public environmental agenda. Yet impressive as their gains in influence have been, in neither country has the environmental experts' greater margin of liberty in advising "the prince" weakened the inherent power of the industrial and economic interests. The experts remain outsiders in the policy process.

7

Public Opinion and Mass Organizations

Of all the parties involved in environmental protection, the public must be considered the greatest outsider of all, sharing none of the economic clout of industry, the political importance of the territorial units, or the expert's access to policymaking councils. The official endorsement of the scientific-technological revolution (STR) as the main means of resolving the man-nature contradiction may have placed the ecological experts in an advantageous position vis-à-vis the decisionmakers. But science cannot have the priority that the STR requires it to have unless the public appreciates its value. Appreciation necessitates a shift in popular attitudes and the mobilization of public opinion in the direction of the new value. This shift is a two-step process. The public must first be made aware of the problems and then educated to what options science can provide for their solution. During the 1970s, the East European and Soviet authorities encouraged the development of programs to educate the public on the importance of a clean environment and the actions it could take to promote environmental protection. The evidence suggests that despite the very real constraints on the expression of public opinion, official environmental education policy is indeed inducing a shift in values, resulting in a perhaps unexpectedly strong public response.

Structural and Regulatory Constraints

Control of public access to environmental information through mass education. Both the Soviet Union and Yugoslavia have incorporated environmental education into the regular grade and high school curricula. There

262

are textbooks that specifically treat environmental subjects, textbooks for the early grades that integrate environmental materials into the main subject matter, and textbooks that specialize in different environmental subjects and take different approaches for the technical and general education schools at the secondary level. Increasing attention is being given to a comprehensive approach to environmental education. The aim is for the student to be presented with ecological materials in every class of instruction in the early grades and then move to a more in-depth study of specific topics in the chemistry, physics, or social science courses of the higher grades.

At the first All-Union Conference on Environmental Education (1979), the conference members noted that

with regard to the scientific-technological revolution and the changes in the natural environment which accompany it, it has become abundantly clear that it is now necessary to explain the goals of the protection of the environment to the general public as a complex, interdisciplinary problem. Subjects relating to this problem should be included in textbooks at various levels of education. There should be improvement of the skills and training of specialists and workers who, in the course of their specific, practical, administrative or scientific work, could apply their acquired knowledge and methods in the interests of the rational use of natural resources and their preservation and renewal.

Education in the field of the environment is intended to make people aware of their responsibility for the state of the environment and to stimulate initiative in solving environmental problems.[1]

To stimulate popular awareness of the environmental obligation, the conference proposed that the USSR Ministry of Education continue its presentation of environmental subject matter in the standard general education program and require student participation from grades four through ten in the upkeep and maintenance of the school area, surrounding parks, and vacant areas. A yearly excursion for each class was also proposed, together with more opportunities for young people to visit nature reserves and take nature field trips. More graphic educational materials as well as textbooks and method books for teaching the environment were requested. An interdisciplinary course, "Man and Nature," was proposed for the last year of secondary education. To improve the teachers' awareness of the need for conservation, the conference demanded that a course on nature protection be mandatory in all pedagogical institutes.

Environmental subject matter is already required in all institutions of higher learning, but the conference thought more could be done in this area by mandating that technical students also be exposed to environmental subject matter. An integrated series of visual and printed aids was proposed, with technical school students participating in the development of these materials.[2] Moscow and Leningrad Universities have interdepartmental faculty committees responsible for supervising the incorporation of environmental education, particularly the impact of society on natural processes, into required course material. The Committee on Environmental Protection at Leningrad University has sixteen members, one from each faculty and two from the faculty of biology. The committee coordinates all the university's academic and research work in the area of the environment. The University of Kiev also has a committee, while others are in the process of organizing one.[3]

There are departments of environmental economics in the main universities and environmental sections in the appropriate natural sciences faculties. In 1983, Michael Soulé and Bruce A. Wilcox's text, *Conservation Biology*, was translated into Russian for use in the faculties of biology in anticipation of the creation of an independent department of environmental biology.[4] A basic environmental text is required for students in the soil sciences.[5] In 1981, Moscow University was the only Soviet university with an environmental department in the law faculty. The department was an outgrowth of the former Department of Kolkhoz Law (*kolkhoznoie pravo*), and it was called the Department of Environmental Protection and Rural (*sel'skoie*) Law. Members of the law faculties at Leningrad and Kiev Universities reorganized their Departments of Kolkhoz Law shortly afterward. With the merger of the smaller collective farms into large conglomerates during the seventies, legal regulation of the Soviet countryside shifted from an absolute division between sovkhoz and kolkhoz legal practice to a more unified concept of rural law. Changes in the countryside made the old kolkhoz law departments an anachronism, and other universities readily followed Moscow University's lead.

According to Petrov and other law professors, experts in environmental law are increasingly in demand in factories and workplaces, but are less wanted by local government. In Czechoslovakia, a pilot program initiated by the law faculty of Charles University, Prague, trained a select group of students to act as environmental legal counsel to local government. But the first graduates of the program in 1981 had great difficulty in getting placed. While local government had initially indicated it would welcome such expertise, it was reluctant to engage it when it was offered.[6]

Textbooks on environmental protection are remarkably free from ideological content, except for the expected assertions that the organization of environmental protection in the "socialist" countries is superior to that in "capitalist" countries because there is no private property. Soviet textbooks also insist that the USSR has done the most for the environment of any country in the world. A representative basic science text, such as *The Foundations of Biology and Ecology* used in the fourth year of gymnasium in Czechoslovakia, takes up such topics as the abiological (sun, air, water, minerals) and biological elements of the environment (plant, animal, and human populations; society), the concept of ecosystem, the geological cycle, conditions for life of an organism, and landscape ecology.[7] The last topic covers land-use planning, using ecological parameters. A text for students in technical courses presents less complex subjects in a more general framework. Thus, two introductory Czech texts on basic theoretical information about environmental protection cover elements of the environment, problems created by human society, the evolution and maintenance of the environment, basic principles of environmental management, a discussion of the protection of the biophysical environment, and the problems of economic development.[8] All three of the books contain excellent charts and graphs. The appendices suggest additional reading, an outline of Czechoslovak and Soviet environmental legislation, and more graphs. The texts prepare the student to accept the value that care and maintenance of the environment is a complex process that must be solved by a comprehensive interdisciplinary approach. American students could profit from such teaching materials.

The advantage of the centipede system is that once the USSR Ministry of Education mandates a program of study, that program is followed in its entirety by every republic in the union. Experimentation in teaching materials and methodology precedes the adoption of the program. Once adopted, teaching manuals instruct the teacher on how to present the materials and when. While the system has obvious rigidities, it has the benefit of providing every schoolchild with virtually the same concepts and information. In the environmental area, this means that thousands of Soviet children are now being sensitized to environmental issues that their parents probably never realized existed.

In the Yugoslav hydra, the strength and depth of the environmental program depends upon the republic. One of the main tasks of the Federal Council for the Protection and Improvement of the Environment is to promote a comprehensive program of environmental education from the lowest level to the highest. In all the republics, children learn basic hygiene in kindergarten. In elementary school, ecological content is integrated into every subject taught in the curriculum. For example, introductory chemistry is not presented as an abstract science, but the danger of certain chemicals to society through air and water pollution is incorporated into instruction on basic chemicals. Ecology is introduced through the basic biology course. In secondary school, environmental education is broken up into special subjects: ecology, environmental economics, society, and nature. As in the Soviet Union, the subject matter differs according to what kind of training the student will have after graduation.

A special program has been developed in Serbia to teach students the technical aspects of environmental protection. The first students graduated from this program in 1980. In other technical programs, environmental education is required to be integrated into the core courses. At the university level, there is as yet no separate faculty for environmental science. However, there is a requirement that all faculties include environmental protection in their curricula. Understandably, the agronomy and forestry faculties devote more time to special aspects of water, air, and land, as these subjects constitute the heart of the discipline. A course in environmental law is offered at Belgrade University and similar courses are being developed at other universities.[9]

An environmental textbook for use in Serbian secondary schools is similar to the Czech texts cited above, only perhaps more interdisciplinary. Its contents cover the purpose of studying environmental protection, the development of pollution in the environment, nature and man-made objects, sources of air pollution, and air pollution control. The text is quite technical, with drawings of different kinds of air filters, the automobile emission system, and a schematic representation of the combustion process, as well as many graphs and charts. The authors' collective is an impressive group of professors from the natural science and mathematics faculty of Belgrade University. The advisers include a member from the Center for Multidisciplinary Studies, a consultant from a biological research institute, and a gymnasium professor.[10] The text attests to the seriousness of the effort to integrate environmental studies into the school curriculum using the multidisciplinary approach.

There are much broader differences between the two countries in the extent of adult or mass media environmental education. The Soviet Union prints a gamut of environmental journals ranging from *Priroda* (Nature) designed for popular consumption to highly specialized scientific journals such as *Okruzhaiushchaia sreda* (The environment). The latest issue of *Priroda* may be bought at most newsstands in the larger Soviet cities. In Yugoslavia, by contrast, there is only one main periodical on the environment: *Čovek i životna sredina* (Man and the environment), which is a scientific publication. It is not available at newsstands and must be purchased through subscription.

Of all the countries in Eastern Europe, the Soviet Union leads the way in the publication of popular books on the environment. In Yugoslavia, visits to bookstores uncovered no adult books and in Belgrade, Ljubljana, and Zagreb, only one or two children's books. In Moscow and Leningrad, by contrast, a goodly number of adult and children's books on the environment could always be found in the appropriate section of the bookstore. The Soviets have a reputation for delightful as well as educational children's books, and those on the environment are no exception. While most of these books are in Russian, the author was pleased to see beautifully designed children's books on environmental topics published in Ukrainian in Kiev and in Belorussian in Minsk. However, popular books on the environment are not distributed equally throughout the country. As foreign scholars in the Soviet Union know, the problem is always to find the particular book you want when and where you need it. It never fails that the one you planned to purchase is sold out. Salespeople in the Moscow bookstores told the author that books on the environment, even the most erudite kind, were very popular and sold out as soon as they appeared. The author herself was very nearly the victim of such popularity. One morning, an English-Russian dictionary of environmental terms was advertised over the radio. In the time it took her to reach the bookstore, there were just two copies left. Twenty-three thousand copies of the dictionary had been issued. Such examples are a convincing indication that the government's environmental book publishing program has clearly been a success. The voracious reading appetite of the Soviet people has eagerly expanded to include the environment.

There are far fewer books published on environmental topics in Yugoslavia because of the high cost of publication and relatively small readership demand. A typical scholarly study on the environment averages between $5.00 and $10.00 and will be issued in 1,500 copies. Such studies are not expected to make a profit, and the publishing houses cannot make up even part of the loss by printing millions of copies of popular literature, as can be done in the Soviet Union. Each republic publishes in its own language, and there are simply not enough readers in any one language. While many Yugoslavs will say they understand and read Serbo-Croatian, Macedonian, and Slovenian with equal facility, fluency in a nonnative language is not common. Moreover, Macedonian and Slovenian books are sold only in special stores in Belgrade, and one would have to go to Skopje or Ljubljana to have access to all the titles. Market limitations coupled with the self-management principle oblige the publisher to choose his manuscripts and his retail outlets very carefully.

Yugoslavs obtain most of their information about the environment from publications imported from abroad or from the mass media. The expense of Western books generally puts Western environmental studies beyond the means of the average person. Students learn Russian so they can buy the cheaper Soviet textbooks. The greatest demand is in the traditional areas of natural science, and the author found only a few specialized environmental studies from the USSR in Yugoslav bookstores. Newspapers, however, are cheap and plentiful. As can be seen from newspaper references in this study, newspaper reporting is constant and provides the Yugoslav man in the street with a steady if not very large flow of material on the environment.

Both governments have taken steps to educate the public in on-site nature conservation. At the entrance to parks and recreation areas in and around Moscow, prominently displayed signs inform visitors of the proper behavior expected of them if the area has been set aside for nature conservation. For example, radios and loud noises are prohibited. Citizens are urged to protect nature as a national heritage, and in some of the parks there are posters with pictures of protected plants that citizens are forbidden to pick. Yugoslav parks carry similar signs. A sign at the entrance to Durmitor National Park urges Yugoslavs to protect nature. Plitvice Lakes Park is particularly well marked to indicate to tourists where cars, camping, boating, and other activities are permitted and where walking only is allowed. One of the most impressive efforts to educate tourists to maintain a clean environment is at the Zlaty Bor Campsite near Split on the Adriatic coast. The campsite is operated by the Yugoslav army. Tourists are instructed that they may camp only in designated areas and not on the beach. Rules of behavior are handed to each incoming tourist with the warning that he may be asked to leave if the rules are not obeyed. Unlike so much of the Adriatic coastline, which is characterized by people-litter, the camp beach is unspoiled, and the recreation areas spotless.

Environmental programs on radio and TV are perhaps the weakest part of the environment efforts in both countries. During the five months that the author watched the evening news on Moscow TV, the only environmental references were the beautiful scenes that accompanied the weather forecast. While there were a few nature programs during the day on such topics as how to recognize mushrooms, the author saw no wildlife or environmental programs during the "prime time" evening hours. In Yugoslavia, academics and environmental experts go on TV from time to time to speak on pollution problems, as did Dr. Todorović and the staff from Belgrade's Institute of Public Health during the Sava River controversy. Moreover, the Federal Council for the Protection and Improvement of the Environment sees to it that the nightly news programs report Yugoslav scientific contributions to pollution control. However, full-length programs of an environmental nature are rare, and those that are presented come generally from abroad (for example, "Wild Kingdom"). The average viewer, at least of Belgrade television, is not likely to see many environmental programs in the course of the year. Federal Council staff admitted that environmental programming had yet to be fully integrated into network broadcast schedules.

On balance, the average Yugoslav citizen is probably exposed far less to environmental information than his Soviet counterpart. However, in both countries, what environmental information is obtained is highly selective.

269

In the Soviet Union, the generally positive presentation of environmental news represents a careful selection of the facts designed to encourage the public to think along certain lines while keeping it ignorant of the real state of affairs. Thus, the public is given sufficient information that an attentive reader would be able to determine what the environmental problems are, but unable to assess their full impact. To determine the extent of a problem he would have to have access on a systematic basis to newspapers and periodicals from all over the USSR. All he can gather from local mass media reporting is that there is a problem; the party and government are aware of it; and steps have been, are being, or will be taken to correct it. Should he want to carry his investigation further, the privileged nature of information denies him access to environmental data from central institutions without permission.

The public official, the researcher, and the layman all face a similar information problem. The difference is in degree, not kind, with the public at the bottom of the information ladder. One of the main tasks of the Czechoslovak Federal Council on the Environment is to inform the public on environmental matters. Yet, it publishes a wide range of material stamped on the back of the front page "not for public consumption," or "for internal use only." The two journals relating planning and the environment published by the Czech Ministry of Construction and Technology also stipulate that the material contained therein is not for public use. Behind the published journals there are many more in-house documents to which the layman has no access whatsoever. In Yugoslavia, similar although less rigorous restrictions pertain if one is interested in obtaining information from a state institute or using a university or institute library.

The tendency toward information monopoly is a characteristic of all bureaucratic organizations. The United States has recognized the tendency in the passage of right-to-know legislation. Even with such guarantees, the American layman is not assured of being able to get the facts. One needs reliable contacts within the bureaucracies, as had Rachel Carson,[11] before one can obtain a clear picture of the dimensions of any one environmental problem. In the Soviet Union and Yugoslavia, information access is even more dependent upon personal contacts, because of the legal existence of censorship and the dissemination of information on a need-to-know basis.

The official environmental public education programs of the two countries thus demand that the individual accept what he hears at face value and engage in environmental activities marked out for him. Should the layman seek to know more, he will find his path blocked by bureaucratic obstacles and closed doors.

Mobilization of the public for environmental purposes. System constraints in both countries provide the citizen scope for action in environmental matters in only three areas: in the workplace; in an officially recognized environmental or youth organization; and in the local community. In all of them, public participation is voluntary. In the Soviet Union, the centipede system directs the environmental volunteer toward the more organized formations of the first two areas, while the greater flexibility and decentralization of the Yugoslav hydra urges more popular involvement at the local community level. It cannot be emphasized sufficiently that the leaderships of the two countries have an interest in seeing their environmental programs realized. But each has more urgent priorities, in particular, the resurrection of the economy. The regimes' mobilization of public participation in environmental matters is thus not merely cosmetic. Rather, it must be seen as a means to provide some public pressure and supervision, in an area where the state authorities prefer to devote less energy and expense, to see that the law, at least minimally, is carried out. The relation between the mobilizing authorities and the mobilized public is a dynamic one, opening up possibilities for the public to extend its influence beyond the permitted limits.

In the Soviet Union, the legal basis for environmental control at the workplace is contained in a 1973 resolution of the Presidium of the Central Council of Trade Unions (CCTU) outlining the participation of the trade unions in fulfilling the 1972 USSR Council of Ministers' resolution on improving environmental protection,[12] and in the 1978 USSR Council of Ministers' resolution calling for additional measures to strengthen environmental protection. Among these measures are instructions for the establishment of environmental committees in every branch ministry down to the factory level. A second measure empowers the republican nature protection societies to realize "social control" over the fulfillment of environmental regulations.[13]

According to the trade union resolution, factory, enterprise, and local

271

trade union committees are required to participate with management in the evaluation of questions relating to reducing the amount of pollution in the factory. The trade union committees are also mandated to make recommendations on ways to control pollution and to bring pollution problems to the attention of management. The CCTU is authorized to work together with management in the implementation of tasks connected with pollution control, drawing on specialists, "rationalizers," and "inventors" to get a particular job done. The CCTU is further to maintain "strict social control over the quality of the decision regarding the design of new objects" (Articles 2 and 3 of Trade Union resolution). Implementation of the resolution proceeded slowly since guidelines had to be drawn up for trade union activity in every industrial branch. In 1977, an environmental commission was established in the CCTU. The competencies assigned to the commission are impressive. If every one were put into practice, they would give the trade unions broad control over the factory environment, ranging from mandatory consultation by the responsible ministry and the CCTU on decisions relating to the factory environment to control over the monitoring of environmental practices at the workplace.[14]

The use of trade union commissions to monitor enterprise fulfillment of environmental regulations is not yet very advanced, and there is a considerable gap between legislation and practice. Petrov indicated that workers were only beginning to realize the effects of noise, air, water, and other forms of pollution on their health, and that, as more information came down from the CCTU, the workers would become more active. Factory workers, he said, were already organizing worker environmental protection committees to monitor factory observance of environmental work regulations. When the question was raised as to whether workers who complained of their work conditions might lose their jobs, he responded with an allegedly true story.

A plant director had called in some workmen to cut down a large old tree in the factory grounds so that he could have a place to park his car. The workmen refused to cut down the tree, saying it beautified the factory area. The workmen were fired. In protest, they took their case to the local soviet. Other workmen were hired to cut down the tree, but eventually the factory director was brought to justice, and the workmen who had lost their jobs were reinstated.

The story confirms that the worker stands to lose a great deal if he goes against management in an environmental question even as small as this one undoubtedly was, but also suggests that if the worker's case has substance and is not too costly to right, it may be upheld by the local authorities. Unfortunately, the story also indicates that the workers were helpless to prevent the degradation of the environment, even though justice eventually prevailed. It would seem therefore that the constraints within which the factory worker works would not encourage him to join in an all-out effort to insist on pollution controls but would rather urge him in the opposite direction, to inaction and apathy.[15]

"Social control" through the republican nature conservation societies, environmental *druzhiny* (parapolice force), and recognized student environmental groups is becoming increasingly widespread and vocal in the Soviet Union. In its 1966 Constitution, the All-Russian (now Soviet) Society for the Preservation of Nature was given the legal authority to organize and administer the social inspection of environmental protection in the RSFSR. The 1982 Constitution expanded this authority and gave the society a new power to make legislative recommendations. The society may further locate and propose natural monuments for inclusion in the nature protection system under the jurisdiction of the local soviets, and it is accorded its own press for the purpose of disseminating environmental information.[16]

Society officials recognize three distinct tasks for its members: the organization and dissemination of environmental protection "propaganda," social or citizen assistance to the authorities in realizing environmental measures, and environmental control. The network of environmental mass organizations is large, with a total all-union membership of 60 to 70 million persons and a 32-million membership in the RSFSR alone. The education functions of the societies are extensive: Most local newspapers have a social section reserved especially for environmental protection issues to which the organization contributes. The All-Russian (Soviet) Society maintains its own news service, which it puts at the disposition of editors of journals, radio, and TV. The society conducts a two-year institute, called the "People's University of Environmental Protection," in technical schools (VUZy), universities, and factories. Upon completion of the course, graduates may become public speakers, members of speaking groups (*lektorskiie*

273

grupy), social inspectors in environmental protection, and volunteer consultants on town beautification and park programs (*po zeleneniiu*). It is also possible to be certified as a *kinolektor*, or public speaker for films. In addition, in all the large cities of the republic, the society maintains and administers nature houses (*doma prirody*). These are centers where all environmental protection activities are held: environmental seminars, the "People's University" lectures, environmental programs organized by the party, programs for professionals and managers, public lectures, and environmental exhibits. In 1980, the Yaroslavl Nature House held a special course for deputies to the local soviet.

To perform its task of assistance to the authorities in environmental protection, the All-Russian (Soviet) Society has a sizable staff organized into thirteen departments representing the major environmental areas, as well as a committee on special problems, such as interrepublican river basins. University and state experts head these departments. Like every other Soviet organization, the departments are organized hierarchically and territorially. Thus, the society's scientific-technical council organizes and supervises the worker technical commissions at the factories, where management, engineers, and workers evaluate environmental control measures for their factory. As an incentive, the society holds a yearly competition among the commissions for the best design of factory environmental controls. The society also mobilizes citizens in their communities to assist local government in town improvement measures, such as tree planting, municipal beautification, and city cleanups. When, for example, the Moscow Gorispolkom (Executive Committee) environmental protection committee calls for citizen action groups, or *aktivy*, the society assumes the major responsibility for mobilizing volunteers.

The public inspection system operates at the workplace and in the community at large. After certification by the "People's University," the new inspector is placed in a basic organization. A small factory might have three to four inspectors; a large factory more. The public inspector works with the official state inspector in the local SES and other government agencies responsible for environmental control. When he determines the law has been broken, he delivers a citation of violation to the local authorities.[17] In addition to the public control exercised by the nature protection societies, there are the people's control commissions organized by local government and the hunting inspectorates established through the appropriate republican ministries in charge of hunting and fishing. Essentially, the participation of the public is the same. The would-be inspectors attend certification classes and then go to work under the supervision of state personnel. Every citation has to be verified by a government supervisor.

There is little grass roots spontaneity about the public's role in these associations. Every member is told what the limits of his activity are and is guided in that activity. Resident scientists and experts exercise leadership of local chapters. The layman has virtually no authority to initiate action. Every step must be cleared with a supervisor, and the citizen faces almost insurmountable bureaucratic hurdles if he goes beyond what is clearly authorized in the society constitutions. Nevertheless, from the citizen's standpoint, the solicitation of his involvement even within the constraints set for his participation identifies an area of opportunity that is denied him as a single isolated individual.

As the authorized vox populi, the nature protection societies, especially in the non-Russian republics, have become increasingly active in recent years. The press has particularly cited the efforts of the Kazakh Society for the Protection of the Natural Environment,[18] the Tadzhik Society for the Protection of Nature,[19] and the Kirgiz Nature Conservation Society.[20] The Georgian Nature Protection Society was only organized in 1980 by a joint party and Georgian Council of Ministers' resolution, but it has also received commendation by the press.[21] Clearly, there are proenvironmental party and government authorities who attach considerable importance to raising the public's environmental consciousness and mobilizing it for environmental objectives. Public opinion can act as a check on irresponsible behavior by the economic and party hierarchies. As a Georgian party official expressed it, "[the analysis of public opinion] is a kind of investigation of republican industry's readiness to implement party and government resolutions on improving the economic machinery, . . . [It] helps improve party committees' organizational and educational work and makes their efforts more effective."[22]

Among the most independent of the nature organizations in the Soviet Union are the student environmental groups. Surprisingly, these groups are not organized hierarchically, but are formed on an ad hoc basis where there is sufficient student interest. In 1979, there were twenty-nine such groups representing an active membership of around three thousand young people.

The MGU (Moscow State University) Young People's Council on Environmental Protection was the pioneer among these organizations. The council originated in the faculty of biology, but quickly became interdepartmental. It now recruits students from every discipline. As might be expected, it runs an information program for students at the university. But it also is involved in several projects that are unique to the group and appear to be run primarily at the students' initiative. These projects have included a study program of recreational resources (*zapovedniki*, nature reserves in the Moscow area and elsewhere, and recreational areas); a garbage disposal project; *Vystrel* (the Shot), where student volunteers go into the woods to control poaching; and *Khoziain o Moskve* (Landlord about Moscow), a project that evaluates problems of environmental control, regulations, and land use in the Moscow area. Students participate in these programs on the basis of their university specialty. If a student is accepted for an expedition to study pollution in Lake Sevan, for example, then he must have taken course work to prepare him for the field experience. The permanent *aktiv* is composed of about fifty students, but in each faculty group, there are probably a hundred students who may be called upon for mass campaigns. The most extensive of these and one for which the council has established a formidable reputation is the New Year's tree campaign. About a thousand students fan out into the railroad stations and the main highways coming into Moscow to check all persons arriving in the city with a fir tree in their possession. Unless an individual can show a receipt of purchase, the chances are he has illegally cut down a tree and is thus liable for a fine. The students catch hundreds of Muscovites annually in their control net.

Once a year, there is a conference where students come from their various universities to attend educational seminars and exchange experiences. Each conference meets in a different university city and is devoted to a special theme or problem. In 1976, the conference in Kirov proposed two new activities, "Fakt" and "Recreation." In 1977, the conference in Perm voted to create a Coordinating Council for the Student Movement in Environmental Protection. The conference is the centerpiece of the MGU Environmental Youth Council's educational program. Other aspects include a newsletter, *Vystrel*, circulated to student groups around the USSR, a general course for students by students in environmental protection, and recreational evenings of films and lectures by faculty and specialists. The annual budget runs to a healthy 15,000 rubles. The council is registered with the International Youth Federation for Environmental Studies and Conservation in Switzerland.[23]

Reports in the MGU Youth Council newsletter indicate considerable activity among the student groups. In 1977, for example, some 3,200 young people were reported as having arrested 3,158 violators, including 226 poachers, 270 speculators, 626 woodcutters, and 499 illegal fishermen. The record for 1978 was as good: 3,018 were caught, among them 181 hunters, 644 fishermen, 1,585 violators of forest regulations, and 213 speculators in the sale of protected birds, flora, and fauna. In addition, members uncovered twenty instances of pollution, wrote 151 articles for the press, and made thirty radio appearances. In 1978, fifteen research groups completed five scientific expeditions, and six other groups worked on identification and data collection for potential nature reserves.[24]

The university environmental groups do not operate independently of all supervision. However, the Moscow University council developed in a rather unique way that appears to have set a precedent for the development of subsequent environmental student organizations. MGU faculty have historically had close ties with the All-Russian Society for the Protection of Nature. At its first conference in 1934, the society elected an MGU scientist as head. At the second congress in 1947, thirty-six of the forty-one individuals elected to the society's executive committee were associated with MGU, eighteen of whom were scientists, and thirteen of whom were members of the MGU Council of Representatives. A youth section for the society was organized in 1941, and in 1960, student environmental groups obtained the right to organize. Students in the MGU geography and biology faculties were the most active and pressed forward with support from their professors. After an initial two-year experimental period, a consolidated MGU Environmental Youth Council obtained its first funding through the Communist Youth League (Komsomol) in 1974.[25]

While the council's plans of activities have to be approved by the league, the council organizationally remains outside the league and is authorized to coordinate environmental campaigns in which youth groups participate either through local government or through the Komsomol. The council thus must gain the support of local government for all community activities. Despite these constraints, the university group appears unique among Soviet organizations in having considerable independence of action with no institutional accountability to a superior unit within its own organization or a supervising umbrella organization embracing all environmental youth groups. The Komsomol still does not have its own environmental subgroup, but it relies on the university organizations, and on the MGU Environmental Youth Council, in particular, for leadership in environmental matters. Apparently, the council has not been required to seek an all-union affiliation with any mass organization. The council is understandably proud of its status and achievements. Conversations with council members revealed an enthusiasm and motivation that was entirely lacking in discussions with the professional administrators of the All-Russian Society.

Given its location at MGU, the MGU Youth Council represents an elite group of students coming mostly from the natural and social science fields. These students form the nucleus of the future environmental "invisible college" networks between the Academy of Sciences institutes (where no doubt the majority will go after graduation), the universities, and the branch ministerial research institutes. Advised and encouraged by the older generation of scientists, they carry on and transfer to the next generation the environmental concern of their professors. At the annual conferences, young environmentalists from all over the Soviet Union come in contact with one another and share similar experiences. Clearly, the student environmental groups of today are the heart of the scientific environmental lobby of tomorrow, the future leaders of the environmental mass organizations, and next generation of consultants to state and party authorities.

The final area of public involvement in environmental protection is in the community. Mention was made in chapter 5 of the recruitment of the public into the environmental *aktivy* organized by the municipal environmental protection subcommittees. Here again, public participation is solicited and is intended to produce the results that are desired and orchestrated by those in charge. The public may express its unsolicited desires through the "voters' requests," the write-in petitions addressed to deputies at election time. A review of the bulletins of the executive committees of the Moscow and Leningrad city soviets from 1970 to 1981 reveals a surprising number of these requests concerned with environmental matters. Voter requests in Leningrad filed in November 1974 included requests to improve a district water supply, take down a compressor station on the banks of the Obvod Canal, have a forestry commission upgrade Nevsky Forest as a recreation area, and complete the reconstruction of the city's children's park. Out of three hundred requests, 125 involved improvement of the environment, or 42 percent.[26] During the same election year, similar requests were addressed to deputies to the Moscow City Soviet, although the proportion of petitions regarding the environment was lower. Deputies are obligated to implement these requests. Implementation may take a long time, but the status of the requests is a matter of public knowledge and must be published from time to time in the gorispolkom bulletins. The number of environmental requests suggests a strong association in the public's mind between an aesthetic and clean environment and acceptable living conditions. Individuals also have limited opportunities to speak up in public meetings or in their residential areas. Citizen protest spared many trees during the restoration of residential blocks in the Old Town of Prague and resulted in the planting of trees in a new residential complex in the outskirts of Leningrad.

The local chapter of the nature protection society can play a leading role in representing the public's views on a community environmental issue. Since the newspapers do not carry accounts of these efforts, it is difficult to measure how widespread they are. In Banská Bystrica in Czechoslovakia, the author learned that the militancy of the local Defenders of Nature organization had successfully prevented the cutting down of some old trees lining a city boulevard. The chapter had also worked hard to have a certain meadowland set aside as a protected area.

The involvement of the Yugoslav layman in environmental protection is not nearly as well organized or as strongly promoted by the government as in the Soviet Union. First of all, although workplaces are now required to implement environmental measures, and workers' councils must set aside monies for environmental protection before they decide what to do with the unallocated factory profit, the trade unions have yet to become involved in the overseeing of environmental performance at the workplace. Since self-management posits worker ownership of the factory, in theory it is the task of the worker in his role as self-managing plant owner to ensure the proper pollution controls, not the trade union.

Second, there is no sociopolitical organization for environmental protection like the Soviet variant that the layman may join. The closest is the system of councils for the protection and improvement of the human environment that extend from the federal to the local level. But these councils are primarily mobilizers of public activity. The public per se does not join them. Rather, the councils work with local government, the republican and local health services, and the research institutes to develop environmental campaigns (*akcije*) in which the public is urged to participate. The main function of the Federal Council for the Protection and Improvement of the Environment is to orchestrate popular participation through the sponsorship of environmental action and educational campaigns under the auspices of the republic and town environmental organs. It is not a mass organization.

An example of a Federal Council *akcija* may be found in the 1981 campaign, "88 Roses for President Tito." In the spring of that year, the Federal Council sponsored and organized a nationwide tree-planting campaign to commemorate the first anniversary of Tito's death. Tito was 88 when he died. A town, factory, or school could honor his death by planting in his memory 88 bushes or trees, which were supplied through the council at little or no cost. The campaign had a political and environmental educational goal. The political goal was to unite the entire country in paying public respect to the father of modern Yugoslavia. The environmental goal was to help beautify the local community and thereby assist the country's much needed reforestation program. The two goals together were designed to promote public awareness of the fact that environmental protection was an integral and necessary component of socialist Yugoslavia's development. According to the former secretary general of the council, Milivoje Todorović, a campaign of this kind may be considered a "typical" Yugoslav environmental *akcija*, combining the political with the environmental.

Action campaigns in Yugoslavia are voluntary in a different sense than in the United States. On March 25, 1981, the Niš paper, *The People's News*, reported that the town of Aksintsa was one of the first to vote to plant the 88 trees.[27] On March 27, 1981, the Permanent Conference of

Towns and Opštini formally approved the campaign.[28] On March 29, the Macedonian Council for the Protection and Improvement of the Human Environment gave its approval to the action.[29] By April 1, 3,200 local communes had approved the project.[30] Once the commune has approved an *akcija*, it is obligated to carry it out. The aim of the Federal Council was to persuade all 15,000 communes of Yugoslavia to join the program; 100 percent approval would mean the campaign was a success. Since, however, the public had nothing to do either with the initiation of the program or with its implementation, the volunteering of services in effect indicated little about public attitudes regarding the environment.

Within the Socialist Alliance, there are the Yugoslav professional societies mentioned in chapter 6 that are concerned with the protection of a specific environmental area, such as air or water. However, membership in these societies is confined mainly to specialists, and when they speak out on environmental issues, their opinion, as noted in the previous chapter, is given from the expert's perspective, not from the layman's point of view.

It is a pity that no lay environmental organization functions in Yugoslavia. Unlike the Soviet Union, Yugoslavia does not have a century-old environmental tradition, nor has it inherited a nature protection society from precommunist times. Yugoslavs attribute their failure to develop a popular environmental conscience to the long period of Turkish rule and the focus of national effort on national independence. There is, of course, no reason today why a nature society could not be formed. The fact that none yet exists attests to the continuing absence of strong popular awareness of environmental issues. Seen in this light, campaigns such as the "88 Roses" have a special relevance and urgency.

The two organizations most oriented toward popular participation are youth groups: the Gorani Movement (*Pokret Gorani*) and the Organization of Young Researchers (*Mladi istraživaci*). As with most institutions in Yugoslavia, the two movements exist in every republic but are more active in some than in others.

Every Yugoslav may belong to the Gorani Movement. Membership is neither formal nor permanent. However, mostly young people are actively involved. The movement began some twenty-five years ago with the aim of promoting reforestation and antierosion programs among the public. It expanded its activities to include beautification and the education of young people in nature conservation. The movement conducts lectures and education and nature conservation demonstration programs. The hope is that once young people begin to appreciate the environment, they will be more interested in its protection and more willing to vote the money to protect it.

The organization has a brigade in every primary school and local community. One to three delegates are elected from every brigade to serve a two-year term in the opština body. There are 150 opština bodies in Serbia. The yearly program is determined by the opština organizations that meet once every four years for a regional conference. In typical Yugoslav administrative fashion, the regional conferences elect representatives to the republican conference, which elects a one-term president and praesidium. The presidium and lower executive committees are voluntary offices, but the presidium has a central office with eight paid staff. The presidium draws up general five-year and one-year plans as guidelines for the lower organizations. Financing is provided by the opština and the regional and republican forestry service. Local work organizations contribute upon request, and when technicians, specialists, or transport are needed, these are provided free of charge by the work organizations.

Large reforestation projects involving a thousand hectares are organized at the Gorani Movement republican level, as they require around three hundred volunteers for at least two months. Lesser projects are based on opština reforestation plans, where local foresters determine the numbers and kinds of trees needed. The Gorani volunteers decide how many people are required to do the job and provide tents, food, and the small necessities. Much of the tree planting is done during the school term. The children's brigades elect an executive committee, commander, secretary, and child in charge of the food. The projects take place on weekends, and only the larger ones occur during the summer months. In general, these are sponsored by the communist youth organization rather than the school. In addition, the movement conducts environmental education programs in the schools and organizes community lectures by environmental specialists. Once or twice a year, there is a membership drive to recruit new students.

So far, no study has been conducted to determine what influence the movement may have had in changing popular attitudes about the environment. The movement leadership believes it has been substantial. Fifteen years ago, it says, the peasants were against reforestation on fertile ground. Now they are eager to receive trees or to have the school children plant in their town. There is no doubt that the reforestation effort has been effective. In 1960, according to the forestry service, 200,000 hectares of land needed to be reforested in Serbia alone. Since that time, 140,000 of those have been reforested by the Gorani Movement. An additional 25,000 hectares have been planted with communal greenery and 35,000 with grass. There are still 1.2 million hectares requiring reforestation in the rest of Yugoslavia, and Gorani volunteers will plant close to two-thirds of that. Approximately 20,000 hectares are planted each year.[31]

With the decrease in funding from central sources after the adoption of self-management, the movement was hard pressed to maintain its momentum. One forestry enthusiast in the town of Bečej in the Vojvodina conceived of the idea of starting a Gorani nursery and having the movement raise the trees needed for reforestation. After nine years of talking and persuading, Miša Pejović succeeded in raising 50,000 dinars from volunteer contributors and persuaded the town of Bečej to donate ten and a half hectares to the project. Today, the Gorani headquarters building and the nursery cover four of those hectares, and six make up the Gorani Movement's Park of Brotherhood and Unity. The nursery's trees are distributed all over Yugoslavia. Those designated for reforestation by the movement are donated; other organizations must pay.[32]

For all its impressive record, the Gorani Movement remains an organization run for young people by authorized, interested adults for a specific purpose. The secretary of the Serbian conference is an older person as is Miša Pejović, the founder of the Gorani Nursery. There is little room within the movement for youth initiative. On the contrary, the movement's leadership seeks to direct youthful energy toward appropriate preselected environmental goals. In its pedagogical aims and dependence on public funds, it resembles the Soviet nature societies, but with a more narrow application.

The Organization of Young Researchers was founded in 1976 to promote scientific interest primarily among university students. Affiliated with the communist youth organization, its membership is not rigid but open to all students with a scientific bent. Of its basic organizations, twenty-six are in Belgrade University alone, in the faculties of biology, geology, and geography. The rest of the groups are widely dispersed in fifty other cities. The organization has grown from two local societies in 1975 to the present number organized into regional and republican conferences. Like the MGU Environmental Youth Council, the Organization of Young Researchers has strong ties with the Yugoslav communist youth organization and the scientific community. The yearly program is drawn up by an appointed commission, of whom ten represent the Young Researchers, nine belong to the Youth Organization, and two are drawn from interested scientific and social institutions.

The Young Researchers' principal activity is the administration of some fifty summer programs involving supervised research in various academic disciplines. Most of the programs are in the sciences, but there are also a few in architecture, art, and archeology. About half the programs involve research in an environmental or environmentally related area. The programs are chosen on the basis of expressed need by a scientific or social organization. According to the leadership, every program must contain three elements: it must be of interest to youth; there must be an organization that can use the research results; and it must demonstrate a benefit to society, namely, the promotion of science in education. Every program is supervised by the sponsoring organization, which also provides equipment free. Transportation to the research site is provided free of charge by the transport industry, while food and lodging are generally provided by the commune in which the study area is located. Environmental projects of a long-term nature include the identification of rare species in Durmitor National Park and the sampling and testing of water at fifty-five points along the Sava River under the supervision of the Slovenian, Croatian, and Serbian hydrometeorological institutes. In 1981, the Serbian organization tested the water supply of Eastern and Central Serbia.[33]

The constraints upon participation are obvious. Each program is highly organized and requires the active cooperation of a large number of bureaucracies, from scientific institutes, to the transport industry, to republican and local governmental institutions. Within these limits, initiative from the young people is sought and encouraged. The author was privileged to attend an organizational meeting to launch the Sava River project in the spring of 1981. The meeting was composed of representatives from the Young Researchers, the Serbian Public Health Department, the communist youth organization, Belgrade University, and Belgrade TV. In the give and take of discussion, the young people were treated on an equal basis with the adults. The two members of the Researchers' Presidium were thoroughly prepared. They explained the project clearly, answered questions without hesitation, and asked questions in turn. Their interest and enthusiasm made the project seem as much theirs as anyone's. At the meeting, the representatives from the interested scientific and social organizations gave their verbal agreement to sponsor the project and offered equipment and expertise.[34] While strong direction and support was provided by the scientific professionals and the political organizations, the students themselves were left to decide whether to undertake a project, and then they had to do most of the legwork to assure its realization.

In organization and modus operandi, the Yugoslav groups mentioned above differ little from the Soviet model. Each form of organization has a pedagogical purpose. Neither country has a truly federal mass environmental organization. Like the Yugoslav organizations, the Soviet nature societies operate on a republican basis, some being more active than others. Like their Yugoslav counterparts, the republican leadership holds the main levers of control. Assuredly, the self-management principle provides for a little more grass-roots flexibility and initiative, witness the founding of the Gorani Tree Nursery, but the necessity of finding outside funding means more direct cooperation with industry than is the case in the Soviet example. Both systems rely heavily on assistance from the state health and environmental agencies.

Where Yugoslavia differs most from the Soviet Union is in the degree of public influence possible at the local community level. Two incidents will illustrate the kinds of opportunities that exist.

The first is the public controversy over the proposed location of a nuclear power plant on Vir Island, one of the less frequented spots along the Adriatic coast. The town fathers were compelled to refuse the project amid mounting public concern about the safety of the plant.[35] The second is the reclamation of Lake Palić. This action was started by the principal of the local high school in the city of Subotica just south of the Hungarian border in the Vojvodina. The principal, a chemist by profession, was also one of the founding members and head of the Subotica Council for the Protection and Improvement of the Human Environment. Due to his initiative and the cooperation of local scientists, the community voted the necessary funds to drain and clean the lake and install a water treatment system. Suboticans are justly proud of the fact that the project was a product of the self-management system. The money was raised locally, local science contributed the expertise, and local contractors did the work. By the mid-seventies, the lake water was probably cleaner than at any time during the past century. The lake was stocked with fish, Yugoslav and Hungarian tourists began flocking to the resort, and the restaurant and motel business picked up.

The two examples suggest the scope of the opportunities available in Yugoslavia for the public to provide input into local environmental decisions. While legally it is possible for the republican or federal authorities to override a local decision if they determine a compelling social interest, it is significant that in the sensitive Vir Island case, they did not choose to exercise this option. At Lake Palić, the cleaning of the lake might have had a less positive outcome if federal or republican monies had been needed to complete it, but the commune is free to undertake any environmental initiative so long as no outside funding is required and the public approves. It is difficult to see the public having either of these opportunities in the Soviet Union.

Significantly, in neither of the countries is the public organized to express itself nationwide on environmental issues. In Yugoslavia, the hydra system clearly discourages the formation of transrepublican associations. And the Soviet leadership has not yet seen fit to establish one. The decentralization of the expression of public opinion on environmental matters is the most serious structural constraint on the public's ability to influence environmental policymaking.

Regulation. As with expertise, both countries attach great importance to the rules and regulations on popular participation in environmental matters. Activities that have not been sanctioned by law or, in the Yugoslav case, by contract, are not only suspect but in most instances not permitted. The legal environmental organizations have thus a vested interest in seeing their participation officially sanctioned in every document that pertains to environmental matters. As environmental groups have discovered in the United States, there is no arguing with legal standing or the fact that it opens doors to new and expanded forms of action.

Earlier, we mentioned the tasks assigned by special government resolution to the Soviet trade unions in the monitoring of environmental protection in the factories. In his classroom lectures on environmental law, Dr. Petrov mentioned a few incidents where factory trade union councils had protested their conditions citing the relevant passages in the 1971 Fundamental Labor Law guaranteeing labor safety (Articles 59–62) and the guidelines for union control over the observance of labor safety and worker health (Article 96).[36] In his opinion, these protests marked the beginning of worker activism in environmental matters. As the local councils became more aware of the protection afforded by the regulations, they would insist on their strict enforcement.

Petrov further identified a new environmental role for trade unions in the supervision of worker recreation. In 1980, there was an agreement between the CCTU Council on Tourism and the Administration for Nature Protection, Nature Reservations, and Forest and Game Preserves on trade union responsibility for law enforcement in national parks. According to the agreement, instructors and responsible personnel at trade union camps became liable for any action taken by those under their supervision. If the trade union tourist broke the law, the instructor was required to bring him to justice. Since the trade union organizations are involved in a great many tourist activities, strict enforcement of the agreement could reduce environmental damage at campsites and fragile areas frequented by hikers and nature lovers.

Under Article 88 of the RSFSR Civil Code, the trade union organization is responsible for damage done by a worker during his work hours. The law requires the individual to pay a third of the assessed damage if the incident occurred accidentally. If it was deliberate, he must pay the entire assessed cost. By extension, therefore, the Council on Tourism is responsible for the worker during his recreation time. If the damage is accidental, the worker pays one-third and the council two-thirds. If it is deliberate, the worker must pay all, and the payment may be deducted from his wages. In Petrov's view, Article 88 of the Civil Code virtually guarantees a worker's interest in preventing environmental damage. Because he is legally liable for the deliberate commission of a pollution offense, the worker will want to cooperate with the factory trade union committees to ensure a cleaner environment.[37] The argument is reasonable. However, worker activism in recreational matters and in the factory would seem to depend more on the attitude of the trade union environmental protection committee toward a

287

factory's or individual's infringement of environmental regulations and the receptivity of factory management to environmental controls than on an article in a civil code. Petrov agreed that trade union initiative might be low at the present time, but he believed it would rise as workers learned more about the value of regulation in preventing health hazards. In his view, "social control" through the trade unions was a method whose time had not quite come.

Personnel in the All-Russian Society for the Protection of Nature also placed great emphasis on the legal description of its permissible activities, stressing that where there were no specific legal guidelines, it was illegal for society members to engage in that activity. In areas where the society could legally operate, the society staff saw many opportunities to be effective. In their view, the republican associations had been particularly active in the discovery and promotion of new nature reserves. Their zeal in this domain had been so strong that the preservation of protected land had taken on national cultural overtones. Landmarks associated with the national past of a republic's dominant ethnic group were increasingly finding their way into the reserve system. The societies were also actively engaged in writing letters to the press and offering opinions on local and republican environmental legislation, as stipulated in the 1972 Council of Ministers' resolution and the revised society constitutions. However, the All-Russian Society officials stressed that legal competence stopped at the republican level. The republican societies' constitutions do not allow them to give an opinion on fundamental environmental legislation (*osnovy*), or on regulations that pertain to the central ministries outside the jurisdiction of the republics.

Legal standing was also very important to the MGU Youth Council. Its leadership expressed particular satisfaction over its relatively independent status and the broad scope of its authorized activities. The obtention of the right to organize in 1960 represented a great step forward for the group, as did the receipt of the first Komsomol funds in 1974. Without legal standing, the group would not be able to undertake summer research programs, publish a legal journal, or hold public seminars. Most important, it would be unable to receive any state financial support.

Regulation also makes it possible for citizens to be active at the local level and send "voters' requests" to local delegates at election time. The same regulation requires that local soviets act on these requests. While one can argue that all of these rules are too insignificant to enable the public to exercise any real influence, the fact remains that they are there to be utilized. The tremendous growth in environmental reporting over the past ten years indicates that not only is the public becoming increasingly sensitized to the environmental degradation around it but that there is public interest in the issues and thus indirect pressure to report progress, particularly when local environmental chapters are involved.

In Yugoslavia, legal standing is equally important. An action initiated by the Federal Council for the Protection and Improvement of the Environment, such as the "88 roses," requires legally binding republican and local approval before it can be carried out. It took nine years for the Gorani Nursery to obtain official approval and contracts from work organizations and the town to go into business. The Young Researchers must reach agreement with a whole range of bureaucratic institutions to conduct the summer research programs, and these compacts have the force of law. Some agreements are more easily reached than others. While the Serbian organizations welcomed the Young Researchers' project on the Sava River, the Croatian and Slovenian organizations were not as enthusiastic, and only the first phase of the plan was implemented. Without agreement of support from the necessary organizations, the Young Researchers could not carry on their research. Regulation not only permits a group to act but defines the scope of its activities and designates funding. As with the environmental agencies and expertise, regulation is the most important factor promoting the public's input into environmental policymaking.

Numbers and Need

The two greatest assets possessed by the public are numbers showing the growing incidence of environmentally related diseases, and the dependence of the environmental authorities upon the mobilization of the public to help achieve its environmental goals.

Numbers. Environmentally induced illness, changes in the mortality rate due to environmental reasons, sterility, lost work days related to environmental causes: these factors more than any other except the exhaustion of resources motivate governments to environmental action, particularly when the problem extends to large numbers of the population. Mention was made in chapter 5 of Dr. Mitrović's calculations of cost and savings in health care when pollution is reduced. At the first USSR/USA Symposium on the Economic Aspects of Environmental Protection, held at Yerevan in October 1977, Dr. V. V. Bulgakov of the Kiev Scientific Institute of General and Public Health investigated the cost of air pollution in terms of pollution-related illness and loss of working time in ferrous metallurgy plants in the Ukraine. He concluded that per thousand persons, the medical costs just for the treatment of an additional number of people suffering from pollution-induced illness was 1,827 rubles per year, and production losses for one hundred workers in terms of disability payments and national income loss was 3,500 rubles.[38] These figures are for one region in the Ukraine only. Bulgakov did not include every cost into his calculations, and he omitted payments to parents who must absent themselves from work to care for sick children. Still, his estimate is useful in that it does provide a crude measure of the cost of pollution to public health. Although the sums involved may seem trivial when applied to a hundred workers or a thousand members of the population, when multiplied over the total population of the USSR, they become substantial.

Statistical evidence that environmental conditions do contribute to the incidence of sickness and serious disease in the Soviet Union is increasingly finding its way into Soviet scientific publications. E. Z. Danilova has reported that among women workers in the chemical industry, there is a higher percentage of premature births, newborn mortality, and birth of handicapped children than in the normal population. In the rubber industry, women exposed to harmful chemicals experienced interrupted menstruation, and the average number of pregnancies was two times less than in a control group not exposed to the same chemicals. Women working in the presence of toxic materials and paints were observed to have a higher incidence of complications during pregnancy and to suffer from more gynecological disturbances than those working in other conditions. It is worth noting that at the present time, the majority of workers working with paints and toxic materials in machine construction, the electronics industry, aviation, and other branches of industry are women.[39]

Based on a highly detailed study of public health in a Leningrad district from 1958 to 1973, V. A. Miniaev and I. V. Poliakov found that in the ten most important branches of industry in Leningrad, the highest incidence of illness in the study period was in the textile, light metallurgy, chemical, and paper and wood processing industries where there was greater pollution, and the lowest was in the autotransport, communications, and construction materials industries. They further found that problems most associated with the growth in temporary work incapacity in all ten industrial branches were inflammation of the lungs, hypertension, and bronchitis. Among the other factors contributing to increased illness was the length of time spent traveling to and from work every day. Significantly, traveling time of over an hour each day tended to increase the incidence of lost work days no matter what the age cohort. While the authors explain the increase as being mainly due to psychological factors, they did not rule out the possibility that car and bus emissions also played a role. Most important, the authors document a change in the type of illness characteristic of large cities, and stress the increased incidence of cancer, which they attribute to environmental factors, as well as diseases associated with the respiratory and cardiovascular systems.[40] The authors join demographer M. S. Bednyi in urging reform in the public health care system and greater emphasis on improving living conditions.[41] A Yugoslav study of the effects of air pollution on respiratory ailments in school children in two Serbian towns, one highly polluted and the other less so, likewise found that children in the heavily polluted town tended to exhibit significantly more cases of nasal congestion, tonsilitis, and chronic bronchial cough.[42]

Soviet scientist Iu. V. Medvedkov has proposed a model of the interaction between man and his urban environment as a basis upon which to calculate the impact of urban environmental conditions on human health.[43] Both the Twenty-sixth and Twenty-seventh CPSU Congresses took notice of the country's changing public health picture in their promise to strengthen the preventive health program, expand the health care network, and improve the production of pharmaceutical products. But they were silent on improving the urban environment.[44]

The public health problem is the passive aspect of the "numbers" asset. Pollution is affecting increasing proportions of the populations of the two countries, forcing the authorities to take remedial action. However, at the present time, probably a very small percentage of the people realize the degree to which pollution has jeopardized their health. In both countries, water remains the number one pollution-related public health danger, and there is definitely some popular awareness of the associated risks. If there was ignorance before, the oil spillage into the Sava River certainly served to bring the problem to the forefront of at least the Serbian public's attention. Unfortunately, it is characteristic of environmental problems that they generally occur within a confined area. Water contamination threatens only Belgrade, not the Slovenian and Croatian cities upriver. Air pollution, including transboundary effects, is also a regional phenomenon, whether it be in Ekibastuz, Alma-Ata, or Skopje, while noise is the most location-specific of all pollution forms. The localization of environmental problems tends to discourage active public involvement. Where groups have organized for environmental causes in the United States, including the Alaska pipeline, the cause has tended to be a regional problem but with global implications (saving endangered species), not a nationwide problem. Indeed, one reason for U.S. federal foot-dragging on transboundary air pollution is that the effects of acid rain are felt in a circumscribed area with a small population, while the costs of additional controls have an impact on a more populous and more economically important industrial area.

The public's limited access to information, and the regional segmentation of its activities, makes it difficult if not impossible for the layman to mount the sort of mass action that would be effective in persuading governments to take strong remedial action where the public's health is threatened. National organization would seem to be required to enable a popular environmental lobby to mobilize sufficient pressure to influence effectively the solution of a regional environmental problem. Numbers make a difference. In the absence of transnational environmental associations in the Soviet Union and Yugoslavia, numbers remain a potential asset that provides tangible evidence of environmentally induced illness to spur government enforcement of pollution controls.

Need. In both countries, the environmental agencies and government administrations need the public to implement their environmental programs. Downing has shown the importance to the EPA of building local constituencies to support air quality standards after the passage of the Clean Air Act of 1970. Toward this end, the agency stimulated public participation at public hearings and encouraged the formation of local coalitions capable of monitoring the implementation of the standards. During the implementation phase, the EPA was forced into a process of complex bargaining with the states and industry that were seeking to undermine agency power and prevent the agency's rigid enforcement of the law. The public, organized into environmental groups, became a necessary party in the bargaining process to hold up higher standards against intense political pressure on the agency from industry and the state administrations to settle for lower ones.[45] The EPA would forfeit its right to exist if it were perceived to have been "bought" by the regulated interests, as the public outcry against Gorsuch proved. To secure its legitimacy and its influence, it must be able to mobilize a mass environmental constituency.

Some of these findings may be applied to the Soviet and Yugoslav situations. The environmental agencies of both countries need a constituency to secure their legitimacy and to serve as a reason for the expansion of their regulatory activities. If they are not to be completely drawn into the *kompromis* with industry, they need environmental activists to monitor the implementation of environmental regulations. Scientists and specialists may be of use in the policy input stage in delineating the importance of the problem and its possible solutions; but the goal of environmental management is not to serve the interests of scientists but to guarantee a better life for the mass of the population. The public needs to demand quality environmental protection and to be in a position to make its presence felt when that is not provided. Moreover, so long as neither government is able to allocate the funds necessary to mount a comprehensive and effective enforcement system, public volunteers can fill in the most serious gaps.

The monitoring and inspection powers delegated to the nature protection societies and the people's control agencies in the Soviet Union, even though highly circumscribed, are indicative of the special relationship between the environmental agencies and the public in the implementation of environmental regulations. They further prove that this relationship is recognized by those within the ruling circle who are concerned with environmental protection. The absence of any bona fide mass organization in Yugoslavia suggests that the Yugoslav leadership either is still unaware of the importance of this relationship or does not yet consider the environmental issue to be of sufficient proportions to launch a serious attempt to implement the tangle of environmental laws. On the other hand, press

293

criticism is becoming increasingly outspoken on the existence of myriad environmental regulations and compacts to which environmental inspectors turn a blind eye. Perhaps the environmental agencies themselves may be beginning to recognize the tie between the mobilization of public demand and their ability to implement the law.

Like the numbers asset, the dependency of the environmental agencies upon mobilized public support remains a potential rather than actual source of popular proenvironmental influence in both countries. The commendations given in the Soviet press to the activities of environmental groups, especially to their assistance in bringing an enterprise into compliance with the law, are indications that it might not take much to transform a potential asset into an actual instrument of public pressure, even within the constraints of public participation. The initiative shown by the MGU Environmental Youth Council is a case in point. In order that such a transformation occur, however, the leaderships in both countries must be convinced that environmental protection is a matter of priority and that mobilization of the public toward this end will not undermine their position in society. Given the dependence of the Communist party upon the economy as an instrument to safeguard its power, one cannot expect any rapid change in attitude. Yet the Soviet leadership has changed its attitude toward its scientific personnel. The threat that environmental pollution represents to public health and to economic development suggests that the regimes will seek to encourage the relationship between the environmental agencies and the public as an important means of assuring implementation of environmental objectives.

Costs and Benefits

There is virtually no information on the actual cost to the state in maintaining the environmental organizations, but given their volunteer status, the costs are small. From the party and government's point of view, low cost is the ultimate benefit in the utilization of volunteers in the implementation of environmental programs. Moreover, local chapters of the nature protection societies in the Soviet Union, for example, do not require as much funding as the central offices of the republican associations. Some idea of cost may be found in the budget of the Yugoslav Organization of

Young Researchers in Serbia. To run the programs and to cover administrative expenses for a permanent republican office, seminars and the annual conference, the Researchers had an annual budget of 2 to 3 million dinars in 1980 and 1981, about $50,000 to $75,000 at the time. Of these funds 50 percent came from the republican SIZOVA (education, culture, water, health) and the funds for forestry and the underdeveloped areas. The other 50 percent came from the Serbian organizations who used the research results. Given that the total public budget of the Republic of Serbia was 191 million dinars,[46] the Young Researchers' budget funded from public sources represents barely 0.5 percent of the total. This figure does not represent a separate budget item, but is included in the annual SIZ allocations. The Young Researchers' budget thus represents only a minor input from state sources, and the Gorani Movement receives no state funding at all. The country is thus obtaining scientific and environmental benefits at a minimum cost outlay.

On the other hand, the lay environmental activist is not free in either country to go out and raise money for a project of his own invention. Every environmental project must be carried out by a recognized, authorized group that receives funds either through the state budget via the ministries and mass organizations, as in the Soviet Union, or by contract agreements with the appropriate funding parties, as in Yugoslavia. The impossibility of private funding rules out the formation of environmental groups whose environmental objectives the leadership may not be in agreement with, such as an antinuclear organization.

In both countries, the cost to the layman of personal involvement in environmental matters would seem to outweigh the benefits. Unless one works through a legal organization, one is breaking the law. Moreover, as Petrov's story about the workman indicates, acting within the law against established interests may result in losing one's job, although the risk is less severe in Yugoslavia. Direct input into substantive environmental policy is not possible, and the bureaucratic structure of involvement frustrates participation. Political apathy has not been confined to the Soviet variant of communist one-party states. One of the chief criticisms that has surfaced in the discussion of reform in Yugoslavia has been the distance between the worker and the bureaucracies that purport to represent him. A 1984 survey of 13,200 local communities reported that 2,500 of them felt their

295

delegates did not represent them.[47] Caught between the self-management principle and the representation of workers' interests, Yugoslav trade unions are popularly viewed primarily as instruments of government propaganda. In 1984, there were 176 illegal strikes in Yugoslavia.[48] The public finds little response in the delegate system or trade union representation. Residents living near a cement factory or the Zastava Automobile Plant may complain about fumes or pollution, but there is no solution without recourse to a long bureaucratic process the results of which are uncertain. Under these conditions, why get involved?

The only place where the benefits are tangible with virtually no costs involved is at the local community level. Here, a tree that is saved from the woodsman's axe is visible, and a new local park or recreational area, particularly if it can be associated with regional or national cultural history, gives the group that promoted it an immediate sense of gratification. In terms of individual rewards, we have seen how several of the Soviet republics have taken to commending the nature protection societies for their efforts in environmental protection, notably in Kazakhstan, Tadzhikistan, and Kirgizia.[49] Environmental actions are also praised in some Soviet factories. In Yugoslavia, neither the trade unions nor any other mass organization are in a position to give such commendations. Recognition tends to come through the community. The respective opštini were loud in their appreciation of the Gorani Nursery at Bećej and the cleaning of Lake Palić. Nevertheless, as elsewhere in the world, the reward for environmental involvement is primarily personal. Those who have a definite environmental concern that they want to see remedied derive the most personal satisfaction. Miša Pejović is one such person. Members of the local chapters of the Soviet nature protection societies are others. For these people as for environmentalists the world over, the knowledge that they have contributed to building a better environment, and that they have been able to make their contribution within the constraints imposed upon them, is all the reward they need.

Such benefits are not sufficient to mobilize mass public involvement in face of the considerable risks. Censorship has served its purpose. Understandably, the authorities want to direct the public's energies to objects of their choosing. Charter 77 attacked the Czechoslovak government for its secrecy in environmental matters and for its attempt to create the impression that environmental degradation was a manageable problem in the process of being resolved. The Chartists proposed an open public discussion on the state of the environment in Czechoslovakia and the free election of environmental committees. These committees would act as watchdogs in plants and would have the right to halt plant production and stop capital construction.[50] While public awareness of specific local environmental problems may be adequate, what is out of sight is out of mind. Few individuals see any reason to pressure the authorities on a broader front. When the political climate becomes freer and the facts about pollution become public knowledge as they did in Poland, mobilization occurs spontaneously and leads to immediate remedial action by the authorities.

Strategies

Because public activity in the environmental domain is mainly confined to the local area, there is little information about it in the national press. Much of what follows has been learned from personal communication to the author. The public in both countries appears to be beginning to expand the opportunities afforded them by the regulatory principle, mainly through the use of formal channels and mass protest. A second strategy is one we have seen successfully utilized by both the territorial administrations and the experts, namely, recourse to the press.

Exploitation of formal channels. Formal channels in the Soviet Union involve the "voters' requests" and the activities of the chapters of the nature protection societies. As was shown earlier, a large number of voters' requests are in the environmental area. Since these requests are not individually inspired, they represent a consensus on the issues brought forward. Voters' demands for a cleaner environment thus reflect a general attitude among the public rather than any one individual's desire to have a tidy lawn in front of his apartment complex. The only direct contact that the author had with the activities of a nature protection association was in Czechoslovakia. Since it is similar in structure and organizational style to the Soviet societies, the Czechoslovak example is indicative of the type of action open to officially recognized environmental organizations.

The Slovak Society of the Defenders of Nature was organized soon after

297

the 1969 federal division of Czechoslovakia and immediately became very active. The success of the society's chapters in directing official attention to stopping local environmental degradation has been in large measure dependent upon the degree to which local authorities have been sensitive to environmental issues and willing to listen to local society chapters. The city of Banská Bystrica in Central Slovakia is known for its proenvironmental municipal administration. When the local environmental chapter protested the felling of a row of venerable trees to make way for new construction, the town fathers listened. The trees still stand, and the construction area is now a park. In the local chapter meeting rooms, wall posters and maps highlight environmental trouble spots in the chapter's territory. At the time of the author's visit, the chapter was very concerned about the increasing pollution of the Hron River by factories upstream from Banská Bystrica. Its immediate worry was the pollution of a tributary of the Hron, the Bystrica River, caused by one of Slovakia's largest pulp and paper plants. The chapter was demonstrating its formal concern by writing letters to the local newspapers and opening chapter meetings on the topic to the public.

The chapter was also engaged in a thorough study of two small parcels of land just outside Banská Bystrica in preparation for drawing up a proposal that these parcels be set aside by the municipal government as protected areas. The area was recommended for preservation by local scientists who were members of the chapter. Identification and recommendation of local reserves are among the competencies of individual chapters, and the Banská Bystrica chapter had undertaken the project entirely on its own initiative. As part of the chapter's contribution to beautifying the city, chapter member John Lupek had organized an environmental brigade from members of the local unit of Young Pioneers and planted different varieties of roses around his apartment complex. The young environmentalists tended the bushes after school under John's guidance as the authorized supervisor and representative of the Defenders of Nature.

The Slovak society does not have its own press nor the massive educational program of the All-Russian Society, but it has a contract with a publishing house in Bratislava for the publication of the society's newsheet, *Poznaj a chraň* (Know and protect). The journal now has a circulation of 12,000. To further its educational goals, the organization sponsors two international environmental camps every summer. These are attended by

environmental groups from all over Europe with the majority of participants from the socialist states. Each camping session is devoted to a specific
theme. Participants sign up for study groups in which they work for the
ten days' duration of the camp. Some of the groups study a particular
environmental or conservation issue, others go out into the field to collect
data on wildlife or flora or make a study of the habitats of protected
species. Still others spend their time at the parcels of land under consideration as nature reserves collecting data to determine whether the area meets
the legal requirements to qualify. Each group is led by a specialist who
volunteers his time and is sponsored by the Slovak society and the Slovak
Ministry of Culture.[51] While the focus of the society's activities is primarily
on nature conservation, the education program during the summertime
and in chapter meetings also addresses sensitive environmental issues.

The Banská Bystrica chapter was well aware of the limits to its activity
and of its supporting role to the state in environmental education and
policy implementation. Nevertheless, its activities prove that the individual
chapters can exercise considerable initiative and leadership in local environmental matters. In the Soviet Union, the nature societies have become
more and more visible at the republican level. In Kazakhstan, a leading
journal carried a thousand-word article by the senior agitator of the propaganda division of the Kazakh Society for the Protection of the Natural
Environment lamenting the lack of nature reserves in the republic.[52] A
press report on the work of the Kirghiz Nature Protection Society is worth
citing at length as it provides an excellent description of the kind of influence a republican society and its chapters can have:

The increased level of activity of the society's subdivisions and their ability to tackle
urgent questions concerning the protection of natural resources in a businesslike and
highminded fashion is also evidenced by the fact that, following their intercession, . . . a
number of local Ispolkoms have examined concrete questions of nature conservation at
their sessions and meetings and that decrees were adopted at the suggestion of the
Central Council by the Kirgiz ssr Supreme Soviet Presidium aimed at the implementation of measures to ensure nature conservation of the coastal zone of Lake Issyk-Kul'
and the protection of waters in Ishskaia oblast'.[53]

In drawing up its suggestions, the central council was described as having
worked closely with the Kirgiz Academy of Sciences in the study of certain
polluted areas.

Citizens may also make public recommendations or complaints in their towns outside the purview of the nature societies. People reportedly spoke out vehemently at public meetings in Ekibastuz over the air pollution coming from the coal mines and thermoelectric plants. Upon receipt of a complaint, local government must order an investigation. In 1981, a public complaint was issued at Dzayrem in Kazakhstan regarding a leakage into the countryside of contaminated wastewaters from mining in the area. The responsible environmental agent from the Kazakh Ministry of Geology investigated the matter and affirmed that the complaint was justified. The Dzayrem soviet then initiated measures to bring the polluters to justice.[54]

The increasing exploitation by the Soviet nature societies and individual citizens of official channels underscores the nature of the link between the proenvironmental scientific institutes, an environmentally minded public administration, and the legal environmental organizations. In the examples given, the environmental organization was the vox populi for the promotion of ecological values desired by the regional scientific and political elites. The nature societies performed the essential function of expressing the popular will, to which science and government could then properly claim to be responding in their demands upon their superiors for material or financial support.

In Yugoslavia, the formal opportunities for mass public action are more clearly defined than in the Soviet Union and relate more directly to the outcome of local environmental decisions. In the case of Lake Palić, strongly positive public support backed by the voting of public funds resulted in the reclamation of a valuable environmental and recreational resource. Active popular backing also produced a new public water and water treatment system in Sarajevo in time to be completed before the 1984 Winter Olympics.

The location of a nuclear power plant on Vir Island provides an excellent example of the efficacy of public protest in Yugoslavia. The investor's position was that the plant was economical at that location, but residents insisted that it was dangerous to health and to tourism, the principal source of their income. The decision went first to the opština government, which decided to hold a public referendum. The vote went strongly against the project. When the opština authorities realized there was solid opposition to the proposal, they also turned it down. The matter then went to the republican government, which, according to the constitution, may override a self-management decision if there is a compensating social interest. The republican authorities understandably did not want to make the decision. They hesitated and urged the investor to find another location. Eventually, the town of Prevlaka near Zagreb agreed to let the power plant be built on its territory. The decision produced a new wave of popular outcry, this time from Zagreb. In addition, scientists voiced their concern that the plant's effluent might raise the temperature of the Sava and risk plant and fish life. But by this time, the town fathers had approved the plant; the opština decision stood.

Legal action by both the Vir Island and Prevlaka residents took the form of sending citizen representations to their local opština and work-place delegates, signing of petitions, and writing letters to the local press. On Vir Island, the tourist interests in particular spoke out strongly. There were no sit-ins as is common in the United States under such circumstances, but the opposition was loud enough to urge the opština officials to a negative vote.[55]

A similar environmental protest occurred in the city of Ulcinj near Bar on the Adriatic coast. An aroused public held up the construction of an offshore plant, backed by French and American money, to get ferromagnesium out of seawater. Once again the tourist industry expressed strong negative views, and the investors sought a new location. After considerable negotiations, necessitated again by a concerned public, Split agreed to permit the plant's construction, but only after firm guarantees regarding antipollution controls had been written into the contract.[56]

Of note in all cases is the fact that a major economic force, the tourist industry, strongly supported the public protest. At Kragujevac and the cement plant outside of Belgrade, by comparison, there was no counter-vailing commercial opposition and the complaint involved the costly retro-fitting of existing plants. Significantly, the town fathers have failed to reach a decision on what to do about the problems. In both the Soviet Union and Yugoslavia, then, the public use of formal channels has had the greatest impact where public opinion has reflected and served the special interests of one of the other environmental players. So far, there is no evidence that public opinion on its own can influence a policy decision without the support of a third party.

Recourse to the press. A second strategy open to the layman in both countries is the use of the press, either by writing letters or reporting successfully completed actions. It is impossible to know how many letters on environmental topics are written since the letters that do get published are carefully selected. Most published letters on environmental problems come from either scientists or local government officials. However, Soviet newspapers appear to have become increasingly eager to publish reports of public protest and public action in environmental matters. It is difficult to ascertain with any degree of certainty a direct linkage between the nature societies and the Soviet mass media outside the authorized press column that is permitted to the societies. Whether reporters uncover the stories themselves or the stories are told to them is impossible to tell. But press activism in the environmental area is of such stature that one can almost say that papers such as *Literaturnaia gazeta* have become the public's environmental "conscience." The press literally acts as an instructor in public participation. Most Soviet newspapers daily expose their wide readership to accounts of miscarriage of environmental law and tales of the polluter brought to justice. Stories of the success of a nature society or a public complaint in seeing that justice is done and the law upheld contain much personal interest and assuredly exert influence on some persons to become more involved in their community's official environmental activities. Given the role the press can play in forming public attitudes, and the right accorded to the nature societies to publish in the press, there is good reason to assume a close relationship between the two as part of the environmental organizations' strategy to have input into the conduct of environmental management.

There is no doubt about the linkage between the press and the public environmental organizations in Yugoslavia. According to officials at the Federal Council for the Protection and Improvement of the Environment, the council has a definite policy of communication with the press. As part of its monitoring program, it keeps a file of newspaper clippings reporting local environmental events throughout the country, especially press reports of council actions such as the "88 Roses for President Tito." The council is also responsible for promoting environmental programs on TV. The problem in using the Yugoslav mass media as a means of policy input is its limited circulation. Stories of popular environmental activism in Croatia tend to be found only in Croatian papers, Macedonian stories in Macedonian papers, and Serbian in Serbia. A Soviet reader of *Pravda* or *Literaturnaia gazeta* will find a great deal of environmental news from all over the country. A Serbian reader of *Politika* will generally find news items confined to Serbia. Only when the issue reaches transnational proportions, as did the Tara River dam, does reporting of it find its way into a leading newspaper in another republic. In this area as in so many others, republican parochialism is one of the main drawbacks of the Yugoslav hydra.

The successful protests at Vir Island and Ulcinj are evidence of a dawning public appreciation of the relation between environmental protection and the quality of life, and they argue in favor of the Yugoslav self-management system in terms of the possibilities of public input into governmental and industrial environmental decisions. In the Soviet Union, decisions regarding the location of plants are made centrally. No manner of public protest can change a decision once the investment monies and starting date of construction have been incorporated into the plan.[57] Nevertheless, for all the public mobilization at the local level in Yugoslavia, popular action strategies at the higher levels of government are so far lacking. It may be, as scientists assert, that the public conscience is not yet sufficiently aroused. Perhaps more education is necessary before the public becomes convinced that environmental controls are not a luxury. Since Yugoslavia is not centrally organized, there is nothing in theory to prevent the organization of a republican or even a transrepublican environmental association from today's grass-roots activism. While the republican authorities might attempt to manipulate it for their own purposes, the example of the Young Researchers suggests that self-management has erased some of the compulsion of hierarchy and that dialogue in the search for funding and programs could be the rule.

Conclusion

The similarities between the Yugoslav and Soviet one-party systems with regard to constraints upon public participation in environmental policy-making are more striking than the differences: Censorship conceals the seriousness of environmental problems through public education and par-

Figure 7.1   Relationship between Experts, Environmental Agencies,
Political Leadership, and the Public in Communist One-Party States

Key:

——————Directives

— — — — —Feedback

ticipation programs and the control of the public's access to information.
All popular activity is limited to the local level. In Yugoslavia, the greater
freedom of citizen initiative within the opština has not yet been fully exploited for environmental purposes, although certain communities have
demonstrated the possibilities for environmental activism.

Of critical importance to the future of citizen participation in both countries is the quadrilateral relationship between the political leadership, the
environmental agencies, the experts, and the public. The relationship may
be expressed by figure 7.1.

As the experts and environmental agencies strive to expand their regulatory powers, they seek support from proenvironmental party leaders. At
the same time, to legitimate their activities, they need a public constituency.
Someone has to recognize and monitor environmental degradation and to
demand its correction. The experts lead and advise the environmental organizations, such as the Soviet nature societies and the Yugoslav Federal
Council for the Protection and Improvement of the Environment, and the
knowledge they impart to the layman defines in essence the scope of the
latter's activities. An expert's environmental militancy in its turn is chan-

neled by the relevancy of the particular environmental issue to the political leadership. The experts thus direct public interest toward areas that will be acceptable to the party and government authorities. On their part, the environmental agencies need the public to report back and protest violations of the law in order to secure stronger regulatory powers. They have an interest, however, in keeping popular participation within local confines lest public concern get out of hand and mount a serious challenge to their authority.

As the fourth partner in the relationship, the public has been given a considerable range of regulatory powers that, up to the present, have remained largely untapped. Given the stress on environmental education in both systems, and the fact that each year a new group of students graduates with an even higher level of environmental education, the public's role in environmental policymaking may be expected to grow. It may well be that the leaderships have launched a process that cannot be stopped. Milbraith and Honnold have shown in the case of the United States and Western Europe that there is a threshold beyond which attitudinal change becomes permanent.[58] Moreover, the mounting evidence of environmental degradation suggests that the leaderships will not want to arrest the change. On the contrary, in their search for an inexpensive yet effective environmental management policy, they will be eager to give the public increased monitoring authority. Nevertheless, the potential future role of the Soviet and Yugoslav publics should not be overstressed. Without a permanent transnational organizational base, lay activism will probably remain limited by its present constraints to a volunteer and marginal phenomenon.

8

Structure and Regulatory Principle Revisited

The question posed at the beginning of this study was which of the two organizational features, the politicoeconomic system or the regulatory principle, plays a greater role in communist one-party states in defining the politics of environmental management? In chapter 1 we identified four essential features of the communist one-party politicoeconomic system and seven typical environmental regulatory measures common to environmental regulatory practice. The two countries chosen as the subject of the study were the Soviet Union and Yugoslavia because they are both federal states but represent opposite poles on the centralization-decentralization continuum. Chapter 2 described the environmental management system of the two countries in greater detail. For simplicity, the Soviet centralized pluralistic model of environmental policymaking was labeled "the centipede"; the more decentralized, republic-focused Yugoslav model, "the hydra." The subsequent chapters looked at the role of each of the five principal actors in terms of the structural and regulatory constraints imposed upon them, their tangible and intangible assets, the costs of their involvement in environmental policymaking, and the strategies developed to improve the weight of their input into the environmental policymaking "game."

The investigation provides no clear answer to the question initially posed. The regulatory principle applied to environmental management has not changed the basic features of the two countries' politicoeconomic systems. On the contrary, regardless of degree of decentralization, the regulatory effect has always been blunted at the point where the regulatory principle has run hard against the basic politicoeconomic realities of the

306

one-party system and the interdependency between the economic enterprises and one-party rule. In this sense, the regulatory principle has had
little influence on the fundamental power balance existing in the two countries. Although in its delegation of implementation authority, regulation
has created new environmental organs, these have failed to develop sufficient power to offset the structural advantage of industry. Where environmental agencies have been created in existing ministries that are engaged
in resource exploitation, the environmental component has been undermined by the traditional production orientation of these institutions.

Regulation has designated the territorial administrative units as the en-
forcers of environmental policy, but here again, these units have experienced great difficulty in driving a wedge into the industry-party alliance. In
the Soviet Union, republican laws may not be applicable to the centrally
managed branch industries, and republican planning is helpless against
the economic decisions taken by the center. In Yugoslavia, regional administrative authorities openly court industry as a guarantee of regional
employment and community financing. In Yugoslavia, as well, interrepublican rivalries have inserted themselves into environmental issues, causing
the distortion of environmental goals for political purposes.

Regulation has not changed the basic employee-employer relationship
of the experts to the central power structures of the party and the industrial
ministries. On the contrary, regulation has further institutionalized it. Environmental experts are only identified by their position in an existing
bureaucratic structure. They are thus subject to the structural constraints
thrust upon them, fragmentation of their efforts where interdisciplinary
cooperation is required, and bureaucratic control of information and communication. In Yugoslavia, specialist influence is further weakened politically by three additional factors: the absence of a solid domestic research
program; the need for each research institute to be self-managing (tied to
the demands of clients, the institutes are unable to engage freely in research
projects necessary for appropriate environmental solutions); and the con-
sequent need to seek scientific and technological answers abroad to solve
environmental problems.

Finally, regulation has thrust some delegation of implementation authority upon the public, particularly in the Soviet Union, as monitor of environmental compliance. However, the content and form of popular partici-

pation is strictly controlled, and despite evidence of popular protest in Yugoslavia, the public in both countries remains a passive observer of the spectacle of rising environmental degradation.

Industry has emerged from the environmental policy game with its needs and demands intact. Indeed, as in Western countries, it has used regulation as a means to delay necessary environmental action and to reinforce its production objectives. On the other hand, by its very creation of new structures and delegation of new authority, regulation has had a positive impact on environmental management in both countries. For one thing, regulation defines the authority and jurisdiction of the environmental agencies and assigns expertise on environmental problems to specialist institutions. It makes no difference whether this assignment is by central fiat or by inter-institution compact (*sporazum*).

In the Soviet Union, demands for stricter observance of environmental rules by the territorial units and the experts have fostered and encouraged the expansion of the regulatory authority of the environmental agencies. In Yugoslavia, the growth in the regulatory competence of the environmental agencies has been at a slower pace because of the country's present economic and constitutional crises. There is reason to expect that once these have been resolved, expansion of regulatory agency competence will proceed more quickly. In the Soviet Union in particular, the environmental agencies have been able through their technical and monitoring functions to acquire power in the first of the four areas identified by Crozier and Friedberg as sources of influence in the policy game: mastery of technical expertise and information.

The experts have been the group that has benefited most from the regulatory principle. Through their membership in research centers as expert authorities in environmental matters, the Soviet environmental experts have secured institutional bases around which has formed an unofficial environmental scientific lobby held together by the informal ties of the "invisible college." In Yugoslavia, where the current economic crisis has made environmental matters partisan issues, the experts have been able to utilize the sociopolitical professional organizations as the basis for a still nascent environmental lobby, bound together as well by an "invisible college" network. The principal source of the specialists' power is their command of technical expertise. The need for technical advice by the "prince" is particularly evident in the Soviet Union, as that country seeks to mobilize science and technology through the scientific-technological revolution to reduce uncertainty in its decisions regarding economic development and resource use. Yugoslavia is also experiencing the need for the application of science to her economic problems, and as the country continues its development path, it may be anticipated that the importance of science will also grow. Investment by Yugoslavia into her own domestic science program may be expected to decrease the party and government leaderships' distrust of expertise and enhance the experts' status, as it has in the Soviet Union.

Regulation finally has brought the public into the implementation of environmental management policies, either as in the Soviet Union, through the monitoring and control function, or as in Yugoslavia, through the direct participation in management programs, such as reforestation, and desired republican and industry research projects. Both countries have seen the public begin to take advantage of their delegated authority, in the Soviet Union through the nature societies and letters to local authorities, and in Yugoslavia through popular action at the local level in support of or protest against proposed environmental developments. While the public has no access to any of Crozier's four sources of power, it is still a significant factor as the recipient of environmental services. As such, it has potential power in numbers and in the need for the environmental agencies and the experts to seek mass support to expand their own opportunities for input and influence.

Thus, the study does not provide an unequivocal answer to the question which of the two organizational factors contributes more to environmental policy management. It can be argued that regulation creates structure and thus modifies existing power structures as it delegates competence and authority. The findings suggest that although regulation may create new regulatory institutions, it cannot challenge the basic socioeconomic structure of a society, unless "the prince" so decides, or there is a social revolution.

We have seen that at those moments when the expansion of regulatory competence starts to infringe on structure, for example, the Soviet experts' proposals for a centralized single-purpose environmental agency or the adoption of an environmental-economic model as the basis for the planning process, the party-industry alliance solidifies into a determined policy of "don't rock the boat." The study has suggested a latent power residing in the population at large to demand a better quality of life. Here, too, however, the socioeconomic structure intervenes. Both countries appear to have understood the marginal quality of popular involvement in politics and have permitted public participation at the local government level. Beyond that, the political arena becomes the province of professionals: experts, party members, government functionaries, and industrial bureaucrats.

One is forced to conclude that environmental regulatory practice in the two countries has been neither a vehicle for revolutionary change redefining power relations in society so as to accommodate the environmental urgencies of the hour, nor a means by which we can anticipate the emergence of a liberated public opinion or an expertise independent of its bureaucratic employer. However, the leaderships' search for a more efficient environmental management system has given the public and the experts, particularly in the Soviet Union, an input into policymaking that they otherwise might not have had. And it has provided a permanent position for the environmental regulatory agencies in the firmament of state institutions. In both cases, these three actors have profited from the environmental policy game to develop an expansion of political opportunity and a concomitant enlargement of Crozier's "margin of liberty" that were unthinkable even twenty years ago. But when all is said and done, the fact remains that the alliance between the party and industry has the last word, whether in its centipede form in the Soviet Union, or its hydra manifestation in Yugoslavia.

What applications can be made from these findings to the Western regulatory experience, and especially to the environmental politics of the United States? The first is the need for a sobering reevaluation of the tendency to believe in regulation as the ultimate solution for environmental management. It is probable that the one-party, centrally planned, state-owned politicoeconomic system frustrates the regulatory effort to a greater degree than may be the case in the United States. French jurist Laurent Cohen-Tanugi, writing about differences in French and American legal practice, argues that regulation in the American context maintains the separation of "natural functions" between the state as legislator, the state as indirect regulator through the regulatory agencies, and the regulated enterprises.

Nationalization abolishes these distinctions when the state assumes all the functions at one and the same time. The advantage for Cohen-Tanugi in the existence of the three differentiated categories is the maintenance of an objective relationship between them, enabling the state to regulate the private sector without being party to the economic risk-taking implicit in the regulation. Under a situation of nationalization, the state as owner, may try to play "the good prince" and permit enterprise autonomy, but in fact is compelled to intervene in management and submit industry's activities to "the whims [*arbitraire*] of the prince and the hazards of '*la politique generale.*'" [1]

In the absence of accurate data regarding the status of environmental protection in the Soviet Union and Yugoslavia, we cannot accept a priori Cohen-Tanugi's thesis in the area of environmental regulation. Bad news tends to be published more than good news, and the Western reader takes consolation in learning of environmental disasters in the East. There is no doubt that both countries have seriously undertaken environmental programs that have an impact on their most critical air and water problems. It is also certain that headway has been made, although not at the rate that was initially anticipated.

In the United States, statistics also indicate that progress in pollution control has been slow. Since the passage of the major environmental legislation of the early 1970s, there has been a reduction in the nationwide total air pollution emission estimates. But emissions are far from their 1940 level, and the reductions fail to meet the Clean Air Act goal of zero health effects projected for the eighties. As regards water, a 1980 Council on Environment Quality report stated that "the quality of surface waters nationally has not changed much in the last five years," although some localities had experienced substantial improvement in water quality. Many of the reasons cited for these humble results could be applied to the Soviet and Yugoslav situations as well: rapid growth of the economy outpacing emission reduction capacity; inadequate staffing and funding of the environmental agencies; recalcitrant territorial administrations (the Yugoslav hydra) fearful of losing business; political pressure from industry; bureaucracy; and technological unfeasibility when emission levels are set too low to be realizable by existing technology. [2] Some fifteen years of environmental regulation in the United States have thus reached only modest targets

311

despite billions of dollars spent and a highly active and vocal environmental lobby.

A second lesson the experiences of Yugoslavia and the Soviet Union suggest is that the question of whether the vertical centralization or the horizontal decentralization of decisionmaking provides more efficient environmental management may not be an issue at all; or it may be the wrong issue. The ecology movement of the 1960s saw in the formation of a central federal environmental agency an answer to the inability of the states to pass or enforce their own environmental laws because of fear of their impact on business. With its administrative decentralization, Yugoslavia finds itself in a position similar to the United States prior to NEPA, where the republics are under pressure to give priority to the economy. But the United States has also seen that a federal agency is no more immune to pressure from the regulated interests than are the states and local government. The Soviet Union appears particularly sensitive to pressure from the regulated interests at the top of the centipede in view of the economy's second function in Soviet society. Indeed, it is precisely the centralized industrial pressure that in the Soviet case prevents the republican and local governments from exercising the environmental control authority delegated to them.

A third lesson to be learned is that science is not a natural handmaid of the regulatory process. Crucial to the adoption of a scientific proposal is the credibility of the scientist. Credibility involves not only his record as a scientist, but also his loyalty to the policymakers. In Yugoslavia, where scientists are still suspect, science has not had the impact in the environmental area it might have had if science had been able to come out from under its ideological cloud. In the Soviet Union, "establishment" senior scientists from the prestigious Academy of Sciences institutes and experts assigned to the environmental policymaking councils may be appropriately compared to the scientific advisers attached to the U.S. executive who are chosen for their sympathy with the president's political views, or to the National Academy of Sciences scientists with their penchant for publishing noncommittal reports designed to offend no one. The reader will recall that when the National Academy finally issued a report that unequivocally opposed a presidential opinion by supporting the link between sulphur dioxide and acid rain, the Reagan administration called the academy "too biased" and appointed its own committee.[3] Experts privy to the councils of the prince tend to reflect his views or to consent to the majority view in order to maintain their advisory influence.

A fourth lesson is that experts separated from the environmental problem tend to produce ideal regulations that are technologically unfeasible. In Yugoslavia, experts are criticized for failing to address themselves to the specific environmental problems requiring urgent solution. The Soviet Union has the greatest number of standards and highest norm levels of any country in the world. But what purpose does an optimum standard serve if it cannot be realized and if industry and the environmental agencies are forced into the inevitable *kompromis*? In the United States, the insertion in the air and water laws of unreasonably early dates for achieving air and water safe for human health provides an analogous example of idealized norm setting, undermining the enforcing agency's authority and encouraging resistance on the part of the regulated industry.

Fifth, the study suggests that regulation imposed on an immature environmental political culture results in a weaker and less comprehensive environmental regulatory framework than that applied to a more environmentally aware society. The Soviet Union, like the United States, has a tradition of environmental protection dating back into the last century. This tradition flowered in the conservation movement of the twenties that espoused Kozevnikov's "web of life" holistic approach to ecology. It was also behind the dominant role played by Moscow University biologists in the formation of the Soviet continuation of the nineteenth-century nature conservation societies. The 1970 environmental legislative corpus may be seen as the outgrowth of the failure of earlier Soviet resource exploitation laws to provide adequately for resource conservation. The contemporary legacy of the Soviet environmental tradition is a comprehensive environmental regulatory program and a core of experts sensitized to environmental issues.

By contrast, throughout their entire history, Yugoslavs have been absorbed in questions of national liberation and national identity. Although environmental laws were passed in the immediate post-World War II period, the absence of an environmental tradition forestalled serious consideration of environmental protection until rising international concern for global pollution in the seventies turned national attention to domestic

313

evidence of environmental degradation. The study suggests that environmental education may be of critical importance in promoting a shift in public opinion to attitudes more receptive to environmental regulation. The majority of Soviet and Yugoslav economic managers today have been raised in the Marxist materialist production-oriented paradigm. The next generation of enterprise directors in both countries will have been exposed to a consideration of environmental problems to a degree unknown by previous managerial elites.

Finally, the Soviet and Yugoslav experience teaches us that no matter what the politicoeconomic system, as long as the regulatory principle is the basis for environmental policy, environmental management will remain highly political. Contrary to Marxist thinking, state ownership of the means of production and environmental resources combined with central planning does not depoliticize environmental issues. It merely changes the configuration of environmental politics. In the United States, the game is played out by state and federal legislatures, enforcing agencies, private industry, and the environmental lobbies. In the Soviet Union and Yugoslavia, it takes the form of intergovernment and interterritorial bureaucratic rivalry.

In the United States and Western Europe, private industry may indeed pursue its nefarious bent for profit, but it is difficult to distinguish private industry's destruction of the environment from that of state-owned or self-managed enterprises. Nor can one readily differentiate between the efforts of private industry to modify environmental regulation to their interests and the *kompromis* or deliberate neglect of the law practiced by firms under social ownership. In each case, regulation creates a juggling for position between interdependent political actors, and in each case the stronger players' interests, particularly when they are coupled with the state interest, prevail. The principle difference between capitalist and communist politicoeconomic systems is the communist states' assurance of the permanent identity of state interest with economic development interests because of the state's structural dependency for survival upon the alliance between the single party and industry.

If the regulatory principle produces ambivalent results in terms of less-than-efficient environmental management and failure to modify the fundamental politicoeconomic structure to give adequate expression to the environmental dimension, are there other alternatives?

One alternative being increasingly advocated by specialists in both the East and West is the application of economic incentives. Society must find it unprofitable to perpetrate environmental degradation. A growing number of American economists have become disillusioned with the present emphasis on regulation and urge a return to economic considerations.[4] In its study of decisionmaking in the EPA, the National Research Council recommends: "The current regulatory framework used by EPA should be revised and supplemented to allow the use of management strategies that may be more *cost-effective in achieving environmental objectives and that experiment with greater use of economic incentives, including effluent charges.*"[5] (My italics.) Although realizing that lack of accurate information on control costs, damages and other variables can be a major problem in developing appropriate economic incentive strategies, the Committee on Prevention of Significant Deterioration (PSD) of Air Quality of the National Academy of Sciences suggested that even in such a difficult area as PSD, a salable emission permit strategy might make up for information gaps and promote efficient control.[6]

Evidence has been produced in this study that Soviet and Yugoslav specialists are also turning to economic incentives. Gofman and Gusev of TSEMI and Todorović of the Yugoslav Association of Engineers and Technicians are enthusiastic promoters of a pollution tax or pollution payment.[7] Economists have also tackled the thorny problems of assigning value to natural resources,[8] and determining the cost-effectiveness of capital investment in environmental protection based on an estimate of social and economic damage resulting from nonapplication of environmental controls. The Soviet government has recognized the validity of the economic incentive strategy by taking several concrete steps in this direction. It has tied managerial and worker bonuses to the fulfillment of the environmental as well as production section of the yearly plans. It has introduced the concept of marginal profitability in evaluating the loss due to mining ventures, and it has levied a water fee.

A second strategy is the adoption of environmental-economic planning models and strict adherence to them in the formation of long-term regional development plans. In this area, the Soviet Union is well advanced in the theoretical level, but behind in practical application. A common problem noted by American and Soviet experts alike is that of obtaining sufficient information for adequate forecasting.[9] Equally important is the question of jurisdiction when, for example, a river basin or economic regional management plan, such as the Siberian TICs, covers several territorial administrative units. The fact that studies treating this topic are being published in the Soviet Union is indicative that the Soviet leadership is giving the matter serious consideration. A third problem in economic-environmental planning is commitment versus flexibility. As the delays in the adoption of territorial plans in Yugoslavia indicate, regions and industry are reluctant to lock themselves into a plan that in effect dictates their future options in economic development. The Soviet experience demonstrates that unless territorial plans are rigidly adhered to, they can be easily modified for reasons of economic expediency. The American tradition has tended to minimize planning of any kind, and present state environmental plans are deficient in their focus, concentrating on single environmental targets rather than the complex picture.

A final strategy is the mobilization of moral outrage to force recalcitrant industries and government to implement environmental protection. As Jones points out in his discussion of the politics preceding the adoption of the Clean Air Act of 1970,[10] the marginality of public participation in policymaking and the public's tendency to demand extreme solutions suggests that this strategy cannot be advanced by itself alone. The Soviet experience indicates the ease with which public participation can be channeled and manipulated. Americans on their part have charged that mandated public hearings are frequently pro forma only, with the chief purpose of the hearing to persuade the public that the decision already taken is the right one. More important perhaps, moral outrage subsides, leaving industry and the regulatory agencies to work out the implementation of poorly conceived environmental regulations. A more suitable strategy is the broadening of participation in environmental policymaking to include all organized environmental interest or political groups with a long-term commitment to environmental policy goals. The last two decades, particularly in the United States and West Germany, have seen significant expansion of organized public participation in the environmental policy area. Neither the Soviet Union nor Yugoslavia has taken any serious steps in this direction. When the moral argument is advanced solely by scientists and specialists, as it is almost exclusively in the two countries under study, it has not nearly the same urgency or force as has aroused popular opinion. The objectivity of science is a central value of contemporary society,[11] and science is diminished in stature when aligned with partisan views. However, virtually all modern political regimes in principle subscribe to the view that governments in some way are supposed to serve the people.

It can be readily seen that all three of the alternative strategies do not do away with the regulatory principle. Nor would it be advisable to do so. Some kind of regulation is necessary to provide coherence and standardization in environmental policymaking. And some kind of central agency, be it a state regulatory agency or an interterritorial committee as in Australia, must have the authority to oversee the global environmental management picture. What the three alternative strategies aim to do is to reform the present command regulatory structure to what Cohen-Tanugi terms an "autoregulatory" system.[12]

In their now classic study of implementation in the United States, Wildavsky and Pressman demonstrate that the command regulatory principle mobilizes so many competing and opposing forces that it is amazing a regulatory program is carried out at all.[13] By contrast, autoregulation takes place between the regulated interests. In the environmental area, direct state intervention is replaced by indirect governmental tutelage to foster conditions where industry finds it economical to institute environmental controls, and territorial units discover regional benefits in adhering to a development plan based on regional ecological capabilities. Under conditions of autoregulation, the environmental organs carry out their monitoring and control functions not as policing or punitive agents but in order to assist industry and localities to optimize their economic and environmental choices. And the moral pressure exercised by the public ceases to be a self-righteous confrontational force directed solely at the polluters, as the public modifies its accusations of "freeloader" and "polluter-pays-all" to pay its share in the financing of environmental controls, either through increased taxes or higher prices.

Neither the centralized pluralism of the Soviet Union nor Yugoslavia's self-management system would seem at the present time in a position

317

to implement a genuine economic incentive strategy. Implementation demands a loosening of the command regulatory principle and letting the economy make its decisions based on economic factors, not political needs. In effect, an economic incentive strategy requires some form of market economy. While the Soviets have done much theoretical research in cost-benefit analysis, the economists complain that it is difficult to apply the theory because of lack of adequate information. The Commission on National Resources has expressed the same thought another way: "The amount of detailed information that any single party must acquire to participate in a market is considerably less than the amount a centralized agency would need if it were to try to substitute for and duplicate the results of a market."[14]

Liberalization of the economy is now under intense scrutiny in such diverse countries as Yugoslavia, China, West Germany, and France. One tends to forget that *étatisme* has a long and venerable history in France, and that only recently has the policy of *dirigisme* begun to be challenged, primarily because of the vitality shown by the American economy on the other side of the Atlantic. French advocates of diminishing the power of the French state argue that the transition to an autoregulatory society where economic incentive strategies can operate to their best advantage requires two conditions. There must be national consensus on fundamental values and the organization of the state, and the state must have confidence that political divisions are not so large that the dismantling of the command regulatory structure will undermine the foundations of government.[15]

Such consensus exists in few modern societies, the United States being perhaps an outstanding exception. The democracies of Western Europe have not been able to reach agreement on the foundations of the economic and social order for various reasons unconnected with a one-party state. While Yugoslavia's discussion of its political and economic crisis questions the relevance of one-party rule, a large part of the crisis can also be attributed to the perpetuation of traditional national rivalries that Tito's constitutional solution was unable to accommodate. As we have seen, expert opinion has tended to take sides in the crisis, weakening the leadership's confidence in the experts' loyalty to the Yugoslav state. In the Soviet Union, the nationality issue may be more submerged but is nonetheless present.[16] Religious and political dissent is reinforced by the nationality problem,[17] and now the question of the future direction of economic development may become an additional divisive factor.

The principle of the general will institutionalized in the absolute political ascendency of the majority party was accepted by the French as an appropriate way to handle the absence of consensus regarding the constitution of the French state. In the Soviet Union and Yugoslavia, this principle has been carried to its extreme by the institutionalization of the permanent rule of a single party. Hence, the difficulties inherent in modifying the command regulatory principle in a democratic multiparty system become intensified under single-party rule. In its positing of a market economy, the autoregulatory system in effect attacks the foundations of the Soviet and Yugoslav politicoeconomic systems by abolishing one of the fundamental structural features of the communist one-party state, and undermining the other three. Modification then not only risks splintering the frail regime-imposed format of national consensus, but the very survival of the two states in their currently constituted form.

Under these circumstances, it cannot be expected that an economic incentive strategy based on autoregulation will be endorsed by the leadership in either country. The command regulatory structure will remain. Given the serious nationality problems confronting the USSR, it can also not be expected that administration will be decentralized to permit regions to have control of their economic development in formulating their regional territorial plans. In Yugoslavia, many would argue that it is precisely decentralization that has precipitated the present constitutional crisis. Hence, there are voices that urge recentralization lest the country be split asunder. Finally, the insistence on a single ideology and a single party means that the leadership can never have confidence that the free public expression of opinion will not be used against it. Until it can be sure, the moral force of public opinion cannot be given free reign to expose the dangers for "spaceship Earth" of a continued adherence to economic growth or to argue for alternative life-styles.

Both countries must then make do with the command regulatory structure, with its inevitable submission of environmental objectives to political and economic priorities. Given these conditions, the outlook for the environment in the Soviet Union would seem to be the progressive adoption of those forms of economic incentives that are not based on autoregulation, and that conform to the present politicoeconomic structure; more power assigned to both the central environmental agencies and the regional agencies such as the river basin authorities and local soviets; and the imposition of increasingly severe legal penalties. In other words, the attempt to rationalize the command regulatory structure will continue. Not excluded is the mobilization of massive state resources if, for example, the ecology of Siberia becomes seriously threatened. In Yugoslavia, the disorganized practice of environmental management that seems to feed on interrepublican rivalry more than likely will move toward some form of centralized environmental authority if the Sava River case is any indication. Possibly, the Soviet experience of moving environmental policymaking from the republican to the transnational level will be replicated, but if the transfer occurs, self-management will ensure that the central structure is less rigid and has fewer jurisdictional competencies. Planned progress in this direction will no doubt continue to be impeded by economic requirements, and the likelihood is high that industrial development will continue to outpace efforts to reduce the impact of industry upon the environment. The impact of these developments upon the environmental policy actors is an ever-expanding area of opportunity for both the environmental agencies and the experts, always constrained by the industrial imperative. Public opinion will maintain its sideline role, unless some national catastrophe provides the triggering mechanism to propel it to the foreground.

The United States is in the fortunate position of having experimented with the command regulatory strategy and found it wanting, not only in the environmental area but in virtually every area of government intervention. Experiments in deregulation are currently under way. We have now had enough experience of the command regulatory strategy in pollution control to realize that it does not provide the fast, reliable solutions desired by the environmentalists. And we now know much more about the working of market economies and the phenomenon of "externalities" than did the nineteenth-century conservationists who, fearful of the demon profit, preferred to adhere to the statist strategies of their European forebears than to risk uncharted autoregulatory seas.[18] The Soviet and Yugoslav examples should provide sobering illustrations of the intrinsic weakness of adherence to an ideological position once events have outpaced its relevance. There is no evidence that state ownership of natural resources provides more effective environmental control than private ownership, just as there is no indication that the elimination of the profit incentive prevents environmental degradation. While the more centralized Soviet regulatory system appears better organized and more comprehensive than the decentralized Yugoslav model, there is no evidence that centralized regulation is more efficient at environmental protection than decentralized. The United States is in a position to try an autoregulatory system without sacrificing its ideological identity to a degree that is impossible in either of the two countries studied, with their insistence on a single ideology and single political party. More important, its politicoeconomic structure is not threatened. On the contrary, the American politicoeconomic system has proven highly conducive to autoregulation in other areas. Uncertainty exists because economic incentives within the framework of regional, ecologically based land-use planning have not been tried.

Even more critical, political acceptance is hampered by the game position of the present constellation of actors, particularly that of industry and the environmental lobby. In not having to respond to economic incentives, industry has used its economic leverage to press forward a politics of delay, mixing threats of unemployment and recession with claims for special subsidies and tax benefits for undertaking environmental controls. In this respect, arguments and behavior of U.S. industries have differed little from their Soviet and Yugoslav counterparts. In the courts and in the legislature, regulation has given the environmentalists a special political "space" in which to urge their demands with a creditable record of wins. Three Mile Island and Love Canal indicate how readily the public makes industry the environmental scapegoat and testify to the power of moral outrage in producing a political response roughly commensurate with the intensity and source of the outcry. While not denying either the environmental interests or the public access to policymaking, the autoregulatory strategy would probably diminish their activity in court and scale down their legislative lobbying effort, as industry made its equipment conform to national standards through market rather than administrative pressures. Nevertheless, more efficient environmental management, however it occurs, ought to please the most ardent advocate of state environmental intervention. Moreover, in the last analysis, moral outrage remains the primary and most necessary way of stimulating government to take the requisite regulatory measures. Hence, environmentalists and the public will continue to be the moral force urging the protection of our environment if mankind is to survive on this planet.

The Soviet and Yugoslav experiences indicate that the command regulatory strategy imposed on a communist one-party politicoeconomic structure augments the primacy of politics and political will in solving environmental problems. The advantage of the autoregulatory strategy is that it reduces the purely political component of environmental protection by referring environmental problems to the economic and social context where they naturally occur. The United States has an opportunity to uncouple environmental protection from politics and develop the requisite market and social mechanisms to ensure environmental control. The risks of acceptance of the experiment are great, and our information is still insufficient to provide assurance of certain success. The risks of rejection are also high. The command strategy has proved insufficient to the task in all countries where it has been tried. Time may be running out. If we are serious in our desire to conserve the world for future generations, prudence suggests an alteration of course.

Postscript Chernobyl

April 26, 1986, marked a watershed in environmental history. The fallout from the Chernobyl disaster went literally around the world. While only a dedicated number could get excited about the effects of long-range transboundary acid precipitation, the panic produced in Europe by fear of the effects of the transboundary transmission of radioactivity was in many respects out of proportion to the actual levels of radiation measured on the ground.

Food and soil contamination were particularly sensitive issues. To soothe the concerns of their anxious citizens and to score political points with their agricultural lobbies, the members of the Common Market voted to stop the importation of agricultural products from Eastern Europe. However, at the request of West Germany, East Germany, which lay directly in the path of "the cloud," was excluded from the embargo. In an extraordinary measure, Italy forbade the import of French agricultural products, although there was literally no difference in radiation levels between Italian Sardinia and French Corsica. Medical personnel everwhere theorized on the number of cancer patients that might be expected as a result of the disaster, painting grisly scenes of future invalid populations.

Western public opinion was quick to express its solidarity with Chernobyl's victims and with the USSR's efforts to manage the disaster. There was virtually no popular outcry against the Soviet Union's behavior or against Soviet failures to assure the safety of its nuclear plants. While the EEC did demand compensation for agricultural damage, there was no way any of the victims, at home or abroad, could sue the Soviet government, as the victims of the chemical disaster in Bophal sued Union Carbide. Europeans turned inward and vented their anxieties against their own governments. Protest against nuclear power quickly devolved into a renewed crusade against the bomb and NATO.[1] Primitive man's terror of things

323

unseen and beyond his control, dressed in the ultimate modern shape, provoked one of the oldest responses of the human race: escapism. Technology is fearful. Away with it and its advocates.

In the plethora of newsprint immediately following the disaster, the reader was able to learn a great deal about Soviet reactor technology or the absence thereof. But there was a curious silence on the organization of the Soviet nuclear enterprise and the monitoring and inspection system that was supposed to ensure plant safety. There are obvious reasons for this silence. One kettle cannot call the other black. Although all civilian nuclear power production is not state-owned in the Western industrialized countries, construction and operation are totally regulated by administrative rulings, compliance with which is monitored by government organs. Every Western country with nuclear power has had its nuclear power accidents of substantial proportions. Windscale in England and Three Mile Island in the United States are the best known, and the latter, the best publicized. On May 4, 1986, there was a minor breakdown in a West German plant that the government tried to hush up, fearful of the public's certain negative reaction. Investigation in every Western case revealed human error at the bottom of the accident and bureaucratic indulgence at the top.

Second, there are strong nuclear lobbies in all the advanced industrialized countries. These lobbies have close links to the government institutions concerned with the military uses of atomic energy. The lesson of Kashtim in 1958 is instructive. The nuclear disaster in the Urals was unknown to the world public until Zhores Medvedev happened to mention it casually to British reporters in 1976 following his decision to seek asylum in Great Britain. The U.S. and British governments denied the story. Medvedev sat down to prove it had occurred. His findings documented American and British complicity in keeping the disaster a secret. Assuredly, the publication in 1958 of a catastrophe of those proportions would have cut short the initial public honeymoon with "Atoms for Peace," as certainly as Chernobyl undermined confidence in nuclear power in 1986. It is difficult to believe that none of the satellites circling the earth that April night would have been placed to record the accident when it occurred, and that the United States had to wait to learn the news until Swedish monitors picked up radiation information a day later. Given the public nervousness over nuclear power, no government wants to be the bearer of bad tidings, even if the trouble was not on its territory. Perhaps the major powers hoped that in some way the problem would go away before it became a public scandal.

The Accident

The Chernobyl tragedy brings into sharp focus the major findings of this book about the failure of environmental regulatory policy in general, and in communist one-party states in particular. The Chernobyl AEC was a very large operation with four reactors on line and a fifth under construction. The 960-megawatt graphite reactors were of a kind that exists nowhere else outside the Soviet Union.[2] The model was originally developed to produce plutonium for nuclear weapons and was adapted for electricity production. Because of its "dual-use," like other graphite reactors it cannot receive the approval of IAEA under the terms of the nonproliferation treaty. In addition, the Soviet RBMK model lacks many of the common Western safety features, especially the containment dome, all of which came under strong criticism at the IAEA conference in August 1986.[3]

It is not publicly known whether in the time preceding the accident the Chernobyl reactors were producing plutonium as their primary goal and electric power on the side, whether the production of plutonium was a by-product of their production of electricity, or whether they were producing weapon's quality plutonium at all.[4] However, the fact that graphite reactors have a neutron spectrum that yields this grade of plutonium would automatically put the plant under the control of the USSR Ministry of Defense and the USSR Ministry of Medium Machine Building, the code name for the organization in charge of making nuclear bombs since the end of World War II. On the formal institutional level, civilian nuclear power production is separate from military nuclear power production and is subordinated officially to the State Committee on the Utilization of Nuclear Energy and the Committee for Nuclear Industry Safety. However, both Andronik Petrosiants, who has been chairman of the state committee since 1962, and Evgenii Koulov, head of the Committee for Nuclear Industry Safety, spent the early part of their careers in the Ministry of Medium Machine Building. We have here all the ingredients of diffusion of administrative responsibilities at the top characteristic of environmental policy-

325

making in the Soviet "centipede," with the civilian arm of the nuclear power industry clearly in an inferior position vis-à-vis the military. Neither Petrosiants nor Koulov are even candidate members of the Central Committee of the Soviet Communist party.[5]

The dual purpose of the Chernobyl power plant and the prior careers of the men responsible for Soviet civilian nuclear power throws into stark relief the special relationship between the Soviet Communist party leadership and the military-industrial complex. Soviet graphite reactors are designed for on-line, continuous fuel recycling and do not have to be shut down to replace spent rods, thus providing constant plutonium output. This feature surely did not escape the notice of the Soviet high command when the decision on what kind of reactors to build for energy production was made in the mid-fifties. However, the reactors have the distinct disadvantage that the graphite core tends to heat up. Periodically, it must be cooled by liberating a certain quantity of energy. Because of the reactor's "positive void coefficient," if the balance between water and steam in the circuit is altered by improper cooling, the temperature of the core rises, increasing fission activity, which in turn raises the reactor's heat in an ever-upward cycle. Such was the case at Windscale in Great Britain in 1957, where the accident was severe enough for the authorities to forbid the sale of milk products produced in the 200-square-mile zone around the plant.[6] Although a more complex event, the Chernobyl tragedy was the direct product of the "positive void" effect.

The official Soviet report submitted to the IAEA chose to place primary blame not on reactor design but on six violations of safety rules and the poor training of the plant operators.[7] The alleged carelessness and haste are incredible to read about but highly believable. It was late at night and the end of the month. The grid supervisor had reportedly asked for a twelve-hour delay, but his opinion was overridden. Monthly accounts on plan fulfillment were doubtless due, and failure to fulfill established norms constitutes a breach of Soviet law. Good as these reasons may be, however, they do not really explain why the operational experiment had to be undertaken at that particular time or why so many blunders were made simultaneously.

The description by Liubov Kovalevska, a senior manager at Chernobyl, of problems in the building of the fifth reactor suggests more than human error may have been at issue. Pressure to maximize production may also have been a factor. Kovalevska's remarkable and prophetic report was published almost a month to the day prior to the accident, on the front page of *Literarni Ukraina*, the Ukrainian counterpart to *Literaturnaia gazeta*. According to the author, construction on the new reactor had been advanced by one year, leaving no time to eliminate the structural mistakes present in the construction of the earlier reactors. The shortening of construction time further promoted disregard for conformance to required standards of safety and reliability. Construction materials were slow in arriving, and when they did arrive, came in insufficient quantities. Much of the concrete, she said, was of substandard quality. The shortage of materials and increasing problems in construction undermined the workers' feeling of responsibility for their work. A highly trained and experienced crew, the workers first appealed to their superiors to improve the situation. When their appeals brought no response, they became indignant. Gradually, indignation gave way to indifference and "worker despair."[8]

So far, the Soviet Union has been completely silent as to what agency ordered the test and why. Which electro-technical institutes under which responsible ministry carried out the experiment? Was it a subordinate institute of the armaments industry or associated with the military-industrial complex? Was the test in response to military demands for stepped-up production, or a hastily conceived effort to control safety conditions outside the regular military production program? Or did the test have nothing to do with the military but lay entirely within the framework of civilian power production? Soviet investigation may show that prior to Kovalevska's article, civilian nuclear power monitoring agencies did indeed register complaints against plant safety conditions. However, as the poor relatives of the armaments industry, their criticisms could be easily set aside. In chapter 4, we saw the arrogant disregard by civilian heavy industry of complaints made by environmental officials. According to Petrosiants, the ill-fated experiment at Chernobyl was not even discussed with the scientists responsible for safety within the plant. Given its military connections, the plant management may not have been required to consult them because plant activities did not fall wholly under civilian control.

The IAEA conference in August 1986 was not the first time that Soviet nuclear reactors came under public censure. In 1975 a group of British engineers of Babcock Power visited several Soviet nuclear power plants. In a report published in 1977, they concluded that Soviet reactor safety features compared badly with those in the West. They were particularly critical of the construction of a RBMK-type channel reactor they saw in Leningrad, similar to those at Chernobyl, faulting especially the absence of a containment vessel. The Soviet authorities were informed of the British evaluation, and some changes were apparently made, but not enough. With one exception, every point raised in the British report was subsequently admitted as an RBMK design defect by Victor Legasov, head of the Soviet delegation to the August 1986 IAEA conference.[9] In 1979 a critical article was published in the official party journal, *Kommunist*. One of the authors was the builder of the first Soviet atomic reactor, Nicolai Dolezhal. Expressing reservations about the current state of Soviet nuclear technology, he urged that nuclear power plants not be built close to large population centers or in the European part of the Soviet Union.[10]

The construction workers' appeals to the Committee for Nuclear Industry Safety or other civilian authorities probably fell on deaf ears. If sent forward, they could easily have been overridden by the military in the interests of national security. M. Slavski, the 89-year-old head of the Ministry of Medium Machine Building, had spent twenty-five years producing bombs for the armaments industry.[11] If the ministry had any say in setting production and other norms, then it was up to the plant to meet those norms regardless of the consequences, particularly since these were not considered very risky. Maksim Rilsky, Ukrainian minister of energy, was quoted in *Soviet Life*, the American journal designated for sale in the Soviet Union, as assessing the probability of a core meltdown at Chernobyl as one in ten thousand.[12] The evidence suggests a scenario where safety conditions at Chernobyl were known to be problematic, but for whatever reason were consistently played down or lost in the bureaucratic intrigues at the top of the nuclear power hierarchy.

The situation evidently sapped plant morale. According to official reports, the accident occurred in an administrative environment of poor work discipline and lackluster leadership. Whatever the technical reason for the catastrophe, the plant administration clearly panicked when it occurred. Both *Pravda* and *Izvestia* carried stirring reports of the heroism of the firemen called to fight the emergency, but senior administrators were singularly absent from the list of heroes. On the contrary, *Pravda* publicly condemned virtually all of them, naming one vice-director for having run away, and another for failing to perform his assigned duties. A large number of plant foremen and senior technicians also were said to have "taken a powder," while 177 members of the party committee in Pripiat apparently had disappeared from view.[13] Bad morale in the plant carried over to its suppliers. The first group to be sanctioned was a transport company associated with the nuclear plant. The company was accused of "indifference and inertia," and failure to lend assistance when asked.[14] Did the drivers refuse to move? It was to be expected that the entire senior plant management should have lost their jobs. But it is significant that they were faulted not for their failure to maintain proper safety precautions but for their failure to assess correctly the seriousness of the accident and to behave responsibly at the height of the crisis. As of this writing, the only group to be censored for preaccident performance is the plant trade union committee, which alone was faulted for showing "little concern for the strengthening of discipline and the ensuring of work safety."[15] Although admittedly the facts are sparse, the picture painted of plant work conditions and attitudes prior to the accident is strongly reminiscent of the tensions and dissatisfactions described as prevailing between administrative and lower personnel in NASA before the *Challenger* tragedy. Americans know from that bitter experience what can happen when the pressure is on and the upper bureaucracy refuses to consider opinions contrary to their own needs and ideas.

A third weakness in Soviet environmental policymaking underscored by Chernobyl is compartmentalization. We do not know when Chief Engineer Fomin decided to inform his superior about what had occurred. We know even less about to whom and at what time Director Briukhanov made his first report outside the plant. Quite possibly it was to his regional military and/or armaments industry superiors. The news probably went from there to the center and then to the republican level, with regional party and government officials the last to hear. Official Soviet information suggests that the first report to the center might have been misleading, showing plant personnel in control of the situation and minimizing radiation fallout.[16]

As we saw in chapter 3, compartmentalization tends to reduce contact between personnel working in different bureaucracies. It would be quite in order, as *Izvestia* reported, particularly in view of Chernobyl's military and nuclear assignments, that there was no contact between the monitoring personnel inside the plant and the agency monitoring radioactivity outside.[17] We have no knowledge of what actions the external agency might have taken in the crisis. Given the nature of Soviet bureaucratic thinking, and lacking supplementary information, quite possibly it took none. According to a Solidarity report, when his Geiger counter suddenly went berserk, a monitoring official in northeastern Poland logically thought it was broken. He changed his mind only after a detail of the Polish army occupied his laboratory.[18] The world may rightfully protest a lack of information from the Soviet Union, but the fact that no one was evacuated until thirty-six hours after the accident, and the 20,000 living in the area immediately surrounding the plant were not taken out until almost a week later, indicate a severe breakdown in judgment and communication at the very spot where they were most crucial.[19]

We may never know how much of the Soviets' initial silence was deliberately imposed and how much was the product of bureaucratic compartmentalization. This study suggests that a considerable part may be attributable to the latter. At first, the top leadership lacked hard information. Only after it had learned the facts was it able to mobilize the mass media to "cover up" the bureaucratic inadequacies. During the period of information uncertainty, the world witnessed the grotesque spectacle of smiling May Day dancers in sunny downtown Kiev at the same time as children were arriving at the railroad station for evacuation from the city. Then the media launched their campaign that likened the catastrophe to war. On one side were the heroes, primarily the firemen and others from *outside the plant* and probably ignorant of its purpose and politics, who gave their lives to prevent the tragedy from getting worse. On the other were the plant management and plant workers guilty of poor discipline and even poorer responsibility. The media placed great emphasis on the fact that the accident at Chernobyl was a world first without precedent. The official line was that as it felt its way along uncharted paths, the Soviet Union was performing a major service to mankind in pioneering the management of one of the most critical problems of our time. In the same way, the USSR had taken the lead in defeating Germany in World War II.

The Soviet people responded enthusiastically and touchingly to the war theme, offering their money, services, and lives to the cause. Chernobyl brought about the USSR's first money-raising rock concert for the benefit of the victims. The vigor and intensity of the media campaign indicate that despite official talk about *glasnost* (openness), nothing was done to open up channels of communication and end compartmentalization. In its treatment of Chernobyl, the government simply switched channels to suit its purpose, closing off some, namely information from the plant, and opening others: top government leaders, international specialists, artists, and the mass media.

Unless radically different new data indicate otherwise, Chernobyl is a tragic but classic example of the problems of environmental management in a one-party state of the Soviet variant. It casts serious doubt on the ability of regimes of this type to master a serious environmental problem. Similarly, it cast doubts on the ability of pluralistic regimes to promote effective controls where the potential polluter is a civilian or military state-owned enterprise, a public utility, or major company receiving partial government subsidies and seeking to co-opt the regulatory agency. Chernobyl may be the product of faulty technology. But it is much more the result of inept bureaucratic management.

The Yugoslav Response

In Yugoslavia, the news of Chernobyl followed an extended period of national discussion over the immediate future of nuclear energy in the country. In December 1985 the Federal Executive Council approved the purchase of four new nuclear reactors to the tune of billions of dollars. Immediately the Union of Engineers and Technicians of Yugoslavia organized a roundtable discussion to which it invited both foreign and domestic energy, economic, and other experts. The press was also invited, and reports of the meeting were carried nationwide. The discussion revealed deep divisions among the experts on Yugoslavia's energy problem and the best way to solve it. Oil and coal specialists accused the nuclear experts of undervaluation of cost and risk, while the nuclear specialists insisted on the viability of nuclear energy despite its serious attendant problems.[20]

The publicity given the roundtable generated a wave of controversy all over the country about the wisdom of borrowing billions of new dollars for an uncertain enterprise at a time of grave economic crisis. Nuclear experts were called to give their opinions on television, and the views of economic experts were solicited. The discussion particularly caught the public's imagination because elections to the Federal Parliament were held in April and there was hope that public opinion might influence the new government. Members of the Communist Youth League (CYL) drew up a petition calling for the end of nuclear energy in Yugoslavia and managed to recruit some 120,000 signatures! Public input, however, had only a minor impact. When the new government assumed office in early April, among its first acts was a decision to purchase one of the four proposed reactors.[21]

On April 26, Chernobyl occurred. The news broke at a most opportune moment, when the Yugoslav public was focused on the nuclear issue. For the second time in a year, the nuclear experts were called to give their opinions on TV. But this time they talked more about safety, the disposal of nuclear waste, and the outdatedness of Yugoslavia's Westinghouse reactor. On May 10, hundreds of young people under the auspices of the Communist Youth League demonstrated in Ljubljana against the risks of planetary pollution and the construction of nuclear power stations in Yugoslavia. Protesting the lack of information coming from the Soviet Union, they urged the Slovene authorities to nominate a commission to evaluate the consequences of the accident for the Yugoslav economy and demanded the payment of damages with interest from the USSR.[22]

Perhaps Chernobyl had its strongest impact upon Yugoslavia's nuclear community. The first victim was "Prevlaka," the reactor the government had just agreed to order. At the suggestion of the Council for Associated Labor, the Croatian Sabor (legislature) dropped the construction of the reactor from its medium-range plans.[23] Nuclear specialists were apparently surprised by the amount of radioactive fallout in the country. While they agreed that the highest levels were recorded during the first days of May, many expressed deeper concern over the evidence of low-level radiation, some of which would be a factor in the Yugoslav environment for thousands of years to come. Although I had not yet asked, one expert was quick to assure me that milk in Belgrade was safe. The plant that produced it took its milk from cows that never went outdoors and ate imported grain! That information must have not reassured most Yugoslavs; for powdered milk, generally readily available in Yugoslavia, seemed to have disappeared from the market shelves. During the first days of May, people were told not to eat fresh fruits and vegetables, but still in mid-June, I was told, the sale of fresh produce was being strictly controlled. A leading specialist on the environmental aspects of radiation said there was no way to tell what harm had been inflicted on the population and over how large an area. Her research had shown fallout patterns typical of long-range acid precipitation. Although she urged me "not to worry," she also was concerned about the future environmental effects of strontium 90 and other radioactive particles with long half-lives that had been registered in Yugoslavia.

The nuclear experts experienced feelings of vulnerability and defenselessness perhaps even more acutely than the rest of the population, because they were more informed about the situation. Reactions took several forms. First, they did not find much reassurance in statements about the accident coming from the United States or Western Europe, which they felt had a common interest with the Soviet Union to suppress information. They pointed out that the early news reports from the United States talked about three thousand casualties. The figure was revised immediately after the first information from the Soviet Union. Where was the truth? There was no way to check Soviet data. Similarly, they believed that the circle of radioactivity was actually much larger than publicly indicated, reaching a radius of at least 1,000 km.

A second reaction focused on the problems of long-term low-level radiation and the difficulty of disposing of radioactive waste, problems the experts had tended to downplay in their pre-Chernobyl discussion about the value of nuclear energy. They were now much less sanguine about waste disposal and indeed wondered whether in a country like Yugoslavia there was a solution. The third reaction called into question the whole issue of nuclear safety, its cost and guarantees. The fact that human error was the cause of the accident made a great impression on them. Yugoslavia, they argued, was essentially an underdeveloped country with little experience in advanced technologies. The Soviet Union might be at a slightly higher industrial level, but the confusion and improper evaluation that attended the accident indicated a population unfamiliar with technology, unused to assessing the degree of seriousness of technological failures and of dealing with them correctly when they occurred. "Can you imagine," one scientist asked, "what would happen in our nuclear plant if three of its technicians came drunk to the job? We have no experience in dealing with problems of this nature. And our plant is in Croatia. What if it were in Kosovo?" In his view, there were very special "clouds" hanging over nuclear power for developing countries. The Soviet difficulties in mastering the catastrophe made it imperative for any nation desiring to acquire nuclear power to have the technical and administrative potential permitting it to face an event that by its very nature was unforeseeable. One drunk, one misjudgment, and—catastrophe. Only the advanced industrial states had the technological foundation and infrastructure to handle a crisis of such proportions.[24]

Pessimism about Yugoslavia's ability to handle nuclear power safely was combined with doubts about the technical possibility of guaranteeing safety. The skyrocketing costs of the construction of nuclear power plants in the United States did not offer much hope to a poor country. Indeed, costs to assure safety had risen so much in America that nuclear power had lost its competitive edge with conventional forms of energy. If safety at any price were the rule in Yugoslavia, it would spell the end of domestic nuclear power production. Perhaps that would be for the best. The West Germans were pouring billions of marks into filters for coal-powered plants. Yugoslavia was rich in coal, and the solution might lie there.

Added to the fears of the population and the skepticism of the nuclear experts are the now serious reservations of the politicians. The cancellation of "Prevlaka" proved that Chernobyl had cast its long shadow over the wisdom of the earlier decision. In a very well-reasoned paper before the Serbian Skupština, Dušan Čkrebić, former chairman of the Serbian Presidency, warned about the divisiveness in seeing the nuclear power issue as one of pro or con. Yugoslavia's energy problem was not a pro/con matter. Before coming to a decision, the country needed to give serious consideration to the role of the human factor in nuclear technology. Nuclear power was not synonymous with the atomic bomb, but its misuse entailed social consequences that made it a "latent ecological bomb." A more immediate ecological problem closely tied to the energy question was water conservation. This was a time bomb waiting to explode in the very near future, and decisions on appropriate forms of energy would have to be made within the strict confines of limiting water consumption and pollution. Yugoslavs thus had to make a sober evaluation of their energy "account." A decision to build four nuclear plants required "serious study" on the basis of economic rationality. Current prices for electric energy were uneconomical, encouraging rather then inhibiting energy consumption. More important, the "logic of the closed economies of the republics and provinces created energy needs and costs that could not be covered in any way, either with or without nuclear power." In his conclusion, Čkrebić carefully sidestepped the nuclear energy issue and called for more economical energy prices, more rational energy consumption, investment in profit-making forms of electrical energy, and the exploitation of all economically feasible domestic resources.[25]

As in the Soviet case, Chernobyl highlighted the problems inherent in environmental management in the Yugoslav "hydra." Prior to the accident, the studied opinions of experts and 120,000 signatures could not override the special relationship between the powerful electric power industry, insistent republican party and government authorities, and the weak federal government. The contract was signed for four reactors. Chernobyl showed the stresses in the system, and thoughtful men were quick to point them out. The new federal government contains twelve university-educated men, more than in any previous body. Yet it is far from certain they will be more willing to listen to the scientists than their predecessors were. Republican autonomy is pulling the country apart, and the population is becoming increasingly dissatisfied with the 100 percent inflation. Politics not economics has priority. Those at the top show no inclination to step down. To remain at the top, they continue to adhere to the old familiar political game rather than seek risky change. The nuclear power issue may have spawned a local demonstration and a successful nationwide effort in signature collection. But neither the LCY nor Slovenia would appear to be the appropriate entities to forge a national environmental movement. The LCY is hardly the right forum for environmental consciousness-raising, and the capitol of the most economically advanced republic was the only place where the protest demonstrations occurred. There were no similar demonstrations in Croatia where the country's nuclear power plant is located. As in the Soviet Union, Chernobyl showed the cracks in the system and raised questions about its ability to handle environmental matters. But the system goes on as before.

Chernobyl was not just a case of an accident bound to happen. The way it started and the way it unfolded were products of the Soviet system, just as the Yugoslav reaction was born of the logic of the "hydra." No nuclear accident in the West has taken lives or scattered radiation over such an enormous area. Significantly, young Croatians told me that the demonstration in Ljubljana was as much a demonstration against "the system" as against nuclear power, confirming a basic fear of communist leaderships that the free expression of opinion will always be used against them. Assuredly, Chernobyl will hasten Soviet efforts to make the command regulatory structure in environmental matters more responsive and responsible, but the prognosis is not optimistic. In both countries, politics and political will dominate all other considerations. The lesson of Chernobyl is not "Away with technology. There but for the luck of the dice go I." The lesson is that technology is only as reliable as the systems devised to manage it and the human beings who run them.

Appendix 1 Representative Environmental Legislation in the Soviet Union

Environmental area	Year	Agent	Description
Constitutional bases	1977	SS SU	Articles 4, 10, 11, 16, 18, 26, 28, 29, 42, 67, 73, 131, 147
General	1956–1963	SS UR	General environmental laws passed by all the union republics
	1961	SS SU	Article 21, state ownership of state property, natural resources
	1964	SS RSFSR	Article 95, state ownership of natural resources
	1967	CM SU	Duty of ministry to protect environment
	1972	SS SU	Resolution to strengthen EP and ENR
	1972	CM SU	Specific implementing instructions to above
	1973	CM SU	Outlines role of militia in EP
	1973	CM SU	Outlines role of state arbitration in EP
	1973	CM SU	Outlines role of State Sanitary Inspection fines in EP
	1974	CM SU	Outlines role of People's Druzhiny in EP
	1975	CM SU	Resolution for scientific-production units to realize EP measures
	1976	CM SU	Instructions on settlement of conflict in EP
	1977	SC SU	Resolution on court EP practice
	1978	CM SU	Additional measures to strengthen EP and ENR
	1981	CM SU	EP Inspection system set up in Defense Ministry
Air	1949	CM SU	First air pollution measures

Appendix 1 (*continued*)

Environmental area	Year	Agent	Description
Air (*cont.*)	1969	SS SU	Fundamental Public Law; includes air pollution provisions
	1972	CM SU	Resolution on noise control in inhabited areas
	1972	CM SU	Chief Administration Hydromet established
	1973	CM SU	Resolution on noise control in industrial enter- prises, towns, and popu- lated areas
	1973	CM SU	State Hygienic and Epidemiological Inspec- tion (SES) established
	1974	CM SU	State Inspection for Control of Gas-Cleaning and Dust-catching equipment established
	1978	CM SU	Hydromet becomes a state committee, Goskomgidromet
	1980	SS SU	Fundamental Law on Air Pollution Control (noise included)
Water	1937	CPK SU	First sanitary water provisions
	1959	CM SU	Strengthens state control over use of underground water
	1960	CM SU	Provides for regulated use and protection of water resources
	1960	SS RSFSR	Article 223, Criminal Code, on criminal liability for breaking WPC laws and regulations; extended to oceans, 1974
	1963	PSS RFSFR	Establishes fines for violating laws
	1963	CM RSFSR	Measures for ending pollution of Moskva River

Appendix 1 (*continued*)

Environmental area	Year	Agent	Description
Water (*cont.*)	1963	CM RSFSR	Measures for ending pollution in Ob-Irtysh basin
	1968	CM RSFSR	Measures for preventing pollution of the Caspian Sea
	1968	CM SU	Role of MinFish in water pollution control (WPC)
	1969	CM SU	Measures for protection and use of Lake Baikal
	1969	CM SU	Role of MinEnerg in WPC
	1969	CM SU	Role of Mincell (Paper Industry) in WPC
	1969	CM SU	Role of MinFor and Lumber in WPC
	1970	SS SU	Fundamental Law on Water Pollution Control
	1971	CM SU	Role of Minvodkhoz in erosion and river basin control
	1972	SS RSFSR	Water Code of RSFSR
	1972	CM SU	Additional jurisdiction given to Minvodkhoz
	1972	CM SU	Measures for preventing sewage pollution of Volga and Ural River basins
	1973	CM RSFSR	On strengthening state organs in regulating use and protection of water in RSFSR
	1974	MVKh RSFSR	On the basin administration of Minvodkhoz for water use and protection in the RSFSR
	1974	CM RSFSR	WPC and EP in Seleger Lake basin
	1974	CM RSFSR	On procedure for establishing water objects as natural monuments
	1974	MVKh and Minzdrav and Minryb SU	Rules of protection of surface waters from sewage pollution

Appendix 1 (*continued*)

Environmental area	Year	Agent	Description
Water (*cont.*)	1974	CM SU	On strengthening the fight against sea pollution
	1974	MVKh, Minmorflot, Minryb and Mingrzha SU	Instructions on informing captains when breaking anti-ocean-pollution laws
	1975	MVKh, Minmorflot, Minryb SU	Rules for registering operations with oil, and oil products in ocean transit
	1975	CM SU	State record of water use established
	1975	CM RSFSR	Reserve created in north part of Caspian Sea
	1976	CM SU	Methodology to develop plan for complex water use
	1976	CM RSFSR	Methodology to develop plan for complex water use
	1976	CM SU	Regulations for forbidding water use of water objects of state, scientific, or cultural value
	1977	CM SU	Regulations for establishing water inventory
	1977	CM SU	Regulations on agreement and issue of special water use permits
	1977	CM RSFSR	Regulations on agreement and issue of special water use permits
Land and soil	1960	SS RSFSR	Article 199, Criminal Code, on criminal liability for breaking laws on LR
	1962	CM RSFSR	Instructions on withdrawal of land for roadways
	1962	CM RSFSR	On parcels ceded to water authorities for special purposes
	1965	CM SU	On increasing role of Minsel in management of kolkhoz and sovkhoz

Appendix 1 (*continued*)

Environmental area	Year	Agent	Description
Land and soil (*cont.*)	1966	CM SU	On massive development of land reclamation for increasing agricultural yields.
	1967	CM SU	Antierosion measures
	1967	CM RSFSR	Antierosion measures
	1968	SS SU	Fundamental Land Law
	1970	SS RSFSR	Land Code
	1970	PSS SU	Administrative liability for breaking land laws
	1970	CM SU	State control over land use
	1971	CM RSFSR	Establishment of All-Russian Kolkhoz Council
	1972	CM RSFSR	On questions of land use
	1973	CM RSFSR	Role of Minsel in soil protection
	1974	Minsel SU Procurator SU	Instructions on ensuring state control over use of land by Minsel construction service
	1974	CM SU	On payment of damages and loss of agricultural production when land is withdrawn from kolkhoz for state and other purposes
	1974	CM RSFSR	On questions of land use when withdrawn for state or societal purposes
	1975	CM RSFSR	On improving organization of fulfillment and increasing of quality of design research in organization of land exploitation
	1975	Minsel, Minfin, Minivst SU	Instructions on payment of damages for temporary withdrawal of land parcels and loss of agricultural production for nonagricultural purposes

Appendix 1 (*continued*)

Environmental area	Year	Agent	Description
Land and soil (*cont.*)	1975	CM SU	Measures to improve antierosion work
	1976	CM SU	Land reclamation, protection and rational use on mining locations
	1977	Minsel SU	Instructions for transfer of reclaimed land from mining operations to other organizations
	1977	CM SU	Establishment of land inventory
	1977	CM RSFSR	Establishment of land inventory
Underground	1960	SS RSFSR	Article 167, Criminal Code, on criminal liability for breaking relevant environmental laws
	1966	CM RSFSR	Measures to prevent unauthorized construction on areas in fields of generally used natural resources
	1966	CM RSFSR	Instructions on procedure for permitting erection of enterprises, towns, villages, structures, water-lines, and other objects on orebeds. Procedure for reviewing applications for land withdrawal for state, social, and other needs
	1968	CM SU	Establishment of State Inspection Committee for work safety in mining industry
	1968	CM SU	Role of Coal Ministry in protection of underground resources (PUR)
	1968	CM SU	Role of Ministry of Ferrous Metallurgy in PUR

342

Appendix 1 (*continued*)

Environmental area	Year	Agent	Description
Underground (*cont.*)	1968	CM SU	Role of Ministry of Non-Ferrous Metallurgy in PUR
	1968	CM SU	Role of Oil Extracting Ministry in PUR
	1968	CM SU	Role of Ministry of Geology in PUR
	1969	CM RSFSR	Role of MinGeoRSFSR in PUR
	1972	CM SU	Establishment of State Committee for Mineral Deposit Reserves
	1975	CM SU	Model constitution for prospectors' *artel*
	1975	SS SU	On measures to further strengthen protection of underground resources and improve their exploitation
	1975	SS SU	Fundamental Underground Resources Law
	1976	SS RSFSR	RSFSR Underground Resources Code
Forests and flora	1947	CM SU	Regulations on cutting of hay and pasturing on state forest land
	1950	CM SU	Role of Ministry of Forestry in protecting forests and establishment of State Forest Protection Service
	1955	CM SU	Logging regulations for state forests
	1959	CM RSFSR	On strengthening fight against forest fires
	1960	SS RSFSR	Articles 98, 99, 168, 169, RSFSR Criminal Code, on criminal liability for breaking forestry laws
	1966	CM RSFSR	On improving management of cedar forests

Appendix 1 (*continued*)

Environmental area	Year	Agent	Description
Forests and flora (*cont.*)	1968	CM SU	On management of forests on collective farms
	1968	CM SU	On procedure and scope of material liability for damages to forest economy
	1968	CM RSFSR	Establishment of tariff for calculation of size of damage caused to forest economy
	1969	CM RSFSR	Procedure for creation of oblast, kraj, republican (ASSR) interkolkhoz forests
	1969	CM SU	Role of Ministry of Forest and Woodworking Industry in forest protection
	1969	CM SU	Establishment of State Forestry Committee (SCF)
	1970	SC SU	On court practice in matters of breaking forestry laws, revised from 1969
	1971	CM SU	Regulations for forest fire security
	1971	PSS SU	On strengthening administrative liability for breaking forest fire security regulations
	1971	CM RSFSR	Role of Ministry of Forestry, RSFSR, in forest protection
	1973	CM RSFSR	Role of Minsel in forest protection
	1973	CM RSFSR	On strengthening material liability for damage caused to forest economy
	1976	SCF SU	Job descriptions of state forest workers in state forest protection service
	1977	SS SU	Fundamental Forestry Law

Appendix 1 (*continued*)

Environmental area	Year	Agent	Description
Wild animals	1955	CM RSFSR	Establishment of Chief Administration of Hunting Economy and Preserves of the RSFSR CM
	1956	CM RSFSR	Organization of local organs of this chief administration
	1956	CM RSFSR	On measures to protect Arctic animals
	1958	CM RSFSR	On measures to improve condition of hunting economy
	1958	CM SU	On measures to improve operation of hunting economy
	1958	CM RSFSR	On measures to improve operation of hunting economy of RSFSR
	1960	CM RSFSR	Legal description of hunting and hunting economy
	1960	CM RSFSR	Article 166, RSFSR Criminal Code, establishing criminal liability for illegal hunting and sale of wild animals
	1961	CM RSFSR	Regulations for spring wild bird hunting
	1961	CM RSFSR	Regulations for hunting sable
	1962	CM RSFSR	On improving management of RSFSR fur industry
	1962	CM RSFSR	Gives additional powers to RSFSR Chief Hunting and Reserve Administration in fish, game, and peltry management
	1962	CM RSFSR	Regulation for shooting wild northern deer
	1965	CAH&NR RSFSR	Establishment of public hunting inspection organ

Appendix 1 (*continued*)

Environmental area	Year	Agent	Description
Wild animals (*cont.*)	1965	CM RSFSR	Measures to improve operation of hunting economy and raise its obligations
	1967	CM RSFSR	On the periods for shooting muskrat
	1969	CAH&NR RSFSR	Instructions for procedure in paying bonuses and rewards for good behavior in hunting inspection service
	1971	CM RSFSR	Regulations for hunting wild hooved animals required
	1971	CAH&NR RSFSR	Instructions on issuing permits for hunting wild hooved animals on territory of RSFSR
	1972	CM SU	Measures for strengthening fight with hunting regulation violators
	1972	PSS SU	On procedure for fining hunting regulation violators
	1973	CM RSFSR	Additional measures against hunting regulation violators
	1974	CAH&NR RSFSR	Model Hunting Regulations
	1974	CAH&NR RSFSR	Constitution of Hunters and Fishermen's Society of RSFSR
	1974	Minsel SU	Establishment of Red Book for endangered species
	1975	CM SU	On implementing Soviet-Japanese Convention on Protection of Endangered Migratory Birds
	1975	CM SU	On protection of endangered migratory birds and their habitat

Appendix 1 (*continued*)

Environmental area	Year	Agent	Description
Wild animals (*cont.*)	1975	CM RSFSR	On strengthening protection of rare animals
	1975	CM SU	Measures to implement Agreement on Protection of White Bear
	1975	CM SU	Measures to implement Convention on water and swamp areas having international significance, especially as habitat for water birds
	1981	SS SU	Fundamental Law on Protection of Wild Animals
Zapovedniki	1961	CM SU	Confirms establishment of network of state reserves and hunting preserves
	1962	CM RSFSR	Confirms establishment of state reserves and hunting preserves under CAH&NR
Fish	1958	CM SU	On the reproduction and protection of fish in the inland waterways of the USSR
	1960	SS RSFSR	Articles 163, 164, 165 of criminal code establishing liability for breaking of fishing laws
	1960	CM SU	Protection of fishing industry in Soviet territorial waters
	1960	CM SU	Establishment of veterinary inspection over fishing industry waters
	1964	PSS SU	On strengthening administrative liability over breaking fishing and fish protection regulations
	1965	Glavryb vod	On taking away violators' fishing tackle

Appendix 1 (*continued*)

Environmental area	Year	Agent	Description
Fish (*cont.*)	1965	Glavrybvod SU	Instructions on organization and activity of councils of public fish protection organization in basins' administration for protection and reproduction of fish, and where fishing under surveillance by fish protection
	1966	Minrybkhoz SU	Rules for production of sea plants and shellfish in Soviet waters
	1966	Minrybkhoz	Establishment of chief administration for protection and reproduction of fish under Minrybkhoz
	1967	Glavrybvod SU	Instruction s on organization and activities of public fish protection service
	1967	Glavrybvod SU	Instructions on procedure for composing judicial protocol, taking into account fishing gear, nature of waterway, and fish
	1967	Minrybkhoz SU	Method of calculating damage to fishing economy by violators of fishing and fish protection regulations
	1968	CM SU	Reconfirms role of Minrybkhoz SU in fish production and protection
	1969	CM SU	Measures for strengthening fish protection in Soviet waters
	1970	Glavrybvod SU	Procedure for changing periods for fishing
	1970	Minrybkhoz SU	Constitution of Fish Protection Service

Appendix 1 (*continued*)

Environmental area	Year	Agent	Description
Fish (*cont.*)	1970	Glavrybvod su	Model proposition for basin administration for fish protection and reproduction, and regulation of fishing
	1971	Glavrybvod su	Rights of basin administration and Fish Protection Service
	1972	Minsel, Minrybkhoz Minvodkhoz su	Measures for preventing fall of poisonous chemicals into Soviet waters
	1973	CM RSFSR	Confirms inventory of all republic waterways where spawning places of salmon and sturgeon exist
	1974	CM RSFSR	Addition of waterways to above inventory where salmon and sturgeon spawn
	1974	Minrybkhoz su	Instructions on methods of sealskin production and seal raising on state and collective farms
	1974	Minrybkhoz su	Method of calculating damage to fishing industry by violators of fishing regulations
	1974	CM su	On strengthening protection of valuable fish, sea mammals, and shellfish in Soviet waters
	1975	Minrybkhoz su	Method of catching dolphins for scientific research purposes
	1975	CM RSFSR	On the setting of a tariff for calculating size of damage by violator of laws regulating fishing and valuable fish in the fishery waters of the oblasts and autonomous republics

Appendix 1 (*continued*)

Environmental area	Year	Agent	Description
Fish (*cont.*)	1975	Minrybkhoz SU	Rules for protection and hunting of sea mammals
	1976	CM SU	Establishment of flood zones around reservoirs in connection with construction of hydroelectric stations
	1976	CM SU	Regulations for sport and amateur fishing
	1977	Minrybkhoz SU	Model Regulations for catching valuable fish with a license
	1977	CM SU	On protection of fish and other living resources in Soviet offshore waters
	1977	PSS SU	Method of implementing Presidium Order 7 on Temporary Measures to protect fish and other living resources in Soviet offshore waters
	1977	CM SU	Procedure for calculating damage to fish and other living resources in Soviet seas and offshore waters
Human environment	1962	CM RSFSR	Regulating cleanliness on Black Sea beaches
	1968	CM RSFSR	On role of kolkhozy in EP
	1969	SS SU	Fundamental health law gives Minzdrav oversight of environment in inhabited areas
	1971	PSS SU	Role of urban soviets in EP
	1971	PSS SU	Role of raion soviets in EP
	1972	SS RSFSR	Law on local soviets provides for administrative EP in their areas
	1973	CM SU	Gives sanitary inspection service authority to monitor EP for damage to human health

Appendix 1 (*continued*)

Environmental area	Year	Agent	Description
Human environment (*cont.*)	1973	CM SU	Establishment of jurisdiction of each level of Soviet administration in monitoring EP in health resorts

Source: Blinov, *Sbornik normativnykh aktov*, and published laws and regulations found in the Soviet press since that date.

CAH&NR	Chief Administration for Game Management and Nature Reserves	Minrybkhoz	Ministry of Fish Industry
CM	Council of Ministers	Minsel	Ministry of Agriculture
CPK	Central Executive Committee of People's Commissars	Minzdrav	Ministry of Health
		MVKh	Ministry of Land Reclamation and Water Management (Minvodkhoz)
EP	Environmental Protection	P	Presidium
Glavrybvod	Chief Administration for Fish Management	RSFSR	Russian Soviet Federated Socialist Republic
Minfin	Ministry of Finance	SC	Supreme Court
Mingrzha	Ministry of Civil Aviation	SFC	State Forestry Committee
Miniust	Ministry of Justice	SS	Supreme Soviet
Minmorflot	Maritime Fleet Ministry	SU	USSR

Appendix 2 Survey of Main Environmental Laws, Yugoslavia[a]

	SFRY	Bosnia-Herzegovina	Croatia
General laws			
Associated labor	53/76	—	—
National defense	22/74	3/70	15/76
Agricultural land			
Agricultural land	25/65	33/75	S
Erosion and flood control	—	—	25/60
Forests, Plants, and			
Animal World			
Forests	26/65	38/71	19/67
Hunting	16/65	36/71	25/76
Marine fishing	10/65	S	11/73
Freshwater fishing	—	38/68	14/73
Water			
Seacoast	2/74	—	—
Water	—	36/75	53/74
Water classification	—	42/67	2/69
Water tax	—	36/75	53/74
Air and water			
Air pollution control	30/65	—	S
Territorial management	—	13/74	—
Nature areas and			
natural wonders			
Nature protection	—	4/65	54/76
Territorial management	—	13/74	—
Historical entities			
and monuments			
Protection of cultural management	12/65	31/65	7/67
Territorial management	—	13/74	—
Urban and rural settlements			
Urban order	—	33/75	8/59
Territorial management	—	13/74	14/73
Determination of city land	5/68	24/68	30/68
Expropriation	11/68	35/72	S
Administration of urban land	—	13/74	14/73
Taxes for the use of urban land	51/67	13/74	14/73
Sale of urban land and buildings	43/65	S	S

Macedonia	Montenegro	Slovenia	Serbia	Kosovo	Vojvodina
—	—	—	—	—	—
12/76	15/75	13/76	27/76	R	R
40/76	S	26/73	47/74	53/75	27/72
—	27/60	—	—	—	—
20/74	29/72	16/74	19/74	12/73	29/75
5/73	17/73	25/76	51/76	22/73	29/71
—	14/73	25/76	—	—	—
15/73	39/76	25/76	8/76	8/75	18/76
—	—	—	—	—	—
47/73	22/74	16/74	33/75	30/76	24/77
—	17/68	—	5/68	R	R
47/73	22/74	16/74	33/75	30/76	24/77
20/74	S	13/75	8/73	R	R
—	—	—	—	—	—
41/73	36/77	7/70	50/75	44/76	10/74
—	—	—	—	—	—
24/73	36/60	SR	28/77	S	11/74
—	—	—	28/77	—	—
5/59	8/59	1/59	10/59	R	R
—	—	—	—	—	—
17/74	18/68	S	32/68	—	10/71
47/73	23/72	22/72	22/73	25/73	27/72
10/73	4/73	22/72	32/75	44/76	15/76
45/72	4/73	7/77	32/75	37/77	16/78
36/75	27/75	19/76	15/74	18/75	1/75

Appendix 2 (*Continued*)

	SFRY	Bosnia-Herzegovina	Croatia
Residences			
Housing relations	—	30/74	33/76
Measures for housing construction	60/70	13/74	32/77
Infrastructure			
Public roads	27/65	30/74	53/74
Railroads	9/65	22/76	19/74
Coastal and inland navigation	22/77	—	—
Ports and harbors	2/68	20/72	19/74
Airline terminals	—	12/74	31/73
Foundations of communications system	24/74	—	—
Water improvement system	—	—	25/60
Planning and construction			
Urban and territorial planning (and administration)	—	13/74	14/73
Land registry	—	16/73	16/74
Water and water objects registry	—	21/77	44/73
Planning and construction	—	13/74	20/75
Standardization	38/77	—	—

Note: R: Appropriate republican law applies. S: Appropriate federal law applies.
Source: Pp. 123–24 of source cited in table 3.1.

Macedonia	Montenegro	Slovenia	Serbia	Kosovo	Vojvodina
36/73	4/74	18/74	29/73	26/73	19/74
S	40/75	5/72	52/74	53/75	10/75
35/67	30/74	51/71	32/75	43/74	7/74
S	27/75	S	32/75	R	R
—	—	—	—	—	—
45/73	S	S	27/77	R	1/78
47/73	S	S	28/75	27/76	—
—	—	—	—	—	—
42/61	27/60	—	31/65	R	—
15/73	23/76	16/67	19/74	37/71	1/76
34/72	34/74	16/74	11/76	12/73	24/77
—	28/77	26/74	31/74	—	—
35/73	36/74	42/73	25/73	39/72	4/76
—	—	—	—	—	—

a. The numerical entry indicates the number of the particular law (numerator) and the year of its enactment (denominator).

Appendix 3 Investment in the Infrastructure, SFRY
(in millions of dinars at current prices)

	Period	SFRY	Bosnia-Herzegovina	Croatia
Roads	1966–70	94.3	17.0	20.0
	1971–75	215.7	49.8	45.3
Railroad tracks	1966–70	24.2	3.3	2.1
	1971–75	37.8	5.1	2.2
Ports and harbors	1966–70	1.5	0	0.6
	1971–75	2.2	0	0.7
Airports	1966–70	2.2	0.3	1.3
	1971–75	4.3	0	2.2
Water management	1966–70	32.0	2.8	6.7
	1971–75	49.3	7.7	7.3
Energy infrastructure	1966–70	50.5	11.0	10.9
	1971–75	106.5	5.8	26.6
Communal infrastructure	1966–70	39.9	4.4	9.9
	1971–75	96.6	14.0	24.5

Source: P. 131 of source cited in table 3.1.

			Serbia		
Macedonia	Montenegro	Slovenia	Serbia proper	Kosovo	Vojvodina
8.2	7.4	7.1	22.7	4.7	7.2
13.7	10.2	33.2	36.3	7.6	19.6
2.4	2.7	3.5	9.2	0	1.0
2.4	10.7	4.8	11.8	0.1	0.7
0	0.1	0.3	0.3	0	0.2
0	0.9	0.5	0	0	0.1
0.2	0.3	0	0.1	0	0.1
0	0.5	1.0	0.5	0.1	0.1
4.1	0.2	2.6	8.9	0.8	5.9
5.1	0.9	6.4	10.5	1.1	10.3
4.1	0.9	6.4	13.7	0.7	2.8
5.9	7.6	12.6	23.1	5.8	9.1
3.6	0.6	5.2	11.6	0.8	3.8
5.7	2.1	13.4	26.5	1.1	9.3

Appendix 4   Share of Construction in National Income, SFRY (percentage)

	Period	SFRY	Bosnia-Herzegovina	Croatia
Housing	1966–70	4.9	12.6	9.7
	1971–75	10.2	13.9	10.7
Urban infrastructure	1966–70	0.4	1.1	0.6
	1971–75	1.2	1.7	0.9
Economic construction	1966–70	1.9	3.7	4.0
	1971–75	3.7	5.1	2.8
Transportation	1966–70	1.4	4.2	2.0
	1971–75	2.1	3.6	1.5
Water	1966–70	0.4	0.3	0.5
	1971–75	0.4	0.6	0.2
Energy	1966–70	0.4	3.2	2.2

Source: Pp. 136–37 of source cited in table 3.1.

			Serbia		
Macedonia	Montenegro	Slovenia	Serbia proper	Kosovo	Vojvodina
10.9	11.2	7.3	11.0	16.2	7.3
8.8	10.7	8.7	10.4	15.4	7.3
1.8	1.4	0.7	0.8	2.0	0.7
1.5	2.1	1.2	1.0	3.4	0.7
6.3	9.0	4.2	3.6	7.3	2.2
4.5	5.0	4.2	2.8	7.0	2.8
8.2	13.2	1.4	3.0	6.4	1.8
2.4	9.8	2.2	1.9	3.4	1.6
1.8	0.1	0.2	0.8	1.0	1.2
0.7	0.4	0.3	0.4	0.4	0.8
1.8	9.7	0.8	1.2	0.9	0.6

Appendix 5 Share of Individual Funds in Total Construction, SFRY (percentage)

	Period	SFRY	Bosnia-Herzegovina	Croatia
Housing fund	1966–70	48.9	48.0	48.5
	1971–75	53.5	51.8	60.5
Urban infrastructure fund	1966–70	4.3	4.4	3.3
	1971–75	6.0	6.2	4.8
Urban economic fund	1966–70	19.1	14.1	20.1
	1971–75	18.7	19.0	16.2
Transportation infrastructure	1966–70	13.9	15.9	10.1
	1971–75	11.0	13.7	8.6
Water	1966–70	3.7	2.1	2.8
	1971–75	2.1	1.9	1.2
Energy infrastructure	1966–70	5.5	12.1	11.1
	1971–75	4.5	3.9	4.5
Communal infrastructure	1966–70	4.6	3.3	4.1
	1971–75	4.1	3.5	4.2

Source: Pp. 131–32 of source cited in table 3.1.

			Serbia		
Macedonia	Montenegro	Slovenia	Serbia proper	Kosovo	Vojvodina
40.9	24.6	46.9	51.8	46.1	48.8
45.0	33.0	49.7	57.8	46.3	50.2
6.9	3.0	4.3	3.9	5.9	5.3
8.0	6.7	7.3	5.5	10.3	4.8
14.0	19.9	27.2	16.6	20.9	15.0
22.5	15.5	24.0	15.8	22.4	19.6
18.3	20.1	9.2	14.0	18.2	12.5
12.1	30.4	10.5	9.3	10.3	10.6
6.9	0.5	2.2	3.8	3.1	8.7
3.8	1.2	1.7	2.0	1.5	5.3
6.9	21.3	5.6	5.9	2.7	4.1
4.4	10.3	3.3	4.4	7.7	4.7
6.1	1.6	4.5	5.0	3.1	5.6
4.2	2.9	3.5	5.1	1.5	4.8

Notes

I The Environmental Problem: Regulation or Structure

1 Alma-Ata, *Kazakhstanskaia pravda*, March 4, 1983, p. 4.

2 Grigory Galazy, *Moscow News*, no. 9, March 6–9, 1983, p. 10.

3 "The Soviets and the Protection of Nature," *Izvestia*, April 28, 1983, p. 1.

4 N. Demidov, "Dark Waters of the Clear Meadow," *Sovietskaia rossia*, August 26, 1981, p. 2.

5 *Pravda*, March 9, 1983, p. 1.

6 *Avtomobil'ny transport*, no. 9 (September 1982): 55.

7 Yerevan, *Sovetakan Ayastan*, August 23, 1983, p. 2.

8 Tashkent, *Sovet Ozbekistoni*, January 16, 1983.

9 Alma-Ata, *Sotsialistik Qazagstan*, January 20, 1983.

10 Belgrade, *Privredni pregled*, March 29, 1979, p. 3; *Politika*, December 25, 1984.

11 Zagreb, *Vjestnik*, October 27, 1979, p. 7.

12 Belgrade, *Privredni pregled*, July 23–25, 1983.

13 Zagreb, *Vjestnik*, December 8, 1979, p. 27.

14 Zagreb, *Sedam dana*, supplement to *Vjestnik*, November 8, 1980.

15 See summary of the change in Soviet perceptions of the global environment in Barbara Jancar, "Soviet Environmental Policy toward the Third World," in W. Raymond Duncan, ed., *Soviet Policy in the Third World* (New York: Pergamon, 1980), p. 51.

16 For a brief discussion of this position, see John Baden and Richard L. Stroup, eds., *Bureaucracy vs. Environment: The Environmental Costs of Bureaucratic Governance* (Ann Arbor: University of Michigan Press, 1981), pp. 2–3.

17 Among the books that should be mentioned are Marshall Goldman, *The Spoils of Progress: Environmental Pollution in the Soviet Union* (Cambridge, Mass.: MIT Press, 1972); Philip R. Pryde, *Conservation in the Soviet Union* (Cambridge: Cambridge University Press, 1972); Donald R. Kelley, Kenneth R. Stunkel, and Richard R. Wescott, *The Economic Superpowers and the Environment: The United States, The Soviet Union and Japan* (San Francisco: W. H. Freeman, 1976); Josef Fullenbach, *European Environmental Policy: East and West* (London: Butterworths, 1981); Boris Komarov, *The Destruction of Nature in the Soviet Union* (White Plains, N.Y.: M. E. Sharpe, 1980) (an "insider" account); Fred Singleton, ed., *Environmental Misuse in the Soviet Union* (New York: Praeger, 1976); W. A. Douglas Jackson, ed., *Soviet Resource Management and the Envi-*

ronment (Columbus, Ohio: American Association for the Advancement of Slavic Studies, 1978); Thane Gustafson, *Reform in Soviet Politics: Lessons of Recent Policies on Land and Water* (Cambridge: Cambridge University Press, 1981); Ivan Volgyes, ed., *Environmental Deterioration in the Soviet Union and Eastern Europe* (New York: Praeger, 1974); and Cynthia H. Enloe, *The Politics of Pollution in a Comparative Perspective* (New York: David McKay, 1975.) The articles are too numerous to be listed here and will be found in the bibliography or cited individually.

18 Among these are John M. Kramer, "The Politics of Conservation and Pollution in the USSR," University of Virginia, 1973; Charles E. Ziegler, "Disaggregated Pluralism in a Socialist System: Environmental Policy in the USSR," University of Illinois, Urbana, 1979; Joan DeBardeleben, "The Environment and Marxism-Leninism: Soviet and East German Perspectives," McGill University, Montreal, Canada, 1983; and Douglas R. Weiner, "Conservation, Ecology and the Cultural Revolution," Columbia University, 1983.

19 Kelley et al., *The Economic Superpowers*, p. 276.

20 Robert J. McIntyre and James R. Thompson, "On the Environmental Efficiency of Economics Systems," *Soviet Studies* 30, 2 (April 1978): 173–92.

21 Marshall I. Goldman, "Externalities and the Race for Economic Growth in the USSR: Will the Environment Ever Win?" *Journal of Political Economy* 80 (March 1972): 313–27.

22 David E. Powell, "Politics of the Urban Environment, the City of Moscow," *Comparative Political Studies* 10, 3 (October 1977): 433–54.

23 Kelley et al., *The Economic Superpowers*, p. 243; Charles E. Ziegler, "Economic Alternatives and Administrative Solutions in Soviet Environmental Protection," University of Louisville, *Policy Studies* 11, 1 (September 1982): 115–27.

24 Pryde, *Conservation in the Soviet Union* p. 174; Goldman, *Spoils of Progress*, pp. 46–48; Fullenbach, *European Environmental Policy* pp. 95–104.

25 For example, one of the foremost proponents of more centralized management as a corrective to present environmental administrative difficulties is Oleg Kolbasov, a leading environmental lawyer and head of the Environmental Law Section of the Institute of State and Law of the USSR Academy of Sciences. This position is argued in *Ekologiia: Politika-pravo* (Ecology: policy-law) (Moscow: Izdatel'stvo "Nauka" [Science Publishing House], 1976).

26 John M. Kramer, "Environmental Problems in the USSR: The Divergence of Theory and Practice," *Journal of Politics* 36, 4 (November 1974): 886–99.

27 See Ziegler, "Disaggregated Pluralism."

28 K. Bush, "Environmental Problems in the USSR," *Problems of Communism* 11 (July–August, 1972): 21–31.

29 Paul B. Downing, *Environmental Economics and Policy* (Boston: Little, Brown, 1984), pp. 16–17.

30 Marshall I. Goldman, "The Convergence of Environmental Disruption," *Science*, October 2, 1970, pp. 37–42.

31 Terry L. Anderson and Peter J. Hill, "Property Rights as a Common Pool Resource," in Baden and Stroup, *Bureaucracy vs. Environment*, pp. 22–45.

32 For an excellent East-West comparison, see Fullenbach, *European Economic Policy*, particularly pp. 82–92.

33 Kelley et al., *The Economic Superpowers*, p. 269.

34 Among these are Jerry F. Hough, *The Soviet Prefects: The Local Party Organs in Industrial Decision-making* (Cambridge, Mass.: Harvard University Press, 1969); Erik P. Hoffmann and Frederic J. Fleron, eds., *The Conduct of Soviet Foreign Policy* (London: Butterworths, 1971); Jerry F. Hough, *The Soviet Union and Social Science Theory* (Cambridge, Mass.: Harvard University Press, 1977); Gordon B. Smith, ed., *Public Policy and Administration in the Soviet Union* (New York: Praeger, 1980); Graham T. Allison and Morton H. Halperin, "Bureaucratic Politics: A Paradigm and Some Policy Implications," in Raymond Tanter and Richard H. Ullman, eds., *Theory and Policy in International Relations* (Princeton: Princeton University Press, 1972), pp. 40–80; James H. Seroka, "Local Political Structures and Policy Outputs in the Yugoslav Commune," *Studies in Comparative Communism* 12, 1 (Spring 1979): 632–73; Paul Cocks, "Rethinking the Organizational Weapon: The Soviet System in a Systems Age," *World Politics* 32, 2 (January 1980): 228–57; and Karen Dawisha, "The Limits of the Bureaucratic Politics Model: Observations on the Soviet Case," *Studies in Comparative Communism* 13, 4 (Winter 1980): 300–26.

35 See Joseph LaPalombara, "Monoliths or Plural Systems: Through Conceptual Lenses Darkly," *Studies in Comparative Communism* 13, 3 (Autumn 1975): 304–32.

36 See further discussion in Barbara Jancar, "Review Article—Political Culture and Political Change," *Studies in Comparative Communism* 17, 1 (Spring 1984): 69–82.

37 H. Gordon Skilling, *Interest Groups in Soviet Society* (Princeton: Princeton University Press, 1971).

38 The diversity of interests within these states has been termed variously by Hough as "institutional pluralism"; Brown, "diversity within monism"; and Nove, "centralized pluralism." For recent discussions of pluralism in communist systems, see Susan Gross Solomon, ed., *Pluralism in the Soviet Union: Essays in Honour of H. Gordon Skilling* (New York: St. Martin's Press, 1983) and Alec Nove, *The Soviet Economic System*, 2d ed. (London: George Allen & Unwin, 1982), chap. 3.

39 Hough, *The Soviet Prefects*; Donald R. Kelley, "Interest Groups in the USSR: The Impact of Political Sensitivity on Group Influence," *The Journal of Politics* 34, 3 (August 1972): 860–88; Peter H. Solomon, *Soviet Criminologists and Criminal Policy: Specialists in Policy Making* (New York: Columbia University Press, 1978) and John Lowenhardt, *Decision Making in Soviet Politics* (New York: St. Martin's Press, 1981). See also Paul Cocks, Robert V. Daniels, and Nancy Whittier Herr, eds., *The Dynamics of Soviet Politics* (Cambridge, Mass.: Harvard University Press, 1976).

40 Lowenhardt, *Decision Making in Soviet Politics*, chap. 5.

41 Peter H. Solomon, *Soviet Criminologists*, chap. 10.
42 Rudolf Tokes, ed., *Dissent in the USSR* (Baltimore: Johns Hopkins University Press, 1976), Introduction.
43 John M. Kramer, "The Environmental Crisis in Eastern Europe: The Price for Progress," *Slavic Review* 42, 2 (Summer 1983): 220; Enloe, *The Politics of Pollution*; and Volgyes, *Environmental Deterioration*.
44 See especially chap. 1 of Michael Crozier and Erhard Friedberg, *L'Acteur et le système* (The Actor and the system) (Paris: Édition du Seuil, 1977), pp. 35–54.
45 For Crozier and Friedberg's excellent discussion of the relationship between the actor, the organization, and power summarized in the next few paragraphs, see ibid., chap. 2, pp. 55–77.
46 Randall B. Ripley and Grace A. Franklin, *Bureaucracy and Policy Implementation* (Homewood, Ill.: Dorsey, 1982), pp. 132–33. See also by the same authors the discussion of regulatory policymaking in *Congress, the Bureaucracy, and Public Policy*, 2d ed. (Homewood, Ill.: Dorsey, 1980).
47 For a discussion of these aspects of environmental regulation, see Downing, *Environmental Economics and Policy*, pp. 2–9.
48 Rodney D. Fort and John Baden, "The Federal Treasury as a Common Pool Resource and the Development of a Predatory Bureaucracy," in Baden and Stroup, *Bureaucracy vs. Environment* pp. 9–21.
49 Goldman, "Externalities," pp. 323–24.
50 Author interview in Belgrade, May 1981.
51 Guy Benveniste, *The Politics of Expertise*, 2d ed. (San Francisco: Boyd and Fraser, 1977), p. 38.
52 See DeBardeleben, "The Environment and Marxism-Leninism," for a longer discussion of this point.
53 Charles D. Jones, *Clean Air: The Policies and Politics of Pollution Control* (Pittsburgh: University of Pittsburgh Press, 1975).
54 Ripley and Franklin, *Bureaucracy and Policy Implementation*, pp. 4–5.
55 See Charles O. Jones's discussion of "The Public Agenda," *An Introduction to the Study of Public Policy*, 2d ed. (North Scituate, Mass.: Duxbury Press, 1977), pp. 51–53. For agenda-building, see Roger W. Cobb and Charles D. Elder, *Participation in American Politics. The Dynamics of Agenda-Building* (Baltimore and London: Johns Hopkins University Press, 1972), and Roger Cobb, Jennie-Keith Ross and Marc Howard Ross, "Agenda Building as a Comparative Political Process," *The American Political Science Review* 70, 1 (March 1976): 126–38.
56 Lowenhardt makes good use of such refinements in his discussion of agenda-building as it relates to Soviet politics. (Lowenhardt, *Decision Making in Soviet Politics*, pp. 27–33.)
57 Notably Lowenhardt, *Decision Making in Soviet Politics*; Peter Solomon, *Soviet Criminologists*; and Donald R. Kelley, "Interest Groups in the USSR: The Impact of Political Sensitivity on Group Influence," *The Journal of Politics* 34, 3 (August 1972): 860–88; Philip D. Stewart, "Soviet Interest Groups and the Policy Process:

The Repeal of Production Education," *World Politics* 22 (October 1969); Milton Lodge, "Groupism in Soviet Politics," in Frederic J. Fleron, Jr., ed., *Communist Studies and the Social Sciences: Essays on Methodology and Empirical Theory* (Chicago: University of Chicago Press, 1969), pp. 254-78; Joel J. Schwartz and William R. Keech, "Public Influence and Educational Policy in the Soviet Union," in Roger E. Kanet, ed., *The Behavioral Revolution and Communist Studies* (New York: Praeger, 1971), pp. 151-86; and Peter H. Juviler, "Family Reforms on the Road to Communism," in Peter H. Juviler and Henry W. Morton, eds., *Soviet Policy-Making: Studies of Communism in Transition* (London: George Allen & Unwin, 1967), pp. 29-60.

58 Lowenhardt, *Decision Making in Soviet Politics*, pp. 192ff.

59 Donald R. Kelley, "Environmental Policy-Making in the USSR: The Role of Industrial and Environmental Interest Groups," *Soviet Studies* 28, 4 (October 1976): 570-789.

60 The concept is carried over from Cobb, Ross, and Ross's discussion of the "inside" and "outside" initiative model relative to agenda-building. See Cobb, Ross, and Ross, *Agenda Building*.

61 Gabriel A. Almond and G. Bingham Powell, Jr., *Comparative Politics: A Developmental Approach* (Boston and Toronto: Little, Brown, 1966), p. 76.

62 For general discussion about groups in Soviet politics, see in particular H. Gordon Skilling, *Interest Groups*, chap. 2; Lowenhardt, *Decision Making in Soviet Politics*, chap. 1; Lodge, "Groupism in Soviet Politics," pp. 254-78; Joseph LaPalombara, "Parsimony and Empiricism in Comparative Politics," in Robert T. Holt and John E. Turner, eds., *The Methodology of Comparative Research* (New York: 1970), pp. 123-49; Linda L. Lubrano, "Scientific Collectives: Behavior of Soviet Scientists," in Linda L. Lubrano and Susan Gross Solomon, eds., *The Social Context of Soviet Science* (Boulder, Colo.: Westview, 1980), pp. 101-36; Susan Gross Solomon, ed., *Pluralism in the Soviet Union*.

63 In the conclusion to his dissertation, Kramer stresses the importance of the natural scientists. (Kramer, "Conservation and Pollution in the USSR," Conclusion.)

64 The rising role of both lawyers and economists will be discussed in the chapter on experts (chap. 6).

65 See especially Ružena Vintrová, Jan Klacek, and Václav Kupka, "Ekonomický růst v ČSSR, jeho bariery a efektivnost," *Politická ekonomie* (Political economy) no. 1, 1980, pp. 29-42.

66 Ripley and Franklin, *Bureaucracy and Policy Implementation*, p. 193.

67 For example, the National Goals Research Staff in 1970 identified two types of complementary approaches to policymaking for improving our environment: corrective actions, which include water treatment, solid waste treatment, and air pollution control; and preventive actions, the aim of which is to minimize or optimally to avoid environmental destabilization before it occurs. National Goals Research Staff, "Environmental Policy," *Towards Balanced Growth: Quantity to Quality, Report of the National Goals Research Staff* (Washington, D.C.: U.S. Government Printing Office, 1970), pp. 66-75.

2 The Centipede and the Hydra

1 For a general description of the system, the reader is referred to, among others, Nove's classic, *The Soviet Economic System*; Robert W. Campbell, *The Soviet-Type Economies, Performance and Evolution*, 3d ed. (Boston: Houghton Mifflin, 1974); James R. Millar, *The ABC's of Soviet Socialism* (Urbana and Chicago: University of Illinois Press, 1981); J. Wilczynski, *The Economics of Socialism*, 4th ed., vol. 2 of *Studies in Economics*, ed. Charles Carter (London: George Allen & Unwin, 1982); and E. Cherevik and Y. Shvyrkov, *An ABC of Planning* (Moscow: Progress, 1982).

2 An excellent commentary on the 1977 Constitution is to be found in Robert Sharlet, ed., *The New Soviet Constitution of 1977: Analysis and Text* (Brunswick, Ohio: King's Court Communications, 1978).

3 The text of this document may be found in V. M. Blinov, ed., *Sbornik normativnykh aktov po okhrane prirody* (Collection of normative acts on environmental protection) (Moscow: "Iuridicheskaia literatura" [Legal literature press], 1978), pp. 11–23.

4 V. V. Petrov, *Pravovaia okhrana prirody* (The legal protection of nature) (Moscow: Moscow University Press, 1980), chap. 4. This book was the required text in environmental law at Moscow University, fall 1980.

5 For example, Fyodor I. Kushnirsky, *Soviet Economic Planning, 1965–1980* (Boulder, Colo.: Westview, 1982), pp. 72–76.

6 Peter Blandon, *Soviet Forest Industries* (Boulder, Colo.: Westview, 1983), pp. 53–58.

7 In 1980, there were 15 union republics; 20 autonomous republics, representing minor nationality groupings; 8 autonomous provinces, representing lesser nationalities; 10 autonomous regions (*okrugi*) representing even smaller national entities; 6 regions (*kraje*), 121 provinces (*oblasti*), 3,176 districts (*raiony*), and 2,074 cities. Prezidium verkhnogo sovieta Soiuza sovietskikh sotsialisticheskikh respublik (Praesidium of the Supreme Soviet of the Union of Soviet Socialist Republics), *SSSR: Administrativno-territorial'noe delenie soiuznykh respublik* (USSR: Administrative territorial divisions of the union republics) (Moscow: Izdatel'stvo "Izvestiia sovietov narodnykh deputatov SSSR" [News of the Soviets of the People's Deputies of the USSR Publishing House], 1980), p. 87.

8 Blandon, *Soviet Forest Industries*, p. 54.

9 Nove, pp. 80–81.

10 The RSFSR celebrated the twentieth anniversary of the passage of the RSFSR environmental protection law in the fall of 1980.

11 Kushnirsky, *Soviet Economic Planning*, p. 79.

12 Carol Lewis, "Economic Functions of Local Soviets," in Everett M. Jacobs, ed., *Soviet Local Politics and Government* (London: George Allen & Unwin, 1983), p. 65.

13 Kramer, "Conservation and Pollution in the USSR."

14 According to official data, the fulfillment of mandates has risen 100 percent since

the reforms of the sixties. Such figures are difficult to evaluate because of ignorance of the base starting point. If nothing else, meetings with constituents and the processing of electors' mandates have become regularized. (L. G. Churchward, "Public Participation in the USSR," in Jacobs, *Soviet Local Politics*, pp. 40–42.)

15 Kramer, "Conservation and Pollution in the USSR."

16 Robert F. Rich, ed., "Symposium on the Production and Application of Knowledge," *American Behavioral Scientist* 22, 3 (January–February 1979): 420–34.

17 Guy Benveniste, *The Politics of Expertise*, 2d ed. (San Francisco: Boyd and Fraser, 1977), chap. 1 and p. 249.

18 For a Yugoslav interpretation, see Kiro Gligorov, "The Basis of Self-management," in Radmila Stojanović, ed., *The Functioning of the Yugoslav Economy*, (Armonk, N.Y.: M. E. Sharpe, 1982), pp. 3–5.

19 *Program of the League of Communists of Yugoslavia* (New York: Praeger, 1958).

20 See Barbara Jancar, "Dissent and Constitutionalism in Yugoslavia," Annual meeting of the Midwest Slavic Conference, Ann Arbor, Michigan, May 5–7, 1977.

21 See Basic Principles and chap. 1, pt. 2, *The Constitution of the Socialist Republic of Yugoslavia*, trans. Marko Pavičić (Ljubljana: "Delo," 1974), pp. 53–78 and 131–70.

22 The text of the Associated Labor Act may be found in *The Associated Labour Act*, trans. Marko Pavičić (Novi Sad: Prosveta, 1977).

23 The factory obtains a lease on the land for a specified period of time, commonly for ninety-nine years.

24 Vladimir Stipetić, "The Development of the Peasant Economy of Socialist Yugoslavia," in Stojanović, *The Functioning of the Yugoslav Economy*, p. 181.

25 Savet za čovekovu sredinu i prostrono uredjenje, Saveznog izvršnog veća i izvršnih veća republika i pokrajina (Council on the Environment and Territorial Planning, Federal Executive Council and executive councils of the republics and provinces), *Čovekova sredina i prostrono uredjenje u Jugoslaviji: Pregled stanja* (The human environment and territorial planning in Yugoslavia: an overview) (Belgrade: OOUR Izdavačko delatnost, 1979), p. 38.

26 Stipetić, *Peasant Economy* pp. 170–74.

27 *Čovekova sredina*, p. 16.

28 Ibid., p. 38.

29 Interview with Milvoje Todorović, former secretary-general of the Federal Council for the Protection and Improvement of the Human Environment, December 1984.

30 Ilija Vuković and Ratko Marković, *Socijalistički samoupravni sistem SFRJ* (Socialist self-management system SFRY) (Belgrade: "Privredni pregled," [Economic review] 1978), pp. 235–37.

31 Preface to *The Constitution of the Socialist Republic of Yugoslavia*, p. 25.

32 Interview with the director of Plitvice Lakes Park, May 1981.

33 Interview with SIZ for Una River, August 1981.

34 For a Yugoslav discussion of the SIZ, see Božidar Durović, ed., and Marko Pavičić, trans., *The Constitutional System of Yugoslavia* (Belgrade: "Jugoslovenski pregled" [Yugoslav review], n.d.), pp. 28–30.

35 Ibid, p. 132.
36 For example, Vuković and Marković, *Socijalistički samoupravni*, pp. 362–78; Najdan Pasić, ed., *Osnove marksizma i sotsijalističko samoupravljanje* (Fundamentals of marxism and socialist self management), text for the third level of directed education (Belgrade: Zavod za učbenike i nastavna sredstva [Institute for Textbooks and Institutional Aids], 1982), pp. 127–52.
37 See especially *Politika*, June 13, 14, 21 and 29, 1984, where the delegate system, the role of the LCY, and changes in the economic system are candidly discussed.
38 David Granick, *Enterprise Guidance in Eastern Europe* (Princeton: Princeton University Press, 1975), pp. 351–95.
39 James H. Seroka, "Local Political Structures and Policy Outputs in the Yugoslav Commune," *Studies in Comparative Communism* 12, 1 (Spring 1979): 63–73.
40 *Politika*, June 22, 1984, p. 5. The article urges a return to "the interests of the workers" in the factories.
41 Milivoje Todorović, *Moguća rešenja u sistemu čovek-društvo-životna sredina* (Possible solutions in the system man-society-environment) (Belgrade: Mladi istraživače Srbije—Republička konferencija [Young Researchers of Serbia—Republican Conference], 1983).
42 V. V. Petrov, ed., *Pravovye problemy ekologii: Sbornik obzorov* (Legal problems of ecology: Review of the literature) (Moscow: USSR Academy of Sciences, Institute of Scientific Information on the Social Sciences, 1980), p. 56.
43 "Animals are a basic component of the natural environment and an important part of natural riches. They serve as a source for material riches to meet the needs of industry, pharmaceutical production, the food industry, the people. . . . Animals are used for scientific, educational, aesthetic purposes," reads the introduction to the Kazakh Law on the Protection of Wild Animals, passed in 1981. (Text of the law published in Alma-Ata, *Sotsialistik Qazagstan*, June 1, 1981, p. 3.)
44 For a fascinating presentation of the early days of Soviet environmentalism, see Douglas Weiner, "The Historical Origins of Soviet Environmentalism," *Environmental Review* 6, 2 (Fall 1982): 42–62.
45 This quotation is cited in the opening paragraph of chap. 1, Petrov, *Pravovaia okhrana prirody*, p. 4.
46 As cited in Ivan Frolov, "The Marxist-Leninist Understanding of the Ecological Problem," authors collective, *Society and the Environment* (Bratislava: Priroda, 1978), p. 11.
47 I. P. Gerasimov, ed., *Man, Society and the Environment* (Moscow: Progress, 1975), p. 331.
48 Dennis C. Pirages and Paul R. Ehrlich, *Ark II, Social Response to Environmental Imperatives* (San Francisco: W. H. Freeman, 1974), pp. 45–51.
49 Notes from lectures of V. V. Petrov in Environmental Law, Moscow University, fall 1980.
50 The first section covers what are termed "general propositions," establishing the fact of state ownership, the fact that the resource comprises a single state fund, the jurisdiction of the union and the union-republics in regulating the use of the re-

source, the definition of the resource, and identification of its legal users. In addition, the first section contains paragraphs affirming state control and administration of the resource, basic liability, and the right of the state to forbid a user the resource. The central sections are devoted to the details relating to the exploitation of the resource, followed by a section outlining protection of the resource. The last sections establish legal norms for monitoring, control, liability, and the settling of disputes. The union-republic law contains more specifics as to how the law affects local government. The complete texts of the principal all-union and RSFSR environmental laws together with the important ministerial resolutions are found in Blinov, *Sbornik normativnykh aktov*, passim. This book provides a wealth of information on the legal organization of environmental protection in the Soviet Union. Unless there is need for specific recognition, no further reference will be made to a particular law or regulation if it is found in this collection.

51 Published in *Izvestia*, January 9, 1982.

52 I. P. Kirpatovskii, *Okhrana prirody: Spravochnik dla rabotnikov neftepereravbatyvaiushchei i neftekhimichesksoi promyshlennosti* (Nature protection: Handbook for workers in the oil refining and petrochemical industry) (Moscow: "Khimia," 1980), pp. 254–59.

53 Notes from lectures of V. V. Petrov, fall 1980.

54 Goskomgidromet is responsible for the national inventory of pollutant emissions by industrial polluters. Given the large number of pollutants required to be measured and the sophistication needed to measure them, not to mention the size of the country and the inaccessibility of many regions, information on all 200 contaminants throughout the USSR may prove to be unobtainable. Goskomgidromet officials anticipate completing the inventory of pollution emission levels of industrial polluters in the urban areas on the basic pollutants only, some time before the end of this decade. (From material from Goskomgidromet personnel, January 1981.)

55 *Bulletin' Moskovskogo gorodskogo ispol'nitel'nego komiteta* (Bulletin of the Moscow City Executive Committee) 895, 1 (January 1979): 11.

56 Notes from lectures of V. V. Petrov, fall 1980.

57 "On the Strengthening of Material Responsibility for Damage to the Forest Economy," Resolution of the RSFSR Council of Ministers, August 8, 1973, as cited in Blinov, *Sbornik normativnykh aktov*, pp. 401–3.

58 Leonore Shever Taga, "Externalities in a Command Society," in Fred Singleton, ed., *Environmental Misuse in the Soviet Union* (New York: Praeger, 1976), pp. 75–94.

59 For example, G. N. Polianskaia, "Zakony ob okhrane prirody—novaia forma prirodookhranitel'nogo zakonodatel'stva" (Nature protection laws—a new form of environmental protection legislation), *Pravnye voprosy okhrany prirody v SSSR* (Legal questions of environmental protection in the USSR) (Moscow: Izdatel'stvo "Nauka," 1963), pp. 57–73; Kolbasov, *Ekologia: Politika-pravo*, p. 226; and Petrov, *Pravovye problemy ekologii*, p. 63.

60 Under the Serbian water law, for example, individuals can be fined up to 30,000 dinars for damaging the water supply, while enterprises may be fined up to 500,000 dinars for "economic violations." The former is equivalent to about $500 and the latter to around $8,000. (For the text of the law, see *Službeni glasnik* SIZ *Serbia* 31, 33 (July 28, 1975), pp. 689–720.)

61 For general information on Yugoslav republican legislation on territorial planning, see *Čovekova sredina*, pp. 122–30.

62 For a discussion of urbanization and urban planning, see SFRJ Savezni zavod za medjunarodnu naučnu, prosvetno-kulturnu i tehničku saradnju i Koordinacioni odbor za čovekovu sredinu prostorno uredjenje i stambene i komunalne poslove SIV-a i izvršnih veća socijalističkih republika i socijalističkih autonomnih pokrajina, *Nacionalni izveštaj: "Stanje i politiká čovekove sredine u SFR Jugoslaviji"* (National report: Environmental conditions and policies in SFR Yugoslavia) (Belgrade: Servis za birotehničke poslove saveznih organa uprave i saveznih orgnizacija, 1985), chap. 2.

63 Author interview at Urbanistični Institut SR Slovenije, August 1981.

64 *Čovekova sredina*, p. 124.

65 Petrov, *Pravovaia okhrana prirody*, pp. 74–75.

66 Process described to the author by staff in Moscow State University's economics faculty.

67 For GKNT's role in the planning of scientific and technological research, see Louvan F. Nolting, *The Structure and Functions of the U.S.S.R. State Committee for Science and Technology*, Foreign Economic Report, no. 16, Bureau of the Census, U.S. Department of Commerce (Washington, D.C.: U.S. Government Printing Office, December 1979).

68 V. F. Afanasev and editorial group, *Upravlenie sotsialisticheskogo vospoizvodstva* (Administration of socialist production), 3d ed. (Moscow: Ekonomika, 1978), pp. 563–68. This book is the authoritative text on Soviet economic administration for university students. The pages cited refer to the administration of environmental protection.

69 In developing their regional zoning concept, Soviet scientists have taken an interest in U.S. regional analyses. See, for example, N. Glickman, *Economic Analysis of Regional Systems*, trans. from the English by A. N. Arianin, A. R. Monfor, O. S. Pchelinetsev, and M. Iu. Shchukin (Moscow: Progress, 1980). Significantly, the American study does not deal with the environmental aspects of regional planning, but focuses purely on economic performance.

70 See the relevant chapters on regional economic and environmental planning, such as M. Ia. Antonovskii, F. N. Semevskii, and S. M. Semonov, "Prognosis and Evaluation of the Condition of Ecologo-economic Systems," in M. Ia. Lemeshev and L. B. Dunaevskii, eds. *Upravlenie okruzhaiushchei sredy* (Environmental management) (Moscow: Izdatel'stvo "Nauka," 1980), pp. 26–63, 73–84.

71 The TIC was approved at the Twenty-fourth CPSU Congress as a "form of organization of the economy of areas within which important national economic tasks are

being tackled." (M. K. Bandman, "The Significance, Sequence, and Instrument of Optimising the Formation of Territorial Industrial Complexes," *Territorial Industrial Complexes: Optimisation Models and General Aspects*, trans. from the Russian by H. Campbell Creighton (Moscow: Progress, 1980), pp. 15–18.

72 Charles E. Lindblom, *The Intelligence of Democracy: Decision Making Through Mutual Adjustment* (New York: Free Press, 1965).

73 For a description of the Yugoslav planning process, see Stojanovic, "Planning Economic Development," *The Functioning of the Yugoslav Economy*, pp. 22–45.

74 Interview with Dr. Srečan Mitrović, Section on the Protection of the Human Environment, Federal Planning Board of Yugoslavia, May 1981.

75 Plans approved prior to that date may be exempt. For example, Belgrade appears to be exempt, although its 1975 plan lacks minimal environmental criteria, such as traffic control regulations, building standards, smoke stack regulations, and systematic zoning. (Interview with Dr. Srečan Mitrović, May 1981.)

76 *Čovekova sredina*, p. 127.

77 *Politika*, June 10, 1984, p. 7. The article criticizes the cities of Yugoslavia for "uncontrolled growth" and asks who is responsible for the chaotic conditions.

3 The Environmental Agencies

1 Oleg S. Kolbasov, *Ekologia: Politika-pravo*, pp. 176, 180, 188, 197–98.

2 S. B. Baisalov and L. E. Il'yashenko, *Pravo i okhrana prirody* (Law and environmental protection) (Alma-Ata: Navka, 1976), pp. 3–5.

3 V. V. Petrov, class lectures, fall 1980.

4 Interview with E. B. Serebriakov, deputy head of the Department of International Relations, Dr. N. N. Khramtsov, chief, Department of Forest Protection, Dr. A. I. Chilmov, chief, Department of Science and Introduction of New Technology, Mrs. N. N. Larienova, engineer, Department of International Relations, State Committee on Forestry, December 1984.

5 Figure derived from Paul J. Culhane, *Public Lands Politics: Interest Group Influence on the Forest Service and the Bureau of Land Management*, Resources for the Future (Baltimore: Johns Hopkins University Press, 1981), pp. 42 and 44.

6 Gustafson, *Reform in Soviet Politics*, pp. 101–21.

7 See, for example, "The Economy, Ecology and Ethics," *Novy mir* Round-Table Discussion among Writers and Scientists, *Ekonomika i organizatsia promyshlennogo proizvodstva* (Economics and the organization of industrial production), no. 3 (March 1982): 147–94.

8 *Pravda*, August 28, 1983.

9 For a full discussion of the organization and administration of protected nature reserves, see Petrov, *Pravovaia okhrana prirody*, pp. 214–28.

10 *Literaturnaia gazeta* (Literary gazette), December 24, 1980.

11 See Kolbasov's discussion of the natural-geographic zoning principle evident in the river basin system in *Ekologia: Politika-pravo*, pp. 178–79.

12 "Resolution on Basin (Territorial) Administration for the Regulation of the Use and Conservation of Water of the Ministry of Land Reclamation and Water Economy RSFSR," May 24, 1974, as cited in Blinov, *Sbornik normativnykh aktov*, pp. 287-93.

13 Articles 2.3, 2.4, 2.6, 2.11 and 2.13 of the above Resolution.

14 Pavičić, *The Associated Labor Act.*

15 The discussion on changes in the water resource management system was summarized from M. Miloradov, "Water Management in the SFR Yugoslavia," *Transactions* of the Jaroslav Cerni Water Resources Institute, nos. 60-63, 1977, pp. 44-45.

16 See Pedro Ramet's informative paper, "Federal Relations in Socialist Yugoslavia: Inter-republican Cooperation in Control of Water Pollution," unpublished, pp. 9-10.

17 The Serbian law, "Zakon o šumama" (Law on forests) was passed in 1974. See *Službeni glasnik SR* Serbia (Official Register SR Serbia), no. 19, April 30, 1974, pp. 824-37.

18 The latest revision was in 1981: See *Službeni glasnik SR* Serbia, no. 39, July 3, 1981, pp. 2705-10.

19 Drago Kocijančić, "Protection of Agricultural Land in the SR Slovenia," *Čovek i životna sredina* (Man and the environment), no. 2, 1980, pp. 32-33.

20 For a brief discussion of the formation of the SFRY Council on the Environment and Territorial Planning, see Conseil de l'environnement et l'aménagement du territoire, "L'Environnement en Yougoslavie" (Rapport national), unpublished paper, Belgrade, June 1978.

21 Interview with Vladimir Čavić, secretary of the Department of Environmental Protection, Permanent Conference of Towns and Opštini of Yugoslavia, Belgrade, April 1981.

22 Author interview with M. Hasara, chief of Department of General Hygiene, Belgrade Municipal Institute of Public Health, March 1981.

23 Author interviews with Dr. Pera Stepanov, director, Institute for Hygiene and Environmental Protection, and Dorelje Minjević, secretary, Serbian Republican Institute of Public Health, April 1981; Dr. Dominik Komadina, director, and Dr. Felix Radmilo, chief, Department of Hygiene, Federal Institute of Public Health, April 1981; Dr. Bratislav Anić; Dr. Slavko Maksimović, assistant director for Meteorology; Dr. Miomir Cirić; and Dr. Đura Jovanović, Department on Water Quality, Republican Hydrometeorological Institute, SR Serbia, April 1981.

24 Interview with Dr. Milorad Miloradov, director general, J. Cerni Water Resources Institute and Milan Đukić, Department for Water Supply, Sewage, and Air Pollution Control, Belgrade, April 1981.

25 As cited in the USSR Council of Ministers Resolution of August 8, 1977, in Blinov, no. 723, *Sbornik normativnykh aktov*, p. 550.

26 As cited from the Resolution of the RSFSR Council of Ministers of August 8, 1977, no. 417, in Blinov, *Sbornik normativnykh aktov*, p. 403.

27 Letter to the editor, *Literaturnaia gazeta*, December 24, 1980.

28 Statutes 166, 167, and 223 of the RSFSR Criminal Code as cited in Petrov, *Pravovaia okhrana prirody*, pp. 102–7.

29 Iu. S. Shemshuchenko, V. L. Muntian, B. G. Rosovskii, *Iuridicheskaia otvestvennost' v oblasti okhrany okrushaiushchei sredy* (Legal liability in the field of environmental protection) (Kiev: Izdatel'stvo "Nauka," 1979), p. 90.

30 Resolution of the Praesidium of the USSR Supreme Soviet, June 2, 1977, as cited in Blinov, *Sbornik normativnykh aktov*, p. 62.

31 Register of the Supreme Soviet.

32 Case presented during Petrov lectures, Moscow University, fall 1980.

33 Ibid.

34 "Counter Claim," *Izvestia*, July 22, 1979.

35 *Sotsialisticheskaia industria*, February 2, 1980, p. 2.

36 L. B. Sheinin, "Compensatory Relations in the National Economy in the Case of the Transformation of the Countryside," in M. Ia. Lemeshev and L. V. Dunaevskii, principal eds., *Upravlenie prirodnoi sredy* (Environmental management) (Moscow: Izdatel'stvo "Nauka," 1979), pp. 34–41.

37 *Ekonomicheskaia gazeta*, no. 45 (November 1979):15.

38 *Službeni glasnik SR* Serbia, no. 8 (February 21, 1981):593.

39 Ibid., no. 33, July 28, 1975.

40 According to official Yugoslav figures, the average annual emission of SO_2 per inhabitant in the United Kingdom is 89 kg.; in West Germany, 60 kg.; in Greece, 78 kg.; and in Yugoslavia, 36 kg. *Nacionalni izveštaj*, p. 89.

41 Skopje, *Nova Makedonija* (New Macedonia), February 16, 1982.

42 Oil consumption in 1980 decreased 16 percent from its 1979 level. *Ekonomska politika* (Economic policy), January 25, 1982, p. 21.

43 For a commentary by Flora Lewis, see *International Herald Tribune*, November 26, 1984.

44 *Ekonomska politika*, pp. 19–20.

45 Interview with Dr. Milica Kačarević, director, Department for Environmental Protection, Institute for Technology of Nuclear and Other Raw Materials, March 1981.

46 Interview with Jelena Vuković, chief engineer of Zastava Automobile Plant, Kragujevac, April 1981.

47 *Vjesnik*, June 5, 1982.

48 *Privredni pregled* (Economic review), March 29, 1979, p. 8.

49 See Pedro Ramet's discussion of the council, in Ramet, *Control of Water Pollution*, p. 11.

50 *USSR in Figures, 1979* (Moscow: Statistika, 1980), p. 200 and *Narodnoe khozaistvo SSSR v 1984g.; Statisticheskii ezegodnik* (The national economy of the USSR 1984; Statistical yearbook) (Moscow: "Financy i statistiki" [Finances and statistics], 1984), pp. 379 and 405.

51 Percentages derived from figures presented in *The RSFSR in Figures, 1979* (Moscow: Statistika, 1980), p. 98.

52 *Narodnoe khozaistvo 1984*, p. 405.

53 Ibid., p. 379.

54 From 1966 to 1973, between 59 percent and 61 percent of all Soviet industrial investment went into the construction of the industrial infrastructure (new construction) rather than into equipment (technology). (United States, Joint Economic Committee of the Congress, *Soviet Economy in a New Perspective* [Washington, D.C.: U.S. Government Printing Office, 1976], p. 451–52.) In the Eleventh Five-Year Plan, although the share of new construction in total industrial investment had dropped to around 30 percent, it was still higher than investment in technology (20 percent). (*Narodnoe khozaistvo 1984*, p. 380.)

55 *Soviet Economy in a New Perspective*, p. 494.

56 As calculated from figures on "primary income for financing public and collective requirements," *Statistical Pocket Book of Yugoslavia 1980* (Belgrade: Federal Statistical Office, 1980), p. 60.

57 Ramet, *Control of Water Pollution*, p. 9.

58 As calculated from *Statistical Pocket Book of Yugoslavia 1980*, p. 60.

59 The Belgrade Institute of Public Health, for example, receives 60 percent of its financing from the Serbian health siz. (Interview with Dr. Hasara, Belgrade Institute of Public Health.)

60 Author's conversations with V. V. Petrov and O. S. Kolbasov, fall 1980.

61 Kramer, "Conservation and Pollution in the USSR."

62 See, for example, the interview with the head of the Belorussian State Regional Inspectorate for Gas-purification and Dust-catching Installations, *Sovietskaia Bielorussia* (Soviet Bielorussia), August 22, 1979; and an article by O. Yekatov, deputy chief engineer of the Administration for Water Pollution Prevention, Soil Bank Fire Control and Soil Reclamation together with S. Sharov, chief scientific assistant of the USSR Coal Research Institute, *Freundschaft* (Friendship), June 14, 1979.

63 O. Ocheretianii, senior engineer-inspector of the Moscow-Oka Administration of the rsfsr Minvodkhoz, accuses several enterprises in Kalininskaia oblast for failure to reach established water purification norms or to improve sewage treatment plant operations to reach those norms and to operate at full capacity (*Ekonomicheskaia gazieta*, no. 26, June 1979, p. 16). Following the Kiev 1979 Campaign against Air Pollution by Motor Vehicles, A. Geletko, inspector with the State Motor Vehicle Inspectorate of the Ukrainian Ministry of the Interior, faults motor vehicle enterprises in particular for failure to familiarize themselves with the established vehicle emission norms and to take emission control seriously *Rabochaia gazeta* (Workers gazette), October 27, 1979, p. 4.

64 Article by L. Yefremov, first deputy chairman of the USSR State Committee for Science and Technology, is found in *Sotsialisticheskaia industria* (Socialist industry), June 6, 1979, p. 2.

65 Eugene Bardach, *The Implementation Game: What Happens after a Bill Becomes a Law* (Cambridge, Mass.: mit Press, 1977), pp. 65–178.

66 For a short and pithy biography of Mr. Gorbachev, see Bernard Ullmann, "Mikhail Gorbatchev, la relève du Kremlin?" (Mikhail Gorbachev, the changing of the guard at the Kremlin?), *L'Express*, no. 1752 (February 1–7, 1985): 108–9.

67 Saulius Girnius, "Changes in the Lithuanian Government," *Radio Free Europe Research* (Baltic Area SR/1) 10, 4 (January 25, 1985): 9–10.

68 For a description of the organization of GKNT, see Nolting, *USSR State Committee for Science and Technology*, pp. 19–24.

69 Interview with representatives of the USSR Ministry for Land Reclamation and Water Resources, October 1980.

70 For example, see *Zaria vostoka*, July 3, 1979, discussing the status of environmental protection in Georgia; *Sovietskaia Bielorussiia*, June 5, 1980, discussing the same in Bielorussia; and *Kazakhstanskaia pravda*, April 11, 1980, urging greater efforts toward land conservation. The list is endless. For every report of progress, there is recognition that much needs still to be done.

71 Zhores A. Medvedev, *Soviet Science* (New York: W. W. Norton, 1978).

72 For a discussion of whether the *nomenklatura* includes or excludes intellectuals, see Michael Voslensky, *La Nomenklatura: les privilegiés en URSS* (The nomenklatura: The privileged in the USSR), trans. from the German by Christian Nugue (Paris: Pierre Belfond, 1984), pp. 33–41.

73 For a list of the agreements, see Jancar, "Third World."

74 Belgrade TV interview, January 10, 1985. The vice-president of Yugoslavia's Federal Chamber stated that "without science, Yugoslavia has no future."

75 Observation made from watching some four months of Yugoslav TV over 1981, 1983, and 1984–1985.

76 Bardach's emphasis is on implementation games. Nevertheless, some of his "games" seem to be valid action strategies, including "keeping the peace" and "design strategies for dealing with monopoly power" (Bardach, *The Implementation Game*, pp. 65–178).

77 Blinov, *Sbornik normativnykh aktov*, pp. 11–23.

78 Published in *Pravda*, January 6, 1979.

79 The text of the Law on Air Quality was published in *Pravda* and *Izvestia*, June 27, 1980.

80 See O. Kolbasov's article in *Izvestia* of January 16, 1980 on the significance of the air quality law. Dr. Kolbasov expressed his views on the need for one central environmental protection organization in an interview with the author in October 1980. He has also expressed those views in writing as cited in chapter 2.

81 *Izvestia*, January 9, 1982.

82 *Pravda*, June 5, 1982, p. 3.

83 For the story of the political demise of the Ministry of Electrification and Power (Hydropower), see Gustafson, *Reform in Soviet Politics*, chap. 3. The assignment to Minvodkhoz of more supervisory competence over irrigation projects was reported in *Izvestia*, January 4, 1981.

84 See V. Afremov's short commentary in *Ekonomicheskaia gazieta* (Economic gazette), no. 2, January 1982, p. 10.

85 V. Danilov, "How Much Water Will Be Lost?", *Sovietskaia rossia*, December 9, 1983.

86 Yerevan, *Kommunist*, October 3, 1979.

87 *Trud*, January 3, 1980.

88 *Pravda*, July 10, and August 11, 1982.

89 Text of "The Principles of Legislation of the USSR and the Union Republics on Administrative Law Violations" was published in *Pravda*, October 25, 1980, pp. 1–2.

90 Author interviews, fall 1980. See Gustafson's similar comment on the same subject, Gustafson, *Reform in Soviet Politics*, p. 48.

91 *Službeni glasnik SR* Serbia, no. 31, July 30, 1977, p. 1729.

92 Article 52, Amendments to Forestry Law, ibid., no. 39, July 3, 1981, p. 2709.

93 Yerevan, *Kommunist*, April 6, 1980.

94 Ibid., October 19, 1980.

95 *Izvestia*, May 6, 1982.

96 *Meditsinskaia gazeta* (Medical gazette), October 23, 1981.

97 *Pravda*, February 7, 1984.

98 Interview at USSR Ministry of Agriculture, Glavnoe upravlenie zemedel'nogo ustroistva (Chief administration for land reclamation), October 1984.

99 A partial listing of these may be found in I. P. Kirpatovskii, *Okhrana prirody*, pp. 179–202, 254–259.

100 Author interview with Goskomgidromet officials, January 1981.

101 Iurii A. Izrael, "On the Evaluation of the Condition of the Biosphere and the Basis for Monitoring," *Lectures of the USSR Academy of Sciences* 226, 4 (1976): 955–957; and Iurii A. Izrael, "Towards a Strategy of Protecting and Regulating Environmental Quality," *Vodnye resursy* (Water resources), no. 6 (1977), pp. 6–12.

102 Except where indicated, the definitions of terms have been translated from V. V. Petrov's excellent section defining environmental terminology in *Pravovyie problemy ekologii*, pp. 101–33.

103 I. Petranov, Iu. A. Izrael, Ev. Teverovskii, and F. Krotov, "Proposal for the Elaboration and Establishment of PDV for Pollution Point Sources," *Pravda*, August 2, 1972.

104 See the description of TSEDS in *Okhrana okrushziushchei sredy i eio sotsial-noekonomicheskaia effektivnost* (Environmental protection and its social-economic effectiveness), T. S. Khachaturov, responsible ed., (Moscow: Izdatel'stvo "Nauka," 1980), pp. 192–93.

105 *Statistical Pocketbook of Yugoslavia 1980*, p. 63.

106 Author interview with Dr. Petar Paunović, director, Institut za zdrastvenu zaštitu (Institute for Public Health), Timok, May 1981.

107 Ramet has also stressed the overlap in environmental legislation (*Control of Water Pollution*, p. 7).

108 Interview with environmental officials, Melbourne, Australia, June 1980.

109 *Službeni glasnik SR* Serbia, no. 68, December 31, 1981, pp. 4281–82.

110 Interview at the Institute of Public Health, May 1981.

111 For Serbian ambient air quality norms, see *Službeni glasnik SR* Serbia, no. 8 (March 3, 1973): 275; and no. 31 (July 30, 1977): 1729.

112 *Literaturnaia gazeta* (Literary gazette), June 14, 1981.

113 Ibid., May 25, 1983.

114 *Pravda*, January 5, 1984.

115 *Politika*, May 20, 1985.

116 *Vjesnik*, June 5, 1982.

117 *Vjesnik*, January 26, 1983.

4 The Economic Enterprises

1 There is an excellent literature on industrial organization and management in the Soviet Union, but perhaps the all-time classic is again Nove's *The Soviet Economic System*. See also the very lucid presentation of the Soviet economic system in Millar, *The ABC's of Soviet Socialism*. The reader is referred to the bibliography for other sources.

2 Much less has been written on Yugoslav industrial organization under the conditions of self-management, but Granick's and Stojanovic's studies provide a solid basis for understanding the system: David Granick, *Enterprise Guidance in Eastern Europe* (Princeton: Princeton University Press, 1976) and Stojanović, *The Functioning of the Yugoslav Economy*.

3 Barbara Jancar, *Czechoslovakia and the Absolute Monopoly of Power* (New York: Praeger, 1971), chap. 2.

4 Nove, *The Soviet Economic System*, p. 321.

5 Voslensky, *La Nomenklatura*, pp. 195-96.

6 For two excellent and insightful discussions of what "building socialism" means in practice, see Alain Besançon, *Anatomie d'un Spectre: l'economie politique du socialisme réel* (The anatomy of a specter: The political economy of real socialism) (Paris: Calmann-Lévy, 1981); and Michel Heller and Aleksandr Nekrich, *L'Utopie au pouvoir: Histoire de l'U.R.S.S. de 1917 à nos jours* (Utopia in power: the history of the USSR from 1917 to our time) (Paris: Calmann-Lévy, 1985).

7 Speech of Andropov, published in *Pravda*, March 19, 1983.

8 Author interview with Belgrade University economists, December 1984.

9 Hélène Carrère d'Encausse argues that the success of Brezhnev in consolidating his rule lay precisely in his tacit agreement with the "gestionnaires" that their positions and privileges would not arbitrarily be touched as was the case under Stalin. [Hélène Carrère d'Encausse, *Le pouvoir confisqué: gouvernants et gouvernés en U.R.S.S.* (Confiscated power: The rulers and the ruled in the USSR) (Paris: Flammarion, 1980), pp. 137-86.] Gorbachev today finds it difficult to crack down on corruption because management's privileges (the "nomenklatura") lie at the heart of the problem.

10 *TANJUG*, October 16, 1984.

11 In the fall of 1984, Milka Planinć, then Yugoslav prime minister, told a group of

managers in Zagreb that she was "shocked" by the claim that was being made that "we have completed the stabilization program; . . . I am not exaggerating, it is a catastrophic illusion." (Belgrade, *Duga*, October 7, 1984).

12 Three Macedonian leaders were investigated for investment failures at the end of 1984 (Belgrade, *Večernje novosti*, September 29, 1984).

13 Kushnirsky, *Soviet Economic Planning*, pp. 49–54; and Nove, *The Soviet Economic System*, pp. 90–95. Kushnirsky stresses the centralizing tendency of the reform while Nove centers on the issue of managerial autonomy.

14 The ecological devastation of the Estonian coast was discussed in Aina Zarins, "Scientists Protect the Devastation of Nature in Estonia," Radio Liberty Research Bulletin 224/1977.

15 For a discussion of the failure of some of the reorganization schemes required by the USSR Council of Ministry Decree of 1973, see *Pravda*, July 31, 1974.

16 September 1968 Decree of USSR Council of Ministers. For a description of the reform, see Louvan E. Nolting, *The 1968 Reform of Scientific Research, Development and Innovation in the U.S.S.R.*, Foreign Economic Report no. 11, U.S. Department of Commerce, Bureau of Economic Analysis (Washington, D.C.: U.S. Government Printing Office, September 1976), passim.

17 Nove, *The Soviet Economic System* pp. 61–62, 85.

18 According to Duniaev, the share of specialized ministries in the production of many items is 60–80 percent, although the percentage is substantially lower for others, for example only 38 percent for washing machines. E. P. Duniaev, *Obedinenia predpriiatii kak forma obshchestvlenia proizvodstva* (Enterprise associations as a form of generalization of production) (Moscow: Izdatel'stvo "Nauka," 1974), p. 120. (Cited in Nove, *The Soviet Economic System*, p. 63.)

19 *Long-term Forecast for the City of Prague*, prepared by the Prague National Committee, 1980.

20 The exceptions are the electric, ferrous and nonferrous metallurgy, and rail transport industries. (Stojanović, "Planning Economic Development," p. 43.) In 1978, there were approximately 20,000 organizations of associated labor (OUR) and 286 composite OUR. *Statistical Pocket Book of Yugoslavia 1980* (Belgrade: Federal Statistical Office, 1980), p. 15.

21 For the legal details on the establishment of basic and work organizations, see Pavičić, *The Associated Labor Act*, pt. 3, chap. 1, pp. 219–55.

22 Pedro Ramet, "Yugoslavia's Uncertain Stability and the Threat of Internal and External Discontent," unpublished manuscript, 1984, pp. 2–8.

23 Author interview with Belgrade University economists, December–January 1984–1985.

24 Barbara Jancar, *Women under Communism* (Baltimore: Johns Hopkins University Press, 1978), pp. 84, 101–2.

25 Story put together from personal interviews and from a reading of *Politika*, May through December 1984.

26 *SP SSSR*, no. 8 (1974): 38.

27 See I. P. Kirpatovskii, *Okhrana prirody*, pp. 50–56, for the details for setting up an environmental section in the Ministry of Petroleum Refining and Petrochemical Industry.

28 USSR Council of Ministers' resolution of January 12, 1978.

29 The four parts were general understandings, the organization of technical work, scientific-technological work, and the schedule for construction work. "On the Order of Implementing Environmental Protection Work in the Enterprises and Organizations of Sverdlovsk Oblast," Resolution of the Executive Committee of the Sverdlovsk Oblast Soviet, June 10, 1977.

30 The foregoing information on the procedure for setting up a factory environmental section has been summarized from Viktor V. Kruglov, "Prava i obiazannosti promyshlennogo predpriiatia po okhrane okruzhaiushchei sredy" (The rights and obligations of industrial enterprises in environmental protection), unpublished *Candidat nauk* dissertation, Moscow State University, 1980, mimeographed, pp. 1–55. The author was privileged to be present at the defense of the dissertation.

31 Ibid., pp. 74–90.

32 Author interviews in the Soviet Union, fall 1980.

33 For example, the Serbian Law on the Protection of Nature requires every work organization to establish an expert section (stručna sluzba) for environmental protection. *Službeni glasnik SR* Serbia, no. 50, December 13, 1975, p. 1101.

34 Author interview with first engineer Jelena Vuković, Zastava Automobile Plant, Kragojevac, April 1981.

35 Author interview with engineer Milica Kačarević, director, Environmental Protection Department, Institute for Technology of Nuclear and Other Raw Materials, March 1981.

36 The concept of the TIC was endorsed by the Twenty-fourth CPSU Congress. The general plan of a complex was approved in the 1971–1975 plan, where five TICs were identified (Bandman, "Territorial Industrial Complexes," pp. 15–18). During the 1970s, increased attention was given to the formation of TICs in Siberia, and a "Siberia Program" was developed by the USSR Academy of Sciences Siberian Section and approved in 1978. The guidelines for economic and social development adopted by the Twenty-sixth Party Congress stressed further growth of the TICs. Three special purpose programs were approved for Siberia. The Eleventh Five-Year Plan calls for two TICs to be formed, one in the Angara-Yenesei Region. The South Yakutia TIC has already been created in the BAM zone. [The Guidelines for the Five-year Plan approved at the Twenty-sixth Party Congress (1981) calling for the working out of "uniform economic and legal principles for the creation of TICs" were published in *Pravda* and *Izvestia* on March 7, 1981.] Discussion of the Siberian Program translated into English may be found in *The Current Digest of the Soviet Press* 30, 13 (1978): 22 and 33, 7 (1981): 8, 19–20.

37 Academician A. Aganbegyan, "Behind the Lines of the Basic Guidelines: The Siberia Program," *Sotsialisticheskaia industria* (Socialist industry), May 8, 1981.

38 Bandman, "Territorial Industrial Complexes," passim. A good discussion of the environmental impact of economic development upon Siberia is found in S. G.

Beirom, N. V. Vostriakova, and V. M. Shirokov, *Izmenenie prirodnykh uslovii v strednei Obi posle sozdanii Novosibirskoe GEX* (Changes in the natural conditions of the middle Ob after the creation of the Novosibirsk hydroelectric station) (Novosibirsk: ANSSSR, Sibirskoe otdelenie, Geographicheskoe obshchestvo SSR, Novosibirsk Otdel; Izdatel'stvo "Nauka," Siberian Division, 1973).

39 Nove, *The Soviet Economic System*; Kushnirsky, *Soviet Economic Planning*, David Granick, *The Red Executive* (Cambridge, Mass.: Harvard University Press, 1956).

40 L. Sharikov, *Okhrana okruzhaiushchei sredy: spravochnik* (Environmental protection: A handbook) (Leningrad: "Sudostroienie," 1978), pp. 203–18.

41 The operating efficiency of the air treatment installations was reported at 93 percent and 98.5 percent, according to the newspaper's account, yet the air was black with soot. (Alma-Ata, *Qazagstanskaia pravda*, March 4, 1983.)

42 Petrov lectures, fall 1980.

43 *Trud*, June 5, 1982.

44 *Literaturnaia gazeta*, June 17, 1982.

45 Warsaw, *Perspektywy*, no. 4 (January 25, 1980): 11.

46 *Sovietskaia rossia*, August 18, 1981.

47 *Social Plan of Yugoslavia 1981–1985* (Belgrade: SFRJ Parliamentary Office, 1981), p. 191.

48 Interview with Dr. Srečan Mitrović, Section on the Protection of the Human Environment, Federal Planning Board of Yugoslavia, May 14, 1981.

49 Belgrade, *Privredni pregled* (Economic review), February 20–22, 1982, p. 2.

50 SFRJ, *Nacionalni izveštaj*, p. 18.

51 In Yugoslavia, in 1977, approximately 64 percent of total realized investment went to industrial construction and equipment. Figures derived from *Statistical Pocket Book of Yugoslavia 1979* (Belgrade: Federal Statistical Office, 1979), p. 60.

52 According to Nolting, decentralized resources are primarily used for low-cost, low-risk projects (*The Financing of Research, Development, and Innovation*, Foreign Economic Report no. 9 [April 1976], p. 23).

53 V. G. Lebedev, V. K. Poltorygin, and V. I. Kyshlin, *Sotsial'no-ekonomicheskaia effecktivnost' perspektivnykh vlozenii* (Social-economic efficiency of prospective investment) (Moscow: Izdatel'stvo "Mysl'," [Thought Publishing House], 1979), pp. 30–31, 73, 101–2.

54 Godfrey Boyle, David Elliott and Robin Roy, *The Politics of Technology* (London: Longman Group, in association with the Open University Press, 1977), p. 204.

55 Resolution No. 898 of December 29, 1972.

56 Interview at TSEMI, fall 1980.

57 Kushnirsky, *Soviet Economic Planning*, p. 131.

58 Charter 77, Document on Environmental Pollution, 1978.

59 Author interview with Srečan Mitrović.

60 Crozier's analysis of the automatization process may be found in Crozier and Friedberg, *L'acteur et le système*, pp. 148–54.

61 A striking example of this phenomenon may be found in Freeman Dyson's descrip-

tion of his attempt to induce the British Air Command to modify the Lancaster bomber to reduce the number of lives lost in air bombings over Germany during World War II (*Disturbing the Universe* [New York: Harper & Row, 1979], pp. 19–32.)

62 A good account of this situation is given in David A. Dyker, "The Crisis in Yugoslav Self-Management," *Contemporary Review* 242, 404 (January 1983): 9–13.

63 Interview with representatives of the USSR State Committee on Forestry, December 1980.

64 Interview with first deputy minister of forestry of the Kazakh SSR, Zhumabek Daurenbekov, as reported in *Qazag Adebieti* (Alma-Ata), June 26, 1981.

65 *Ekonomika i organizatsia promyshlennogo proizvodstva* (Economics and the Organization of Industrial Production), no. 3 (March 1982):147–94.

66 Author interview with M. F. Grishaev, deputy chief of the State Administration for Land Development, USSR Ministry of Agriculture, October 26, 1980. See also T. S. Khachaturov, ed., *Okhrana okruzhaiushchei sredy i ee sotsial'no ekonomicheskaia effectivnost'* (Environmental protection and its socioeconomic effectiveness) (Moscow: Izdatel'stvo "Nauka," ANSSSR, Institut ekonomiki, 1980), p. 91.

67 Grishaev's statements on the status of reclaiming old land must be taken with some caution. In 1979, he wrote an article claiming that land reclamation was proceeding at a pace incommensurate with the amount of new hectares being disturbed by mining. However, his criticism had more to do with newly mined areas rather than with land mined before 1968 (*Ekonomicheskaia gazeta*, no. 45, November 1979, p. 15.)

68 Khachaturov, *Okhrana okruzhaiushchei sredy*, p. 42.

69 Ibid, p. 147.

70 *Sotsialisticheskaia industria*, July 23, 1981, p. 2.

71 *Pravda*, August 30, 1981, p. 3.

72 Khachaturov, *Okhrana okruzhaiushchei sredy*, p. 133.

73 Ibid, pp. 111–44.

74 Interview with Andelko Kalpić, president of the Yugoslav Council on the Protection and Improvement of the Environment, *Privredni pregled* (Economic Review), July 23–25, 1983, pp. 7 and 12.

75 Peter Vanneman, *The Supreme Soviet: Politics and the Legislative Process in the Soviet Political System* (Durham, N.C.: Duke University Press, 1977), p. 64.

76 As cited from Soviet sources in ibid., p. 141.

77 Anatoly Agranovsky, "The Soviet Parliament: A Working Body," *World Marxist Review*, May 1971, pp. 78–79.

78 Author interview with representatives of the Una River SIZ, summer 1981.

79 Interviews with Milivoje Todorović.

80 Robert T. Nakamura and Frank Smallwood, *The Politics of Policy Implementation* (New York: St. Martin's Press, 1980); and Ripley and Franklin, *Bureaucracy and Policy Implementation*, pp. 152–53.

81 In Bardach's classic formulation, implementation is "the continuation of politics by

other means." For his identification of "games," see particularly Bardach, *The Implementation Game*, pp. 36–37, 85, 153.

82 Jones, *Clean Air*, p. 275; and Downing, *Environmental Economics and Policy*, pp. 52–59, 121–29.

83 Kruglov, "Prava i obiazonnost promyshlennogo predpriiatia." The whole dissertation documents this point.

84 *Vjesnik*, June 5, 1982, p. 5.

85 See in particular the article by I. Novikov, deputy chairman of the USSR Council of Ministers and chairman of the Commission for Environmental Protection and Rational Utilization of Natural Resources under the Presidium of the USSR Council of Ministers, *Pravda*, June 5, 1983.

86 For example, see *Sel'skaia zhizn'*, May 28, 1983, p. 3. The newspaper reported a session of the environmental protection commission attached to the USSR Council of Ministers, where the committee "made it mandatory" for officials of the Food Industry and Meat and Dairy Industry ministries "to strengthen environmental protection work."

87 *Vjestnik*, June 6, 1982.

88 Project "Adriatic III" indeed said that the greatest value of the Adriatic lay in its unique combination of land and sea (*Vjestnik*, April 2, 1980, p. 5).

89 Ibid., November 8, 1980, p. 21, and June 5, 1982.

90 *Sovietskaia rossia*, October 29, 1979, p. 3.

91 *Vjestnik*, November 9, 1980, p. 5.

92 *Privredni pregled*, July 23–25, 1983.

93 *Vjestnik*, December 8, 1979, p. 27.

94 *Izvestia*, July 22, 1979.

95 "The Economy, Ecology and Ethics," pp. 147–94.

96 A report on ecological devastation in Estonia may be found in Saulius Girnius, "Ecological Perils in Northeast Estonia," *RFE Research Report* 10, 25 (January 1985): 3–8.

97 Dragoljub Drašković, "Combating Pollution Created by Coal Burning Generation Plants in Yugoslavia," *Environment*, March 1981, p. 120.

98 *Politika*, June 9, 1984.

99 *Pravda*, December 20, 1983.

5   The Party and Territorial Administrations

1 *Ocnovnye napravlenia ekonomicheskogo i sotsial'nogo razvitia SSSR na 1981–1985 gody i na period do 1990 goda* (Guidelines for the economic and social development of the USSR for 1981–1985 and for the period up to 1990) (Moscow: "Politizdat," 1981), chap. 9, pp. 69–70. The draft program was published in *Pravda*, October 26, 1985, pp. 1–7.

2 *Ob osnovnykh napravleniakh ekonomicheskogo i sotsial'nogo razvitia SSSR na 1986–1990 gody i na period do 2000 goda* (Guidelines for the economic and social

development of the USSR for 1986–1990 and for the period up to 2000), *Pravda*, March 6, 1986, chap. 11, p. 5.

3 *Social Plan of Yugoslavia 1976–1980* (Belgrade: "Kultura," 1980), pp. 35–39, 48–49, 56–57, 91–92, 109–12, 124–25.

4 Gustafson, *Reform in Soviet Politics*, pp. 11–122.

5 *Moscow News* interview with Grigory Galazy, director of the Baikal Limnological Institute of the Siberian Department of the USSR Academy of Sciences and a corresponding member of the USSR Academy of Sciences, *Moscow News*, no. 9 (March 6–13, 1983): 10. For an official description of environmental measures taken in the Baikal area, see V. Saganov, chairman of the Buriatskaia ASSR Council of Ministers, "Multiply the Wealth of Nature," *Izvestia*, August 15, 1979, p. 3.

6 See chap. 3 for the discussion of Chernenko's appointment of an experienced agricultural official to the Estonian Minvodkhoz.

7 *Pravda*, November 23, 1985, p. 2.

8 As reported in ibid., July 3, 1985, pp. 2–3.

9 Ibid., July 19, 1985, p. 2.

10 The author was in Belgrade for December–January 1984–1985 and read the Belgrade press for the preceding five months. In addition, during her stay in Belgrade, she spent a portion of most evenings watching Belgrade television. The pollution of the Sava River over this period was a veritable cause célèbre. For a good short discussion of the issue, see *NIN*, no. 1768 (November 18, 1984): 24.

11 "Rezolucija o zadačima Saveza komunista Jugoslavije u ostvarivanja politike ekonomske stabilizacije" (Resolution on the tasks of the League of Communists of Yugoslavia in the creation of a policy of economic stabilization), *12 Kongres Saveza komunista Jugoslavije, referat, rezoljucije, statut SKJ, završna rec* (12th Congress of the League of Communists of Yugoslavia, Speeches, Resolutions, LCY Statutes, Closing Speech) (Belgrade: Centar komunist, 1982), pp. 147–51.

12 For accounts of LCY disunity, see Stjepan Pabrenovic's excellent article, "Podjeljena budučnost" (Divided future), *NIN*, no. 1768 (November 18, 1984): 14–15. See also *RFE Reports* 9: 51 (December 20, 1984): 7–13, and "Background Report: Eastern Europe in 1984," *RFE Reports* 10: 1 (January 11, 1985), pp. 48–52.

13 In this connection, it is interesting to note a return to militarism in Czechoslovakia, where public statements have strongly supported the role of the military in national security and the need for a strong defense. Defense expenditures for 1985 are expected to rise 4.5 percent above their 1984 level of 7.6 percent of the total budget. (Radio Prague, December 11, 1984.) The preoccupation with defense and all things military may be noted in expert and journalistic writings, specifically in an article on the armed forces and the economy by Miloš Chrastil and Zbynek Siň in *Historie a vojenství* (History and the military), no. 5 (1984): 73–87.

14 For a discussion of this point, see Ota Šik, *The Communist Power System* (New York: Praeger, 1981), pp. 45–54.

15 Petrov, *Pravovaia okhrana prirody*, pp. 76–77.

16 *RFE Research Reports* 10: 4 (January 18, 1984), Baltic Area SR/1, pp. 6–7.

17 Article 49 of the Fundamental Law on the Protection of Underground Resources, Blinov, *Sbornik normativnykh aktov*, p. 181.

18 Tallinn, *Sirp ja Vasar* (Hammer and sickle), December 28, 1984.

19 Yerevan, *Kommunist*, October 10, 1983, and Yerevan, *Sovetakan Ayastan* (Soviet Armenia), September 24, 1983.

20 Tbilisi, *Komunisti*, August 2, 1983.

21 *Pravda*, October 12, 1981.

22 Gustafson, *Reform in Soviet Politics*, pp. 11–122.

23 *Pravda*, October 12, 1981.

24 *Sovietskaia rossia*, February 8, 1981.

25 Vil'nius, *Kommunist*, February 2, 1983.

26 "The Project of the Century," *Literaturnaia gazeta*, March 10, 1982.

27 Edward Kardelj, "Directions of the Development of the Political System of Socialist Self-Management," June 1977, as cited in Leonard Cohen, *Political Cohesion in a Fragile Mosaic: the Yugoslav Experiment* (Boulder, Colo.: Westview, 1983), p. 153. See also Cohen's discussion, pp. 152–55.

28 For a detailed discussion of the federal decisionmaking process, see Steven Burg's superb analysis of the Yugoslav federal system in *Conflict and Cohesion in Socialist Yugoslavia: Political Decision Making Since 1966* (Princeton: Princeton University Press, 1983), pp. 242–300, 265–71. Burg argues that the relation between the delegate to the Chamber of Republics and Provinces, his delegation, and the republican or provincial assemblies has been a subject of much controversy. The chamber staff has urged greater freedom of the delegations from republican or provincial assembly tutelage in order to speed up the process of negotiation.

29 Articles 284–96, *The Constitution of the Socialist Federal Republic of Yugoslavia* (Ljubljana: "Delo," 1974), pp. 236–46.

30 See Serbian party secretary Slobadan Milosević's speech at the Serbian CC Plenum in November 1984, as published in *Politika*, November 24, 1984.

31 A reading of the Belgrade press suggests that Dolanć may be the more likely instigator of the trials. *Borba*, April 19, 1984, indicated that Dolanć had visited the Belgrade Secretariat of Internal Affairs the night before the police raid.

32 A Serbian defense of its position in favor of "integration" against the conflicting claims of autonomy may be found in *Politika*, January 10, 1985. During interviews in Ljubljana, Zagreb, and Skopje at the end of 1984, the author was struck by the fervent expressions of nationalism and the desire of the respondents to set forth their nation's special contribution to Yugoslavia.

33 See especially Articles 24–26. The entire text was published in *Službeni list SFRJ* 30: 2 (January 10, 1974), pp. 9–12.

34 *Službeni list SFRJ*, no. 5 (February 1, 1980): 181–84.

35 *Politika*, December 25, 1984.

36 *Politika*, December 29, 1984.

37 *Politika*, January 9, 1985.

38 *Borba*, December 27, 1985.

39 This and other information on the Tara comes out of a statement written by the chairman of the Federal Conference of the Socialist Alliance (SSRNJ), Marjan Rožić, and published in *Čovek i životna sredina* (Man and the environment), no. 3, (May–June 1984): 4–5. The article is entitled "Sačuvajmo kanjon Tare" (Let's save the Tara Canyon).

40 *Politika*, May 29, 1984.

41 The Neretva River agreement is a further instance of interrepublican discord leading to environmental inaction.

42 The author's request to attend a meeting of the Moscow or Leningrad environmental committees went unfilled, but she was able to interview a member of the Leningrad Environmental Committee as well as the then deputy chairman of the Moscow Environmental Committee. The report that follows is derived from those interviews.

43 The members were the chief of the North-Western Basin Territorial Administration for Water Conservation, the deputy chairman of the Chief Architectural-Planning Administration for the City of Leningrad, the deputy chairman of the Chief Public Health Administration, the chief public doctor for the city, the deputy chairman of the State Auto Inspectorate of the Chief Administration of the Interior, the head of the Leningrad State Regional Inspection for Performance Control of Gas and Dust Scrubbers, the deputy director of the main Geophysical Observatory, the director of the Central Scientific Research Institute of Autotransport, the deputy director of the State Hydrometeorological Institute, the director of the Museum of the Botanical Institute of the ANSSR, and the chairman of the geochemical faculty of Leningrad State University. The secretary of the committee was chief of the section for the monitoring and control of environmental pollution of the regional Hydromet. ("Resolution on the Environmental Protection Committee of the Leningrad City Soviet of People's Deputies," *Bulletin of the Executive Committee of the Leningrad City Soviet*, April 7, 1979, pp. 13–14.)

44 Interview with Professor V. F. Barabanov, chairman, geochemical faculty of Leningrad State University, November 11, 1980.

45 The Moscow Gorispolkom's first special session on the environment was held in 1973, and the session was made a permanent practice in 1979. The environmental protection committee was formed in 1975. (Interview with Margarita V. Shesterina, M.D., deputy director for Scientific Work, Moscow Research Institute for Tuberculosis, Ministry of Public Health, RSFSR, January 20, 1981.) Dr. Shesterina had served five years on the Moscow Gorispolkom Environmental Committee when the author met her. Before that she had served on the City Construction and Public Health Committees. At the time of the interview, she still served on the latter committee.

46 Figures from *The Bulletin of the Executive Committee of the Leningrad Soviet of People's Deputies*, January 1, 1977, p. 12.

47 Blair A. Ruble, "Romanov's Leningrad," *Problems of Communism* 32: 6 (November–December 1983): 36.

48 Vladimir Djorjevíc et al., *Zaštita i unapredjivanje životne sredine* (The protection

and improvement of the environment), for the third level of directed education (Bor: "Bakar," 1979), pp. 22–23. See also Milivoje Todorović, *Moguća rešenja*, pp. 122–38.

49 *Politika*, June 10, 1984.

50 Of these, 460,000 had migrated from Bosnia-Herzegovina, and 568,500 had migrated to Serbia.

51 The figures are taken from the Council for the Human Environment and Territorial Management of the Federal Executive Committee and executive committees of the republics and provinces of Yugoslavia, *Čovekova sredina*, pp. 14–28.

52 For the Macedonian perspective on Ohrid, see *A History of the Macedonian People*, Mihaylo Apostolski, principal ed., trans. Graham W. Reid (Skopje: Macedonian Review Editions, 1979), pp. 23–49.

53 The watchword was "Ohrid shall not become another Baikal."

54 To give some idea of the size of the project: forty-four studies were prepared with the help of OECD. Three institutes in Macedonia contributed their expertise. Cooperation was secured from the universities at Belgrade, Ljubljana, and Zagreb, and an Institute for Territorial Planning was established at the lake. The institute has thirty members, most of them with advanced degrees, but students are invited to develop a doctoral thesis on a topic associated with the lake, and they are given a scholarship to come and finish their work at the institute. The hope is that some of them will want to remain. The preliminary investigation alone resulted in a thousand-page, twenty-volume study.

55 In the construction of the sewage system, four options were considered ranging from the construction of five separate systems with five treatment plants to a single system with a single plant. The Ohrid Planning Institute selected the fourth option.

56 The plan was to be realized in three stages, with the first stage to be the building of the water treatment system at the north end. The second stage would extend the system to all the towns along the Yugoslav coast, and the final stage would see the completion of the system's infrastructure. As of 1981, no completion dates or funds had been agreed upon for the second and third stages.

57 Zoning Map of Lake Ohrid, and interview with Vasilka Zarova, architect and planner, Institute for Territorial Planning, Ohrid, May 16, 1981.

58 In his environmental law lectures, V. V. Petrov dwelt especially on the fact that Soviet investment monies for pollution control come mostly from central investment funds earmarked for the purpose and distributed through the branch ministries, relevant state committees, and other central organs. Indeed, one of his suggestions for more effective implementation of legal regulations was to let the enterprises finance environmental protection measures from their own resources.

59 *Narodnoe khozaistvo SSSR v 1984 g.; Statisticheskii ezegodnik* (The national economy of the USSR 1984; Statistical yearbook) (Moscow: "Financy i statistiki," 1984), p. 379.

60 N. N. Nekrasov and E. Mateev, eds., *Sotsialisticheskoe prirodopol'zovanie: Ekonomicheskie i sotsial'nye aspekty* (Socialist nature resource use: Economic and social aspects) (Moscow—Sofia: Izdatel'stvo "Ekonomika," Partizdat, 1980), p. 60.

61 *Osnovnye napravlenia 1981–1985*, p. 7.

62 According to official statistics, of the total USSR state budgetary expenditure for 1980, 52 percent was for the financing of material production, 33 percent for socio-cultural measures, and 8 percent for "other purposes." As derived from figures from *Narodnoe khozaistvo SSSR* (National economy USSR) for representative years by Wilczynski in *The Economics of Socialism*, p. 158.

63 For a discussion of the difficulties in knowing the size of the Soviet military-industrial complex and Soviet military expenditures, see Andrew Cockburn, *The Threat: Inside the Soviet Military Machine* (New York: Vintage, 1983), pp. 120–49. Cockburn gives credence to John Prados' estimate of 58 billion rubles as the real Soviet defense budget. (Cited from John Prados, *The Soviet Estimate* [New York: Dial, 1982], p. 247, in Cockburn, *The Threat*, p. 475.) For more recent presentation of the problems of evaluating the Soviet military budget, see Franz Waltery, "Trends in Soviet Defense Expenditures: Facts and Speculation," Federal Institute for East European and International Studies, FRG, ed., *The Soviet Union 1984/1985* (Boulder and London: "Westview Special Studies on the Soviet Union and Eastern Europe"; Westview Press, 1986), pp. 159–68.

64 Kushnirsky, *Soviet Economic Planning*, pp. 52 and 68.

65 Ibid., pp. 69–76. As Wilczynski rather pompously states in his uncritical study of socialist economics, local budgets form an integral part of the "state budget" because "the Socialist State cannot remain indifferent to the independent raising and spending of finances, as these might conflict with the State's overall financial policy." Wilczynski, *The Economics of Socialism*, p. 155.

66 Under these circumstances, it is not surprising that Friedgut should have failed to observe "a vigorous debate" on the budget at the budget session he attended in the Oktiabr Borough in Moscow. All the important decisions had been made beforehand. (Theodore H. Friedgut, "A Local Soviet at Work: The 1970 Budget and Budget Discussion of the Oktyabr Borough Soviet of Moscow," in Everett M. Jacobs, ed. *Soviet Local Politics and Government* (London: George Allen & Unwin, 1983), p. 158.

67 Kushnirsky, *Soviet Economic Planning*, p. 74. Moscow and Leningrad, as noted later in the text, are the exceptions.

68 Of the total income available for financing public services in 1979, the SIZ absorbed 47 percent, local government less than 1.5 percent, the federal government 12 percent, the republican governments 14 percent, and the communes and towns, 7 percent. See *Statistical Yearbook of Yugoslavia 1980* (Belgrade: Federal Statistical Office, 1980), p. 60.

69 Komarov, *The Destruction of Nature*.

70 Philip P. Micklin is probably correct in arguing this point. See Mecklin, "Environmental Factors in Soviet Interbasin Water Transfer," *Environmental Management*, 2, 6 (1978): 578.

71 For a lucid discussion of Soviet regional economic trends, see Leslie Dienes, "Regional Economic Development," in Abram Bergson and Herbert S. Levine,

eds. *The Soviet Economy: Toward the Year 2000* (London: George Allen & Unwin, 1983), pp. 268ff.

72 See, for example, the description of the dire consequences of accelerated economic development in the Siberian TICs in *Soviet Review* (Winter 1981), pp. 20–31. See also Hermann Clement's excellent evaluation of the cost/benefits of the Soviet development of Siberia in "Siberia: Resources or Burden?," *The Soviet Union 1984/ 1985*, pp. 169–78. No less a recognized expert than Soviet economist V. Perevendentsev has argued against the Siberian river diversion project in favor of greater investment in Central Asia (*Literaturnaia gazeta*, March 10, 1982, p. 10).

73 Kushnirsky makes this same point about the ability of local communities to obtain funding for infrastructure and basic community needs. (Kushnirsky, *Soviet Economic Planning*, p. 73.)

74 "General Design-Research and Construction Plan for the Elimination of Pollution in the Baltic Sea Basin," Decision of the Leningrad Gorispolkom, no. 8, January 9, 1978, as published in *Bulletin of the Leningrad Gorispolkom*, February 4, 1978, pp. 6–17.

75 B. Ivanov, Minister of Power and Electrification of the Kasak SSR, "Light Cities Must Be Clean," *Kazakhstanskaia pravda*, April 7, 1981.

76 The 1974 Constitution provides that the Socialist Alliance, "headed by the Communist Party, . . . lay down common criteria for the elections of delegations . . . and delegates" (Sect. 8, "Basic Principles"). In practice, the provision assigns the decision on electoral candidates to the LCY. The question of whether to have one or more candidates was recently discussed in the Committee for Social Affairs of the Vojvodina Assembly, whose chairman said that multiple candidacy was possible, but it should take place gradually to avoid the "anarcholiberalism" that took hold of the province in 1968. (*Politika*, January 9, 1985.)

77 *Politika*, December 25, 1984.

78 According to official statistics, investment in environmental protection in Leningrad from 1976 to 1980 totaled 272.64 million rubles. Leningrad's water system has been in a chronic state of disrepair ever since it was rapidly rebuilt after World War II. Warnings to visitors not to drink tap water, such as those commonly issued by the U.S. Embassy in Moscow, bring home the urgency of improving water quality. The figures are from *Bulletin of the Executive Committee of the Leningrad City Gorispolkom*, January 1, 1977, p. 12, and "On the Strengthening of Environmental Protection and Improving Sanitary Conditions in the City," *Bulletin*, no. 18 (September 1972): 12–13.

79 "Measures for the Fulfillment of the Decree of the Council of Ministers and the Communist Party of the Soviet Union of September 13, 1978, on the realization of the 10th Five-year Plan in the City of Moscow," *Bulletin of the Moscow Gorispolkom*, no. 1 (January 1978): 1–10.

80 "Plan for the Comprehensive Economic and Social Development of the City of Moscow for 1980 and Report on the Progress of the Fulfillment of the Plan for the Comprehensive Economic and Social Development of the City of Moscow for

1979," *Bulletin of the Moscow Gorispolkom*, no. 3 (February 1980): 1–16. Moscow now boasted that the environment was "cleaner than ever before" in the capital city. Forty-four square meters of greenery had been planted per citizen. Most of Moscow's enterprises had dust-catching filters and other pollution controls. Most of the dirty enterprises had been liquidated, including 4,500 small boiler rooms. Trucks were being switched to liquified-gas fuel. Water treatment facilities had the capacity to treat over six million cubic meters of water per day, more than the city consumed. And the cleanup of the Moskva River had virtually been completed. (TASS broadcast, June 26, 1979.)

81 Investment in environmental protection in Leningrad increased 250 percent between the eighth and ninth Plans, and 150 percent between the ninth and tenth.

82 Dienes, "Regional Economic Development."

83 Author interview with Srečan Mitrović, Federal Social Planning Board, May 1981.

84 For the most recent published inventory on the state of the environment in Yugoslavia, see SFRJ, *Nacionalni izveštaj*.

85 The author was shown the survey maps at a meeting with water quality experts at the J. Černi Water Resources Institute, April 1981.

86 Author interview with Republican Institute of Public Health SR Serbia, spring 1981.

87 A. D. Lebedev, ed., *Okruzhaiushchaia sreda i zdorov'e cheloveka* (The environment and human health) (Moscow: Izdatel'stvo "Nauka," 1979). The chapter on the effects of urbanization is perhaps the most interesting in regard to its discussion of the specific effects of urbanization on Soviet city residents.

88 L. G. Mel'nik, "Questions of the Long Range Forecasting of Losses Accruing to the National Economy as a Result of Air Pollution," *Economic Evaluation and the Rational Use of Natural Resources* (Moscow: TSEMI, USSR Academy of Sciences, 1972).

89 M. S. Bednyi, *Demographicheskie factory zdorov'a* (Demographic factors of health) (Moscow: "Financy i statistika," 1984).

90 "The Economy, Ecology and Ethics," pp. 147–94.

91 *Krasnyi arkhiv* (Red archive), 311515/82.

92 Data from *Narodnoe khozaistvo SSSR v 1975 godu* (National economy of the USSR, 1975) (Moscow: "Statistika," 1976), pp. 191, 199; "O predvaritel'nykh itogakh Vsesoiuznoi perepisi naselenia 1979 g", *Pravda*, April 22, 1979; and A. A. Titlianova, "Okhrana pochv," (Soil conservation), *Problemy sokhranenia okruzhaiushchei sredy* (Problems of environmental protection) (Novosibirsk: Izdatel 'stvo "Nauka," 1977), and *Pravda*, December 20, 1978.

93 *Gigienicheskie aspekty raionnoi planirovki i gradostroitel'stva v Kemerovskoi oblasti* (Hygienic aspects of raion planning and construction in Kemerovo oblast) (Novosibirsk: Izdatel'stvo "Nauka," 1978), p. 31.

94 *Soviet Review* (Winter 1981): 21–22.

95 A. V. Bolotinyi, "Gigenicheskoe znachenie pervichnogo raspredelenia pestitsidov v okrushaishchei srede" (Hygienic significance of primary distribution of pesticides

in the environment), *Gigiena i sanitaria* (Hygiene and health), no. 4 (April 1984): 81.

96 *Corriere della sera*, December 9, 1984.

97 SFRJ, *Nacionalni izveštaj*, pp. 36, 68, and 74.

98 Author interview with Dr. Srečan Mitrović.

99 R. L. Raiatskas, and V. P. Sutkaitis, "K probleme modelirovania vzaimosvazei obshchestva i prirody" (On the problem of modeling the interaction of society and nature), *Ekonomika i matematicheskie metody* (Economics and mathematical methods) 14: 3 (1978).

100 Stojanović, "Planning Economic Development," p. 42.

101 Questions suggested by Dienes, "Regional Economic Development."

102 Yerevan, *Kommunist*, October 10, 1982.

103 Alma-Ata, *Sotsialistik Qazagstan*, December 23, 1981, and *Izvestia*, June 15, 1980.

104 *Literaturnaia gazeta* (Literary gazette), June 19, 1981.

105 V. Orlov, "The Smoke Percentage," *Pravda*, August 13, 1980.

106 Report of a special interview by the Swedish press with the Estonian vice-minister of the environment in Helsinki, *Hufvudstadsbladet*, July 9, 1980.

107 Yerevan, *Kommunist*, April 6, 1980.

108 Vil'nius, *Kommunist*, no. 2 (February 1983): 61–64.

109 Alma-Ata, *Kazakhstanskaia pravda*, April 7, 1981.

110 Riga, *Sovietskaia Latvia*, January 11, 1983.

111 Tbilisi, *Komunisti*, March 1, 1980.

112 *Sovietskaia rossia*, February 8, 1981.

113 Author interview, Institute of Geography, Polish Academy of Sciences, Warsaw.

114 Alma-Ata, *Sotsialistik Qazagstan*, October 10, 1981.

115 Alma-Ata, *Sotsialistik Qazagstan*, August 20, 1981.

116 A good example of a positive report on environmental protection measures is the account of a meeting of the ESSR Council of Ministers in the summer of 1979 published in Tallinn, *Sovietskaia Estonia*, July 4, 1979. See also report of M. Kassik, head of the Department of Environmental Protection of the ESSR Gosplan in *Sovietskaia Estonia*, March 19, 1981.

117 Helsinki, *Hufvudstadsbladet*, July 9, 1980.

118 Tbilisi, *Kommunisti*, March 1, 1980 and Yerevan, *Kommunist*, April 6, 1980.

119 *Ekonomicheskaia gazeta*, no. 43, (October 1979): 24.

120 *Izvestia*, August 15, 1979.

121 Bardach, *The Implementation Game*, pp. 198–220.

122 Interview with Dr. Srečan Mitrović.

123 In this respect, Yugoslavia may be usefully perceived as a south Slav variant of the Common Market.

124 Bardach, *The Implementation Game*, p. 213.

125 Stojanović, "Planning Economic Development," pp. 41–45.

126 V. Sitnikov, "Our Concern for Nature," Moscow, *Trud*, June 3, 1980.

127 For example, see Ashkhabad, *Sovet Turkmenistan*, June 4, 1981, where local farms

are criticized for their wasteful use of water, and Alma-Ata, *Qazag adebieti*, June 5, 1981, where the local karakul sheep farms come under criticism.

128 See especially, Hélène Carrère d'Encausse, *Decline of an Empire: The Soviet Socialist Republics in Revolt* (New York: Harper Colophon Books, 1979).

129 Interview at Department of Environmental Economics, Moscow University, fall 1980.

130 For examples of press reports of increasing pollution of the Adriatic, see "Cleaner Wastes, Cleaner Sea," *Vjestnik*, December 8, 1979, and *Oslovodjenje*, April 8, 1981.

6   The Experts

1 There is a vast Western literature on the role of experts in policymaking in the United States and the Western industrialized countries, and a growing body of both Western and Eastern scholarship on their role in the communist countries. Among these may be mentioned Philip D. Stewart, "Soviet Interest Groups and the Policy Process: The Repeal of Production Education," *World Politics*, vol. 22 (October 1969); Peter Solomon, *Soviet Criminologists*; Lowenhardt, *Decision Making in Soviet Politics*; and, in particular, Radovan Richta, *Civilization at the Crossroads* (Prague: International Arts and Sciences Press, 1969), and Sharon Wolchik, "The Scientific-Technological Revolution and the Role of Specialist Elites in Policy-making in Czechoslovakia," in Michael J. Sodaro and Sharon L. Wolchik, eds., *Foreign and Domestic Policy in Eastern Europe in the 1980s: Trends and Prospects* (London: Macmillan, 1983), pp. 111–32.

2 Allan Schnaiberg, "Obstacles to Environmental Research by Scientists and Technologists: A Social Structural Analysis," *Social Problems* 24 (June 1977): 500–520.

3 See Wolchik's excellent discussion of this point in Wolchik, "The Scientific-Technological Revolution," p. 112.

4 Benveniste, *The Politics of Expertise*, pp. 4–5.

5 For a thoughtful presentation of the Soviet discussion on the STR as it relates to the conduct of Soviet foreign policy, see Erik Hoffmann and Robbin F. Laird, *"The Scientific-Technological Revolution" and Soviet Foreign Policy* (New York: Pergamon, 1982).

6 Richta, *Civilization at the Crossroads*, passim.

7 Hoffmann and Laird, *"The Scientific-Technological Revolution,"* pp. 82–88.

8 Yugoslav television, January 10, 1985.

9 See Robert Rich, ed., "Symposium on the Production and Application of Knowledge," *American Behavioral Scientist* 22, 3 (January–February 1979): 420–34.

10 Louvan E. Nolting and Murray Feshbach, *Statistics on Research and Development Employment in the U.S.S.R.*, International Population Reports, ser. P-95, no. 76, Bureau of the Census, U.S. Department of Commerce, Foreign Demographic Analysis Division (Washington, D.C.: U.S. Government Printing Office, 1981), p. 47.

11 *Statistical Pocket Book of Yugoslavia 1980* (Belgrade: Federal Statistical Office, 1980), p. 141, and SFRJ, *Nacionalni izveštaj*, p. 39.

12 The Lake Baikal story is hard to put together, since each published account of it in the West is different. The reader is referred to Komarov, *The Destruction of Nature*, pp. 6–13; Goldman, *The Spoils of Progress*, pp. 178–79; Kelley, "Environmental Policy Making in the USSR," pp. 570–89; and Lowenhardt, *Decision Making in Soviet Politics*, pp. 70–76.

13 Schnaiberg, "Obstacles to Environmental Research," p. 501. See also Lewis Mumford, *The Myth of the Machine: The Pentagon of Power* (New York: Harcourt Brace Jovanovich, 1970), pp. 123–27.

14 When Leningrad, for example, prepared to implement a technical plan for ending the dumping of raw sewage into waterways leading to the Baltic, the city mobilized its local organs of expertise (the local branches of the head special organs) to provide the solutions. See "On the General Plan of Design-research and Construction Work Development for the Stopping of Pollution of the Baltic Sea Basin," decision of the Leningrad Gorispolkom, January 8, 1978, as published in *Bulletin of the Executive Committee of the Leningrad Soviet*, February 4, 1978, pp. 6–7.

15 Blinov, *Sbornik normativnykh aktov*, pp. 11–23.

16 Author interview with the chairman of the department of biology, Moscow State University, fall 1980.

17 Nolting, *Planning of Research*, pp. 14–15.

18 "The Economy, Ecology and Ethics," pp. 147–94.

19 *Izvestia*, January 30, 1985, p. 2.

20 "The Economy, Ecology and Ethics," pp. 147–94.

21 A supplemental discussion of the role of these meetings for expert policy input in general may be found in Lowenhardt, *Decision Making in Soviet Politics*, pp. 87–89, 138–48.

22 Ibid.

23 The second section was added after the passage of the Serbian Environmental Protection Law in 1975.

24 Author interview with Stepan Nikolić, director, Republican Institute for Environmental Protection, SR Serbia, March 1981.

25 One recent publication on the nutrition of children in public educational institutions is *Ishrana dece u jazlama, vrtićima i školama* (The nutrition of children in creches, kindergartens and schools) (Belgrade: Municipal Institute for Public Health, 1980).

26 Author interview with M. Hasara, chief of the Department of Hygiene, Belgrade Municipal Institute of Public Health, March 1981.

27 Interview with Djordje Minjević, secretary of the Institute of Hygiene and Epidemiology, Council for the Human Environment and Territorial Management, SR Serbia, April 1981.

28 A list of the institute's contracts may be found in *Transactions*, No. 63, published on the thirtieth anniversary of the founding of the J. Černi Water Resources Insti-

tute in honor of the institute's being awarded the AVNOJ prize in recognition of its contribution to the development of Yugoslavia in the field of engineering (Belgrade: J. Černi Water Resources Institute, 1977).

29 Dobrivoje Tosković, *Urbanizacija Libije: poreklo, utičajni faktori i prostorno-fizički efekti* (The urbanization of Libya: Origins, influential factors and spatial-physical effects) (Belgrade: Yugoslav Institute for Urban Planning and Construction, 1980).

30 The list represents contracts received by the firm since 1968. SMELT '80 Reference List published by SMELT, Ljubljana.

31 *Vjestnik*, June 5, 1982.

32 Admission requirements include a university degree, preferably but not necessarily in one of the sciences, high grades, and knowledge of a foreign language.

33 Author interview with Dr. Radoslav Radoslavjević, docent, chair, Department for Economic Studies, Center for Multidisciplinary Studies, Belgrade University, March 1981. See also the brochure put out by the center: University of Belgrade, *Center for Multidisciplinary Studies*, M. M. Ristić, ed. (Belgrade: "October 10" Publishing House, 1980).

34 Belgrade, *Borba*, October 24, 1982.

35 SFRJ, *Nacionalni izveštaj*, p. 19, and author interview with Dr. Milica Kačarović, director, Department of Environmental Protection, Institute for the Technology of Nuclear and Other Raw Materials, May 1981.

36 Author interview with Goskomgidromet staff, January 1980.

37 Nolting, *Planning of Research*, pp. 14–15.

38 Kushnirsky, *Soviet Economic Planning*, p. 131.

39 The reader will recall the impression made upon the Polish public when environmental data were made available in the Polish press during the Solidarity period. The outcry was sufficient to force the closing of one of the most polluting factories near Cracow.

40 *Listy*, no. 6 (November 1981): 34–40.

41 Zhores A. Medvedev, *Soviet Science* (New York: W. W. Norton, 1978), pp. 162–70.

42 W. Leontiev and D. Ford, "Mezhotraslevoi analiz vozdiestvia struktury ekonomiki na okruzhaiushchuu sredy" (Interbranch analysis of the influence of the structure of the economy on the environment), *Economika i matematicheskie metody* (Economics and mathematical methods) 8, 4 (1972).

43 The reader is particularly referred to M. Ia. Lemeshev and L. V. Dunaievskii, eds. *Upravlenie prirodnoi sredy—Sotsial'no-ekonomicheskie i estestvenno-nauchnye aspekty* (The management of nature—Social-economic and natural science aspects) (Moscow: "Nauka," 1979).

44 R. L. Raiatskas and V. P. Sutkaitis, "A System of Ecological and Economic Models for Environmental Planning and Control," Martin Cave, Alastair McAuley, and Judith Thornton, eds., *New Trends in Soviet Economics* (Armonk, N.Y.: M. E. Sharpe, 1982), pp. 366–405.

45 Schnaiberg, "Obstacles to Environmental Research," p. 500.

46 The plan is developed on the basis of the guidelines published in the five-year

Communist Party Program. Basic forecasting of national importance is done jointly by GKNT, the USSR Academy of Sciences, Gosplan, and Gosstroi. Forecasting of interbranch R&D is carried out by the ministries and agencies in charge of the relevant branches within the framework of the general forecast. The five-year national plan is compiled by the four supervisory agencies on the basis of the forecast, while implementation planning occurs through the assignment of interbranch scientific and technical programs to the appropriate ministries. A lead ministry or agency is designated to coordinate the program. In some cases, where assignment proves difficult, GKNT divides up the program tasks among agencies of its own selection. (Nolting, *Planning of Research*, passim.)

47 Ibid., p. 1.

48 Office of Technology Assessment, *Technology and Soviet Energy Capability* (Boulder, Colo.: Westview, 1982), p. 10.

49 Abram Bergson, "Technological Progress," in Bergson and Levine, *Toward the Year 2000*, p. 52.

50 *SSSR v tsifrakh 1979* (USSR in figures 1979) (Moscow: Central Statistical Administration, 1979), pp. 87 and 179.

51 *SSSR v tsifrakh 1980* (USSR in figures 1980) (Moscow: Central Statistical Administration, 1980), pp. 81 and 169. Bergson uses the National Science Board figure, developed for 1975, of 3.5 percent of gross national income (GNI) (Bergson, "Technological Progress," p. 84). It is fascinating that nowhere in this book dealing with the future economic performance of the USSR are the problems of the Soviet environment even mentioned.

52 *Narodnoe khozaistvo SSSR v 1984 g.: Statisticheskii ezhegodnik* (The national economy of the USSR 1984: Annual statistical yearbook) (Moscow: "Financy i statistiki," 1985), pp. 378–79 and 405.

53 Federal Committee of Information, *Social Plan of Yugoslavia 1976–1980* (Belgrade: "Kultura" stamparsko preduzece [Culture printing house], n.d.).

54 Author interview with Dr. Stepan Nikolić, director, Republican Institute for Environmental Protection SR Serbia, March 1981.

55 Author interview with Dr. Pera Stepanov, Institute for Hygiene and Environmental Protection, Republican Institute for Public Health, April 1981.

56 Author interview with Dr. Hasara, March 1981.

57 Author interview with Dr. Stepan Nikolić.

58 Medvedev, *Soviet Science*, pp. 19–120.

59 For a review of the early literature, see Diana Crane, "The Nature of Scientific Communication and Influence," *International Social Science Journal* 12, 1 (1970): 28–41.

60 See, for example, I. I. Leiman, "Nauchnyi kollektiv, ego struktura, tipologia i funksti" (The scientific collective, its structure, typology and functions), in V. Zh. Kelle and S. R. Mikulinski, eds., *Sotsialogicheskie problemy nauki* (Sociological problems of science) (Moscow: Izdatel'stvo "Nauka," 1974), pp. 414–52. Leiman even uses the term "invisible college," and postulates that these networks rarely form on the basis of personal affinity, but derive from professional interests for the

"facilitation of scientific contact, the acceleration of information exchange, and the improvement of operational efficiency" (p. 442).

61 I. V. Sergeeva, "Kollektiv i lichnost' v nauke" (The collective and personality in science), *Sotsial'nye issledovania* (Social research), no. 3 (1970): 178–88.

62 G. G. Diumenton, "Issledovanie seti nauchnykh kontaktov i ego prakticheskoe znachenie" (Research on the scientific contact networks and its practical significance), in Kelle and Mikulinski, *Sotsialogicheskie problemy nauki*, pp. 348–68.

63 Richard F. Vidmer, "Soviet Studies of Organization and Management: A 'Jungle' of Competing Views," *Slavonic Review* 40, 3 (fall 1981): 404–22.

64 Professor and Academician T. S. Khachaturov is a good example. In 1980, he was the chair of the Department of Environmental Economics and also a member of the USSR Academy of Sciences.

65 Zhores A. Medvedev, *Nuclear Disaster in the Urals*, trans. George Saunders (New York: Vintage, 1980), pp. 18–26. For a Western analysis of the Soviet nuclear accident in Cheliabinsk Province during 1957–58, see John R. Trabalka, L. Dean Eyman, and Stanley I. Auerbach, "Analysis of the 1957–1958 Soviet Nuclear Accident," *Science* 209, 4454 (July 18, 1980): 345–53. The analysis draws on numerous Western and Soviet sources and essentially confirms Medvedev's findings.

66 Thomas J. Allen and Stephen I. Cohen, "Information Flow in Research and Development Laboratories," *Administrative Science Quarterly* 14, 1 (March 1969): 12–19.

67 Michael Crozier, *The Bureaucratic Phenomenon* (Chicago: University of Chicago Press, 1964), p. 229.

68 Karen Dawisha, "The Limits of the Bureaucratic Politics Model: Observations on the Soviet Case," *Studies in Comparative Communism*, 12, 4 (winter 1980): 300–346.

69 Gustafson, *Reform in Soviet Politics*, p. 47.

70 It is interesting to recall that Kunyaev seconded Gorbachev's nomination as first secretary. (*International Herald Tribune*, March 19, 1985.)

71 Schnaiberg, "Obstacles to Environmental Research," pp. 507–16.

72 For an overview of the trial, see Zdenko Antić, "The Belgrade Trial, Its Outcome and Analysis," RFE-RL Radio Free Europe Research, Yugoslavia/2, February 12, 1985, pp. 3–8.

73 Medvedev, *Soviet Science*, chap. 4.

74 Nolting and Feshbach, *Statistics on Research*.

75 Lowenhardt, *Decision Making in Soviet Politics*, pp. 70–76.

76 For highly differentiated accounts of the report writing, see Komarov, *The Destruction of Nature*, pp. 6–13; Goldman, *The Spoils of Progress*, pp. 178–79; Kelley, "Environmental Policy Making," pp. 570–89; and Lowenhardt, *Decision Making in Soviet Politics*, pp. 70–76.

77 Boffey, for example, faults the U.S. National Academy of Sciences for its reluctance to risk its reputation on controversial issues, its stress on middle-of-the road consensus positions, and the leadership's general hesitation to oppose the government. (Phillip M. Boffey, *The Brain Bank of America: An Inquiry into the Poli-*

tics of Science (New York: McGraw-Hill, 1975).) Primack found only two cases where the presidential adviser had gone public with his concerns: the SST and the building of the ARM system. In both instances, the publicity led to a reversal of the presidential decision. The presidential environmental "hit list" is not new to the Reagan Administration. (*Science* 219, no. 18: 1303.) The three scientists who led the Colorado Committee for Environmental Information in questioning the public health hazard of three federal activities in the state changed their careers to public interest science to escape the constraints of the bureaucratic or industrial consultant relationship. (Joel Primack and Frank von Hippel, *Advice and Dissent: Scientists in the Political Arena* [New York: Basic Books, 1974], pp. 74–84, and 174.)

78 See Steven Burg's cogent discussion of the legislative process in Burg, *Conflict and Cohesion*, chap. 5.

79 Vanneman, *The Supreme Soviet*, p. 141.

80 Ibid., p. 147.

81 Author interview at USSR Academy of Sciences Institute of State and Law, October 1980.

82 Benveniste, *The Politics of Expertise*, p. 155.

83 Gustafson, *Reform in Soviet Politics*, pp. 48–49, 65–66, 101–10.

84 For a discussion of the role of experts in the Yugoslav federal legislative process, see Burg, *Conflict and Cohesion*, pp. 261–63, 271–74.

85 Author interview with Dr. Srečan Mitrović, spring 1981.

86 Books of note by these men include V. V. Kriuchkov, *Sever: priroda i chelovek* (The north: nature and man) (Moscow: Izdatel'stvo "Nauka," 1979); V. V. Vorob'iev and A. V. Belov, eds.-in-chief, *Geographicheskie problemy zony BAM* (Geographic problems of the BAM zone) (Novosibirsk: Siberian Division of "Nauka," 1979); and I. P. Gerasimov, chairman of editorial collective, *Okruzhaiushchaia sreda i zdorov'e cheloveka* (The environment and human health), USSR Academy of Sciences Institute of Geography (Moscow: Izdatel'stvo "Nauka," 1979).

87 Downing, *Environmental Economics and Policy*, chap. 2.

88 See especially K. G. Gofman, A. A. Gusev, A. F. Mudretsov, "The Determination of Marginal Costs of the Products of the Resource Exploitation Branches," *Ekonomika i matematicheskie metody*, 11: 4 (1975): 695–706; T. S. Khachaturov, ed., *Okhrana okruzhaiushchei sredy i eio sotsial'no-ekonomicheskaia efektivnost* (Environmental protection and its social-economic effectiveness) (Moscow: Izdatel'stvo "Nauka," 1980); M. Ia. Lemeshev and L. V. Dunaievskii, eds., *Upravlenie prirodnoi sredy — Sotsial'no-ekonomicheskie i estestvenno-nauchnye aspekty* (The management of nature — social-economic and natural science aspects) (Moscow: Izdatel'stvo "Nauka," 1979); M. N. Loiter, "Methods and Practice for the Determination of the Effectiveness of Capital Investment and New Technology," *Sbornik nauchnoi informatsii* (Collection of scientific information), no. 28 (Moscow: "Nauka," 1977), pp. 61–64; O. F. Balatskii, "Economic Aspects in Establishing the Maximum Permissible Substances in the Atmosphere," *First U.S./USSR Environmental Economics Symposium*, U.S. Department of Commerce, Office of

Environmental Affairs, Projects 02.11.21 (December 1978), pp. 134–42. For other sources, the reader is referred to the bibliography.

89 M. T. Meleshkin, A. P. Zaitsev, Kh. Marinov, *Ekonomika i okruzhaiushchei sredy* (Economics and the environment) (Moscow: "Ekonomika," 1979), pp. 123–25.

90 K. G. Gofman, "Financial Accountability and the Right to Use Resources," in Cave, McAuley, and Thornton, *New Trends in Soviet Economics*, pp. 406–12, and his longer work, *The Economic Evaluation of Natural Resources under the Conditions of a Socialist Economy* (Moscow: Izdatel'stvo "Nauka," 1977). See also Judith Thornton's excellent introduction to the environmental economics section, pp. 329–38.

91 Gofman, *Economic Evaluation*, chaps. 3 and 4.

92 N. Fedorenko and K. Gofman, "Problems of Optimization in the Planning and Control of the Environment," *Voprosy ekonomiki* (Problems in economics), no. 10 (1972), pp. 24–38.

93 Leontiev and Ford, "Mezhotraslevoi analiz."

94 In a recent book on the concept and formation of TICs, there is not one mention of environmental demands. See Creighton, *Territorial Industrial Complexes*. For information on the Siberia Program, see A. Aganbegyan, "Behind the Lines of the Basic Guidelines: The Siberia Program," *Sotsialisticheskaia industria* (Socialist industry), May 8, 1981, p. 2; and V. Koptiug, chairman, USSR Academy of Sciences' Siberian Division, "According to Comprehensive Programs: Siberian Dimensions," *Pravda*, February 15, 1981, p. 3. The program comprises some thirty special-purpose scientific programs dealing with factors in comprehensive planning. The three Siberian regions are the West Siberian petroleum and gas complex, the Angara-Yenesei region from the Arctic Ocean in the north to Krasnoyarsk and Irkutsk in the south, and the BAM zone.

95 For example, Iu. I. Tiutekin, *Priroda, obshchestvo, zakon* (Nature, society, law) (Kishinev: Izdatel'stvo "Nauka," 1976), p. 109.

96 Resolution of the Praesidium of the Supreme Court of June 2, 1977, as published in Blinov, *Sbornik normativnykh aktov*, p. 62.

97 Iu. S. Shemshuchenko, V. L. Muntian, B. G. Rosovskii, *Iuridicheskaia otvetstvennost' v oblasti okhrany okruzhaiushchei sredy* (Legal liability in the field of environmental protection) (Kiev: Izdatel'stvo "Nauka," 1979), p. 90.

98 Milivoje Todorović, "Tretman životne sredine u ZUR-u i reperkusije na kvalitet životne sredine" (The treatment of the environment in law on social labor and its repercussions on environmental quality), paper presented at the Conference on the Meaning of Environmental Health in General and for National Defense in Particular, Brdo kod Kravja, May 31–June 1, 1985 (unpublished).

99 *Vjesnik*, April 2 and June 5, 1980.

100 "The Economy, Ecology, and Ethics," pp. 139–48.

101 Rich, "Symposium on Knowledge," pp. 125–45, 327–470; and Holcomb Research Institute, *Environmental Modeling and Decision Making: The United States Experience* (New York: Praeger, 1976). Greeneburger in particular indicates that operations models are more likely to be utilized than more comprehensive general

models because of their more immediate applicability, lesser political complexity, and hence reduced risk potential for the bureaucrat. [Martin Greeneberger, Matthew A. Crenson, and Brian L. Cissey, *Models in the Policy Process: Public Decision Making in the Computer Era* (New York: Russell Sage Foundation, 1976).]

102 See in particular the selection of articles by leading Soviet scientists urging that the Northern Rivers – Volga Diversion Project be dropped. "Debating the Need for River Diversion," published in *The Current Digest of the Soviet Press* 38, 7 (March 19, 1986): 1–4.

103 See T. A. Busheva and P. S. Dagel', "The Object of Criminal-Legal Environmental Protection," *Sovietskoe gosudarstvo i pravo* (Soviet state and law), no. 8 (1977): 77–79; and Iu. I. Liapunov, *Criminal Law, Environmental Protection and the Organs of the Ministry of Internal Affairs* (Moscow: Izdatel'stvo "Nauka," 1974).

104 Part 2, Statutes 166, 167, and 223 of the RSFSR Criminal Code. Statute 163 of the RSFSR Criminal Code included the illegal production of goods and illegal fishing equipment, such as nets, fishing rods, etc.

105 Gofman, *Economic Evaluation*, 1977. See also M. M. Voronovitskii, K. G. Gofman, A. A. Gusiev, V. A. Spivak, "Ekonomicheskie osnovy platy za zagriasnenie okruzhaiushchei sredy" (Economic basis of payment for environmental pollution), *Ekonomika i matematicheskie metody* (Economics and mathematical methods) 11: 3 (1975): 483–90.

106 See Fullenbach's discussion of West German appraisal of the emission tax in *European Environmental Policy*, pp. 116–17.

107 A pollution tax has failed to be adopted in the United States as well, for the same reason.

108 USSR Council of Ministers' Resolution on the Strengthening of Environmental Protection, December 29, 1978.

109 *Politika*, February 22, 1985.

110 Professor Jovan Mirić published a series of articles called "The System and the Crisis" attacking the 1974 Constitution for destroying the unity of the Yugoslav market and increasing republican autonomy. (Belgrade, *Borba*, October 12–25, 1984.)

111 Dr. Radojić Kljajić, "Uloga i značaj zaštite hrane od hemijskih i bioloških agensa, posebno sa stanovišta civilne zaštite" (Task and meaning of protection of food from chemical and biological agents, especially from the viewpoint of civil defense), *Čovek i životna sredina*, no. 4 (1983): 15–19.

112 Both organs were criticized for failing to perform their coordinating and supervisory functions properly. (*Pravda*, August 28, 1983.)

113 Goldman, *The Spoils of Progress*; Komarov, pp. 6–10; Lowenhardt, pp. 70–77. The experts have not let down their vigilance on Lake Baikal. The controversy continues between the environmentalists and the authorities about whether adequate pollution controls are yet in place, with the former insisting they are not. See V. Yermolayev, A. Ilyin and V. Orlov, "Along Both Sides of Lake Baikal," *Pravda*, January 11, 1986, p. 3, and V. Rasputin, "We Have Only One Baikal," *Izvestia*,

February 17, 1986, pp. 3 and 6. The second article concerns the author's interview with officials of the Ministry of the Timber, Pulp-and-Paper and Lumber Industry.

114 For a discussion of Soviet literature and activity in this area, see Micklin, "Soviet Interbasin Water Transfer Policy," pp. 567–80.

115 Namely the organization to make the land around the Kara Deg Volcano in the Crimea a protected area. V. Sitnikov, "Our Concern for Nature," *Trud* (Moscow), June 3, 1980.

116 For a discussion of the problematic relationship of the party to the Alliance, see April Carter, *Democratic Reform in Yugoslavia: The Changing Role of the Party* (Princeton: Princeton University Press, 1982), pp. 96–110. Another area where the sociopolitical organizations have shown a capacity for transnational action is in belles-lettres. When the Yugoslav writers met in Novy Sad in April 1985, many thought the conference would dissolve into interrepublican accusations and counteraccusations. Instead, the writers united to decry what they termed was the "unexplained absolutism" of the current situation, and they demanded the suppression of Article 133 of the Penal Code, permitting writers be sentenced for ten years for expressing "hostile propaganda." (*Le point*, no. 185 [April 29–May 5, 1985], p. 86.)

7 Public Opinion and Mass Organizations

1 "Recommendations of the First All-Union Conference on Education in the Field of the Environment," *Bulletin of the Ministry of Higher and Secondary Education of the USSR*, no. 9 (September 1979):28.

2 Ibid., pp. 32–34.

3 Author interview with Dr. V. F. Barabanov, chair, Committee for Environmental Protection, Leningrad University, November 1980.

4 Michael E. Soulé and Bruce A. Wilcox, eds., *Biologia okhrany prirody* (Conservation biology), trans. S. A. Ostoumov and A. V. Iablokov (Moscow: "Mir," 1983).

5 Cf. B. G. Rozanov, *Osnovy uchenia ob okruzhaiushchei srede* (Fundamentals of the study of the environment) (Moscow: Izdatel'stvo Moskovskogo universiteta, 1984).

6 Author interview with Dr. Olga Vidláková, summer 1981.

7 Dana Kvasnićková, Council for Environmental Protection for the Government of the ČSR, *Foundations of Biology and Ecology*, "Educational Basis for the Care of the Environment" Series, Dr. Antonin Šum, adviser (Prague: Research Institute of Construction and Architecture, 1981).

8 Josef Riha and Antonin Šum, Council for Environmental Protection for the Government of the CSR, *Introduction to Basic Theoretical Information about Care for the Environment*, pts. I and II (Prague: Research Institute of Construction and Architecture, 1981).

9 Author interview with Milivoje Todorović, at that time general secretary of the Federal Council for the Protection and Improvement of the Human Environment, March 1981.

10 Dragoslav Joković, ed.-in-chief, *Zaštita i unapredjivanje životne sredine* (The protection and improvement of the environment) (Belgrade: "Bakar" 1979).

11 Allan Schnaiberg, "Obstacles to Environmental Research by Scientists and Technologists: A Social Structural Analysis," *Social Problems* 24 (June 1977):506.

12 "On the Participation of the Trade Union Organizations in the Fulfillment of the Resolution of the CC CPSU and the USSR Council of Ministers" (On the Strengthening of Environmental Protection and the Improvement of Natural Resource Use), February 23, 1973, as published in L. P. Sharikov, compiler, *Okhrana okruzhaiushchei sredy* (Environmental protection) (Leningrad: "Sudostroenie," 1978), pp. 62–64.

13 The relevant passage of the resolution is found in Kirpatovskii, *Okhrana prirody* pp. 10–12.

14 Among the competencies that should be mentioned are "social control" over ministerial decisions affecting workers and their environment; assisting the Presidium of the CCTU in implementing control measures; participating in the elaboration of all ministerial and organizational plans involving environmental protection; educating workers to the latest technological advances in environmental protection; monitoring the lower trade union committees in controlling environmental conditions at the workplace; working with these committees in monitoring pollution control equipment; elaborating more effective and economic treatment methods; and checking the inclusion of pollution control requirements in blueprints and plans. ("Regulations concerning the Commission for Environmental Protection of the Central Committee of the Chemical and Petrochemical Workers Union," Protocol no. 9, September 21, 1977, as printed in Kirpatovskii, *Okhrana prirody* pp. 47–48.)

15 Author interview with V. V. Petrov, December 1980.

16 For the text of the 1966 Constitution of the All-Russian Society of Nature Protection, see Blinov, *Sbornik normativnykh aktov*, pp. 59–61. The new constitution changes the name of the society from "All-Russian" to "Soviet" and includes provisions whereby the society may make legislative recommendations.

17 Author interview with staff of the All-Russian Society for Environmental Protection, Moscow, December 1980.

18 Alma-Ata, *Madeniyet zhane turmys*, no. 10 (October 1982):16–17.

19 Dushambe, *Kommunisti Tojikiston*, no. 8 (August 1983): 72–78.

20 Frunze, *Sovietskaia Kirgizia*, January 12, 1982, p. 12.

21 Moscow, *Sovietskaia kultura* (Soviet culture), June 6, 1980, p. 3.

22 G. Yenukidze, secretary of the Georgian CP Central Committee, "Party Life: The Quality of Ideological Work: By Dint of Public Opinion," *Pravda*, January 13, 1982.

23 Author interview with Dr. Igor Rusin, chairman, Young People's Council on Environmental Protection, MGU, January 1981.

24 *Vystrel* (The shot), no. 2, 2999 (January 28, 1978), and no. 6, 3052 (February 9, 1979).

25 *Vystrel*, no. 38, 2772 (September 27, 1974), and no. 41, 2779 (November 19, 1974).

26 *Bulletin of the Executive Committee of the Leningrad City Soviet*, November 19, 1974.

27 As reported in *Borba* (Belgrade), March 28, 1981.

28 Belgrade, *Borba*, March 31, 1981.

29 Ibid.

30 *Politika*, April 1, 1981.

31 Author interview with Momcilo Dozoterić, secretary of the Republican Conference of the Gorani Movement, SR Serbia, March 20, 1981.

32 Author interview with Misa Pejović, Bečej Opština Conference, Gorani Movement, March 1981.

33 Author interview with Vladimir Beličeavić, chairman, and Vigor Majić, secretary, Republican Conference of Young Researchers SR Serbia, March 1981.

34 Meeting of representatives of the Young Researchers and the Communist Youth Organization with representatives of interested scientific and social institutions to plan Sava River Project, April 13, 1981.

35 Author interview with Djordje Minjević and Sofija Borovonica, senior adviser to the secretary of the Federal Council for the Human Environment and Territorial Management attached to the Executive Council of the SFR Yugoslavia, April 1981.

36 The text of the Fundamental Labor Law may be found in *Labor Legislation in the USSR*, (Moscow: Novosti Publishing House, 1972).

37 Author interview with V. V. Petrov, December 1980.

38 V. V. Bulgakov, "Economic Effectiveness of the Elimination of Air Pollution in the Region of Ferrous Metallurgy Plants of the Ukrainian SSR," *First USSR/USA Symposium on "Economic Aspects of Environmental Protection"*, Yerevan, October 16–23, 1977 (Washington, D.C.: U.S. Government Printing Office, 1977), pp. 100–103.

39 E. Z. Danilova, *Sotisal'nyie problemy truda zenshchiny-rabotnitsy (Trud zhenshchiny-rabotnisty i materinstvo)* (Social problems of the work of the woman worker [the woman-worker's work and maternity]) (Moscow: Izdatel'stvo "Mysl'," 1968), p. 31.

40 V. A. Minyaev and I. V. Poliakov, *Zdravookhranenie krupnogo sotsialisticheskogo goroda* (Public Health in the Large Socialist City) (Moscow: "Meditsina," 1979), chap. 2, esp. pp. 124, 130.

41 M. S. Bednyi, *Demographicheskie faktory zdorov'a* (Demographic factors of health) (Moscow: "Financy i statistika," 1984).

42 SFRJ, *Nacionalni izveštaj*, p. 94.

43 Iu. V. Medvedkov, *Chelovek i gorodskaia sreda* (Man and his urban environment) (Moscow: Izdatel'stvo "Nauka," 1978).

44 *Osnovnye napravlenia*, pp. 67–68. Significantly, letters from the public at large poured into the Congress expressing concern about existing conditions in the health care system.

45 Downing, *Environmental Economics and Policy*, pp. 226–42.

46 *Statistical Pocket Book of Yugoslavia 1980* (Belgrade: Federal Statistical Office,

1980), p. 60, and author interview with the Young Researchers, Belgrade, spring 1981.

47 *Politika*, August 2, 1984, p. 4.

48 Zagreb, *Danas*, November 13, 1984.

49 Alma-Ata, *Sotsialistik Qazagstan*, June 5, 1981, p. 4.; Dushanbe, *Kommunisti Tajikistan*, no. 8 (August 1983):72–78.; Frunze, *Sovietskaia Khirghizia*, January 12, 1982, p. 3.

50 The report was published in *Listy*, no. 6 (November 1981):24–30.

51 Author interview with Jan Kleinert of the Banska Bystrica Chapter of the Slovak Society of the Defenders of Nature, July 1981.

52 Alma-Ata, *Madeniyet zhane turmys*, no. 10 (October 1982):16 and 17.

53 Frunze, *Sovietskaia Khirghizia*, January 12, 1982.

54 Alma-Ata, *Qazaqstanskaia pravda*, March 4, 1983, and *Sotsialistik Qazagstan*, October 10, 1981.

55 The putting into trial operation of the Krsko nuclear power plant was postponed because of failure to apply all the necessary environmental protection measures. (Zagreb: TANJUG, April 24, 1981.)

56 Author interviews with Sofija Borovonica, Djordje Minjević, and Srečan Mitrović of the Federal Planning Board SFRY, April 1981.

57 Author interviews with Professor Antonin Kerner, Law Faculty, Charles University, Prague, summer 1981.

58 Lester W. Milbraith, "Environmental Values and Beliefs of the General Public and Leaders in the United States, England, and Germany," and Julie A. Honnold, "Predictors of Public Environmental Concern in the 1970s," in Dean Mann, ed. *Environmental Policy Formation: The Impact of Values, Ideology and Standards* (Lexington, Mass.: Lexington Books, 1981), pp. 43–86.

8 Structure and Regulatory Principle Revisited

1 Laurent Cohen-Tanugi, *Le droit sans l'état: Sur la démocratie en France et en Amérique* (Law without the state: Democracy in France and in America), preface by Stanley Hoffmann ("Recherches politiques") (Paris: Presses Universitaires de France, 1985), pp. 141–43.

2 The foregoing paragraph has been summarized from Downing, *Environmental Economics and Policy*, pp. 9–17.

3 *Nature* 303 (January 26, 1983):270. For a piercing discussion of science politics and the U.S. National Academy of Sciences, see Boffey, *The Brain Bank of America*. For the political interaction between scientists and the White House, see Edward J. Burger, Jr., *Science at the White House: A Political Liability* (Baltimore: Johns Hopkins University Press, 1980.)

4 Robert Dorfman and Nancy S. Dorfman, eds., *Economics of the Environment, Selected Readings*, 2d ed. (New York: W. W. Norton, 1977), particularly chap. 1; Philip E. Graves and Ronald J. Krumm, *Health and Air Quality: Evaluating the Effects of Policy* (Washington, D.C., and London: American Enterprise Insti-

tute for Public Policy Research, 1981); Downing, *Environmental Economics and Policy*; and Baden and Stroup, *Bureaucracy vs. Environment*. See also, R. J. Anderson, Jr., R. O. Reid, and E. P. Siskin, *An Analysis of Alternative Policies for Attaining and Maintaining a Short-Term NO2 Standard* (Princeton, N.J.: Mathtech, 1979); S. E. Atkinson and D. H. Lewis, "Determination and Implementation of Optimal Air Quality Standards," *Journal of Environmental Economics and Management* 3 (1976): 363–80; and A. Marin, "The Choice of Efficient Pollution Policies: Technology and Economics in the Control of Sulphur Dioxide," *Journal of Environmental Management*, 5 (1979): 44–62.

5 National Research Council, Commission on Natural Resources, *Decision-making in the Environmental Protection Agency* (Washington, D.C.: National Academy of Sciences, 1977), p. 141.

6 Commission on Natural Resources, Environmental Studies Board, Committee on Prevention of Significant Deterioration of Air Quality, *On Prevention of Significant Deterioration of Air Quality* (Washington, D.C.: National Academy Press, 1981), pp. 107–12.

7 A. A. Gusiev, "K voprosy ob ekonomicheskoi otsenke ushcherba ot zagriaznenia okruzhaiushchei sredy" (The question of economic evaluation of loss from environmental pollution), Academy of Sciences USSR, Scientific Council on the Problems of the Biosphere, Institute of Geography, *Ekonomicheskaia i vneekonomicheskaia otsenka vozdeistvia cheloveka na okruzhaiushchuiu sredu* (Economic and non-economic evaluation of the activity of man on the environment) (Moscow: Izdatel'stvo "Nauka," 1981), pp. 77–80, and N. Federenko and K. Gofman, "Problems of Optimization in the Planning and Control of the Environment," *Voprosy ekonomiki* (Problems of economics), no. 10, 1972.

8 See, for example, "Metodicheskie osnovy ekonomicheskoi otsenki mestorozhdenii poleznykh iskopaemykh" (Methodological basis for valuations of mineral deposits), *Ekonomika i matematicheskie metody* (Economics and mathematical methods) 14, 3 (1978), as translated and published in *Matekon* 15: 4 (1979): 3–27.

9 The problem of information is specifically noted by A. Druzinin, "Optimization of Developing the Agricultural Component of Water," *Water Supply and Management* 3 (1979): 323–33.

10 Jones, *Clean Air.*

11 For a discussion of the origins of scientific "objectivity" and its role in modern culture, see Evelyn Fox Keller, *Reflections on Gender and Science* (New Haven: Yale University Press, 1985), pp. 75–114.

12 Cohen-Tanugi, *Le Droit sans l'état*, chap. 1.

13 Jeffrey L. Pressman and Aaron Wildavsky, *Implementation: How Great Expectations in Washington are Dashed in Oakland*, 2d ed. (Berkeley and Los Angeles: University of California Press, 1979). An excellent example of the problems of regulatory reform was provided by the massive student demonstrations in Paris in early December 1986. The students were protesting a proposed government reform in regulations concerning admission to higher education. The demonstrations

mobilized so many conflicting negative opinions that the government was forced to withdraw its proposal.

14 *On Prevention of Significant Deterioration*, p. 108.

15 Cohen-Tanugi, *Le Droit sans l'état*, pp. 38–58 and pp. 76–77.

16 Hélène Carrère d'Encausse, *Decline of an Empire: The Soviet Socialist Republics in Revolt* (New York: Harper Colophon Books, 1979).

17 For an elaboration of this point, see Barbara Jancar, "Religious Dissent in the Soviet Union," in Rudolf Tokes, ed. *Dissent in the USSR* (Baltimore: Johns Hopkins University Press, 1975).

18 Baden and Stroup, *Bureaucracy vs. Environment*, pp. 22–45.

Postscript Chernobyl

1 Except where specifically indicated, the information presented has been culled from a reading of the May/June 1986 issues of major newspapers, such as the *International Herald Tribune*, the *Wall Street Journal*, the *New York Times*, *The Times* (London), the *Manchester Guardian*, *Le monde*, *Pravda*, *Izvestia*, *Politika*, and the *Washington Post*.

2 *Le monde*, April 1, 1986, p. 8.

3 The *Wall Street Journal* ("Chernobyl's Special Problem," May 14, 1986) insists on the "dual-use" nature of the Chernobyl plant, citing evidence of a former Soviet engineer who helped build nuclear power plants similar to the ones at Chernobyl but who now works for Ebasco Services, Inc. The *Guardian Weekly* (May 18, 1986) also stresses that the plant was used for plutonium production. For a concise description of the RBMK reactor, see U.S. Congress, Congressional Research Service, Science Policy Research Division, Warren Donnelly et al., *The Chernobyl Nuclear Accident: Causes, Initial Effects, and Congressional Response (with Appendices) Updated 08/19/86*, Order Code IB86077. That report as well cites the reactor's "dual-use" purpose.

4 Yugoslav commentator Milos Bačić suggests that official American opinion may be divided on this matter. "Deset dana koji su trasli svet" [Ten Days That Shook the World], *NIN*, no. 1845 (May 11, 1986), p. 10.

5 See the very brief discussion of the organization of the civilian nuclear industry in the USSR in "Le nucléaire civil en URSS: un parent pauvre de l'industrie d'armement" (Civilian Nuclear Power: A Poor Relative of the Armaments Industry), *Le monde*, April 30, 1986, p. 8. The article cited earlier in *NIN* also carries a short description.

6 *Le monde*, May 4, p. 6.

7 Among the many initial explanations of what occurred, see *Le monde*, May 4–5, 1986, p. 6, *New York Times*, May 19, 1986, *Washington Post*, May 25, 1986, and *NIN*, pp. 10–12. For summaries of the Soviet report to the IAEA, see particularly *New York Times*, August 16 and 18, 1986, *Le monde*, May 20, 1986, and *Manchester Guardian*, August 31, 1986, p. 7.

8 Liubov Kovalevska, "Ne privatna sprava" (Not Private Information), *Literarni Ukraina* (Literary Ukraine), March 27, 1986, p. 1.

9 *The Times* (London), May 21, 1986, p. 1, and *Washington Post*, August 26, 1986, p. A14.

10 Article cited in *NIN*, p. 13.

11 Ibid., p. 12.

12 As cited in ibid., p. 9.

13 *Pravda*, June 3, 1986, p. 6, and June 15, 1986, p. 6.

14 *Le monde*, May 13, 1986, p. 48.

15 *Pravda*, June 15, 1986.

16 According to the *Guardian Weekly* (May 11, 1986, p. 6), the British Foreign Ministry was not told anything was unusual until Monday, more than two full days after the accident.

17 *Izvestia*, May 9, 1986, p. 6.

18 *Tygodnik Mazowsze*, no. 169, May 8, 1986, as translated in RFE Polish Underground Extracts 8/86, p. 17.

19 Reported in the *Guardian Weekly*, May 18, 1986, p. 2.

20 The proceedings were recorded on tape, and the author was shown an informal transcript.

21 Much of the following has been derived from personal interviews by the author, who prefers not to name the individuals.

22 The protest statement along with an article on the costs and dangers of expanding the nuclear power industry in Yugoslavia were published in *Mladina*, no. 18, May 18, 1986, pp. 14–17. A brief Western report on the demonstration may be found in *Le monde*, May 13, 1986, p. 9.

23 *NIN*, p. 14.

24 Western commentators writing in *Newsweek* and elsewhere have expressed the same thought. Veronique Maurus comments, "One can imagine the consequences of a similar disaster in countries like Egypt, Turkey or Pakistan." "Nuages sur le nucléaire" (Clouds over Nuclear Energy), *Le monde*, May 20, 1986, p. 15.

25 Dusan Čkrebić, "Atomizirana ekonomija" (The Atomized Economy), *NIN*, no. 1845, May 11, 1986, pp. 14–15.

Selected Bibliography

Government Documents

Belgrade. Municipal Institute for Public Health. *Ishrana dece u jazlama, vrtičima i skolama* (The nutrition of children in creches, kindergartens and schools). Belgrade: Municipal Institute for Public Health, 1980.

Canada. Environment Canada. Atmospheric Environment Service. *Extended Abstracts: Third Symposium on Arctic Air Chemistry.* Downsview, Ontario: Atmospheric Environment Service, 1984.

ČSR and SSR. Environmental Council of the Government of CSR in cooperation with the Government of the SSR. *Environmental Education in Czechoslovakia: Guidelines in Methodology.* Prague: Research Institute of Building and Architecture, 1977.

ČSR. Rada pro životní prostředi při vládě ČSR. (Council on the Environment of the ČSR Government.) *Analýza současného stavu péče o životni prostředí v ČSR. Informační publikáce 4.7.1977* (Analysis of the present status of environmental protection in the ČSR. Information publication 4/7/1977). Prague: Rada pro životní prostředí při vládě ČSR and Secretariat ČSAV, 1977.

————. *Informačni zpravodaj: Nove zakony v SSSR k peče o životni prostředí* (Information bulletin: The new laws in the USSR on environmental protection). Prague: Rada pro životni prostředí ve Státním zemědělském nakladatelství, 1980.

————. *Mimoškolní výchova k péči o životní prostředí, I dil, Základy a současný stav výchovy. Informační publikáce 3.10.1980* (Extracurricular education in environmental protection, pt. 1, The foundations and current status of education. Information publication 3/10/1980). Prague: Rada pro životní prostředí pri vládě ČSR, 1980.

————. *Nekteré otázky doprava a motorismus ve vztahu k životnímu prostředí. Informační publikáce 6.2.1976* (Some questions of transportation and motorism in relation to the environment. Information publication 6/2/1976). Prague: Rada pro životní prostředí pri vládě ČSR, 1976.

————. *Recreace v Krajině, I dil, Základní vztahy; 2 dil, Specifické otázky rekreace. Informačni publikáce 2.11 i 3.11.1981.* (Recreation in the countryside, pt. I, Basic relationships; pt. 2, Specific tasks of recreation. Information Publications 2/11 and 3/11/1981). Prague: Státní zemědělskí nakladatelství, 1981.

————. *Studijni podklady k péči o životni prostředí* (Research foundations of environmental protection), vols. 1, 2, and 3. Prague: Státní zemědělskí nakladatelství, 1981.

407

————. *Úloha krajiny a územního plánování v životním prostředí. Informační publikáce 1.9.1979* (The task of the countryside and territorial planning on the environment. Information publication 1/9/1979). Prague: Státní zemědělskí nakladatelství, 1979.

————. *Vědeckotechnický pokrok, investiční výstava a životní prostředí. Informační publikáce 4.9.1979* (Scientific technological progress, investment policy and the environment. Information Publication 4/9/1979). Prague: Rada pro životní prostředí při vládě ČSR, 1980.

————. *Význam vody v životním prostředí. Informační publikáce 5.10.1980* (The significance of water in the environment. Information Publication 5/10/1980). Prague: Rada pro životní prostředí při vládě ČSR, 1980.

CSR, Environmental Council and SSR, Environmental Council. *Legal Regulation of the Human Environment in the Czechoslovak Socialist Republic.* Prague: Ministry for Construction and Technology, 1973.

————. *Ústava Československé socialistické republiky* (Constitution of the ČSR). Prague: Mlada fronta, 1960.

France. Collection "Environnement." *Evaluation de l'environnement, recueil de textes* (Evaluation of the environment: Collection of texts). Paris: La Documentation Française, 1973.

Japan. Environment Agency. *Environmental Law and Regulations in Japan, Vols. 1-5.* Tokyo: Environment Agency, 1980.

————. *Quality of the Environment in Japan.* Tokyo: Environment Agency, 1978.

————. *Quality of the Environment in Japan.* Tokyo: Environment Agency, 1979.

Leningrad. Gorodskoi soviet. Ispolnitel'nyi komitet. *Bulletin'* (Bulletin of the Executive Committee of the Municipal Soviet of Leningrad). Leningrad: Ispolnitel'nyi komitet Leningradskogo gorodoskogo sovieta, 1960-1980.

Moscow. Gorodskoi soviet. Ispolnitel'nyi komitet. *Bulletin'* (Bulletin of the Executive Committee of the Moscow Municipal Soviet). Moscow: Ispolnitel'nyi komitet Moskovskogo gorodoskogo sovieta, 1960-1970.

New York State. Legislature. Commission on Energy Systems. *Legislating for Energy Independence.* Albany, N.Y.: New York State Legislative Commission on Energy Systems, September 1978.

Nolting, Louvan E. *The Planning of Research, Development and Innovation in the USSR.* Foreign Economic Report No. 14, United States Department of Commerce, Bureau of the Census. Washington, D.C.: U.S. Government Printing Office, July 1978.

————. *The Structure and Functions of the USSR State Committee for Science and Technology.* Foreign Economic Report No. 19, United States Department of Commerce, Bureau of the Census. Washington, D.C.: U.S. Government Printing Office, December 1979.

————. and Feshbach, Murray. *Statistics on Research and Development Employment in the USSR.* International Population Reports, Series P-95, No. 76, United States Department of Commerce, Bureau of the Census, Foreign Demographic Analysis Division. Washington, D.C.: U.S. Government Printing Office, 1981.

OECD. *Perspectives énergétiques mondiales* (World energy prospects). Paris: OECD, 1977.

Prievidza. Okresny narodny vybor-odbor kultury, Okresna pamiakova sprava. *XV tabor okhrancov prirody: Prehlad odbornych vysledkov* (Fifteenth camp of the defenders of nature: Overview of special results). Prievidza: Okresny narodny vobor, 1980.

RSFSR. Ministerstvo iustitsii. *Lesnoi kodeks RSFSR* (The forest code of the RSFSR). Moscow: Iuridicheskaia literatura, 1980.

————. *Ugolovnyi kodeks RSFSR s izmeneniami i dopolneniami po 1 janvaria 1978 g* (Criminal code of the RSFSR with the changes and additions of January 1, 1978). Moscow: Iuridicheskaia literatura, 1978.

————. *Ugolovnyi kodeks RSFSR; Ugolovno-protsessual'nyi kodeks RSFSR; Ispravitel'ni-trudavoi kodeks RSFSR* (Criminal code of the RSFSR; Criminal trial code of the RSFSR; Correctional labor code of the RSFSR). Moscow: Izdatel'stvo "Iuridicheskaia literatura" (Legal Literature Publishing House), 1979.

RSFSR. Ministerstvo vysshego i srednego spetsial'nogo obrazovania. *Sotsial'no-ekonomicheskie problemy prirodopol'zovania* (Social economic problems of natural resource use). Leningrad: Izdatel'stvo Leningradskogo universiteta, 1978.

————. Tsentral'noe statisticheskoe upravlenie. *Narodnoe khozaistvo RSFSR v 1979 g.: Statisticheskii ezhegodnik* (National economy of the RSFSR in 1979: Statistical yearbook). Moscow: "Statistika," 1980.

————. *RSFSR v tsifrakh v 1979 godu; kratkii statisticheskii sbornik* (The RSFSR in figures for 1979: Short statistical collection). Moscow: "Statistika," 1980.

————. *RSFSR v tsifrakh v 1980 godu; kratkii statisticheskii sbornik* (The RSFSR in figures in 1980: Short statistical handbook). Moscow: "Financy i statistika," 1981.

————. *Narodnoe khozaistvo RSFSR v 1984 g.* (National economy of the RSFSR in 1984). Moscow: "Financy i statistika," 1985.

RSFSR. Verkhovnyi Soviet. *Konstitutsia Rossiiskoi sovetskoi federativnoi sotsialisticheskoi respubliki* (Constitution of the Russian Soviet Federated Socialist Republic). Moscow: Izdatel'stvo Izvestia Sovietov narodnykh deputatov SSSR, 1978.

SEV (Soviet ekonomicheskoi vsaimopomoshchi). Sekretariat. *Statisticheskii ezhegodnik stran-chlenov Soveta ekonomicheskoi vzaimopomoshchi* (Statistical yearbook of the member states of CMEA). Moscow: Izdatel'stvo "Statistika," 1980.

SFRJ. Pavičić, Marko, transl. *The Constitution of the Socialist Federal Republic of Yugoslavia.* Belgrade: Delo, 1974.

————. Assembly. *Outline of a Common Policy for Long-Term Development in Yugoslavia until 1985.* Belgrade: Yugoslav Survey, 1975.

————. *The Associated Labour Act.* Novy Sad: Prosveta, 1977.

SFRJ. Federal Committee of Information. *Social Plan of Yugoslavia 1976–1980.* Belgrade: Jugoslovenska stvarnost, 1976.

SFRJ. Federal Institute of Public Health. *The Public Health Service in Yugoslavia.* Belgrade: Beogradski izdavačko-grafički zavod, 1975.

————. Federal Statistical Office. *Statistical Pocket-book of Yugoslavia 1979.* Belgrade: Federal Statistical Office, 1979.

————. *Statistical Pocket-book of Yugoslavia 1980.* Belgrade: Federal Statistical Office, 1980.

————. *Statistical Pocket-book of Yugoslavia 1985.* Belgrade: Federal Statistical Office, 1985.

SFRJ. Savezni zavod za medjunarondnu naučnu, prosvetno-kulturno i tehničku saradnju i Koordinacioni odbor za čovekovu sredinu prostorno uredjenje i stambene i komunalne poslove SIV-a izvršnih veća socijalističkih republika i socijalističkih autonomnih pokrajina. *Nacionalni izveštaj: "Stanje i politika čovekove sredine u SFR Jugoslaviji"* (National report: "Environmental status and policies in the SFR Yugoslavia). Belgrade: Servis za birotehnicke poslove saveznih organa uprave i saveznih organizacija, 1985.

SFRJ. Savezno izvršno veće i izvršna veća republika i pokrajina. Savet za čovekovu sredinu i postorno uredjenje. *Čovekova sredina i prostorno uredjenje u Jugoslaviji: Pregled stanja* (The environment and land use in Yugoslavia: An overview of their status). Belgrade: OOUR Izdavačka delatnost, 1978.

————. Standing Conference of Towns and Communes. *The Yugoslav Commune.* Belgrade: Stalna konferencija gradova Jugoslavije, 1980.

————. *Membership-Organization Activities.* Belgrade: Stalna konferencija gradova Jugoslavije, 1965.

SR Srbije. Mladi istraživači. Republička konferencija. *Statut mladih istraživača Srbije* (Statutes of the young researchers of Serbia). Belgrade: Istrazivačko-izdavački centar SSO Srbije, 1980.

————. Pokret Gorana, Republička konferencija. *15 Godina: Izvestaj o radu Pokreta Gorana Srbije* (15th Anniversary: Report on the work of the Gorani Movement of Serbia). Belgrade: Stampa "Grafika" Prokuplje, 1976.

————. Republički zavod za zaštitu prirode. *Neka pitanja nacionalnih i regionalnih prirodnih parkova u Jugoslaviji.* Posebna izdanja, Knj.11. (Some questions about the national and regional parks in Yugoslavia. Special Edition, Book 11). Belgrade: Republički zavod za zaštitu prirode SR Srbije, 1978.

SSSR. Central Statistical Administration. *USSR in Figures 1979: Statistical Handbook.* Moscow: Central Statistical Administration, 1979.

————. Glavnoe upravlenie gidrometeorologicheskoi sluzhby pri Soviete ministrov SSSR. *Vsestoronnii analiz okryzhaiushchei prirodnoi sredy. Trudy II Sovietsko-amerikanskogo simpoziuma, Gonolulu, Gawaii, 20–26 X 1975* (Comprehensive analysis of the environment: Proceedings of the 2d Soviet-American symposium, Honolulu, Hawaii, October 20–26, 1975). Leningrad: Gidrometeoizdat, 1976.

————. Ministerstva sel'skogo khozaistva, Glavnoe upravlenie po okhrane prirody. *Zapovedniki Sovietskogo soiuza: Kratkii spravochnik* (Nature reserves of the Soviet Union). Moscow: Izdatel'stvo Lesnaia promyshlennost', 1977.

————. Ministerstvo prosveshchenia and vysshego i srednego obrazovanii. *Programma dla srednei obshcheobrazovatel'noi shkoly i srednikh spetsial'nykh ycebnykh zavedenii* (Program for the secondary general education school and secondary specialized training institutions). Moscow: Izdatel'stvo Politicheskoi literatury, 1985.

————. Ministerstvo sel'skogo khozaistva. Glavnie upravlenie zemlepol'zovania i zemleustroistva. *Polozhenie o poriadke peredachi rekul'tivirovannykh zemel'* (Proposition on the procedure for the transfer of recultivated lands). Moscow: "Kolos," 1978.

――――. Ministerstvo zdravookhranenia i Gosudarstvennyi komitet po gidrometeorologii i kontroliu prirodnoi sredy. *Rukovodstvo po kontroliu zagraznenia atmoshery* (Guide to the control of atmospheric pollution). Leningrad: Gidrometeoizdat, 1979.

――――. Prezidium verkhnogo sovieta Soiuza sovietskikh sotsialisticheskikh respublik. *SSSR: Administrativno-territorial'noe delenie soiuznykh respublik* (The USSR: Administrative territorial division of the union republics). Moscow: Izdatel'stvo Izvestiia sovietov narodnykh deputatov SSSR, 1980.

――――. Soviet ministrov. Gosudarstvennyi arbitrazh. *Pravila rassmotrenia khozaistvennykh sporov gosudarstvennymi arbitrazhami* (Rules for the consideration of economic disputes by state arbitration). Moscow: Izdatel'stvo "Iuridicheskaia literatura," 1978.

――――. Supreme Soviet. *Labour Legislation in the USSR*. Moscow: Novosti Press Agency Publishing House, 1971.

――――. Supreme Soviet. *The Rights of Factory and Office Trade Union Committees*. Moscow: Novosti Press Agency Publishing House, 1971.

――――. Tsentral'noe statisticheskoe upravlenie. *Narodnoe khozaistvo SSSR v 1978 g: Statisticheskii ezhegodnik* (National economy of the USSR in 1978: Statistical yearbook). Moscow: Izdatel'stvo "Statistika," 1979.

――――. *SSSR v tsifrakh v 1980 godu; kratkii statisticheskii sbornik* (The USSR in figures in 1980; A short statistical collection). Moscow: "Financy i statistika," 1981.

――――. TsSU i TsSU soiuznykh respublik. *SSSR i soiuznye respubliki v 1979 godu* (The USSR and the Union Republics in 1979). Moscow: "Statistika," 1980.

――――. Verkhovnyi soviet. *Konstitutsia (Osnovnoi zakon) Soiuza sovietskikh sotsialisticheskikh respublik* [Constitution (Fundamental Law) of the Union of Soviet Socialist Republics]. Moscow: Izdatel'stvo "Iuridicheskaia literatura," 1978.

――――. *Zakon SSSR ob okhrane atmosfernogo vozdukha* (Law of the USSR on the protection of atmospheric air). Moscow: Izdatel'stvo Izvestia Sovietov narodnykh deputatov SSSR, 1980.

――――. *Zakon SSSR ob okhrane i ispol'zovanii zhivotnogo mira* (USSR Law on the protection and use of the animal world). Moscow: Izdatel'stvo Izvestia Sovietov narodnykh deputatov SSSR, 1980.

Tokyo. Metropolitan Government. Bureau of General Affairs. Liaison and Protocol Section, ed. *Tokyo Fights Pollution*. Rev. ed. Tokyo: Tokyo Metropolitan Government, 1977.

United Nations. World Health Organization. Lopez, A. D. and Cliquet, R. L., eds. *Demographic Trends in the European Region: Health and Social Implication*. Copenhagen: World Health Organization Regional Publications, European Series No. 17, 1984.

――――. World Health Organization. *Estimating Human Exposure to Air Pollutants*. Geneva: World Health Organization, 1982.

USA. Environmental Protection Agency. Office of Water. *Primer for Wastewater Treatment*. Washington, D.C.: U.S. Environmental Protection Agency, July 1980.

411

————. Environmental Protection Agency. *EPA Noise Control Program, Progress to Date*. Washington, D.C.: U.S. Environmental Protection Agency, March 1978.

————. *The Noise Control Act of 1972 as Amended by the Quiet Communities Act.* Washington, D.C.: U.S. Environmental Protection Agency, December 1978.

————. *First USSR/USA Symposium on "Economic Aspects of Environmental Protection."* Washington, D.C.: U.S. Government Printing Office, 1977.

USA. House of Representatives. Committee on Science and Technology, y 4. Sci 2:97/118. *Hearings: U.S. Science and Technology under Budgetary Stress.* Washington, D.C.: U.S. Government Printing Office, 1982.

USSR. Tsentral'ne statistichne upravlenia. *Ukrainskaia SSR v tsifrakh u 1979 godu: kratkii statistichnii spravochnik* (The Ukrainian SSR in figures in 1979: Short statistical handbook). Kiev: "Tekhnika," 1980.

Vojvodina. Novi Sad. Turistički savez. Predsednistva PK SSRNV. Savet za zaštitu i unapredjivanje čovekove sredine. *Akcija "Ulepšajmo mesnu zajednicu" u povodu 25-godišnjice turističke društvene organizacije Vojvodine* (Action "Let's improve our community": for the 25th anniversary of the tourist social organization in the Vojvodina). Novi Sad: Turistički Savez Vojvodina, February 1979.

————. Novi Sad. Predsednistva PK SSRNV. Savet za zaštitu i unapredjivanje čovekove sredine. *Estetsko i higejensko uredjivanje vaspitno-obrazovnih organizacija i njihove sredine* (The esthetic and hygienic management of educational-cultural organizations and their environment). Novi Sad: Savet za zaštitu i unapredjivanje čovekove sredine, June 1980.

Vojvodine, SAP. *Osnove koncepcije dugoročnog razvoja SAP Vojvodine do 1985 god.* (Basic conception of the long-term development of the socialist autonomous province of Vojvodina until 1985). Novi Sad: Skupština Socijalističke Autonomne Pokrajine Vojvodine, December 1975.

Communist Party Documents

ČSSR. Komunistička strana Československá, Ústřední výbor. Vlada ČSSR. *Ke zdokonaleni plánovitého řízení národního hospodářství po roce 1980: Sborník dokumentů a materiálů* (On the improvement of the planned management of the national economy after 1980: Collection of documents and materials). Prague: Nakladatelství Svoboda, 1980.

————. KSČ. *Dokumenty i materiali zarubezhnykh kommunisticheskikh i rabochikh partii: XV s'ezd Kommunisticheskoi partii Chekhoslovakii, Praga, 12–16 apr 1976* (Documents and Materials of the Foreign Communist and Workers Parties: The Fifteenth Congress of the Communist Party of Czechoslovakia, Prague, April 12–16, 1976). Moscow: Izdatel'stvo "Politicheskoi literatury," 1977.

————. KŠC. *XV s'ezd Komunisticheskoi partii Chekhoslovakii* (15th Congress of the Communist Party of Czechoslovakia). Moscow: Izdatel'stvo "Politicheskoi literatury," 1977.

————. XVI Sjezd KSČ. *Komplexní program dalšího prohlubování a zdokonalování spolupráce a rozvoje socialistické ekonomické integrace členských států RVHP* (Comprehensive program for the future deepening and improvement of cooperation and the development of socialist economic integration of the member states of CMEA). Prague: Nakladatelsví Svoboda, 1973.

———. *Sborník hlavních dokumentu XVI sjezdu Komunističké strany Československa* (Collection of principal documents of the 16th Congress of the Communist Party of Czechoslovakia 6–10 April, 1981). Prague: Nakladatelství Svoboda, 1981.

SFRY. Eleventh Congress of the League of Communists of Yugoslavia. *The League of Communists of Yugoslavia between the 10th and 11th Congress.* Belgrade: STP, 1978.

———. SKJ. *12 Kongres Saveza komunista Jugoslavije, referat, rezoljucije, statut, završna reč* (The 12th Congress of the League of Communists of Yugoslavia, speeches, resolutions, statutes). Belgrade: Centar Komunist, 1982.

SSSR. CPSU. M. C. Gorbachev. *Politicheskii doklad Tsentral'nogo komiteta KPSS, XXVII S'iezdu Kommunisticheskoi partii Sovietskogo soiuza* (Political speech of the CPSU Central Committee, 27th Congress of the Communist party of the Soviet Union). Moscow: Izdatel'stvo "Politicheskoi literatury," 1986.

———. KPSS. *Programma Kommunisticheskoi partii Sovietskogo soiuza* (Program of the Communist party of the Soviet Union). Moscow: Izdatel'stvo "Politicheskoi literatury," 1986.

———. KPSS. XXVII S'ezd. *Proekt: Osnovnye napravlenia ekonomicheskogo i sotsial' nogo razvitia SSSR na 1986–1990 gody i na period do 2000 goda* (Draft: Guidelines for the economic and social development of the USSR for 1986–1990 and up to the year 2000). Moscow: Izdatel'stvo "Pravda," 1985.

———. KPSS. *Materialy plenuma Tzentral'nogo komiteta KPSS, 15 oktiabra 1985 goda* (Material of the KPSS Central Committee Plenum, October 15, 1985). Moscow: Izdatel'stvo "Politicheskoi literatury," 1985.

———. KPSS. *Materialy XXVII S'ezda Kommunisticheskoi partii Sovietskogo soiuza* (Materials of the 27th Congress of the Communist Party of the Soviet Union). Moscow: Izdatel'stvo "Politicheskoi literatury," 1986.

———. KPSS. *XXVI Sjezd KSSS: Dokumenty a materiály, 23 unora–3 brezna 1981* (The 26th Congress of the CPSU: Documents and materials, February 23–March 3, 1981). Prague: Nakladatelství Svoboda, 1981.

———. KPSS. *Ustav Kommunisticheskoi partii Sovietskogo soiuza* (Constitution of the Communist Party of the Soviet Union). Moscow: Politizdat, 1980.

SSSR. KPSS. XXVI S'ezd. *Osnovnye napravlenia ekonomicheskogo i sotsial'nogo razvitia SSSR na 1981–1986 gody i na period do 1990 goda* (Guidelines for the economic and social development of the USSR for 1981–1986 and for the period up to 1990). Moscow: Politizdat, 1981.

Selected Books

Adams, Arthur E.; Matley, Ian M.; and McCagg, William O. *An Atlas of Russian and East European History.* New York: Praeger, 1967.

413

Afanasev, V. F., and editorial group. *Upravlenie sotsialisticheskogo vosproizvodstva* (The administration of socialist production). 3d ed. Moscow: "Ekonomika," 1978.

Aleeva, A. M., and Kurok, M. L. *V Seminarakh po problemam ekologii* (Seminars on environmental problems). Moscow: Moskovskii rabochii (Moscow worker), 1980.

Almond, Gabriel A., and Powell, G. Bingham Jr. *Comparative Politics: A Developmental Approach.* Boston and Toronto: Little, Brown, 1966.

Ananichev, K. *Environment: International Aspects.* Moscow: Progress, 1976.

Anderson, R. J. Jr.; Reid, R. O.; and Siskin, E. P. *An Analysis of Alternative Policies for Attaining and Maintaining a Short-Term NO2 Standard.* Princeton, N.J.: Mathtech, 1979.

Anderson, Terry L., ed. *Water Rights: Scarce Resource Allocation, Bureaucracy, and the Environment.* Cambridge, Mass.: Pacific Institute for Public Policy Research, Ballinger, 1983.

Andreev, S. I. *Effektivnost'funktsionirovania osnovnykh fondov* (The efficiency of the functioning of the basic funds). Moscow: "Ekonomika," 1980.

ANSSSR. Institut ekonomiki mirovoi sotsialisticheskoi sistemy. *Narodnoe khozaistvo sotsialisticheskikh stran v 1979 godu* (The national economy of the socialist countries in 1979. Communication of the statistical administration). Moscow: "Statistika," 1980.

―――――. Institut filosofii, A. V. Katsura, ed.-in-chief. *Chelovek i priroda* (Man and nature). Moscow: Izdatel'stvo "Nauka," 1980.

―――――. Institute of Economics and Industrial Organization of the Academy of Sciences. *Territorial Industrial Complexes: Optimization Models and General Aspects.* Trans. H. Campbell Creighton. Moscow: Progress, 1980.

―――――. Institut sotsiologicheskikh issledovanii, Leningradskii financovo-ekonomicheskii institut. *Planirovanie sotsial'nogo razvitia gorodov* (The planning of urban social development). Moscow: Institut sotsiologicheskikh issledovanii, 1973.

―――――. Leningradskii finansovo-ekonomicheskii institut. Institut sotsialisticheskikh issledovanii. *Perspektivnye problemy sotsial'nogo razvitia monopromyshlennogo goroda* (Future problems of social development of a single industry city). Moscow: ANSSSR, Institut sotsiologicheskikh issledovanii, 1973.

―――――. Nauchnyi soviet po problemam biosfery. Institut geografii. *Ekonomicheskaia i vneekonomicheskaia otsenka vozdeistvia cheloveka na okruzhaiushchuiu sredu* (Economic and noneconomic evaluation of the influence of man on the environment). Moscow: Izdatel'stvo "Nauka," 1981.

―――――. Nauchnyi soviet po effektivnosti osnovnykh fondov. Institut ekonomiki. *Metody i praktika opredelenia effektivnosti kapital'nykh vlozhenii i novoi tekhniki: Sbornik nauchnoi informatsii, Vypusk 31* (The methods and practice of determining the efficiency of capital investment and new technology: Collection of scientific information, No. 31). Moscow: Izdatel'stvo "Nauka," No. 31 Sbornik naychnoi informatsii, 1980.

―――――. TSEMI. *Economic Evaluation and the Rational Use of Natural Resources.* Moscow: USSR Academy of Sciences, 1972.

414

Apostolski, Mihaylo, principal ed. *A History of the Macedonian People*. Trans. from Macedonian by Graham W. Reid. Skopje: Macedonian Review Editions, 1979.

Arab-Ogly, E. A. *Demograficheskie i ekologicheskie prognozy: Kritika sovremennykh burzhuaznykh kontseptsii* (Demographic and ecological forecasts: Critical survey of modern bourgeois conceptions). Moscow: "Statistika," 1978.

Arrow, Kenneth J. *The Limits of Organization*. New York: W. W. Norton, 1974.

Artsybashev, E. S. *Lesnye pozhary i bor'ba s nimi* (Forest fires and the struggle with them). Moscow: Izdatel'stvo "Lesnaia promyshlennost'," 1974.

Authors' Collective. *Spoločnost a životne prostredie* (Society and the environment). Bratislava: Priroda, 1978.

Axelrod, Regina S., ed. *Environment, Energy, Public Policy: Toward a Rational Future*. Lexington, Mass.: Lexington Books, 1981.

Baden, John, and Stroup, Richard L., eds. *Bureaucracy vs. Environment: The Environmental Costs of Bureaucratic Government*. Ann Arbor: University of Michigan Press, 1981.

Baibakov, N. K. *O gosudarstvennom plane ekonomicheskogo i sotsial'nogo razvitia SSSR na 1981–1985 gody, gosudarstvennom plane ekonomcheskogo i sotsial'nogo razvitia SSSR na 1982 god i k hode vypolnenia plana v 1981 godu* (On the state plan for the economic and social development of the USSR for 1981–1985, the state plan for 1982, and report on the progress on the development of the plan in 1981). Moscow: Politizdat, 1981.

Baisalov, S. B., and Iliashenko, L. E. *Pravo i okhrana prirody* (Law and nature protection). Alma-Ata: Izdatel'stvo "Nauka," 1976.

Baisetov, R. C., and Andreev, A. K. *Ekonomika i budzhet Sovietskogo Kazakhstana* (Economics and the budget of Soviet Kazakhstan). Alma-Ata: "Kazakhstan," 1984.

Balezin, V. P. *Pravovoi rezhim zemel' naselennykh punktov* (The legal regimen for land in populated areas). Moscow: Izdatel'stvo "Iuridicheskaia literatura," 1980.

Bannikov, A. G., ed., and Kozlovskii, V. B., compiler. *Zapovedniki Sovietskogo soiuza* (Zapovedniki of the Soviet Union). Moscow: "Kolos," 1969.

Barabanov, V. F. *Nauchno-tekhnicheskaia revolutsia i sud'ba prirody* (The Scientific Technological Revolution and the Fate of Nature). Leningrad: Obshchestvo Znanie RSFSR, (Society "Knowledge" of the RSFSR), 1979.

_____ and Collective, eds. *Nauchno-tekhnicheskaia revolutsia, chelovek, ego prirodnaia i sotsialnaia sreda* (The scientific technological revolution, man, his natural and social environment). Leningrad: Izdatel'stvo Leningradskogo universiteta, 1977.

Bardach, Eugene. *The Implementation Game: What Happens after a Bill Becomes a Law*. Cambridge, Mass.: MIT Press, 1977.

Barney, Gerald O., Study Director. *The Global 2000 Report to the President of the United States, Vol. I*. New York: Pergamon, 1980.

Bartkowski, Tadeusz. *Ksztaltowanie i ochrona srodowiska* (Modeling and Environmental Protection). Warsaw: Panstwowe Wydawnictwo Naukowe, 1981.

Baykov, Alexander. *The Development of the Soviet Economic System*. Cambridge: Cambridge University Press, 1950.

Bednyi, M. C. *Demograficheskie factory zdorov'ia* (The demographic factors of health). Moscow: "Financy i statistika," 1984.

Beliaeva, Z. S., Kolbasov, O. S., Slavin, M. M. *Pravo i okhrana prirody* (Law and the protection of nature). Moscow: ANSSSR, Institut gosudarstva i prava, 1979.

Benveniste, Guy. *Bureaucracy*. San Francisco: Boyd and Fraser, 1977.

————. *The Politics of Expertise*. 2d. ed. San Francisco: Boyd and Fraser, 1977.

Berezin, Vladimir. *Cooperation between CMEA and Developing Countries*. Moscow: Novosti Press Agency Publishing House, 1979.

Bergson, Abram, and Levine, Herbert S. *The Soviet Economy: Toward the Year 2000*. London: George Allen & Unwin, 1983.

Bertsch, Gary K. *Nation-Building in Yugoslavia: A Study of Political Integration and Attitudinal Consensus*. Beverly Hills, Calif.: Sage Publications, 1971.

————. *Value Change and Political Community: The Multinational Czechoslovakia*. Beverly Hills, Calif.: Sage Publications, 1974.

Bialer, Seweryn, and Gustafson, Thane, eds. *Russia at the Crossroads: The 26th Congress of the CPSU*. London: George Allen & Unwin, 1982.

Blandon, Peter. *Soviet Forest Industries*. Boulder, Colo.: Westview, 1983.

Blinov, V. M., ed. *Sbornik normativnykh aktov po okhrane prirody* (Collection of normative acts on environmental protection). Moscow: "Iuridicheskaia literatura," 1978.

Boffey, Phillip M. *The Brain Bank of America: An Inquiry into the Politics of Science*. New York: McGraw-Hill, 1975.

Böhm, Antonin, and Madar, Zdeněk. *Cestovní ruch a životní prostředí* (Tourism and the environment). Prague: Merkur, 1980.

Boyle, Godfrey; Elliott, David; and Roy, Robin. *The Politics of Technology*. London: Longman Group, in association with Open University Press, 1977.

Brown, Lester R. *The Twenty-Ninth Day: Accommodating Human Needs And Numbers to the Earth's Resources*. New York: W. W. Norton, 1978.

Brubaker, Sterling, ed. *Rethinking the Federal Lands*. Washington, D.C.: Resources for the Future, Johns Hopkins University Press, 1984.

Burg, Steven L. *Conflict and Cohesion in Socialist Yugoslavia: Political Decision Making Since 1966*. Princeton: Princeton University Press, 1983.

Burger, Edward J. Jr. *Science at the White House: A Political Liability*. Baltimore: Johns Hopkins University Press, 1980.

Butakov, D. D., ed., Ministerstva financov SSSR. *Mestnye budzhety stran-chlenov SEV*. (Local Budgets of the Member Countries of CEMA). Moscow: "Financy," 1980.

Bystrova, A. K. *Ekologia i kapitalisticheskii gorod*. (Ecology and the capitalist city). Moscow: Izdatel'stvo "Nauka," 1980.

Campbell, Robert W. *The Soviet-type Economies: Performance and Evolution* 3d ed. Boston: Houghton Mifflin, 1974.

Capra, Fritjof, and Spretnak, Charlene. *Green Politics*. New York: E. P. Dutton, 1984.

Carter, April. *Democratic Reform in Yugoslavia: The Changing Role of the Party*. Princeton: Princeton University Press, 1982.

416

Cave, Martin; McAuley, Alastair; and Thornton, Judith, eds. *New Trends in Soviet Economics.* Armonk, N.Y.: M. E. Sharpe, 1982.

Cerný, Borivoj V. *Úvod do podnikového hospodářství v odboru cestovního ruchu* (Introduction to enterprise economics in the tourism sector). Prague: Orbis, 1948.

Cherevik, E., and Shvyrkov, Y. *An ABC of Planning.* Trans. from the Russian by Peter Greenwood. Moscow: Progress, 1982.

Chistobaev, A. I. *Razvitie ekonomicheskikh raionov: Teoria i metody issledovania* (The development of the economic regions: Theory and research methods). Leningrad: Leningradskoie otdeleniia Nauk, 1980.

Clark, Cal, and Johnson, Karl F. *Development's Influence on Yugoslav Political Values.* Beverly Hills, Calif.: Sage Publications, 1976.

Clawson, Marion. *The Federal Lands Revisited.* Washington, D.C.: Resources for the Future, Johns Hopkins University Press, 1983.

Clemens, Walter C. Jr. *The USSR and Global Interdependence: Alternative Futures.* Washington, D.C.: American Enterprise Institute for Public Policy Research, 1978.

Cobb, Roger W., and Elder, Charles D. *Participation in American Politics: The Dynamics of Agenda-Building.* Baltimore: Johns Hopkins University Press, 1972.

Cockburn, Andrew. *The Threat: Inside the Soviet Military Machine.* New York: Vintage Books, 1984.

Cocks, Paul; Daniels, Robert V.; and Herr, Nancy Whittier, eds. *The Dynamics of Soviet Politics.* Cambridge, Mass.: Harvard University Press, 1976.

Cohen, Leonard. *Political Cohesion in a Fragile Mosaic: the Yugoslav Experiment.* Boulder, Colo.: Westview, 1983.

Cohen-Tanugi, Laurent. *Le droit sans l'état: Sur la démocratie en France et en Amérique* (Law without the state: On democracy in France and America). Preface by Stanley Hofmann. Paris: Presses Universitaires de France, 1985.

Colton, Timothy J. *The Dilemma of Reform in the Soviet Union.* New York: Council on Foreign Relations, 1984.

Cross, John G., and Guyer, Melvin J. *Social Traps.* Ann Arbor: University of Michigan Press, 1980.

Crozier, Michel. *La Societé Bloquée* (The blocked society). Rev. ed. Paris: Éditions du Seuil, 1984.

————. *The Bureaucratic Phenomenon.* Chicago: University of Chicago Press, 1964.

————, and Friedburg, Erhard. *L'Acteur et le système: les contraintes de l'action collective* (The actor and the system: The constraints of collective action). Paris: Éditions du Seuil, 1977.

Culhane, Paul J. *Public Lands Politics: Interest Group Influence on the Forest Service and the Bureau of Land Management.* Baltimore and London: Johns Hopkins University Press, 1981.

Dadayan, V. S. *Ocherki o nashei ekonomike* (Outline of our economy). Moscow: Izdatel'stvo "Znanie," 1974.

Daneke, Gregory A., ed. *Energy, Economics, and the Environment: Toward a Comprehensive Perspective.* Lexington, Mass.: Lexington Books, 1982.

Danilova, E. Z. Sotsial'nyie problemy truda zenshchiny-rabotnitsy (Trud zhenshchiny-

417

rabotnisty i materinstvo) (Social problems of the work of the woman workers [the woman-worker's work and maternity]). Moscow: Izdatel'stvo "Mysl'," 1968.

Danilova, N. A. *Klimat i otdykh v nashei strane. Evropeiskii chast' SSSR. Kavkaz* (Climate and Relaxation in Our Country: The European Part of the USSR, The Caucasus). Moscow: Izdatel'stvo "Mysl'," (Thought), 1980.

d'Encausse, Hélène Carrère. *Decline of an Empire: The Soviet Socialist Republics in Revolt.* Trans. Martin Sokolinsky and Henry A. la Farge. New York: Harper Colophon Books, 1981.

———. *Le grand frère: l'Union soviétique et l'Europe soviétisée* (Big Brother: The Soviet Union and Sovietized Europe). Paris: Flammarion, 1983.

———. *Le pouvoir confisqué: gouvernants et gouvernés en U.R.S.S.* (Confiscated power: Governors and governed in the USSR). Paris: Flammarion, 1980.

Denitch, Bogdan Denis. *The Legitimation of a Revolution: The Yugoslav Case.* New Haven and London: Yale University Press, 1976.

Desai, Padma, ed. *Marxism, Central Planning, and the Soviet Economy.* Cambridge, Mass.: MIT Press, 1983.

Djordjević, Vladimir, et al. *Zaštita i unapredjivanje životne sredine za III razred hemijsko-tehničkog smera i IV razred biotehničkog smera prirodno-tehničke struke usmernog obrazovanje* (The protection and improvement of the environment for the third class of the chemical-technical direction and the fourth class of the biotechnical direction of nature-technical field of structured education). Belgrade: Naučna Knjiga, 1979.

Dorfman, Robert, and Dorfman, Nancy S., eds. *Economics of the Environment, Selected Readings,* 2d ed. New York: W. W. Norton, 1977.

Downing, Paul B. *Environmental Economics and Policy.* Boston: Little, Brown, 1984.

Duderstadt, James J., and Kikuchi, Chihiro. *Nuclear Power: Technology on Trial.* Ann Arbor: University of Michigan Press, 1979.

Duncan, W. Raymond, ed. *Soviet Policy in the Third World.* New York: Pergamon, 1980.

Dunyaev, E. P. *Ob'edinenia predpriatii kak forma obshchestvlenia proizvodstva* (The consolidation of enterprises as a form of social production). Moscow: Izdatel'stvo "Nauka," 1974.

Durovčik, Juraj, and Lepulica, Pavol, eds. *Stavebný zákon a súvisiace predpisy* (The construction law and related regulations). Bratislava: Obzor, 1977.

Durovic, Bozidar, ed. *Constitutional System of Yugoslavia.* Trans. by Marko Pavičić. Belgrade: Jugoslovenska stvarnost (Yugoslav actuality), 1980.

Dyker, David A. *The Process of Investment in the Soviet Union.* Cambridge: Cambridge University Press, 1983.

Dyson, Freeman. *Disturbing the Universe.* New York: Harper & Row, 1979.

Ena, V. G. *Zapovednye landshafty Kryma* (The nature reserves of the Crimea). Simferopol': Izdatel'stvo Tavriia, 1983.

Enloe, Cynthia H. *The Politics of Pollution in a Comparative Perspective: Ecology and Power in Four Nations.* New York: David McKay, 1975.

418

Erofeev, B. V.; Krasnov, N. I.; Syrodev, N. A. *Normativnyie akty o zemle* (Normative acts on land). Moscow: "Iuridicheskaia literatura," 1978.

Ershov, I. N., and Serebrianikov, N. I. *Teplofikatsia Moskvy.* (The introduction of a district heating system in Moscow). Moscow: "Energiia," 1980.

Federal Institute for East European and International Studies, ed. *The Soviet Union 1984/1985: Events, Problems, Perspectives.* Westview Special Studies on the Soviet Union and Eastern Europe. Boulder, Colo.: Westview, 1986.

Fedoseev, P. N., ed. *The Fundamental Law of the USSR.* Moscow: Progress, 1980.

Feld, Werner. *The European Community in World Affairs: Economic Power and Political Influence.* Sherman Oaks, Calif.: Alfred Publishing, 1976.

Firestone, David B., and Reed, Frank C. *Environmental Law for Non-Lawyers.* Ann Arbor: Ann Arbor Science, the Butterworth Group, 1983.

Flavin, Christopher. *Nuclear Power: The Market Test.* Worldwatch Paper 57. Washington, D.C.: Worldwatch, December 1983.

Fleishits, Ye., and Makovsky, A. *The Civil Codes of the Soviet Republics.* Moscow: Progress, 1976.

Fleron, Frederic J., Jr., ed. *Communist Studies and the Social Sciences: Essays on Methodology and Empirical Theory.* Chicago: University of Chicago Press, 1969.

Foresta, Ronald A. *America's National Parks and Their Keepers.* Washington, D.C.: Resources for the Future, 1984.

Fullenbach, Josef. *European Environmental Policy: East and West.* Trans. Frank Carter and John Manton. London: Butterworths, 1981.

Galbraith, John Kenneth. *The New Industrial State.* 2d ed. Boston: Houghton Mifflin, 1972.

Garvey, Gerald. *Energy, Ecology, Economy: A Framework for Environmental Policy.* New York: W. W. Norton, 1972.

Gelman, Harry. *The Brezhnev Politburo and the Decline of Détente.* Ithaca, N.Y., and London: Cornell University Press, 1984.

Gerasimov, I. P., ed. *Man, Society and the Environment.* Moscow: Progress, 1975.

Gibbons, John H., and Chandler, William U. *Energy: The Conservation Revolution.* New York and London: Plenum, 1981.

Girusov, E. V. *Sistema "obshchestvo-priroda"* (The system: "Society-nature"). Moscow: Izdatel'stvo Moskovskogo universiteta, 1976.

Gitelman, Zvi Y. *The Diffusion of Political Innovation: From Eastern Europe to the Soviet Union.* Beverly Hills, Calif.: Sage Publications, 1972.

Glikman, N. *Ekonometricheskii analiz regional'nykh sistem* (The econometric analysis of regional systems). Trans. from the English by A. N. Arianin, A. R. Monfor, O. S. Pshelentsev, and M. Iu. Shchykin. Moscow: Progress, 1980.

Gofman, K. G. *Ekonomicheskaia otsenka prirodnykh resursov v usloviakh sotsialisticheskoi ekonomiki* (Economic evaluation of natural resources in the conditions of a socialist economy). Moscow: Izdatel'stvo "Nauka," 1977.

――――, and Gusiev, A. A. *Okhrana okruzhaiushchei sredy: modeli upravlenia chistotoi prirodnoi sredy* (Environmental protection: Models of administering the cleanliness of the natural environment). Moscow: Izdatel'stvo "Ekonomika," 1977.

419

Gokhberg, M. Ia., and Shtul'berg, B. M. *Ekonomicheskoe obosnovanie territorial'nykh planov* (The economic bases of territorial plans). Moscow: Izdatel'stvo "Ekonomika," 1977.

Goldman, Marshall. *The Spoils of Progress: Environmental Pollution in the Soviet Union.* Cambridge, Mass.: MIT Press, 1972.

————. *Ecology and Economics: Controlling Pollution in the 70s.* Englewood Cliffs, N.J.: Prentice-Hall, 1972.

Granger, John V. *Technology and International Relations.* San Francisco: W. H. Freeman, 1979.

Granick, David. *Enterprise Guidance in Eastern Europe.* Princeton: Princeton University Press, 1975.

————. *The Red Executive.* Cambridge, Mass.: Harvard University Press, 1956.

Graves, Philip E., and Krumm, Ronald J. *Health and Air Quality: Evaluating the Effects of Policy.* Washington, D.C., and London: American Enterprise Institute for Public Policy Research, 1981.

Greenberger, Martin; Crenson, Matthew A.; and Crissey, Brian L. *Models in the Policy Process: Public Decision Making in the Computer.* New York: Russell Sage Foundation, 1976.

Gusakovoi, V. A. *Sbornik zadach po kursu "Gosydarstvennyi budzhet SSSR"* (Collection of assignments for the course: "The state budget of the USSR"). Moscow: "Financy," 1980.

Gusarov, A., and Radaev, V. *Besedy o nauchno-tekhnicheskoi revolutsii* (Conversations on the scientific-technological revolution). Moscow: Izdatel'stvo Politicheskoi literatury, 1977.

Gusev, R. K., and Petrov, V. V. *Pravovaia okhrana prirody v SSSR* (The legal protection of the environment in the USSR). Moscow: Vyshaia Shkola, 1979.

Gusieva, V. V. *Predpriatie i budzhet* (The enterprise and the budget). Moscow: Izdatel'stvo "Iuridicheskaia literatura," 1979.

Gustafson, Thane. *Reform in Soviet Politics: Lessons of recent policies on land and water.* Cambridge: Cambridge University Press, 1981.

Healy, Robert G., and Rosenberg, John S. *Land Use and the States.* 2d ed. Baltimore: Johns Hopkins University Press, 1979.

Heller, Michel, and Nekrich, Aleksandr. *L'Utopie au pouvoir: Histoire de l'URSS de 1917 à nos jours* (Utopia in power: The history of the USSR from 1917 to our day). Trans. from the Russian by Wladimir Berelowitch and Anne Coldefy-Faucard. Paris: Calmann-Lévy, 1985.

Himal, Juraj; Kincl, Vladimir (principal ed.); Koutnik, Josef; Zavadil, Jarom, eds. *Za další úspěšný rozvoj československého hospodářství* (For the further successful development of the Czechoslovak economy). Prague: Nakladatelství Svoboda, 1980.

Hoffmann, Erik P., and Fleron, Frederic J., Jr., eds. *The Conduct of Soviet Foreign Policy.* London: Butterworths, 1971.

————, and Laird, Robbin F. *"The Scientific-Technological Revolution" and Soviet Foreign Policy.* New York: Pergamon, 1982.

————, eds. *The Soviet Polity in te Modern Era.* New York: Aldine, 1984.

Holcomb Research Institute. *Environmental Modeling and Decision Making: The United States.* New York: Praeger, 1976.

Holt, Robert T., and Turner, John E., eds. *The Methodology of Comparative Research: A Symposium.* New York: Free Press, 1970.

Hough, Jerry F. *The Soviet Prefects: The Local Party Organs in Industrial Decision-making.* Cambridge, Mass.: Harvard University Press, 1969.

————. *The Soviet Union and Social Science Theory.* Cambridge, Mass.: Harvard University Press, 1977.

House, Peter W. *The Art of Public Policy Analysis: The Arena of Regulations and Resources.* Beverly Hills, Calif.: Sage Publications, 1982.

Howard, Ross, and Perley, Michael. *Acid Rain: The Devastating Impact on North America.* New York: McGraw-Hill, 1982.

Howitt, Arnold M. *Managing Federalism: Studies in Intergovernmental Relations.* Washington, D.C.: Congressional Quarterly, 1984.

Hutchings, Raymond. *Soviet Economic Development.* 2d ed. New York and London: New York University Press, 1971.

Isachenko, A. G. *Optimizatsia prirodnoi sredy; geograficheskii aspekt* (The optimization of the natural environment; The geographical aspect). Moscow: Izdatel'stvo "Mysl'," 1980.

Jackson, W. A. Douglas, ed. *Soviet Resource Management and the Environment.* Columbus, Ohio: American Association for the Advancement of Slavic Studies, 1978.

Jacobs, Everett M., ed. *Soviet Local Politics and Government.* London: George Allen & Unwin, 1983.

Jancar, Barbara Wolfe. *Czechoslovakia and the Absolute Monopoly of Power.* New York: Praeger, 1971.

Jokovic, Dragoslav, ed.-in-chief. *Zaštita i unapredjivanje životne sredine* (The protection and improvement of the environment). Belgrade: Bakar Printing House, 1979.

Jones, Charles D. *Clean Air: The Policies and Politics of Pollution.* Pittsburgh: University of Pittsburgh Press, 1975.

————. *An Introduction to Public Policy.* 2d ed. North Scituate, Mass.: Duxbury Press, 1977.

Kalter, Robert J., and Vogely, William A., eds. *Energy Supply and Government Policy.* Ithaca, N.Y., and London: Cornell University Press, 1976.

Kanet, Roger E., ed. *The Behavioral Revolution and Communist Studies: Applications of Behaviorally Oriented Research on the Soviet Union and Eastern Europe.* New York: Praeger, 1971.

Karpenko, A. S., and Stavrova, N. I. *Okhrana pastitel'nogo mira v nechernozem'e* (The Protection of the Plant World in the Non-chernozem). Leningrad: Izdatel'stvo "Nauka," 1980.

Kaverin, A. M. *Pravovaia okhrana vod ot zagriaznenia* (The legal protection of water from pollution). Moscow: Izdatel'stvo "Iuridicheskaia literatura," 1977.

———; Krasnov, N. I.; Nemirovskii, E. I.; and Syrodoiev, N. A. *Zakonodatel'stvo o lesakh* (Legislation on forests). Moscow: Izdatel'stvo "Iuridicheskaia literatura," 1978.

Kay, David A., and Jacobson, Harold K., eds. *Environmental Protection: The International Dimension*. Totowa, N.J.: Allanheld, Osmun, 1983.

Keller, Evelyn Fox. *Reflections on Gender and Science*. New Haven and London: Yale University Press, 1985.

Kelley, Donald R.; Stunkel, Kenneth R.; and Wescott, Richard R. *The Economic Superpowers and the Environment: The United States, the Soviet Union, and Japan*. San Francisco: W. H. Freeman, 1976.

Kerner, Antonín, with Collective. *Základy plánovitého řízení národního hospodářství* (The foundations of the planned management of the national economy). Prague: Ústav státní správy, 1978.

Kerr, Anthony J. C. *The Common Market and How It Works*. 2d ed. Oxford: Pergamon, 1983.

Khachaturov, T. S. *Intensifikatsiia i effektivnost' v usloviiakh razvitogo sotsializma* (Intensification and efficiency in conditions of developed socialism). Moscow: Izdatel'stvo "Nauka," 1978.

———, ed. *Okhrana okruzhaiushchei sredy i ee sotsial'no ekonomicheskaia effectivnost* (Environmental protection and its socioeconomic effectiveness). Moscow: Izdatel'stvo "Nauka," ANSSSR, Institut ekonomiki, 1980.

Kirpatovskii, I. P. *Okhrana prirody: Spravochnik dlia rabotnikov neftepererabatyvaiushchei i neftekhimicheskoi promyshlennosti* (Nature protection: Handbook for workers in the oil refining and petrochemical industry). Moscow: "Khimiia," 1980.

Koistinen, Paul A. C. *The Military-Industrial Complex: A Historical Perspective*. New York: Praeger, 1980.

Kolbasov, O. S. *Ekologiia: Politika-Pravo* (Ecology: Politics-law). Moscow: Izdatel'stvo "Nauka," 1976.

———, ed. *Sotsializm i okhrana okruzhaiushchei sredy: pravo i upravlenie v stranakh-chlenakh SEV* (Socialism and environmental protection: Law and administration in the member countries of CMEA). Moscow: Izdatel'stvo "Iuridicheskaia literatura," 1979.

———, principal ed. *Okruzhaiushchaia sreda i pravo* (The environment and law). Moscow: ANSSSR, Institut gosudarstva i prava, 1977.

Koleda, R.; Mokrý, V.; Vincúr, P. *Národohospodárske plánovanie*. (National economic planning). 2d ed. Bratislava: Alfa, 1978.

Kolektiv Avtorov (Authors' Collective). *Spoločnost a životné prostredie* (Society and the environment). Bratislava: Priroda, 1978.

Komarov, Boris. *Le Rouge et le vert: La Déstruction de la nature en URSS* (The red and the green: The destruction of nature in the USSR). Trans. from Russian by Basile Karlinsky. Paris: Éditions du Seuil, 1979.

———. *The Destruction of Nature in the Soviet Union*. Trans. by Michel Vale and Joe Hollander. Armonk, N.Y.: M. E. Sharpe, 1980.

Kotliarov, E. A. *Geografia otdykha i turizma* (The geography of rest and tourism). Moscow: Izdatel'stvo "Mysl'," 1978.

Kotov, F.; Ivanov, Y.; and Prostyakov, I. *Twenty-Fifth Congress of the Communist Party of the Soviet Union; The USSR Economy in 1976-1980.* Moscow: Progress, 1977.

Kozyr', M. I. (principal ed.); Beliaeva, Z. S.; Slavin, M. M.; and Fomina, L. P. *Razvitie agrarno-pravovykh nauk.* (The development of agrarian legal science). Moscow: ANSSSR Institut gosudarstva i prava, 1980.

Kriuchkov, V. V. *Sever: priroda i chelovek* (The north: Nature and man). Moscow: Izdatel'stvo "Nauka," 1979.

Kuehn, Thomas J., and Porter, Alan L., eds. *Science, Technology and National Policy.* Ithaca, N.Y., and London: Cornell University Press, 1981.

Kuligin, P. I. *Khozrashchet i ego razvitie v zarubezhnykh stranakh SEV* (Cost accounting and its development in the foreign countries of SEV). Moscow: Izdatel'stvo "Nauka," 1980.

Kushnirsky, Fyodor I. *Soviet Economic Planning, 1965-1980.* Boulder, Colo.: Westview, 1982.

Kutta, František, and Collective. *Teorie a praxe sociálního plánování a programování v ČSSR* (The theory and practice of social planning and programming in the ČSSR). Prague: "Ekonomie a spolecnost"; Nakladatelství Svoboda, 1980.

Lacko, Rastislav. *Ekorozvoj/ Problémy a perspektívy* (Ecodevelopment: Problems and perspectives). Bratislava: Alfa, 1981.

Lagasse, Charles-Etienne. *L'Entreprise soviétique et le marché: Contrats, Profit, Rentabilité.* (The Soviet enterprise and the market: Contracts, profit, profitability). Paris: Economica, 1979.

Laptev, I. *The Planet of Reason: A Sociological Study of the Man-Nature Relationship.* Moscow: Progress, 1977.

Lebedev, A. D., ed.-in-chief. *Okruzhaiushchaia sreda i zdorov'e cheloveka* (The environment and human health). Moscow: Izdatel'stvo "Nauka," ANSSSR Institut geografii, 1979.

Lebedev, V. G.; Poltorygin, V. K.; and Kushlin, V. I. *Sotsial'no-ekonomicheskaia effektivnost' perspektivnykh vlozhenii* (The social economic efficiency of future investment). Moscow: Izdatel'stvo "Mysl'," 1979.

Lefever, Ernest W. *Nuclear Arms in the Third World: U.S. Policy Dilemma.* Washington, D.C.: Brookings Institution, 1979.

Lemeshev, M. Ia., and Dunaevskii, L. V., principal eds. *Upravlenie prirodnoi sredoi: sotsial'no-ekonomicheskie i estestvenno-nauchnye aspekty* (Environmental administration: Socialeconomic and natural science aspects). Moscow: Izdatel'stvo "Nauka," ANSSSR, TSEMI, 1979.

————, and Panchenko, A. I. *Kompleksnye programmy v planirovanii narodnogo khozaistva* (Comprehensive programs in the planning of the national economy). Moscow: Izdatel'stvo "Ekonomika," 1973.

Levin, V. M. *Sotsial'no-ekonomicheskie potrebnosti: Zakonomernosti formirovania i razvitia* (Social economic needs: The principles of their formation and development). Moscow: Izdatel'stvo "Mysl'," 1974.

Liapunov, Iu. I. *Criminal Law, Environmental Protection and the Organs of the Ministry of Internal Affairs*. Moscow: Izdatel'stvo "Nauka," 1974.

Libecap, Gary D. *Locking up the Range: Federal Land Controls and Grazing*. Cambridge, Mass.: Ballinger, Pacific Institute for Public Policy Research, 1981.

Licitsyn, E. N.; Petrov, V. V.; Petrova, G. V.; and Riabov, A. A. *Pravovyi problemy ekologii: Sbornik obzorob* (Legal problems of ecology: Collection of views). Moscow: Institut nauchnoi informatsii po obshchestvennym naukam, 1980.

Lim, Gill C., ed. *Regional Planning: Evolution, Crisis and Prospects*. Totowa, N.J.: Allanheld, Osmun, 1983.

Lindblom, Charles E. *The Intelligence of Democracy: Decision Making Through Mutual Adjustment*. New York: Free Press, 1965.

Lomovatskii, G. I. *Matematicheskie metody i modeli v ekonomicheskikh issledovanii* (Mathematical methods and models in economic research). Moscow: Izdatel'stvo "Nauka," 1980.

Lowenhardt, John. *Decision Making in Soviet Politics*. New York: St. Martin's, 1981.

Lubrano, Linda, and Solomon, Susan Gross, eds. *The Social Context of Soviet Science*. Boulder, Colo.: Westview, 1980.

Madar, Z., and Mencer, G. *Životní prostředí III: Právní aspekty mezinárodní ochrany životního prostředí* (The environment III: The legal aspects of international environmental protection). Prague: Horizont, 1980.

Madar, Zdeněk. *Československé právo, státní správa a životní prostředí* (Czechoslovak law, state administration and the environment). Prague: Ústav státní správy, 1977.

Makunina, A. A., and Tsvetaeva, Z. N. *Regional'nyi geograficheskii prognoz* (Regional geographic forecasting). 2d ed. Moscow: Izdatel'stvo Moskovskogo universiteta, 1980.

Mann, Dean E., ed. *Environmental Policy Formation: The Impact of Values, Ideology and Standards*. Lexington, Mass.: Lexington Books, 1981.

————. *Environmental Policy Implementation*. Lexington, Mass.: Lexington Books, 1982.

Markarian, E. S. *Integrativnye tendentsii vo vzaimodeistvii obshchestvennykh i estestvennykh nauk* (Integrative tendencies in the interaction of the social and natural sciences). Erevan: Izdatel'stvo AN Armianskoi SSR, 1977.

Matveev, A. N. *Financovo-kreditnye otnoshenia gosudarstva s kolkhozami* (Financial credit relations of the state with the kokhozy). Moscow: "Financy," 1980.

Medvedev, Zhores A. *Nuclear Disaster in the Urals*. Trans. George Saunders. New York: Vintage, 1980.

————. *Soviet Science*. New York: W. W. Norton, 1978.

Medvedkov, Iu. V., ANSSSR Institut geografii. *Chelovek i gorodskaia sreda* (Man and the urban environment). Moscow: Izdatel'stvo "Nauka," 1978.

Meleshkin, M. T.; Zaitsev, A. P.; Marinov, Kh. *Ekonomika i okruzhaiushchaia sreda: vzaimodeistvie i upravlenie* (Economics and the environment: Interaction and administration). Moscow: Izdatel'stvo "Ekonomika," 1979.

424

Mesarovic, Mihajlo, and Pestel, Eduard. *Mankind at the Turning Point: The Second Report to The Club of Rome.* New York: E. P. Dutton, Reader's Digest Press, 1974.

Meyer, Alfred G. *Communism.* 4th ed. New York: Random House, 1984.

Micovic, Vojislav. *The Information System in Yugoslavia.* Belgrade: Jugoslovenska Stvarnost — Medjunarodna politika, 1980.

Mihálik, Štefan, and Collective. *Chránené územia a prírodné výtvory Slovenska* (Protected lands and natural monuments of Slovakia). Bratislava: Slovenský ústav pamiatkovej starostlivosti a ochrany prírody, 1971.

Mikoláš, J., and Pittermann, L. *Riadenie starostlivosti o životné prostredie* (Management of environmental protection). Bratislava: Alfa, 1980.

Millar, James R. *The ABCs of Soviet Socialism.* Urbana, Chicago, London: University of Illinois Press, 1981.

Minyaev, V. A., and Poliakov, I. V. *Zdravookhranenie krupnogo sotsialisticheskogo goroda* (Public health in a large socialist city). Moscow: "Meditsina," 1980.

Mocker, Volkhard, ed. *Was Sie schön immer uber Umweltschutz wissen wollten* (What you would like to know about the environment). Stuttgart, Berlin: Verlag W. Kohlhammer, 1981.

Mumford, Lewis. *The Myth of the Machine: The Pentagon of Power.* New York: Harcourt Brace Jovanovich, 1970.

Nakamura, Robert T., and Smallwood, Frank. *The Politics of Policy Implementation.* New York: St. Martin's, 1980.

National Academy of Sciences. Commission on Natural Resources. Environmental Studies Board. Committee on Prevention of Significant Deterioration of Air Quality. *On Prevention of Significant Deterioration of Air Quality.* Washington, D.C.: National Academy Press, 1981.

———. Committee on Environmental Decision Making. Commission on Natural Resources. *Decision Making in the Environmental Protection Agency.* Washington, D.C.: National Academy of Sciences, 1977.

———. Committee on the Atmosphere and the Biosphere. Commission on Natural Resources. Board on Agriculture and Renewable Resources. *Atmosphere-Biosphere Interactions: Toward a Better Understanding of Acid Precipitation.* Washington, D.C.: National Academy Press, 1981.

Nekrasov, N. N., and Mateev, E. *Sotsialisticheskoe prirodopol'zovanie: ekonomicheskie i sotsial'nye aspekty* (Socialist natural resource use: Economic and social aspects). Moscow-Sofia: Izdatel'stvo "Ekonomika," — Partizdat, 1980.

Nikitin, D. P., and Novikov, Iu. V. *Okruzhaiushchaia sreda i chelovek* (The environment and man). Moscow: Vyshaia shkola, 1980.

Nove, Alec. *The Soviet Economic System.* 2d ed. London: George Allen & Unwin, 1982.

Oldak, P. G. *Sokhranenie okruzhaiushchei sredy i razvitie ekonomicheskikh issledovanii* (Environmental protection and the development of economic research). Novosibirsk: Izdatel'stvo "Nauka," Sibirskoe otdelenie, 1980.

Ophuls, William. *Ecology and the Politics of Scarcity.* San Francisco: W. H. Freeman, 1977.

425

Osipov, N. T., ed. *Problemy pravovoi okhrany okruzhaiushchei sredy v SSSR* (Problems of the legal protection of the environment in the USSR). Leningrad: Izdatel'stvo Leningradskogo universiteta, 1979.

Palamarchuk, M. M.; Gorlenko, I. A.; and Iasniuk, T. E. *Mineral'nye resursy i formirovanie promyshlennykh territorial'nykh kompleksov* (Mineral resources and the formation of industrial territorial complexes). Kiev: Naukova Dumka, 1978.

Pašić, Najdan, ed. *Osnove marksizma i socijalističko samoupravljanje* (Foundations of Marxism and socialist self-management). Belgrade: Zavod za ücbenike i nastavna sredstva, 1982.

Peremyslov, A. S. *Koeffitsient budushchego* (Coefficient of the future). Novosibirsk: Siberian Division, Nauka, 1967.

Petranović, Branko. *Istorija Jugoslavije 1918–1978* (The history of Yugoslavia 1918–1978). Belgrade: Nolit, 1981.

Petrov, V. V. *Pravovaia okhrana prirody v SSSR* (The legal protection of nature in the USSR). Moscow: Izdatel'stvo "Iuridicheskaia literatura," 1984.

―――, ed. *Nauchno-tekhnicheskii progress i pravovaia okhrana prirody: Problemy sovershenstvovania prirodo-okhranitel'nogo zakonodatel'stva v usloviakh nauchno-tekhicheskogo progressa* (Scientific technological progress and the legal protection of the environment: Problems of perfecting environmental protection legislation under the conditions of scientific technological progress). Moscow: Izdatel'stvo Moskovskogo universiteta, 1978.

―――, ed. *Pravovaia okhrana prirody* (The legal protection of the environment). Moscow: Izdatel'stvo Moskovskogo universiteta, 1980.

―――, principal ed. *Pravovye problemy ekologii: Sbornik obzorov* (Legal problems of ecology: Collection of views). Moscow: Akademia nauk SSSR, Institut nauchnoi informatsii po obshchestvennym naukam, 1980.

Pirages, Dennis C., and Ehrlich, Paul R. *Ark II: Social Response to Environmental Imperatives*. San Francisco: W. H. Freeman, 1974.

Plecas-Simić, Zorica, and Filipon-Plecas, Anica. *Ishrana dece u jaslama vrtićima i skolama: Priručnik za planiranje ishrane dece u jaslama, vrtićima i skolama* (The nutrition of children in creches, kindergartens and schools: Handbook of the planning of the nutrition of children in creches, kindergartens and schools). Bačka Palanka: Branko Bajic, 1980.

Pobedinskii, A. V. *Vodookhrannaia i pochvozashchitnaia rol' lesov* (Water protection and soil conservation roles of forests). Moscow: Izdatel'stvo Lesnaia promyshlennost', 1979.

Podgorski, Karol, ed. *Zagadnienia prawne ochrony srodowiska* (Legal issues of environmental protection). Katowice: Uniwersytet Slaski, 1981.

Polianskaia, G. N. *Pravnye voprosy okhrany prirody v SSSR* (Legal questions of conservation in the USSR). Moscow: Izdatel'stvo "Nauka," 1963.

Polska Akademia Nauk. Komitet Naukowy. *"Czlowiek i Srodowisko." Ekspertyza: Ocena aktualnego stanu srodowiska w Polsce* ("Man and the environment." Expertise: Evaluation of the present state of the environment in Poland). Warsaw: Polska Akademia Nauk, 1981.

Popov, A. I., and Trofimov, V. T., eds. *Prirodnye uslovia zapadnoi Sibiri* (The natural conditions of Western Siberia). Moscow: Izdatel'stvo Moskovskogo universiteta, 1980.

Portney, Paul R., ed. *Current Issues in Natural Resource Policy.* Washington, D.C.: Resources for the Future, Johns Hopkins University Press, 1983.

Pressman, Jeffrey L., and Wildavsky, Aaron. *Implementation: How Great Expectations in Washington are Dashed in Oakland.* Berkeley: University of California Press, 1979.

Price, Kent A., ed. *Regional Conflict and National Policy.* Washington, D.C.: Resources for the Future, Johns Hopkins University Press, 1982.

Pryde, Philip R. *Conservation in the Soviet Union.* Cambridge: Cambridge University Press, 1972.

Radović, Dusan, and Petricić, Dusan. *Beogradjani i Beograd* (Belgradians and Belgrade). Belgrade: Gradski secretarijat za urbanizam i zaštitu životne sredine, 1982.

Ramet, Pedro, ed. *Yugoslavia in the 1980s.* Boulder, Colo.: Westview, 1986.

Reimers, N. F., and Shtil'mark, F. R. *Osobeno okhraniaemye prirodnye territorii* (Specially protected natural areas). Moscow: Izdatel'stvo "Mysl'," 1978.

Revel, Jean-François. *Comment les démocraties finissent.* (How the democracies will end). Paris: Bernard Grasset, 1983.

Richta, Rodovan. *Civilization at the Crossroads.* Prague: International Arts and Sciences Press, 1969.

Ripley, Randall B., and Franklin, Grace A. *Bureaucracy and Policy Implementation.* Homewood, Ill.: Dorsey, 1982.

————. *Congress, the Bureaucracy, and Public Policy.* 2d ed. Homewood, Ill.: Dorsey, 1980.

Rokhvarger, A. E., and Sheviakov, A. Iu. *Matematicheskoe planirovanie nauchno-tekhnicheskikh issledovanii (statisticheskii podkhod)* [Mathematical planning of scientific technological research (statistical approach)]. Moscow: Izdatel'stvo "Nauka," 1975.

Rosenbaum, Walter A. *Energy, Politics and Public Policy.* Washington, D.C.: Congressional Quarterly Press, 1981.

Rozanov, B. G. *Osnovy uchenia ob okruzhaiushchei srede* (Fundamentals of the study of environmental protection). Moscow: Izdatel'stvo Moskovskogo universiteta, 1984.

Sagdeev, R. Z., ed. ANSSSR Institut kosmicheskikh issledovanii. *Terminologiia po prirodnym resursam zemli* (Terminology for earth's natural resources). Moscow: Izdatel'stvo "Nauka," 1976.

Sakhipov, M. C., ed.-in-chief. *Priroda i zakon: Sbornik normativnikh aktov po okhrane prirody* (Nature and law: Collection of normative acts on nature protection). Alma-Ata: "Kainar," 1984.

Seleši, Dula. *Jezero Palić odumiranje i sanacija* (Lake Palic: Death and reclamation). Subotica: Fond za sanaciju jezera Palić, 1973.

Sharikov, L. P., ed. *Okhrana okruzhaiushchei sredy: spravochnik* (Environmental protection: A handbook). Leningrad: Izdatel'stvo "Sudostroenie," 1978.

427

Sharlet, Robert, ed. *The New Soviet Constitution of 1977: Analysis and Text*. Brunswick, Ohio: King's Court Communications, 1978.

Shauro, E. A., ed. ANSSSR, Institut ekonomiki mirovoi sotsialisticheskoi sistemy. *Sotsial'no-ekonomicheskiie problemy okhrany okruzhaiushchei sredy i puti ikh resheniia v stranakh-chlenakh SEV* (Social economic problems of environmental protection and ways of resolving them in the member countries of CMEA). Moscow: Sekretariat SEV, 1978.

Shemshuchenko, Iu. S.; Muntian, V. L.; and Rosovskii, B. G. *Iuridicheskaia otvestvennost' v oblasti okhrany okruzhaiushchei sredy* (Legal responsibility in the area of environmental protection). Kiev: Izdatel'stvo "Nauka," 1979.

Shniper, R. I., ed. ANSSSR, Sibirskoe otdelenie, Institut ekonomiki i organizatsii promyshlennogo proizvodstva. *Tendentsii ekonomicheskogo razvitia Sibiri (1961–1975 gg.)* [Tendencies in the economic development of Siberia (1961–1975)]. Novosibirsk: Izdatel'stvo "Nauka," Sibirskoe otdelenie, 1980.

Shukhardin, S. V., and Gukov, V. I., eds. ANSSSR, Institut istorii. *Nauchno-tekhnicheskaia revoliutsia: obshcheteoreticheskie problemy* (The scientific technical revolution: General theoretical problems). Moscow: Izdatel'stvo "Nauka," 1976.

Shultz, Richard H., and Godson, Roy. *Dezinformatsia: Active Measures in Soviet Strategy*. Washington, D.C.: Pergamon-Brassey's, 1984.

Shumskii, Aleksandr. *Chistoe nebo* (Clean sky). Moscow: Izdatel'stvo "Pravda," 1980.

Šik, Ota. *Czechoslovakia: The Bureaucratic Economy*. White Plains, N.Y.: International Arts and Sciences Press, 1972.

———. *The Communist Power System*. Trans. Marianne Grund Freidberg. New York: Praeger, 1981.

———. *The Third Way: Marxist-Leninist Theory and Modern Industrial Society*. White Plains, N.Y.: International Arts and Sciences Press, 1976.

Singleton, Fred, ed. *Environmental Misuse in the Soviet Union*. New York: Praeger, 1976.

Sinyakov, Yuri. *Standing Up for Nature*. Moscow: Novosti Press Agency Publishing House, 1979.

Skilling, H. Gordon. *Interest Groups in Soviet Society*. Princeton: Princeton University Press, 1971.

Smith, Gordon B., ed. *Public Policy and Administration in the Soviet Union*. New York: Praeger, 1980.

Sokić, Sreten. *Industrija i industrijski napredak Jugoslavije* (Industry and industrial progress in Yugoslavia). Belgrade: Institut za političke studije, Fakulteta političkih nauka, 1973.

Sokolov, V. I. *Amerikanskii kapitalizm i problema okhrany okruzhaiushchei sredy* (American capitalism and the problem of environmental protection). Moscow: Izdatel'stvo "Nauka," 1979.

Solomon, Peter H., Jr. *Soviet Criminologists and Criminal Policy: Specialists in Policy-Making*. New York: Columbia University Press, 1978.

Solomon, Susan Gross. *The Soviet Agrarian Debate: A Controversy in Social Science, 1923–1929*. Boulder, Colo.: Westview, 1977.

_____, ed. *Pluralism in the Soviet Union: Essays in Honor of H. Gordon Skilling.* New York: St. Martin's, 1983.

Soulé, Michael E., and Wilcox, Bruce A., eds.-in-chief. *Biologia okhrany prirody* (Conservation biology: An evolutionary-ecological perspective). Trans. from English by C. A. Ostroumov, A. B. Iablokov, eds. Moscow: "Mir," 1983.

Špak, Michal. *Koncentrácia a špecializácia v priemysle ČSSR* (Concentration and specialization in industry in the USSR). Bratislava: Nakladatel'stvo Pravda, 1976.

Spivakova, T. I. ANSSSR, Institut gosudarstva i prava. *Pravo i prirodnye resurcy pribrezhnykh zon (Nekotorye tendentsii v mezhdunarodnom morskom prave)* (Law and natural resources of the coastal zones). Moscow: Izdatel'stvo "Nauka," 1978.

Stepanović, Zivadin, ed. *Istraživački Zbornik: Ješevać i Kotlenik* (Research collection: Ješavać i Kotlenik). Kragujevac: Društvo Mladih istraživača Polet, 1981.

Stobaugh, Robert, and Yergin, Daniel, eds. *Energy Future: Report of the Energy Project at the Harvard Business School.* New York: Ballantine Books, 1979.

Stojanovic, Radmila, ed. *The Functioning of the Yugoslav Economy.* Armonk, N.Y.: M. E. Sharpe, 1982.

Stroup, Richard L., and Baden, John A. *Natural Resources: Bureaucratic Myths and Environmental Management.* Cambridge, Mass.: Ballinger, Pacific Institute for Public Policy Research, 1983.

Tanter, Raymond, and Ullman, Richard H., eds. *Theory and Policy in International Relations.* Princeton: Princeton University Press, 1972.

Tarasov, A. I. ANSSSR, Nauchnyi soviet po problemam biosfery. TSEMI. *Ekonomiki rekreatsionnogo lesopol'zovania.* (The economics of recreational forest use). "Problemy sovietskoi ekonomiki" ("Problems of the Soviet economy"). Moscow: Izdatel'stvo "Nauka," 1980.

Teicholz, Eric, and Berry, Brian J. L. *Computer Graphics and Environmental Planning.* Englewood Cliffs, N.J.: Prentice-Hall, 1983.

Tillmann, Jiri, and Simon, Jiri. *Priručka investora* (The investor's handbook). 3d ed. Prague: SNTL-Nakladátelství technické literatury, 1980.

Tiutekin, Iu. I. *Priroda, obshchestvo, zakon* (Nature, society, law). Kishinev: Izdatel'stvo "Nauka," 1976.

Todorović, Milivoje. *Moguća rešenja u sistemu čovek-društvo-životna sredina* (Possible solutions in the system man-society-environment). Belgrade: Mladi istraživači Srbije-Republička konferencija, 1983.

Tökés, Rudolf, ed. *Dissent in the USSR.* Baltimore: Johns Hopkins University Press, 1975.

Tosković, Dobrivoje. *Urbanizacija Libije: poreklo, utičajni faktori i prostorno-fizički efekti* (The urbanization of Libya: Origins, influential factors, and spacial-physical effects). Belgrade: Yugoslav Institute for Urban Planning and Construction, 1980.

Trudova, M. G., ed.-in-chief. *Statistika okruzhaiushchei sredy* (Environmental statistics). Moscow: "Financy i statistika," 1981.

Tsarfis, P. G. *Rekreatsionnaia geografia SSSR: kurortologicheskie aspekty* (Recreational geography of the USSR: Resort aspects). Moscow: Izdatel'stvo "Mysl'," 1979.

Tsepin, A. I. *Profsoiuzy i trudovye prava rabochikh i sluzhashchikh* (Trade unions and the legal rights of workers and employees). Moscow: Izdatel'stvo "Nauka," 1980.

Tupytsia, Iu. Iu. ANSSSR, Nauchnyi Soviet po problemam biosfery. *Ekologo-ekonomicheskaia efektivnost prirodopol'zovania* (The Ecologo-economic efficiency of natural resource use). Moscow: Izdatel'stvo "Nauka," 1980.

Turchikhin, E. Ia., ed.-in-chief. *Proektirovanie gorodskogo khozaistva* (The planning of the city economy). Text for VUZ (Higher Educational Institution) students studying "The Economics and Organization of the City Economy." 2d ed., rev. and enlarged. Moscow: Stroiizdat, 1983.

Turk, Jonathan, and Turk, Amos. *Environmental Science.* 3d ed. Philadelphia: Saunders College Publishing, 1984.

Urbanek, Jan, and Collective. *Chránime prírodu a krajinu* (Let's protect nature and the countryside). Bratislava: Príroda pre Slovenský zväz ochrancov prírody a krajiny, 1979.

U.S. Congress. Office of Technology Assessment. *Technology and Soviet Energy Availability.* Boulder, Colo.: Westview, 1982.

Valenta, Jiri, and Potter, William, eds. *Soviet Decision Making for National Security.* London: George Allen & Unwin, 1984.

van Lier, Irene H. *Acid Rain and International Law.* Toronto, Canada: Bunsel Environmental Consultants, 1981.

Vanneman, Peter. *The Supreme Soviet: Politics and the Legislative Process in the Soviet Political System.* Durham, N.C.: Duke University Press, 1977.

Vasil'ev, V.; Pisarev, V.; and Khozin, G. *Ekologia i mezhdunarodnye otnoshenia* (Ecology and international relations). Moscow: Izdatel'stvo Mezhdunarodnye otnoshenia, 1978.

Vidláková, O., ed. *Landscape and Man in Socialist Czechoslovakia.* Prague: Orbis, 1977.

Volevakha, M. M. *Water and Air of Our Planet.* Kiev: Naukova Dumka, 1975.

Volgyes, Ivan, ed. *Environmental Deterioration in the Soviet Union and Eastern Europe.* New York: Praeger, 1974.

Volkov, F. M., and Collective. *Vozrastanie roli obshchestvennyhkh nauk v kommunisticheskom stroitel'stve* (The growth of the role of the social sciences in communist construction). Moscow: Izdatel'stvo Moskovskogo universiteta, 1979.

Vorobiev, B. B., ed. *Geograficheskie problemy zony BAM.* (The geographic problems of the BAM zone). Novosibirsk: Izdatel'stvo "Nauka," Sibirskoe otdelenie, 1979.

Vorotilov, V. A., and Cherkasov, G. N., eds. ANSSSR, Institut. *Metodologia sotsial'no-ekonomicheskogo planirovania goroda* (Methodology of municipal social economic planning). Leningrad: Nauka, Leningradskoe otdelenie, 1980.

Voslensky, Michael. *La nomenklatura: les Privilegiés en URSS* (The nomenklatura: The privileged in the USSR). Trans. from the German by Christian Nugue. Paris: Pierre Belfond, 1984.

Vukovic, Ilija, and Markovic, Ratko. *Socijalistički samoupravni sistem SFRJ* (The socialist self-management system of SFRJ). Belgrade: Privredni pregled, 1978.

Wallace, Helen; Wallace, William, and Webb, Carole. *Policy-Making in the European Communities.* London, New York: John Wiley, 1977.

Wenner, Lettie McSpadden. *One Environment under Law: A Public Policy Dilemma.* Pacific Palisades, Calif.: Goodyear, 1976.

Wiatra, Jerzy J., ed. *Wladza lokalna u progu kryzysu: Studium dwu wojewodztw* (Local government in the grips of crisis: A study of two vojvodstvi). Warsaw: Uniwersytet Warszawski, Instytut Socjologii, 1983.

Wickham, Alexandre, and Coignard, Sophie. *La nomenklatura française: pouvoirs et privilèges des élites* (The French Nomenklatura: The powers and privileges of the elites). Paris: Pierre Belfond, 1986.

Wilczynski, J. *The Economics of Socialism.* 4th ed. London: George Allen & Unwin, 1982.

Wolanski, Napolean. *Zmiany srodowiskowe a rozwoj biologiczny czlowieka* (Environmental changes and the biological development of man). Warsaw: Zaklad Narodowy imienia Ossolinskich Wydawnictwo Polskiej Akademii Nauk, 1983.

Young, Oran R. *Natural Resources and the State: The Political Economy of Resource Management.* Berkeley: University of California Press, 1981.

Yugoslavia, The League of Communists of. *Yugoslavia's Way: The Program of the LCY.* Trans. Stoyan Pribechevich. New York: All Nations' Press, 1958.

Zalkind, A. I., and Miroshnichenko, V. P. *Ocherki razvitia narodno-khozaistvennogo planirovania* (Outline of the development of national economic planning). Moscow: Ekonomika, 1980.

Zeković, Velimir. *Socijalističko samoupravljanje* (Socialist self-management). 2d ed. Belgrade: Zavod za učbenike i nastavna sredstva, 1978.

Zinberg, Dorothy S., ed. *Uncertain Power: The Struggle for a National Energy Policy.* New York: Pergamon, 1983.

Monographs

ČSR. Soviet pravitel'stva ČSR po voprocam okruzhaiushchei sredy v sotrudneniem s Sovietom pravitel'stva SSR po voprocam okruzhaiushchei sredy. *Vospitanie zabotlivogo otnoshenia k okruzhaiushchei srede v Chekhoslovakii* (The formation of a caring relationship to the environment in Czechoslovakia). Prague: Nauchno-issledovatel'skii institut stroitel'stva i arkhitektury, 1977.

ČSR. Výzkumny ústav výstavby a architektury. *Report on Activity, 1976–1977.* Prague: Výzkumny ústav výstavby a architektury, 1978.

Dautović, Mirko. *Društveno-ekonomski odnosi osnovnih organizacija udruženog rada* (The social economic relations of the basic organizations of associated labor). Belgrade: Institut za političke studije, Fakulteta političkih nauka, 1974.

Gorbachev, M. C. *Aktivno deistvovat', ne teriat' vremeni* (Actively work, don't lose time). Moscow: Izdatel'stvo "Politicheskoi literatury," 1985.

———. *Korennoi vopros ekonomicheskoi politiki partii* (The root question of the party's economic policy). Moscow: Izdatel'stvo "Politicheskoi literatury," 1985.

————. *Nastoichivo dvigat'sia vpered* (Persistently move ahead). Moscow: Izdatel'stvo "Politicheskoi literatury," 1985.

Kazanskii, N. N., ed. *Problemy razvitia i razmeshchenia proizvoditel'nykh sil Severo-Zapadnyi PTK* (Problems in the development and location of productive forces in the north-western territorial industrial complex). Moscow: Izdatel'stvo "Mysl'," 1978.

Kincl, Vladimír, ed.-in-chief, and Collective. *Za další úspěšný rozvoj československého hospodářství: Názorné pomůcky k Souboru opatření ke zdokonalení soustavy plánovitého řízení národního hospodářství po roce 1980* (For the further successful development of the Czechoslovak economy: Visual aid to the set of measures for the improvement of the system of the planned administration of the national economy after 1980). Prague: Nakladatelství Svoboda, 1980.

Kirkonoše National Park Administration. *Yearbook 1/1977*. Hrádec Králove: Vítězná kridla, 1978.

Kovaliev, C. A., ed.-in-chief. *Biogeograficheskie aspekty prirodopol'zovania. Voprosy Geografii*, (The biogeographic aspects of resource exploitation. Geographic questions), No. 114. Moscow: Izdatel'stvo "Mysl'," 1980.

————. *Ekonomicheskaia i sotsial'naia geografia. Voprosy geografii*, No. 112 (Economic and social geography. Geographic Questions, No. 112). Moscow: Izdatel'stvo "Mysl'," 1980.

Kozlowski, Stefan. *Ochrona krajobraze; Poradnik ochrony przyrody* (The protection of the countryside, environmental protection handbook). Warsaw: Liga ochrony przyrody, 1980.

Lazarev, I. N. *Financirovanie nauchno-technicheskogo progressa: Nekotorye voprosy teori i metodologii* (The financing of scientific technological progress: Some questions of theory and methodology). Moscow: "Financy," 1980.

National Research Council. Committee on Atmospheric Sciences. *Atmospheric Precipitation: Prediction and Research Problems*. Washington, D.C.: National Academy Press, 1980.

————. Committee on Energy and the Environment. *Implications of Environmental Regulations for Energy Production and Consumption*. Vol. 6. Washington, D.C.: National Academy of Sciences, 1977.

Paunović, Petar. *Zbornik Radova, Godina II, Knjiga 2* (Collection of studies, year 2, book 2). Zajecar: Zavod za zdravstvenu zaštitu Timok, September 1980.

Quandt, William B. *The Comparative Study of Political Elites*. Beverly Hills, Calif.: Sage Publications, Comparative Politics Series, 1970.

Reichrtova, Eva. *Biologické účinky magnetizových imisii na živočišný organizmus* (The biological effects of magnetized emissions on animal organisms). Bratislava: VEDA, Biologické práce XXVIII/1 (1982). Edicia Vědeckého kolegia pre biologičko-pol'nohospodářské vědy a Vědeckého kolegia pre biologičko-lékařské vědy SAV (Edition of the Scientific Collegium at the Biological-Agricultural Sciences and the Scientific Collegium at the Biological-Medical Sciences at the Slovak Academy of Science), 1982.

Ristić, M. M., ed. *Center for Multi-disciplinary Studies*. Brochure, University of Belgrade. Belgrade: "October 10" Publishing House, 1980.

432

Savezna konferencija SSRNJ, Goncin, Milorad, ed. *Drustveno-ekonomski značaj male privrede i zadači SSRN* (Socioeconomic significance of small business and the tasks of the SSRN). Belgrade: NIGP Borba-OOUR, n.d.

Savezna konferencija SSRNJ, Milinkovic, Bosko, ed. *Aktualna idejno-politička pitanja u sredstvima informisanja i zadači SSRN* (Current ideological-political questions in the information media and the tasks of the SSRN). Belgrade: NIGP Privredni pregled, 1977.

Shkaratan, O. I., ed.-in-chief, and Borshchevskii, M. B., comp. *Perspektivnye problemy sotsial'nogo razvitia monopromyshlennogo goroda, po materialam izychenia Al' met'evska Tatarskoi ASSR* (Perspective problems of the social development of the single industry city based on study materials from Al'met'evska, Tatar ASSR). Moscow: ANSSSR. Institut sociologicheskikh issledovanii. Leningradskii finansovo-ekonomicheskii institut im. N. A. Voznesenskogo, 1973.

Sodaro, Michael J. *External Influences on Regime Stability in the GDR: a Linkage Analysis*. Washington, D.C.: George Washington University, Institute for Sino-Soviet Studies, 1983.

Thornton, Richard C. *Distant Connections: Superpower Rivalry in the Middle East and Southeast Asia, 1977-79*. Washington, D.C.: George Washington University, Institute for Sino-Soviet Studies, 1984.

Tikhonov, N. A. *Osnovnye napravlenia ekonomicheskogo i sotsial'nogo razvitia SSSR na 1981-1985 gody i na period do 1990 goda* (Guidelines for economic and social development of the USSR for 1981-1985 and for the period up to 1990). Moscow: Politizdat, 1981.

Tito, Josip Broz. *The Struggle and the Development of the CPY Between the Two Wars: Lectures in Kumrovec*. Belgrade: Socialist Thought and Practice, 1977.

Truluck, Phillip N., ed. *Private Rights and Public Lands*. Washington, D.C.: Heritage Foundation, Pacific Institute for Public Policy Research, 1983.

Univerzitet u Beogradu. *Centar za multidisciplinarne studije* (Center for multidisciplinary studies) Belgrade: Univerzitet u Beogradu, 1980.

Vidláková, Olga. *Státní správa ČSSR a životní prostředí* (The ČSSR state administration and the environment). *Studia ČSAV*, No. 12/1977 (Studies of the Czech academy of sciences, No. 12/1977). Prague: Academia, 1977.

Wolchik, Sharon L. *The Scientific-Technological Revolution and the Role of Specialist Elites in Policy-making in Czechoslovakia*. Washington, D.C.: George Washington University, Institute for Sino-Soviet Studies, 1984.

World Bank. *Environment and Development*. Washington, D.C.: World Bank, June 1975.

———. *Environmental Considerations for the Industrial Development Sector*. Washington, D.C.: World Bank, August 1978.

——— (Banque mondiale). *Considérations écologiques, mésologiques, sanitaires et humaines liées aux projets de développement* (Ecological, mesological, health, and human considerations linked to development projects). Washington, D.C.: World Bank, May 1974.

Conference Proceedings

Sanger, Frederick J., ed., with assistance of Hyde, Peter J. *USSR Contribution: Permafrost, Second International Conference.* Washington, D.C.: National Academy of Sciences, 1978.

V. Medzinárodné sympozium o problematike ekologickího výskumu krajiny. *Ekologičká stabilita, odolnost, diverzita, potenciál, produktivita a rovnováha krajiny* (The ecological stability, toughness, diversity, potential, productivity and balance of a region). November 19-23, 1979. Bratislava: Ustav experimentalnej biologie a ekologie SAV, 1979.

Unpublished Papers, Dissertations, and Abstracts

DeBardeleben, Joan. "The Environment and Marxism-Leninism: Soviet and East German Perspectives." Ph.D. thesis, McGill University, Montreal, 1983.

Jancar, Barbara Wolfe. "Dissent and Constitutionalism in Yugoslavia." Annual Meeting of the Midwest Slavic Conference, Ann Arbor, Mich., May 5-7, 1977. Unpublished.

————. Personal notes from interviews in the USSR, Czechoslovakia, and Yugoslavia, made in 1980-81, 1983, 1985, and 1986.

Kramer, John M. "The Politics of Conservation and Pollution in the USSR." Ph.D. thesis, University of Virginia, Charlottesville, 1973.

Kruglov, Viktor Viktorovich. "Prava i obiazannosti promyshlennogo predpriiatia po okhrane okruzhaiushchei sredy" (The rights and duties of industrial enterprises in environmental protection). *Candidat nauk* thesis, Moscow State University, 1980. Unpublished.

Kružíková, Éva. "Právní úprava plánování a stimulování péče o životní prostředí." Disertační práce 68-04-9 (The legal management of the planning and stimulation of environmental protection. Dissertation work 68-04-09). Prague: ČSAV, Ústava státu a práva, 1983.

Lopatina, Myza Nikolaevna. "Pravovoi regulirovanie vozmeshchenia ubytkov zemlepol'zovateliam i poter' sel'skokhozaistvennogo proizvodstva pri iz'iatii zemiel' dlia gosudarstvennykh ili obshchestvennykh nuzd." Avtoreferat. Spetsial'nost No. 12.00.06 (The legal regulation of compensation of loss to agricultural producers and agricultural enterprises for the confiscation of lands for state and society's needs. Ph.D. dissertation no. 12.00.86), Moscow gosudarstvennyi universitet, 1980.

Ramet, Pedro. "Federal Relations in Socialist Yugoslavia: Inter-republican Cooperation in Control of Water Pollution." Unpublished.

Vidláková, Olga. *O tvorbe rozhodnuti městské správy.* (On decisionmaking by local administration). Prague: Československá akademie věd, Vědecké kolegium věd o státu a právu, n.d.

Weiner, Douglas R. *Conservation, Ecology and the Cultural Revolution.* Ph.D. thesis, Columbia University, 1983.

434

Zelenková, Hana. *Makroekonomické aspekty reprodukce životního prostředí. Disertační práce* (Macroeconomic aspects of the reproduction of the environment. Dissertation work). Prague: Karlův universitet, May 1981.

Ziegler, Charles E. "Disaggregated Pluralism in a Socialist System: Environmental Policy in the USSR." Ph.D. thesis, University of Illinois, Urbana, 1979.

Selected Periodicals

ANSSSR. Institut sotsial'nykh issledovania. *Sotsial'nye issledovania* (social research). Moscow: Izdatel'stvo "Nauka," 1970–85.

Čovek i životna sredina, 1980–86.

Current Digest of the Soviet Press. Columbus, Ohio: Current Digest of the Soviet Press, 1960–.

Ekonomika i matematicheskie metody (Economics and mathematical methods). Moscow. 1975–.

Environmental Impact Assessment Review 2, 3 (September 1981). New York: Spring Street Publishers, 1981.

Environmental Review. Pittsburgh: Duquesne University, 1970–86.

Foreign Affairs. New York: Council on Foreign Relations, 1980–86.

Geographic Society of the USSR. Moscow Chapter. *Voprosy geografii* (Questions of geography). Moscow: Izdatel'stvo "Mysl'," 1970–82.

International Affairs. Moscow: Novosti, 1970–1986. In particular, Nos. 11, 1978; 9, 1978; 12, 1978.

International and Comparative Law Quarterly. 1975–86.

International Herald Tribune. Paris and Amsterdam. 1982–86.

Izvestia. Moscow. 1970–86.

Journal of Politics. 1970–85.

JPRS. Washington, D.C.: U.S. Government Printing Office, 1970–86.

Literaturnaia gazeta, 1970–86.

Manchester Guardian Weekly. London: The Guardian Weekly, 1977–86.

Le Monde. Paris. 1982–86.

Moscow News. Moscow. 1970–86.

Moscow State University. *Vestnik Moskovskogo universiteta, Seria 11, Pravo* (Moscow University Review, Ser. 11, Law). Moscow: Moscow State University, 1980–84, particularly June 1980.

Nature. London. 1970–86.

New York Times. 1970–84.

NIN, 1979–86.

Novy mir, 1975–86.

Polar Record. Great Britain. 1976–80.

Politika. Belgrade. 1970–86.

Polska Akademia Nauk. Institut Ekologii. *Ekologia polska* (Polish ecology) Vol. 31, No. 4. Warsaw-Lodz: Polish Scientific Publishers, 1984.

Polska Akademia Nauk. Komitet Ekologii. *Wiadomosci ekologiczne* (Ecological science). A Quarterly. Vol. 30, No. 1. Warsaw: Panstwowe Wydawnictwo Naukowe, 1984.

Poznaj a chraň (Know and preserve). Prague. 4–8/1980.

Pravda. Moscow. 1970–86.

Privredni pregled (Economic Review). Belgrade. 1970–86.

Problems of Communism. Washington, D.C.: U.S. Information Agency. 1970–86.

Radio Free Europe Research Reports: East European and Baltic Areas. Munich: Radio Free Europe (mimeographed.) 1970–86.

Review of Socialist Law. London: 1975–85.

Science. Washington, D.C. 1970–86.

Sedam dana oko sveta (Seven days around the world). Belgrade: Tanjug, 1985–86.

Službeni glasnik SR Srbije (The Official Herald SR Serbia). Belgrade. 1970–85.

Službeni list SFRJ (The official newspaper SFRJ). Belgrade. 1970–85.

Social Problems. 1970–85.

Socialist Thought and Practice. Belgrade. Vols. 3 and 4 (March, April 1984).

Soe, Christian, ed. *Comparative Politics.* Guilford, Conn.: Dushkin Publishing Group: 1970–84.

Soviet Geography: Review and Translation. 1975–85.

Soviet Review. 1970–86.

Sovietskaia rossia (Soviet Russia). Moscow. 1970–86.

Sovietskoe gosudarstvo i pravo (Soviet state and law). Moscow: ANSSSR, Institut gosudarstva i prava, 1960–86.

Správní právo (Administrative law). Prague: Ministry of the Interior CSR. 1975–85.

SR Srbije. Republička konferencija Mladih istraživača. *Bilten* (Bulletin). Smederevska Palanka, 1981.

SR Srbije. Republička konferencija Mladih istraživača. *Istraživač* (Researcher). Belgrade: Beogradski izdavačko-grafički zavod, 1980–81.

Stát a právo (State and law). Prague: CSAV. 1970–1985.

Studies in Comparative Communism. 1970–86.

Survey: Report on Soviet Science. London. No. 52 (July 1964).

The Times. London. 1982–86.

Urban Ecology. Amsterdam: Elsevier Scientific, 1980–85.

Vjestnik (News). Zagreb. 1970–86.

Voprosy ekonomiki (Questions of economics). Moscow: Izdatel'stvo "Nauka," 1972–86.

Voprosy filosofii (Questions of philosophy). Moscow: Izdatel'stvo "Nauka," 1960–85.

Water Supply and Management. Vol. 3. New York: Pergamon, 1979.

Životné postredie (The environment). Bratislava, 1970–85.

Index of Acts and Laws

Index of Institutions

Institutions include academies, committees, commissions, conferences, ministries, societies, unions, universities, and others.

439

Organizations (*continued*)
Organization of Young Researchers of
Yugoslavia, 281–84, 289, 295,
303
Solidarity (Poland), 3, 124, 139, 330
United Nations (UN), 226, 234
Man and the Biosphere Program
(MAB), 37, 180, 186, 197
United Nations Educational,
Scientific, and Cultural
Organization (UNESCO), 180,
186, 233
United Nations Environmental
Program (UNEP), 233
World Bank, 187
World Health Organization (WHO),
90

Parties
Communist party
Czechoslovakia, 214
Kazakh SSR, 196
SFRY League of Communists of
Yugoslavia (LCY), 34–36,
40, 41, 130, 170, 178, 179,
199, 282–84, 332, 335
Soviet Union (CPSU), 27, 131, 196,
207, 227, 256
—Central Committee (CPSU CC),
53, 326
—Politburo, 195, 196
—Twenty-sixth Congress, 162, 167,
169, 175, 291
—Twenty-seventh Congress, 256,
291
Uzbek, 196

Secretariats
SFRY secretariats of agriculture,
forestry, water management, 75
SFRY Republican Secretariat for
Urbanism and Planning, SR
Serbia, 233
Services
Belgrade City Health Service, 233

Federal Hydrometeorological Service,
81
Fish Conservation Service, 73
Self-managing communities of interest
(SIZ-a), 36–40, 46–47, 74–83,
98–106, 140, 184, 187, 208,
223, 233
League of SIZ for Water Manage-
ment, 75, 208
Republican SIZ for Public Health of
Serbia, 233
Serbian SIZ for Science, 83
Serbian SIZ for Social Insurance,
223
U.S. Forestry Service and the Bureau
of Land Management, 68
Societies
All-Russian (Soviet) Society for the
Preservation of Nature,
273–74, 277–78, 288, 298
"People's University of Environ-
mental Protection," 273–74
ČSSR Slovak Society of the Defenders
of Nature, 279, 297–98
Georgian Nature Protection Society,
275
Kazakh Society for the Protection of
the Natural Environment, 275,
299
Kirgiz Nature (Conservation) Protec-
tion Society, 275, 299
Soviets
USSR Leningrad City Soviet
Executive Committee (Goris-
polkom), 181–82
Committee on Environmental
Protection, 181–82
USSR Moscow City Soviet, 180, 279
Executive Committee, 54
Committee on Environmental
Protection, 182
Symposia
U.S./USSR Symposium on the
Economic Aspects of
Environmental Protection, 290

Index of People's Names

Alexandrov, I. G., 252
Andropov, Iurii, 123, 169, 183

Balatskii, O. F., Kharkov Polytechnical Institute, 251
Bednyi, M. S., 200, 291, 416
Belov, A. B., ANSSSR, Institute of Geography of Siberia and the Far East, 250
Bessonenko, V., 201
Brezhnev, L., 32, 52, 169, 174, 214, 252, 255
Briukhanov, director at Chernobyl, 329
Bulgakov, V. V., Kiev Scientific Institute of General and Public Health, 290

Carson, R., 270
Chernenko, C. V., 103, 169
Crozier, M., 8–10, 20, 48, 146, 237, 308–10, 417–18

Danilova, E. Z., 290, 418
Diumenton, G. G., 235
Dolanć, S., Slovenian Federal Minister for Internal Affairs, 178
Dolezhal, N., builder of first Soviet nuclear reactor, 328

Engels, F., 51

Fomin, N., chief engineer at Chernobyl, 329
Ford, D., 229, 252
Friedberg, E., 8–10, 20, 48, 146, 237, 308, 418

Gerasimov, I. P., ANSSSR, Institute of Geography, 51, 52, 104, 241, 250, 419
Gluscevič, B., director, Institute for Socioeconomic Research, Titograd, 226
Gofman, K. G., 229, 251, 252, 315, 420
Gorbachev, M. C., 103, 168–69, 176, 238, 432
Gorsuch, A. B., former head of U.S. EPA, 293
Grishaev, M. F., former deputy chief of the State Administration for Land Development, USSR Ministry of Agriculture, 149
Grzecić, N., manager, Hotel Libertas, 129
Gusev, R. K., 251, 252, 315, 420

Izrael, Iu. A., chair, USSR State Committee on Hydrometeorology and Environmental Protection (Goskomgidromet), 101, 104, 112–13, 247

Jelović, I., 118

Kalpić, A., president, Federal Council for the Protection and Improvement of the Environment, 153
Kardelj, E., 177
Kaznacheyev, V., head, Institute of Clinical and Experimental Medicine, Siberian Branch of the USSR ANSSSR, 201
Kerner, A., director, Law Faculty, Charles University, Prague, 140

446

Index of Place-Names

Index of Concepts

Access: to communications, 227–30, 234; to libraries, 234, 270; public access to environmental information, 270, 292, 304

Accommodation: of experts to party line, 244, 246, 257; industrial accommodation with local interests in Yugoslavia, 159; in reaching compacts in Yugoslavia, 158; strategy of environmental agents, 110–16

Acid rain, 12, 201, 292; National Academy of Sciences report on, 312

Actors: capabilities of political actor, 67; governmental, 29, 65; individual, 22, 48; institutional, 22; nongovernmental, 34, 47, 63, 65; in policymaking, 11; and power, 10; relation to system, 48; subsystem, 5, 14; territorial, 59

Adversarial relations: and regulated interests, 11

Advice: acceptance of expert, 254–55, 261; expert, 34, 47, 119; expert constraints on, 230; Yugoslav expert advice politicized, 257

Agency(ies): Academy of Sciences as, 72; as data collectors, 227–28; interrepublican, 76; lead (*golovyie*), 24, 28, 60–61, 69, 144, 157, 175

Agenda: environment on the public agenda, 215; expert role in setting, 248–49, 258, 261; public, 16, 91, 158, 247

Agreements: Adriatic, 160, 211; on economic and social order, 318; factory agreements with towns, 132; negotia-

tion and, 58–59; on power stations on the Drina and Neretva, 130; republican, 178, 180, 193; self-managing, 77, 83, 98, 110, 141, 147, 184; Sverdlovsk four-plant agreement with local enterprise, 132; Una River, 158; voluntary agreements in Yugoslavia, 119–20

"Agregaty" (industrial conglomerates), 61

Agricultural land: abandonment of in Yugoslavia, 2, 58; degradation, 164; distinction between nonagricultural land and, 87–88; erosion of in Yugoslavia, 202; payments on damage to, 86; regulation, 195; Slovenian land-use law, 58–59, 76

Agricultural policy: national Yugoslav, 35–36, 57, 122, 125, 153, 222; Soviet investment in, 92–97, 190–91; Yugoslav investment in, 98, 232

Air: effects of pollution on respiratory illness, 291; inventory of air quality, 169; quality, 1, 2, 12, 24, 44, 54, 69, 113, 169, 197, 199, 222, 227; quality standards, 13, 54, 115, 292; revision of Yugoslav laws, 110, 313; Soviet investment in air pollution control, 189–90; transboundary pollution, 292

Air pollution, 1, 2, 15, 20, 28, 85, 111, 116–17, 138–39, 162, 185, 196, 200–207, 230, 266, 292, 300; control, 5, 20, 60, 91, 132, 138, 168, 217; control measures, 107–8, 184; point-sources of, 112; regulations, 211; urban, 228

Akcije: campaigns, 43, 210; "88 Roses for President Tito," 280–81, 289, 302

About the Author

The author currently is Co-director of the SUNY Paris Program in the Social Sciences and Professor of Political Science at SUNY Brockport, where she teaches Environmental Policy and International Relations. In the fall of 1980, she was a State University exchange scholar at Moscow State University's Faculty of Law, Department of Environmental Law, where she lectured on environmental law. In the spring of 1981, she held an IREX fellowship to Yugoslavia and Czechoslovakia for research on environmental management and interviews with environmental officials. Since then, she has regularly been in contact with environmental personnel in Poland, Czechoslovakia, Hungary, and Yugoslavia. Her publications include *Czechoslovakia and the Absolute Monopoly of Power* (Praeger, 1971) and *Women under Communism* (Johns Hopkins University Press, 1978), as well as numerous articles and chapters in books.